Church Episcopal

The Cathedral Psalter

Containing the Psalms of David Together With the Canticles...

Church Episcopal

The Cathedral Psalter
Containing the Psalms of David Together With the Canticles...

ISBN/EAN: 9783337021610

Printed in Europe, USA, Canada, Australia, Japan

Cover: Foto ©Lupo / pixelio.de

More available books at **www.hansebooks.com**

NEW EDITION
WITH CANTICLES AS SET FORTH BY THE GENERAL CONVENTION OF 1889.

CATHEDRAL PSALTER

CONTAINING

THE PSALMS OF DAVID

TOGETHER WITH THE

CANTICLES, PROPER PSALMS,

AND

SELECTIONS OF PSALMS

POINTED FOR CHANTING AND SET TO APPROPRIATE CHANTS

ADAPTED TO THE

USE OF THE AMERICAN CHURCH

BY

ALFRED FOX　　　　**D. E. HERVEY**
(OF CLEVELAND, OHIO);　　　(OF NEWARK, NEW JERSEY)

AND

HENRY KING
(OF ST. PAUL'S CATHEDRAL, LONDON, ENGLAND).

NEW YORK & LONDON
NOVELLO, EWER AND CO.
AND
JAMES POTT AND CO.
NEW YORK.

COPYRIGHT (A. D. 1890) BY NOVELLO, EWER & CO.

PUBLISHED BY PERMISSION OF
CHARLES L. HUTCHINS,
SECRETARY OF THE GENERAL CONVENTION.

PREFACE.

THE CHANTS in this Collection have been arranged with the following main principles in view :—

(1) That single or double Chants should be used according to the character and construction of each Psalm.

See Psalms xv. (single); xxiv. (double).

(2) That the construction of each Psalm should as far as possible govern the antiphonal arrangement; *e.g.*, if the parallel or antithesis occurs between the two halves of one verse, each half should be assigned to Cantoris and Decani respectively.

See Psalms xv. xix. l. xc.

(3) That the variations of subject or sentiment in each Psalm should be marked by a change of Chant.

See Psalms xviii. lxxviii.

Should there be any difficulty in following the antiphonal marks (*Dec.* and *Can.*) as they stand, they can be simplified under the direction of the Choirmaster without injury to the general arrangement of the Chants.

1. THE WORDS, from the commencement of each verse and half-verse up to the accented syllable, are called the Recitation.

2. On reaching the accented syllable, and beginning with it, the *music* of the chant commences, in strict time (*a tempo*), the upright strokes corresponding to the bars. The Recitation must therefore be considered as *outside* the chant, and may be of any length. The note on which the Recitation is made is called the Reciting note.

3. If there is no syllable after that which is accented, the accented syllable must be held for one whole bar or measure,* *e.g.*—

If other syllables follow the one accented, the first measure or initial bar of the chant will have to be divided into *parts of a semibreve*.

4. The following general rules will help to explain this, the accented syllable being called *the accent*. If one syllable follows the accent, the first bar is divided into a dotted minim and a crotchet, *e.g.*—

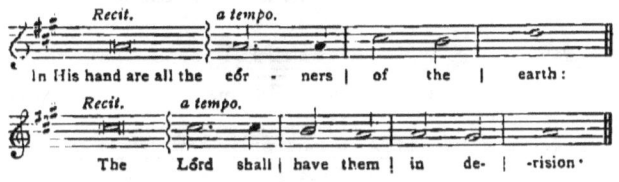

* The melody of the following chant has been used throughout in the examples :—

Sir JOHN GOSS.

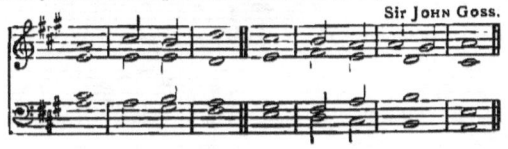

Sometimes, when only one syllable follows the accent, the first bar is divided into two minims, e.g.—

5. If two syllables follow the accent, the first bar is generally divided into a minim and two crotchets, e.g.—

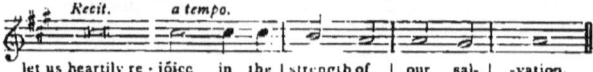

or into two crotchets and one minim, e.g.—

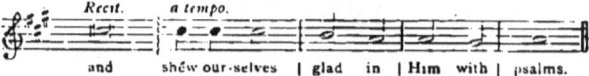

6. If three syllables follow the accent, the first bar is generally divided into four equal parts, or their equivalent value, e.g.—

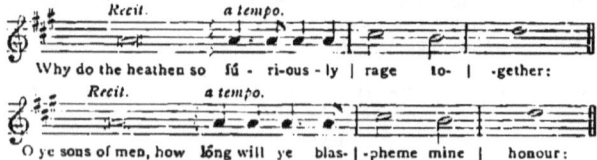

7. In the rare cases in which four syllables follow the accent, the bar will be without difficulty divided into the equivalent of four crotchets, e.g.—

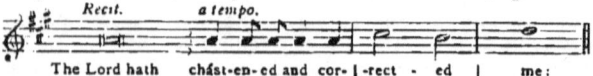

8. Study and experience will show that the most natural rendering of the words will in many instances call for other divisions of the bar, a few of which are here given, e.g.—

9. All stops in this Psalter must be observed as in good reading; those which experience has proved to be unnecessary or detrimental to chanting have been intentionally omitted by the Editors. An asterisk (∗) is a direction to take breath.

10. It is of the utmost importance that no break' or pause should occur between the Recitation and Accent. The words should be deliberately recited; but the reciting note must not be held any longer than is absolutely necessary for this. Hence in some verses the reciting note will be only equal to a *very short* musical note, *e.g.*—

11. When a verse or half-verse commences with an accent, it is evident that there is *no recitation;* the rhythmical music therefore begins at once, *e.g.*—

As the accent holds the position of the first beat of the first bar, it is unnecessary to sing it louder than any of the words recited : its position, musically, will give it quite enough emphasis.

12. A dot is placed between words or syllables belonging to the second bar of the music, when their division would otherwise be doubtful, *e.g.*—

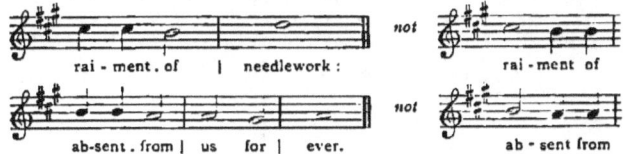

13. Lines placed horizontally show that the preceding syllable must be continued for the space indicated, *e.g.*—

14. F. signifies *Full*, that is, to be sung by both sides of the choir ; *f* signifies *forte*, loud ; *p*, *piano*, soft ; *mf*, *mezzo-forte*, moderately loud ; *2nd part*, directs the choir to repeat the second half of a double chant at the verse to which it is prefixed.

The thanks of the Editors are due to those professional and amateur musicians who have contributed original compositions to this work ; also to those who have granted permission for the insertion of such Chants as have appeared before, or of which they hold the copyright. The Editors likewise offer their apologies for any infringement of copyright of which they may have been unintentionally guilty.

CONTENTS.

	PAGE
PREFACE	iii
TABLE OF PROPER PSALMS	vii
TABLE OF SELECTIONS OF PSALMS	vii
THE CANTICLES:—	
Venite, exultemus Domino	viii
Te Deum laudamus	xiii
Benedicite, omnia opera	xviii
Benedictus	xx
Jubilate Deo	xxi
Magnificat	xxii
Cantate Domino	xxiii
Bonum est confiteri	xxiv
Nunc dimittis	xxv
Deus misereatur	xxvi
Benedic, anima mea	xxvii
THE PSALMS	1

PROPER PSALMS FOR

	Morning	Evening
First Sunday in Advent	114	116
Christmas Day	118	120
Circumcision	123	125
Epiphany	126	128
Purification	130	131
Ash Wednesday	133	134
Annunciation	136	139
Good Friday	140	143
Easter Even	145	147
Easter Day	149	151
Ascension Day	153	154
Whitsunday	156	158
Trinity Sunday	160	161
Transfiguration	162	164
St. Michael and All Angels	165	166
All Saints' Day	168	169
Burial of the Dead		170
Churching of Women		171
Thanksgiving Day		172
Consecration of Churches		172
Institution of Ministers		174

SELECTIONS OF PSALMS:—

	PAGE
First	179
Second	180
Third	182
Fourth	184
Fifth	185
Sixth	186
Seventh	188
Eighth	190
Ninth	191
Tenth	192
Eleventh	193
Twelfth	194
Thirteenth	195
Fourteenth	197
Fifteenth	198
Sixteenth	200
Seventeenth	201
Eighteenth	202
Nineteenth	204
Twentieth	205

TABLE OF PROPER PSALMS ON CERTAIN DAYS

	Morning.	Evening.
First Sunday in Advent	8, 50	96, 97
Christmas Day	19, 45, 85	89, 110, 132
Circumcision	40, 90	65, 103
Epiphany	46, 47, 48	72, 117, 135
Purification	20, 86, 87	84, 113, 134
Ash Wednesday	6, 32, 38	102, 130, 143
Annunciation	89	131, 132, 138
Good Friday	22, 40, 54	69, 88
Easter Even	4, 16, 17	30, 31
Easter Day	2, 57, 111	113, 114, 118
Ascension Day	8, 15, 21	24, 47, 108
Whitsunday	48, 68	104, 145
Trinity Sunday	29, 33	93, 97, 150
Transfiguration	27, 61, 93	84, 99, 133
St. Michael and All Angels	91, 103	34, 148
All Saints' Day	1, 15, 146	112, 121, 149

TABLE OF SELECTIONS OF PSALMS.

	Psalms.
First	1, 15, 91
Second	4, 31 to v. 7, 91, 134
Third	19, 24, 103
Fourth	23, 34, 65
Fifth	26, 43, 141
Sixth	32, 130, 121
Seventh	37
Eighth	51, 42
Ninth	72, 96
Tenth	77
Eleventh	80, 81
Twelfth	84, 122, 134
Thirteenth	85, 93, 97
Fourteenth	102
Fifteenth	107
Sixteenth	118
Seventeenth	123, 124, 125
Eighteenth	139, 145
Nineteenth	147
Twentieth	148, 149, 150

VENITE, EXULTEMUS DOMINO.

VENITE, EXULTEMUS DOMINO (continued).

VENITE, EXULTEMUS DOMINO.

F. f O COME, let us sing | unto . the | Lord : let us heartily rejoice in the | strength of | our sal- | -vation.

F. 2 Let us come before his présence with | thanks- | -giving : and shów ourselves | glad in | him with | psalms.

3 For the Lórd is a | great | God : and a gréat | King a- | -bove all | gods.

4 In his hand are all the córners | of the | earth : and the stréngth of the | hills is | his | also.

5 The séa is his | and he | made it : and his hánds pre- | -pared . the | dry | land.

mf 6 O come, let us wórship and | fall | down : and knéel be- | -fore the | Lord our | Maker.

7 For hé is the | Lord our | God : and we are the people of his pasture * ánd the | sheep of | his | hand. *Ps.* xcv. 1—7.

8 O worship the Lórd in the | beauty . of | holiness : let the whole éarth | stand in | awe of | him.

9 For he cometh, for he cómeth to | judge the | earth : and with righteousness to judge the wórld and the | people | with his | truth. *Ps.* xcvi. 9, 13.

F. f Glory be to the Fáther, | and . to the | Son : ánd | to the | Holy | Ghost;

F. As it was in the beginning * nów, and | ever | shall be : wórld without | end. | A- | -men.

VENITE, EXULTEMUS DOMINO (continued).

VENITE, EXULTEMUS DOMINO (continued).

VENITE, EXULTEMUS DOMINO.

F. f O COME, let us síng | unto . the | Lord : let us heartily rejóice in the | strength of | our sal- | -vation.

F. 2 Let us come before his présence with | thanks- | -giving : and shów ourselves | glad in | him with | psalms.

3 For the Lórd is a | great | God : and a gréat | King a- | -bove all | gods.

4 In his hand are all the córners | of the | earth : and the stréngth of the | hills is | his | also.

5 The séa is his | and he | made it : and his hánds pre- | -pared . the | dry | land.

mf 6 O come, let us wórship and | fall | down : and knéel be- | -fore the | Lord our | Maker.

7 For hé is the | Lord our | God : and we are the people of his pasture ✶ ánd the | sheep of | his | hand. *Ps.* xcv. 1—7.

8 O worship the Lórd in the | beauty . of | holiness : let the whole éarth | stand in | awe of | him.

9 For he cometh, for he cómeth to | judge the | earth : and with righteousness to judge the wórld and the | people | with his | truth. *Ps.* xcvi. 9, 13.

F. f Glory be to the Fáther, | and . to the | Son : ánd | to the | Holy | Ghost ;

F. As it was in the beginning ✶ is nów, and | ever | shall be : wórld without | end. | A- | -men.

✶✶✶ *For Easter Day and Thanksgiving Day see Proper Psalms, pp.* 149 *and* 172.

VENITE, EXULTEMUS DOMINO (continued).

Alternative Chants.

VENITE, EXULTEMUS DOMINO.

F. f O COME, let us sing | unto . the | Lord : let us heartily rejoice in the | strength of | our sal- | -vation.

F. 2 Let us come before his présence with | thanks- | -giving : and shów our-selves | glad in | him with | psalms.

3 For the Lórd is a | great | God : and a gréat | King a- | -bove all | gods.

4 In his hand are all the córners | of the | earth : and the stréngth of the | hills is | his | also.

5 The séa is his | and he | made it : and his hánds pre- | -pared . the | dry | land.

mf 6 O come, let us wórship and | fall | down : and knéel be- | -fore the | Lord our | Maker.

7 For hé is the | Lord our | God : and we are the people of his pasture ✶ ánd the | sheep of | his | hand. *Ps.* xcv. 1—7.

8 O worship the Lórd in the | beauty . of | holiness : let the whole éarth | stand in | awe of | him.

9 For he cometh, for he cómeth to | judge the | earth : and with righteousness to judge the wórld and the | people | with his | truth. *Ps.* xcvi. 9, 13.

F. f Glory be to the Fáther, | and . to the | Son : ánd | to the | Holy | Ghost ;

F. As it was in the beginning ✶ is nów, and | ever | shall be : wórld without | end. | A- | -men.

TE DEUM LAUDAMUS.

Verses 1 to 13.   Dr. R. Woodward.

F. f WE práise | thee O | God : we acknówledge | thee to | be the | Lord.
F. 2 All the éarth doth | worship | thee : thé | Father | ever- | -lasting.
    3 To thee all A'ngels | cry a- | -loud : the Héavens, and | all the | Powers there- | -in.
    4 To thee Chérubin and | Seraph- | in : cón- | tinual- | -ly do | cry,
    5 Hóly | Holy | Holy : Lórd | God of | Saba- | -oth ;
    6 Heaven and earth are fúll of the | Majes- | -ty : óf | thy | Glo- | -ry.

    7 The glorious cómpany | of · the A- | -postles : práise | — | — | thee.
    8 The goodly féllowship | of the | Prophets : práise | — | — | thee.
2nd part. 9 The nóble | army · of | Martyrs : práise | — | — | thee.
    10 The holy Chúrch throughout | all the | world : dóth ac- | -know- | -ledge | thee ;
    11 Thé | Fa- | -ther : óf an | infinite | Majes- | -ty ;
    12 Thíne a- | -dorable | true : ánd | on- | — | -ly | Son ;
    13 A'lso the | Holy | Ghost : thé | Com- | -fort- | -er.

Verses 14 to 25.   Henry Smart.

    14 Thóu art the | King of | Glory : O' | — | — | Christ.
    15 Thou art the éver- | -lasting | Son : óf | — the | Fa- | -ther.
mf 16 When thou tookest upón thee to de- | -liver | man : thou didst humble thysélf to be | born | of a | Virgin.
    17 When thou hadst overcóme the | sharpness · of | death : thou didst open the Kíngdom of | Heaven to | all be- | -lievers.
    18 Thou sittest at the ríght | hand of | God : ín the | Glory | of the | Father.
    19 We believe that | thou shalt | come : tó | be | our | Judge.

    20 We therefore práy thee | help thy | servants : whom thou hast redéemed | with thy | precious | blood.
    21 Make them to be númbered | with thy | Saints : ín | glory | ever- | -lasting.
    22 O Lórd | save thy | people : ánd | bless thine | herit- | -age.
    23 Góv- | — | -ern | them : ánd | lift them | up for | ever.
F. f 24 Dáy | by | day : wé | magni- | -fy | thee ;
F. 25 A'nd we | worship · thy | Name : éver | world with- | -out | end.

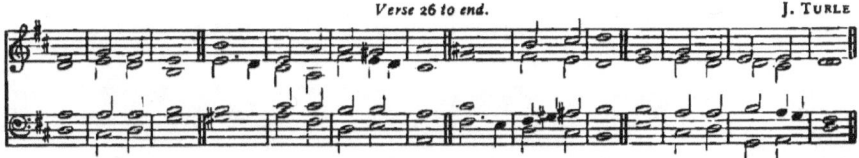

Verse 26 to end.   J. Turle.

mf 26 Vóuch- | -safe O | Lord : to kéep us this | day with- | -out | sin.
    27 O Lórd have | mercy · up- | -on us : háve | mer- | -cy up- | -on us.

    28 O Lord let thy mércy | be up- | -on us : ás our | trust | is in | thee.
    29 O Lord in thée I | have I | trusted : lét me | never | be con- | -founded.

TE DEUM LAUDAMUS (*continued*).

Alternative Chants (First Set).

Verses 1 to 13.   Dr. W. Hayes.

F. f WE praise | thee O | God : we acknowledge | thee to | be the | Lord.

F. 2 All the earth doth | worship | thee : the | Father | ever- | -lasting.

3 To thee all A'ngels | cry a- | -loud : the Heavens, and | all the | Powers there- | in.

4 To thee Cherubin and | Seraph- | in : con- | -tinual- | -ly do | cry,

5 Hóly | Holy | Holy : Lórd | God of | Saba- | -oth ;

6 Heaven and earth are full of the | Majes- | -ty ; of | thy | Glo- | -ry.

7 The glorious company | of · the A- | postles : praise | — | — | thee.

8 The goodly fellowship | of the | Prophets : praise | — | — | thee.

9 The noble | army · of | Martyrs : praise | — | — | thee.

10 The holy Church throughout | all the | world : doth ac-|-know-|-ledge | thee ;

11 The | Fa- | -ther : of an | infinite | Majes- | -ty ;

12 Thine a- | -dorable | true : and on- | — -ly | Son ;

13 A'lso the | Holy | Ghost : the | Com- | -fort- | -er.

Verses 14 to 25.   W. Russell.

14 Thou art the | King of | Glory : O | | — | — | Christ.

15 Thou art the éver- | -lasting | Son : of | — the | Fa- | -ther.

mf 16 When thou tookest upon thee to de- | -liver | man : thou didst humble thyself to be | born of a | Virgin.

17 When thou hadst overcome the | sharpness . of | death : thou didst open the Kingdom of | Heaven to | all be-|-lievers.

18 Thou sittest at the right | hand of | God : in the | Glory | of the | Father.

19 We believe that | thou shalt | come : to | be | our | Judge.

20 We therefore pray thee | help thy | servants : whom thou hast redeemed | with thy | precious | blood.

21 Make them to be numbered | with thy | Saints : in | glory | ever- | -lasting.

22 O Lórd | save thy | people : and | bless thine | herit- | -age.

23 Góv- | — -ern | them : and | lift them | up for | ever.

F. f 24 Day | by | day : we | magni- | -fy | thee ;

F. 25 And we | worship · thy | Name : ever | world with- | -out | end.

Verse 26 to end.   Dr. Stainer.

mf 26 Vouch- | -safe O | Lord : to keep us this | day with- | -out | sin.

27 O Lórd have | mercy· up- | -on us : have | mer- | -cy up- | -on us.

28 O Lord let thy mercy | be up- | -on us : as our | trust | is in | thee.

29 O Lord in thee | have I | trusted : let me | never | be con- | -founded.

TE DEUM LAUDAMUS (continued).

Verses 1 to 13.   W. RUSSELL.

F. ƒ WE práise | thee O | God : we acknówledge | thee to | be the | Lord.

F. 2 All the éarth doth | worship | thee : thé | Father | ever- | -lasting.

3 To thee all A'ngels | cry a- | -loud : the Héavens, and | all the | Powers there- | in.

4 To thee Chérubin and | Seraph- | in : cón- | -tinual- | -ly do | cry,

5 Hóly | Holy | Holy : Lórd | God of | Saba- | -oth ;

6 Heaven and earth are fúll of the | Majes- | -ty : óf | thy | Glo- | -ry.

7 The glorious cómpany | of · the A- | postles : práise | — | — | thee.

8 The goodly féllowship | of the | Prophets : práise | — | — | thee.

2nd purt 9 The nóble | army · of | Martyrs : práise | — | — | thee.

10 The holy Chúrch throughout | all the | world : dóth ac- | -know- | -ledge | thee ;

11 Thé | Fa- | -ther : óf an | infinite | Majes- | -ty ;

12 Thine a- | -dorable | true : ánd | on- | —-ly | Son ;

13 A'lso the | Holy | Ghost : thé | Com- | -fort- | -er.

Verses 14 to 25.   J JONES.

14 Thóu art the | King of | Glory : O' | — | — | Christ.

15 Thou art the éver- | -lasting | Són | óf | — the | Fa- | -ther.

mf 16 When thou tookest upón thee to de- | -liver | man : thou didst humble thysélf to be | born | of a | Virgin.

17 When thou hadst overcóme the | sharpness · of | death : thou didst open the Kingdom of | Heaven to | all be- | -l-ievers.

18 Thou sittest at the ríght | hand of | God : ín the | Glory | of the | Father.

19 We beliéve that | thou shalt | come : tó | be | our | Judge.

20 We therefore práy thee | help thy | servants : whom thou hast redéemed | with thy | precious | blood.

21 Make them to be númbered | with thy | Saints : ín | glory | ever- | -last- ing.

22 O Lórd | save thy | people : ánd | bless thine | herit- | -age.

23 Góv- | — -ern | them : ánd | lift them | up for | ever.

F. ƒ 24 Dáy | by | day : wé | magni- | -fy | thee ;

F. 25 A'nd we | worship · thy | Name : éver | world with- | -out | end.

Verse 26 to end.   K. J. PYE.

mf 26 Vóuch- | -safe O | Lord : to kéep us this | day with- | out | sin.

27 O Lórd have | mercy · up- | -on us : háve | mer- | -cy up- | -on us.

28 O Lord let thy mércy | be up- | -on us : ás our | trust | is in | thee.

29 O Lord in thée | have I | trusted | lét me | never | be con- | -founded.

TE DEUM LAUDAMUS (continued).

—Alternative Chants (Third Set).

Verses 1 to 13. — Henry Lawes

F. ƒ WE praise | thee O | God : we acknowledge | thee to | be the | Lord.
　F. 2 All the earth doth | worship | thee : the | Father | ever- | -lasting.
　3 To thee all A'ngels | cry a- | -loud : the Heavens, and | all the | Powers there- | -in.
　4 To thee Cherubin and | Seraph- | in : con- | -tinual- | -ly do | cry,
　5 Hóly | Holy | Holy : Lórd | God of | Saba- | -oth ;
　6 Heaven and earth are full of the | Majes- | -ty : of | thy | Glo- | -ry.

　7 The glorious cómpany | of · the A- | -postles : praise | — | — | thee.
　8 The goodly féllowship | of the | Prophets ; praise | — | — | thee.
　2nd part 9 The nóble | army · of | Martyrs : praise | — | — | thee.
　10 The holy Chúrch throughout | all the | world : doth ac-|-know-|-ledge | thee ;
　11 The | Fa- | -ther : of an | infinite | Majes- | -ty ;
　12 Thine a- | -dorable | true : and | on- | — -ly | Son ;
　13 A'lso the | Holy | Ghost : the | Com- | -fort- | -er.

Verses 14 to 25. — R. Cooke

14 Thou art the | King of | Glory : O' | — | — | Christ.
　15 Thou art the éver- | -lasting | Son : óf | — the | Fa- | -ther.
　mƒ 16 When thou tookest upón thee to de- | -liver | man : thou didst humble thyself to be | born | of a | Virgin.
　17 When thou hadst overcóme the | sharpness · of | death : thou didst open the Kíngdom of | Heaven to | all be-|-lievers.
　18 Thou sittest at the right | hand of | God : in the | Glory | of the | Father.
　19 We belíeve that | thou shalt | come : tó | be | our | Judge.

　20 We therefore práy thee | help thy | servants : whom thou hast redéemed | with thy | precious | blood.
　21 Make them to be númbered | with thy | Saints : in | glory | ever- | -lasting.
　22 O Lórd | save thy | people : ánd | bless thine | herit- | -age.
　23 Góv- | — -ern | them : ánd | lift them | up for | ever.
　F.ƒ 24 Dáy | by | day : wé | magni- | -fy | thee ;
　F. 25 A'nd we | worship · thy | Name : éver | world with- | -out | end.

Verse 26 to end. — E. J. Hopkins.

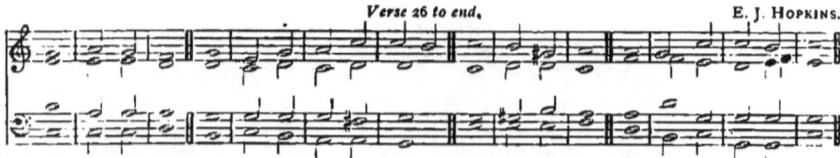

mƒ 26 Vóuch- | -safe O | Lord : to kéep us this | day with- | -out | sin.
　27 O Lórd have | mercy · up- | -on us : háve | mer- | -cy up- | -on us.

　28 O Lord let thy mércy | be up- | -on us : ás our | trust | is in | thee.
　29 O Lord in thée | have I | trusted : lét me | never | be con- | -founded.

TE DEUM LAUDAMUS (continued).

Alternative Chants (Fourth Set)

Verses 1 to 13.   J. S. SMITH.

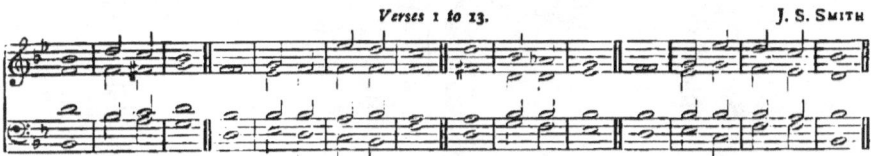

F. f WE práise | thee O | God : we acknówledge | thee to | be the | Lord.
F. 2 All the éarth doth | worship | thee : thê | Father | ever- | -lasting.
3 To thee all A'ngels | cry a- | -loud the Héavens, and | all the | Powers there- | -in.
4 To thee Chérubin and | Seraph- | in : cón- | -tinual- | -ly do | cry,
5 Hóly | Holy | Holy : Lórd | God of | Saba- | -oth ;
6 Heaven and earth are fúll of the | Majes- | -ty : óf | thy | Glo- | -ry.

7 The glorious cómpany | of · the A- | -postles : práise | — | — | thee.
8 The goodly féllowship | of the | Prophets : práise | — | — | thee.
2nd part 9 The nóble | army · of | Martyrs : práise | — | — | thee.
10 The holy Chúrch throughout | all the | world : dóth ac- | -know- | -ledge | thee ;
11 Thê | Fa- | -ther : óf an | infinite | Majes- | -ty ;
12 Thíne a- | -dorable | true : ând | on- | — -ly | Son ;
13 A'lso the | Holy | Ghost : thê | Com- | -fort- | -er.

Verses 14 to 25.   Dr. ALDRICH.

14 Thóu art the | King of | Glory : O' | — | — | Christ.
15 Thou art the éver- | -lasting | Son : óf | — the | Fa- | -ther.
mf 16 When thou tookest upón thee to de- | -liver | man : thou didst humble thysélf to be | born | of a | Virgin.
17 When thou hadst overcóme the | sharpness · of | death : thou didst open the Kíngdom of | Heaven to | all be- | -lievers.
18 Thou sittest at the ríght | hand of | God : ín the | Glory | of the | Father.
19 We belíeve that | thou shalt | come : tó | be | our | Judge.

20 We therefore práy thee | help thy | servants : whom thou hast redéemed | with thy | precious | blood.
21 Make them to be númbered | with thy | Saints : ín | glory | ever- | -lasting.
22 O Lórd | save thy | people : ánd | bless thine | herit- | -age.
23 Góv- | — -ern | them : ánd | lift them | up for | ever.
F. f 24 Dáy | by | day : wê | magni- | -fy | thee ;
F. 25 A'nd we | worship · thy | Name : éver | world with- | -out | end.

Verse 26 to end.   J. BARNBY.

mf 26 Vóuch- | -safe O | Lord : to kéep us this | day with- | -out | sin.
27 O Lórd have | mercy · up- | -on us : háve | mer- | -cy up- | -on us.

28 O Lord let thy mércy | be up- | -on us : âs our | trust | is in | thee.
29 O Lord in thée | have I | trusted ; lét me | never | be con- | -founded.

BENEDICITE, OMNIA OPERA.

Alternative Chants (First Set).

Alternative Chants (Second Set).

BENEDICITE, OMNIA OPERA (*continued*).

———— *Alternative Chants (Third Set).* ————

Verses 1 to 17; 26 to end. Dr. ARNOLD.

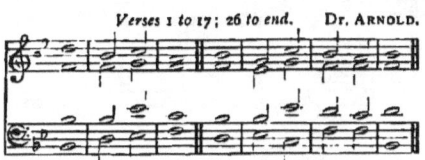

Verses 18 to 25. Dr. ARMES.

mf O ALL ye Works of the Lórd | bless · ye the | Lord : (*f F.*) práise him, and | magnify | him for | ever.*

F. 2 O ye Angels of the Lórd | bless · ye the | Lord : práise him, and | magnify | him for | ever.

3 O ye Héavens | bless · ye the | Lord: práise him, and | magnify | him for | ever.

4 O ye Waters that be above the Fírmament | bless · ye the | Lord : práise him, and | magnify | him for | ever.

5 O all ye Powers of the Lórd | bless · ye the | Lord : práise him, and | magnify | him for | ever.

6 O ye Sun and Móon | bless · ye the | Lord: práise him, and | magnify | him for | ever.

7 O ye Stars of Héaven | bless · ye the | Lord : práise him, and | magnify | him for | ever.

8 O ye Showers and Déw | bless · ye the | Lord : práise him, and | magnify | him for | ever.

9 O ye Winds of Gód | bless · ye the | Lord : práise him, and | magnify | him for | ever.

10 O ye Fire and Héat | bless · ye the | Lord : práise him, and | magnify | him for | ever.

11 O ye Winter and Súmmer | bless · ye the | Lord : práise him, and | magnify | him for | ever.

12 O ye Dews and Frósts | bless · ye the | Lord: práise him, and | magnify | him for | ever.

13 O ye Frost and Cóld | bless · ye the | Lord : práise him, and | magnify | him for | ever.

14 O ye Ice and Snów | bless · ye the | Lord : práise him, and | magnify | him for | ever.

15 O ye Nights and Dáys | bless · ye the | Lord : práise him, and | magnify | him for | ever.

16 O ye Light and Dárkness | bless · ye the | Lord : práise him, and | magnify | him for | ever.

17 O ye Lightnings and Clóuds | bless · ye the | Lord : práise him, and | magnify | him for | ever.

18 O let the Eárth | bless the | Lord : yea let it práise him, and | magnify | him for | ever.

19 O ye Mountains and Hílls | bless · ye the | Lord : práise him, and | magnify | him for | ever.

20 O all ye Green Things upon the Eárth | bless · ye the | Lord : práise him, and | magnify | him for | ever.

21 O ye Wélls | bless · ye the | Lord : práise him, and | magnify | him for | ever.

22 O ye Seas and Flóods | bless · ye the | Lord : práise him, and | magnify | him for | ever.

23 O ye Whales, and all that move in the Wáters | bless · ye the | Lord : práise him, and | magnify | him for | ever.

24 O all ye Fowls of the Aír | bless · ye the | Lord : práise him, and | magnify | him for | ever.

25 O all ye Beasts and Cáttle | bless · ye the | Lord : práise him, and | magnify | him for | ever.

26 O ye Children of Mén | bless · ye the | Lord : práise him, and | magnify | him for | ever.

27 O let Ísrael | bless the | Lord : práise him, and | magnify | him for | ever.

28 O ye Priests of the Lórd | bless · ye the | Lord : práise him, and | magnify | him for | ever.

29 O ye Servants of the Lórd | bless · ye the | Lord : práise him, and | magnify | him for | ever.

30 O ye Spirits and Souls of the Ríghteous | bless · ye the | Lord : práise him, and | magnify | him for | ever.

31 O ye holy and humble Men of héart | bless · ye the | Lord : práise him, and | magnify | him for | ever.

F. f Glory be to the Fáther, | and · to the | Son : ánd | to the | Holy | Ghost ;

F. As it was in the beginning ✶ is nów, and | ever | shall be : wórld without | end. | A- | -men.

* The second part of each verse to be sung *full*.

BENEDICTUS.

BENEDICTUS.—*St. Luke* i. 68.

F. mf BLESSED be the Lórd | God of | Israel : for he hath vísited | and re- | deemed · his | people ;

F. 2 And hath raised up a míghty sal- | vation | for us : in the house | of his | servant | David ;

3 As he spake by the móuth of his | holy | Prophets : which have béen | since the | world be- | -gan ;

4 That we should be sáved | from our | enemies : and fróm the | hand of | all that | hate us ;

5 To perform the mercy prómised | to our | forefathers : ánd to re- | -member · his | holy | Covenant ;

6 To perform the oath which he swáre to our | forefather | Abraham : thát | he would | give | us ;

7 That we being delivered out of the hánd | of our | enemies : might sérve | him with- | -out | fear ;

8 In holiness and ríghteous- | -ness be-|-fore him : áll the | days | of our | life.

9 And thou Child shalt be called the Próphet | of the | Highest : for thou shalt go before the face of the Lórd | to pre- | pare his | ways ;

10 To give knowledge of salvátion | unto · his | people : fór the re- | -mission | of their | sins,

11 Through the tender mércy | of our | God ; whereby the day-spring fróm on | high hath | visited | us ;

12 To give light to them that sit in darkness ✶ and ín the | shadow · of | death : and to guide our féet | into · the | way of | peace.

F. f Glory be to the Fáther, | and · to the | Son : ánd | to the | Holy | Ghost ;

F. As it was in the beginning ✶ is nów, and | ever | shall be : wórld without | end. | A- | -men.

JUBILATE DEO

Dr. P. Hayes.
R. Goodson.
Dr. E. Ayrton.
Rev. Sir F. Ouseley.

JUBILATE DEO.—*Psalm* c.

F. f O BE joyful in the Lórd | all ye | lands : serve the Lord with gladness ✱ and come befóre his | presence | with a | song.

F. 2 Be ye sure that the Lórd | he is | God : it is he that hath made us and not we ourselves ✱ we are his people, ánd the | sheep of | his | pasture.

3 O go your way into his gates with thanksgiving ✱ and ínto his | courts with | praise : be thankful unto hím, and | speak good | of his | Name.

mf 4 For the Lord is gracious ✱ his mércy is | ever- | -lasting : and his truth endureth from géner- | -ation · to | gener- | -ation.

F. f Glory be to the Fáther, | and · to the | Son : ánd | to the | Holy | Ghost ;

F. As it was in the beginning ✱ is nów, and | ever | shall be : wórld without | end. | A- | -men.

MAGNIFICAT.

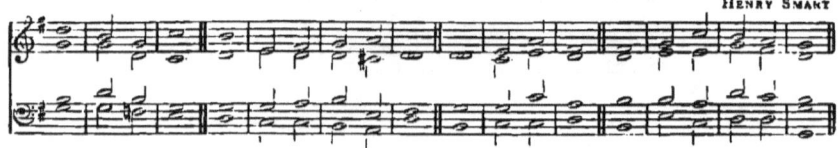

MAGNIFICAT.—*St. Luke* i. 46.

F. mf MY soul doth mágni- | -fy the | Lord : and my spirit háth re- | -joiced . in | God my | Saviour.

F. 2 Fór he | hath re- | -garded : the lówliness | of his | hand- | -maiden.

3 Fór be- | -hold from | henceforth : áll gener- | -ations . shall I call me | blessed.

4 For he that is mighty hath | magnified | me : ánd | holy | is his | Name.

2nd part 5 And his mércy is on | them that | fear him : throughóut | all | gener- | ations.

6 He hath showed stréngth | with his | arm : he hath scattered the proud in the imágin- | -ation | of their | hearts.

7 He hath put down the míghty | from their | seat : and háth ex- | -alted . the | humble . and | meek.

8 He hath filled the húngry with | good | things : and the rích he hath | sent | empty . a- | -way.

9 He remembering his mercy hath hólpen his | servant | Israel : as he promised to our forefathers ✱ A'braham | and his | seed for | ever.

F. f Glory be to the Fáther, | and . to the | Son : ánd | to the | Holy | Ghost ;

F. As it was in the beginning ✱ is nów, and | ever | shall be : wórld without | end. | A- | -men

CANTATE DOMINO.

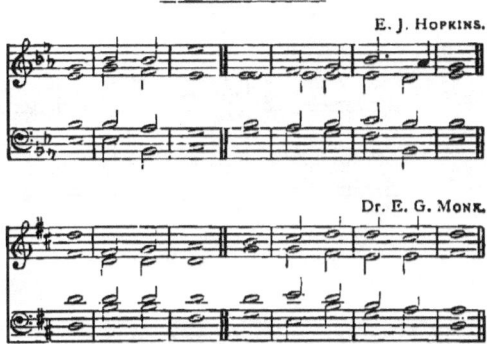

E. J. Hopkins.

Dr. E. G. Monk.

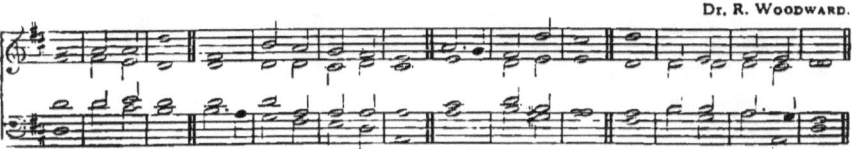

Dr. R. Woodward.

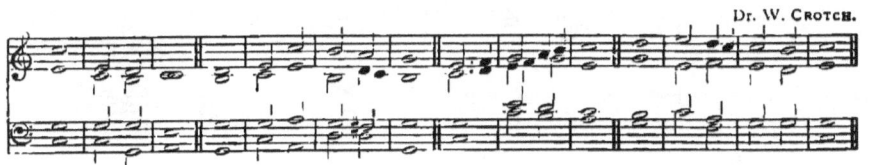

Dr. W. Crotch.

CANTATE DOMINO.—*Psalm* xcviii.

F. f O SING unto the Lórd a | new | song : for hé hath | done | marvellous | things.

F. 2 With his own right hand ✶ and wíth his | holy | arm : háth he | gotten · him- | self the | victory.

3 The Lord decláred | his sal- | vation : his righteousness hath he openly shówed in the | sight | of the | heathen.

4 He hath remembered his mercy and truth, tóward the | house of | Israel : and all the ends of the world have séen the sal- | -vation | of our | God.

5 Show yourselves joyful unto the Lórd | all ye | lands : síng, re- | -jóice and | give | thanks.

6 Praise the Lórd up- | -on the | harp : sing to the hárp with a | psalm of | thanks- | giving.

7 With trúmpets | also and | shawms : O show yourselves jóyful be- | -fore the | Lord the | King.

8 Let the sea make a noise ✶ and áll that | therein | is : the round wórld, and | they that | dwell there- | -in.

9 Let the floods clap their hands ✶ and let the hills be joyful togéther be- | -fore the | Lord : fór he | cometh · to | judge the | earth.

10 With righteousness sháll he | judge the | world : ánd the | people | with | equity.

F. f Glory be to the Fáther, | and · to the | Son : ánd | to the | Holy | Ghost ;

F. As it was in the beginning ✶ is nów, and | ever | shall be : wórld without | end. | A- | -men.

BONUM EST CONFITERI.

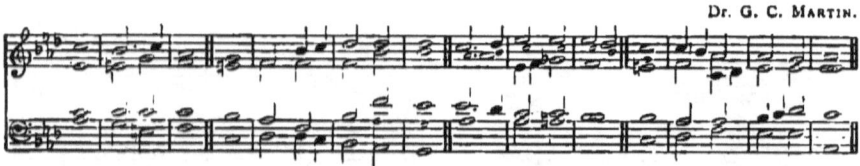

BONUM EST CONFITERI.—*Psalm* xcii. 1—4.

F. ƒ IT is a good thing to give thánks | unto · the | Lord : and to sing praises únto thy | Name | O most | Highest ;

F. 2 To tell of thy loving-kindness éarly | in the | morning : and of thy trúth | in the | night- | -season ;

3 Upon an instrument of ten strings ✱ ánd up- | -on the | lute : upon a loud ínstrument | and up- | -on the | harp.

4 For thou, Lord, hast made me gláscript | through thy | works : and I will rejoice in giving praise, for the óper- | ations | of thy | hands.

F. ƒ Glory be to the Fáther, | and · to the | Son : ánd | to the | Holy | Ghost ;

F. As it was in the beginning ✱ is nów, and | ever | shall be : world without | end. | A- | -men.

NUNC DIMITTIS.

NUNC DIMITTIS.—*St. Luke* ii. 29.

F.mp LORD, now lettest thou thy sérvant | de- | -part in | peace : ác- | -cording | to thy | word.

2 Fór mine | eyes have | seen : thý | — sal- | -va- | -tion,

3 Whĭch thou | hast pre- | -pared : befóre the | face of | all | people;

4 To be a lĭght to | lighten · the | Gentiles : and to be the glóry | of thy people | Israel.

F. f Glory be to the Fáther, | and · to the Son : ánd | to the | Holy | Ghost;

F. As it was in the beginning ✶ is nów, and | ever | shall be : wórld without | end. A- | -men.

DEUS MISEREATUR.

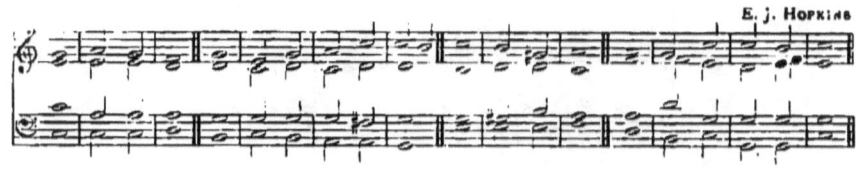

E. J. Hopkins.

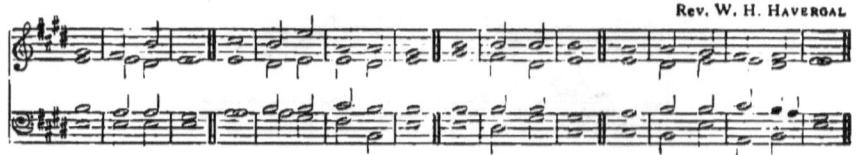

Rev. W. H. Havergal.

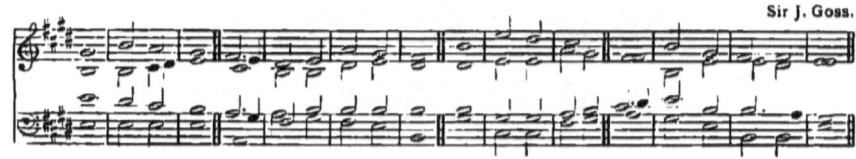

Sir J. Goss.

A. H. Littleton.

DEUS MISEREATUR.—*Psalm* lxvii.

mf GOD be merciful únto | us and | bless us : and show us the light of his countenance ✶ ánd be | merciful | unto | us ;

F. 2 That thy way may be knówn up- | on | earth : thy sáving | health a- | -mong all | nations.

F. 3 Let the people práise | thee O | God : yéa let | all the | people | praise thee.

4 O let the nations rejóice | and be | glad : for thou shalt judge the folk righteously ✶ and góvern the | nations · up- | on | earth.

F. 5 Let the people práise | thee O | God : yéa let | all the | people | praise thee.

6 Then shall the éarth bring | forth her | increase : and God, even our own Gód, shall | give | us his | blessing.

2nd part 7 Gód | shall | bless us : and all the ends of the | world shall | fear | him.

F. f Glory be to the Fáther, | and · to the | Son : ánd | to the | Holy | Ghost ;

F. As it was in the beginning ✶ is nów, and | ever | shall be : wórld without | end. | A- | -men.

BENEDIC. ANIMA MEA.

xxvii

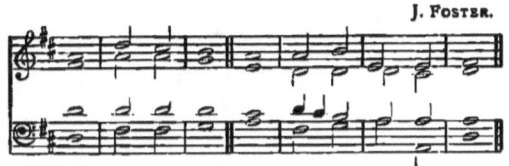

BENEDIC, ANIMA MEA.—*Psalm* ciii. 1—4, 20—22.

F. f PRAISE the Lórd | O my | soul: and all that is withín me | praise his | holy | Name.

F. 2 Praise the Lórd | O my | soul: ánd for- | -get not | all his | benefits;

3 Who forgíveth | all thy | sin: and héaleth | all | thine in- | -firmities;

4 Who saveth thy lífe | from de- | struction : and crowneth thée with | mercy · and | loving- | -kindness ;

5 O praise the Lord, ye angels of his ✱ yé that ex- | -cel in | strength; ye that fulfil his commandment ✱ and hearken únto the | voice | of his | word.

6 O praise the Lórd, all | ye his | hosts: ye sérvants of | his that | do his | pleasure.

2nd part 7 O speak good of the Lord, all ye works of his ✱ in all pláces of | his do- | minion : práise thou the | Lord | O my | soul.

F. f Glory be to the Fáther, | and · to the | Son : ánd | to the | Holy | Ghost;

F. As it was in the beginning ✱ is nów, and | ever | shall be : wórld without end. | A- | -men.

THE PSALMS OF DAVID.

DAY I. MORNING.

S. Wesley.

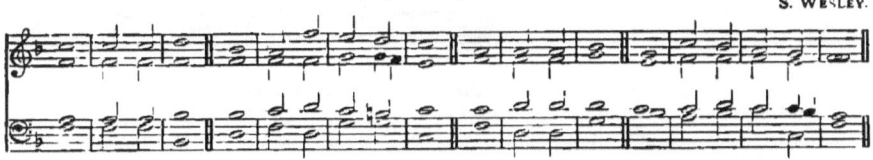

PSALM I.—*Beatus vir, qui non abiit.*

mf BLESSED is the man that hath not walked in the counsel of the ungodly * nor stood in the | way of | sinners : and hath not sát in the | seat | of the | scornful.

2 But his delight is in the láw | of the | Lord : and in his law will he exercíse him- | -self | day and | night.

3 And he shall be like a tree planted by the | water | side : that will bring fórth his | fruit in | due | season.

4 His léaf also | shall not | wither : and look, whatsoéver he doeth | it shall | prosper.

5 As for the ungodly, it is nót | so with | them : but they are like the chaff * which the wind scattereth awáy from the | face | of the | earth.

6 Therefore the ungodly shall not be able to stánd | in the | judgement : neither the sinners in the cóngre- | -gation | of the | righteous.

2nd part. 7 But the Lord knoweth the wáy | of the | righteous : and the wáy of the un- | godly | shall | perish.

J. Turle.

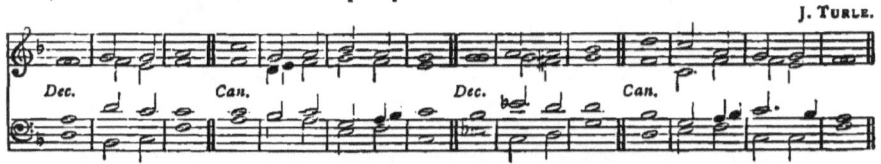

PSALM II.—*Quare fremuerunt gentes?*

f WHY do the heathen so fúriously | rage to- | -gether : and why do the péople im- | -agine · a | vain | thing ?

2 The kings of the earth stand up * and the rúlers take | counsel · to- | -gether : against the Lórd and a- | -gainst | his A- | nointed.

3 Let us bréak their | bonds a-|-sunder : and cást a- | -way their | cords | from us.

4 He that dwelleth in héaven shall | laugh them · to | scorn : the Lórd shall | have them | in de- | -rision.

5 Then shall he speak unto thém | in his | wrath : and véx them | in his | sore dis- | -pleasure.

6 Yét have I | set my | King : upón my | holy | hill of | Sion.

7 I will preach the law * whereof the Lord hath sáid | unto | me : Thou art my Son * this dáy have | I be- | -gotten | thee.

8 Desire of me * and I shall give thee the héathen for | thine in- | -heritance : and the utmost párts of the | earth for | thy pos- | -session.

9 Thou shalt brúise them with a | rod of | iron : and break them in pièces | like a | potter's | vessel.

10 Be wise now thérefore | O ye | kings : be learned, yé that are | judges | of the | earth.

11 Sérve the | Lord in | fear : and re- jóice | unto | him with | reverence.

12 Kiss the Son lest he be angry, and so ye pérish from the | right | way : if his wrath be kindled (yea but a little), * blessed are all théy that | put their | trust in | him.

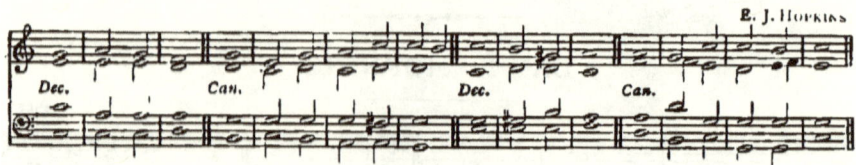

E. J. Hopkins.

PSALM III.—*Domine, quid multiplicati!*

mp LORD, how are they incréased that | trouble | me : mány are | they that | rise a- | -gainst me.

2 Many one there be that sáy | of my | soul : There is no hélp | for him | in his | God.

3 But thou, O Lórd art | my de- | fender · thou art my worship ✶ and the lífter | p of | my | head.

4 I did call upon the Lórd | with my | voice : and he héard me | out of · his | holy | hill

5 I laid me down and slept ✶ and róse | up a- | -gain : fór the | Lord sus- | tained | me.

6 I will not be afraid for ten thóu- sands | of the | people : that have set them- sélves a- | -gainst me | round a- | -bout.

f 7 Up, Lord, and hélp me | O my | God : for thou smitest all mine enemies upon the cheekbone ✶ thou hast bróken the | teeth of | the un- | -godly.

8 Salvation belóngeth | unto · the | Lord : and thy bléssing | is up- | -on thy | people.

Dr. E. G. Monk.

PSALM IV.—*Cum invocarem.*

mf HEAR me when I call, O Gód | of my | righteousness : thou hast set me at liberty when I was in trouble ✶ have mercy upon mé, and | hearken | unto · my | prayer.

2 O ye sons of men ✶ how lóng will ye blas- | -pheme mine | honour : and have such pleasure in vánity and | seek | after | falsehood ?

3 Know this also ✶ that the Lord hath chosen to himself the mán | that is | godly : when I cáll upon the | Lord | he will | hear me.

4 Stánd in | awe and | sin not : com-

mune with your own heart ✶ and ín your chamber | and be | still.

5 Offer the sácri- | -fice of | righteous- ness : and pút your | trust | in the | Lord.

6 Thére be | many · that | say : Whó will | shew us | any | good ?

7 Lórd | lift thou | up : the líght of thy | counte- | -nance up- | -on us.

8 Thou hast put gládness | in my | heart : since the time that their córn and | wine and | oil in- | -creased.

9 I will lay me down in péace, and | take my | rest : for it is thou, Lord, ónly that | makest · me | dwell in | safety.

Anon.

PSALM V.—*Verba mea auribus.*

mf PÓNDER my | words O | Lord : cón- | -sider · my | medi- | -tation.

2 O hearken thou unto the voice

of my calling ✶ my Kíng | and my | God : for unto thée | will I | make my | prayer.

DAY I. MORNING (continued).

3 My voice shalt thou héar be- | -times
O | Lord : early in the morning will I direct
my prayer unto thée | and will | look | up.

4 For thou art the God that hást no |
pleasure . in | wickedness: neither shall
ány | evil | dwell with | thee.

5 Such as be foolish shall not stánd |
in thy | sight : for thou hátest all | them
that | work | vanity.

6 Thou shalt destróy them that |
speak | lies : the Lord will abhor both
the blóodthirsty | and de- | -ceitful | man.

7 But as for me, I will come into
thine house * even upon the múltitude |
of thy | mercy : and in thy fear will I
wórship | toward · thy | holy | temple.

8 Lead me O Lord in thy righteous-
ness * becáuse | of mine | enemies : make
thy wáy | plain be- | -fore my | face.

9 For there is no fáithfulness | in his |
mouth : their ínward | parts are | very
wickedness.

10 Their thróat is an | open | sepulchre:
théy | flatter | with their | tongue.

11 Destroy thou them O God * let
them perish through their ówn im- | -agin- |
ations : cast them out in the multitude of
their ungodliness * fór they | have re- |
belled · a- | -gainst thee.

ƒ 12 And let all them that put their trúst
in | thee re- | -joice : they shall ever be
giving of thanks because thou defendest
them * they that love thy Náme | shall
be | joyful · in | thee.

2nd part 13 For thou Lord wilt give thy bléssing |
unto · the | righteous : and with thy favour-
able kindness wilt thóu de- | -fend him
as · with a | shield.

DAY I. EVENING.

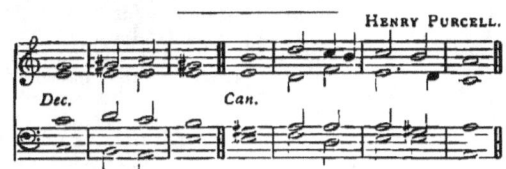

PSALM VI.—*Domine, ne in furore.*

F. mp O LORD rebuke me nót in thine |
indig- | -nation : neither chásten | me in |
thy dis- | -pleasure.

F. 2 Have mercy upon me O Lórd, for |
I am | weak : O Lord héal me | for my |
bones are | vexed.

3 My soul álso is | sore | troubled :
but Lord, how lóng | wilt thou | punish |
me?

4 Turn thee O Lórd and de- | -liver ·
my | soul : O sáve me | for thy | mercy's |
sake.

5 For in death nó man re- | -mem-
bereth | thee : and who will gíve thee |
thanks | in the | pit?

6 I am weary of my groaning * every
night wásh | I my | bed : and wáter my |
couch | with my | tears.

7 My beauty is góne for | very |
trouble : and worn awáy be- | -cause of |
all mine | enemies.

8 Away from me, all yé that | work |
vanity : for the Lord hath héard the |
voice | of my | weeping.

9 The Lord hath héard | my pe- |
tition : the Lórd | will re- | -ceive my | prayer.

10 All mine enemies shall be con-
foúnded and | sore | vexed : they shall be
turned báck, and | put to | shame | sud-
denly.

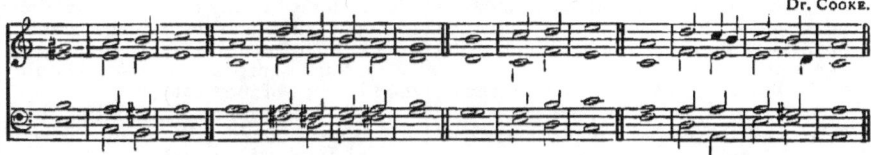

PSALM VII.—*Domine, Deus meus.*

mf O LORD my God, in thée have I |
put my | trust : save me from all them
that pérsecute me | and de- | -liver | me;

2 Lest he devour my soul líke a líon
and | tear it . in | pieces : whíle | there is |
none to | help.

DAY I. EVENING (continued).

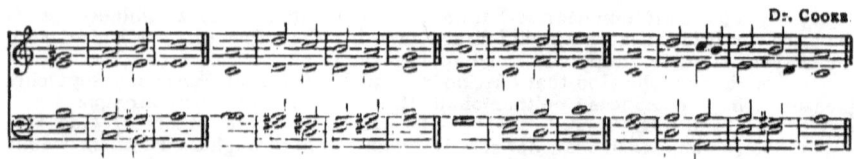
Dr. Cooke.

3 O Lord my God * if I have done | any · such | thing : or if there be any | wickedness | in my | hands;

4 If I have rewarded evil unto him that dealt | friendly · with | me : yea, I have delivered him that without any | cause | is mine | enemy;

5 Then let mine enemy persecute my | soul and | take me : yea, let him tread my life down upon the earth * and lay mine | honour | in the | dust.

6 Stand up O Lord in thy wrath, and lift up thyself * because of the indignà- | tion | of mine | enemies : arise up for me in the judgement | that thou | hast com- | manded.

7 And so shall the congregation of the people | come a- | -bout thee : for their sakes therefore, lift | up thy- | -self a- | gain.

8 The Lord shall judge the people * give sentence with | me O | Lord : according to my righteousness * and according to the innocency | that is | in | me.

9 O let the wickedness of the ungodly | come · to an | end : but | guide | thou the | just.

10 For the | righteous | God : trieth the | very | hearts and | reins.

f 11 My help | cometh · of | God : who preserveth them | that are | true of | heart.

12 God is a righteous Judge | strong and | patient : and God is pro- | -voked | every | day.

13 If a man will not turn he will | whet his | sword : he hath bent his | bow and | made it | ready.

14 He hath prepared for him the instru- | -ments of | death : he ordaineth his arrows a- | -gainst the | perse- | cutors.

15 Behold he travail- | -eth with | mischief : he hath conceived sorrow and | brought | forth un- | -godliness.

16 He hath graven and digged | up a | pit : and is fallen himself into the destruction | that he | made for | other.

17 For his travail shall come upon his | own | head : and his wickedness shall fall | on his | own | pate.

18 I will give thanks unto the Lord according | to his | righteousness : and I will praise the Name | of the | Lord most | High.

Rev. W. Tucker.

PSALM VIII.—*Domine, Dominus noster.*

f O LORD our Governour * how excellent is thy Name in | all the | world : thou that hast set thy | glory · a- | -bove the | heavens.

2 Out of the mouth of very babes and sucklings hast thou ordained strength * because | of thine | enemies : that thou mightest still the | enemy | and · the a- | -venger.

3 For I will consider thy heavens * even the works | of thy | fingers : the moon and the stars | which thou | hast or- | -dained.

4 What is man, that thou art | mindful · of | him : and the son of man that thou | visitest | him ?

5 Thou madest him lower | than the | angels : to crown | him with | glory · and | worship.

6 Thou makest him to have dominion of the works | of thy | hands : and thou hast put all things in sub- | -jection | under · his | feet ;

7 All | sheep and | oxen : yea and the | beasts | of the | field ;

8 The fowls of the air, and the fishes | of the | sea : and whatsoever walketh through the | paths | of the | seas.

9 O | Lord our | Governour : how excellent is thy | Name in | all the | world |

DAY II. MORNING.

I. Sir H. S. Oakeley.

Alternative Chant.

II. Sir J. Goss.

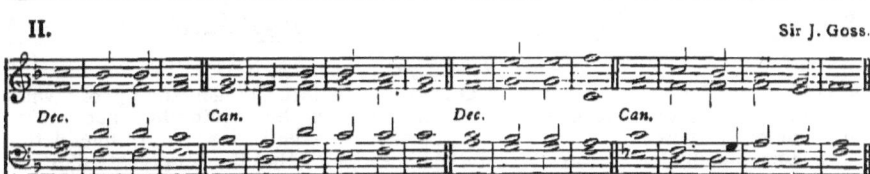

PSALM IX.—*Confitebor tibi.*

mf 1 I WILL give thanks unto thee O Lord, wíth my | whole | heart : I will speák of | all thy | marvellous | works.

2 I will be glád and re- | -joice in | thee : yea, my songs will I máke of thy | Name O ! thou most | Highest.

3 While mine énemies are | driven | back : they shall fáll and | perish | at thy | presence.

4 For thou hast maintained my ríght | and my | cause : thou art sét in the | throne that | judgest | right.

5 Thou hast rebuked the heathen * and destróyed | the un- | -godly : thou hast put oút their | name for | ever · and | ever.

6 O thou enemy, destructions are cóme to a per- | -petual | end : even as the cities which thou hast destroyed * their me- | -morial · is | perished | with them.

7 But the Lórd shall en- | -dure for | ever : he hath álso pre- | -pared · his | seat for | judgement.

8 For he shall júdge the | world in | righteousness : and minister trúe | judge- ment | unto · the | people.

9 The Lord also will be a defénce | for · the op- | -pressed : even a réfuge in | due | time of | trouble.

10 And they that know thy Name will pút their | trust in | thee : for thou, Lord, hast néver | failed | them that | seek thee.

11 O praise the Lórd which | dwell- eth . in | Sion : shéw the | people | of his | doings.

12 For when he maketh inquisition for blood, hé re- | -membereth | them : and forgetteth nót the com- | -plaint | of the | poor.

13 Have mercy upon me O Lord * consider the trouble which I súffer of | them that | hate me : thou that liftest me úp | from the | gates of | death.

14 That I may shew all thy praises within the pórts of the | daughter · of | Sion : I' will re- | -joice in | thy sal- | -va- tion.

15 The heathen are sunk down in the pít | that they | made : in the same net which they hid prívily | is their | foot | taken.

16 The Lord is knówn to | execute | judgement : the ungodly is trapped in the wórk | of his | own | hands.

17 The wicked shall be túrned | into | hell : and all the péople | that for- | -get | God.

18 For the poor shall not álway | be for- | -gotten : the patient abiding of the méek | shall not | perish · for | ever.

19 Up, Lord, and let not mán have the | upper | hand : let the héathen be | judged | in thy | sight.

20 Pút them in | fear O | Lord : that the heathen may knów them- | -selves to | be but | men.

DAY II. MORNING (continued).

PSALM X.—*Ut quid, Domine?*

mp WHY standest thou so far | off O | Lord : and hidest thy face in the | need- | ful | time of | trouble ?

2 The ungodly for his own lust doth perse- | -cute the | poor : let them be taken in the crafty wiliness | that they | have im- | -agined.

3 For the ungodly hath made boast of his own | heart's de- | -sire : and speaketh good of the covetous | whom | God ab- | -horreth.

4 The ungodly is so proud, that he careth | not for | God : neither is | God in | all his | thoughts.

5 His ways are | alway | grievous : thy judgements are far above out of his sight * and therefore de- | -fieth · he | all his | enemies.

6 For he hath said in his heart * Tush, I shall never be | cast | down : there shall no harm | happen | unto | me.

7 His mouth is full of cursing, de- | ceit and | fraud : under his tongue is un- | -godli- | -ness and | vanity.

8 He sitteth lurking in the thievish corners | of the | streets : and privily in his lurking dens doth he murder the innocent * his eyes are | set a- | -gainst the | poor.

9 For he lieth waiting secretly * even as a lion lurketh he | in his | den : that | he may | ravish · the | poor.

10 He doth | ravish · the | poor : when he | getteth · him | into · his | net.

11 He falleth down, and | humbleth · him- | -self : that the congregation of the poor may fall into the | hands | of his | captains.

12 He hath said in his heart * Tush, God | hath for- | -gotten : he hideth away his face, and | he will | never | see it.

13 Arise, O Lord God * and lift up | thine | hand : for- | -get | not the | poor.

14 Wherefore should the wicked blas- | pheme | God : while he doth say in his heart * Tush | thou God | carest · not | for it.

15 Surely | thou hast | seen it : for thou beholdest un- | -godli- | -ness and | wrong.

16 That thou mayest take the matter | into · thine | hand : the poor committeth himself unto thee * for thou art the | helper | of the | friendless.

17 Break thou the power of the ungodly | and ma- | -licious : take away his ungodliness and | thou shalt | find | none.

18 The Lord is King for | ever · and | ever : and the heathen are | perished | out · of the | land.

19 Lord thou hast heard the desire | of the | poor : thou preparest their heart * and thine ear | hearkeneth | there- | -to ;

20 To help the fatherless and poor | unto · their | right : that the man of the earth be no | more ex- | -alted · a- | -gainst them.

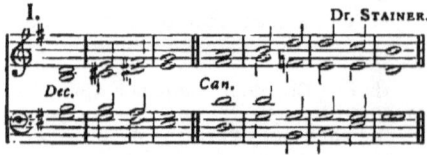
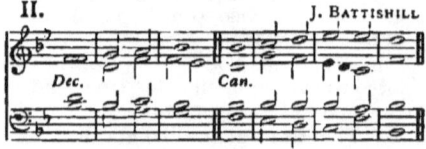

PSALM XI.—*In Domino confido.*

mf IN the Lord put | I my | trust : how say ye then to my soul * that she should flee as a | bird | unto · the | hill ?

2 For lo, the ungodly bend their bow * and make ready their arrows with- | -in the | quiver : that they may privily shoot at them | which are | true of | heart.

DAY II. MORNING (continued).

3 For the foundations will be | cast | down : and what | hath the | righteous | done ?

4 The Lord is in his | holy | temple : the Lord's | seat | is in | heaven.

5 His eyes con- | -sider · the | poor : and his eyelids | try the | children · of | men.

6 The Lord al- | -loweth · the | righteous : but the ungodly and him that delighteth in wickedness | doth his | soul ab- | -hor.

7 Upon the ungodly he shall rain snares ✱ fire and brimstone, | storm and | tempest : this shall | be their | portion · to | drink.

8 For the righteous Lord | loveth | righteousness : his countenance will behold the | thing | that is | just.

DAY II. EVENING.

I. J. TURLE.

Alternative Chant.

II. Dr. STAINER.

PSALM XII.—*Salvum me fac.*

F. *mf* HELP me, Lord ✱ for there is not one | godly · man | left : for the faithful are minished from a- | -mong the | children · of | men.

F. 2 They talk of vanity every one | with his | neighbour : they do but flatter with their lips ✱ and dissemble | in their | double | heart.

3 The Lord shall root out all deceitful | lips : and the tongue that | speaketh | proud | things;

4 Which have said ✱ With our tongue will | we pre- | -vail : we are they that ought to speak, who is | lord | over | us ?

5 Now for the comfortless troubles' sake | of the | needy : and because of the deep | sighing | of the | poor,

6 I will up | saith the | Lord : and will help every one from him that swelleth against him | and will | set him · at | rest.

7 The words of the Lord are | pure | words : even as the silver ✱ which from the earth is tried, and purified | seven · times | in the | fire.

8 Thou shalt keep | them O | Lord : thou shalt preserve him from this | generation · for | ever.

2nd part 9 The ungodly walk on | every | side : when they are exalted, the children of | men are | put · to re- | -buke.

PSALM XIII.—*Usque quo, Domine ?*

mp HOW long wilt thou forget me O | Lord for | ever : how long wilt thou | hide thy | face | from me ?

2 How long shall I seek counsel in my soul ✱ and be so vexed | in my | heart : how long shall mine enemies | triumph | | over | me ?

3 Consider, and hear me O | Lord my | God : lighten mine eyes that I | sleep | not in | death.

4 Lest mine enemy say ✱ I' have pre- | -vailed · a- | -gainst him : for if I be cast down ✱ they that trouble me | will re- | -joice | at it.

f 5 But my trust is | in thy | mercy : and my heart is | joyful · in | thy sal-l-vation.

6 I will sing of the Lord ✱ because he hath dealt so | lovingly | with me : yea, I will praise the Name | of the | Lord most | Highest.

DAY II. EVENING (continued).

PSALM XIV.—*Dixit insipiens.*

mf THE fool hath sáid l in his l heart ; l Thére l is l no l God.

2 They are corrupt, and become abóminable l in their l doings : there is none that dóeth l good l no not l one.

3 The Lord looked down from heaven upon the l children · of l men : to see if there were any that would understánd, and l seek l after l God.

4 But they are all gone, out of the way * they are altogéther be- l ·come a- l bominable : there is none that dóeth l good l no not l one.

5 Their throat is an open sepulchre * with their tóngues have l they de- l ·ceived : the póison of l asps is l under · their l lips.

6 Their mouth is full of l cursing · and l bitterness : their féet are l swift to l shed l blood.

2nd part. 7 Destruction and unhappiness is in their ways * and the way of péace have l they not l known : there is no féar of l God be- l ·fore their l eyes.

8 Have they no knowledge, that they are áll such l workers · of l mischief : eating up my people as it were bréad, and l call · not up- l ·on the l Lord ?

9 There were they brought in great fear * éven where l no fear l was : for God is in the géner- l ·ation l of the l righteous.

10 As for you * ye have made a mock at the cóunsel l of the l poor : because he pútteth l his l trust l in the l Lord.

11 Who shall give salvation unto Israel out of Sion ? * When the Lord turneth the captivity l of his l people : then shall Jacob rejóice, and l Israel l shall be l glad.

DAY III. MORNING.

PSALM XV.—*Domine, quis habitabit ?*

mf LORD, who shall dwéll in thy l l taber- l nacle : or who shall rést up- l ·on thy l holy l hill ?

2 Even he that léadeth an l uncorrupt l life : and doeth the thing which is right * and spéaketh the l truth l from his l heart.

3 He that hath used no deceit in his tongue * nor done évil l to his l neighbour : ánd l hath not l slandered · his l neighbour

4 He that sétteth not by himself * but is lówly in his l own l eyes : and maketh múch of l them that l fear the l Lord.

5 He that sweareth unto his neighbour * and dísap- l ·pointeth · him l not : though it l were · to hís l own l hindrance.

6 He that hath not given his móney up- l ·on l usury : nor táken re- l ·ward a- l ·gainst the l innocent.

7 Whóso l doeth · these l things : sháll l nev- l ·er l fall.

DAY III. MORNING (continued).

PSALM XVI.—*Conserva me, Domine.*

mf PRESÉRVE | me O | God : for in thée | have I | put my | trust.

2 O my soul, thou hast sáid | unto • the | Lord : Thou art my Gcd * my góods are | nothing | unto | thee.

3 All my delight is upon the sáints that are | in the | earth : ánd upon | such as • ex- | -cel in | virtue.

4 But they that run áfter an- | -other | god : shall | have | great | trouble.

5 Their drink-offerings of blóod will | I not | offer : neither make méntion of their | names with- | -in my | lips.

6 The Lord himself is the portion of mine inhéritance and | of my | cup : thóu | shalt main- | -tain my | lot.

7 The lot is fallen unto mé in a | fair | ground : yéa I ' have a | goodly | heritage.

8 I will thank the Lord for | giving • me | warning : my reins also chásten me | in the | night- | -season.

9 I have set Gód | always • be- | -fore me : for he is on my right hánd | there- fore • I | shall not | fall.

10 Wherefore my heart was glád and my | glory • re- | -joiced : my flésh | also • shall | rest in | hope.

11 For why * thou shalt not léave my | soul in | hell : neither shalt thou suffer thy Hóly | One to | see cor- | -rup- tion.

12 Thou shalt shew me the path of life * in thy presence is the | fulness • of | joy : and at thy right hánd there is | plea- sure • for | ever- | -more.

I. TOMLINSON.

II. A. H. LITTLETON.

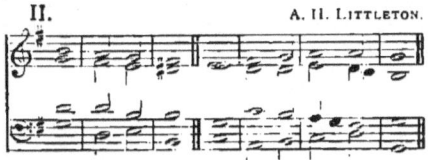

PSALM XVII.—*Exaudi, Domine.*

mp HEAR the right O Lord * consíder | my com- | -plaint : and hearken unto my prayer * that góeth not | out of | feigned | lips.

2 Let my sentence come fórth | from thy | presence : and let thine eyes look upón the | thing | that is | equal.

3 Thou hast proved and visited mine heart in the night-season * thou hast tried me, and shalt find no | wickedness | in me : for I am utterly purposed thát my | mouth shall | not of- | -fend.

4 Because of men's works that are done against the wórds | of thy | lips : I have kept me fróm the | ways of | the de- | -stroyer.

5 O hold thou up my góings | in thy | paths : thát my | footsteps | slip | not.

6 I have called upon thee O Gód, for | thou shalt | hear me : incline thine ear to mé, and | hearken | unto • my | words.

mf 7 Shew thy marvellous loving-kind- ness * thou that art the Saviour of them which pút their | trust in | thee : from súch as re- | -sist thy | right | hand.

8 Keep me as the ápple | of an | eye : hide me únder the | shadow | of thy | wings,

9 From the ungódly that | trouble | me : mine enemies compass me round about to | take a- | -way my | soul.

10 They are enclósed in their | own | fat : and their móuth | speaketh | proud | things.

11 They lie waiting in our wáy on | every | side : turning their éyes | down | to the | ground ;

12 Like as a lion that is grédy | of his | prey : and as it were a lion's whélp | lurking • in | secret | places.

13 Up, Lord, disappóint him and | cast him | down : deliver my soul from the ungódly which | is a | sword of | thine ;

14 From the men of thy hand, O Lord * from the men I say, and fróm the | evil | world : which have their portion in this life * whose bellies thou fillest | with thy | hid | treasure.

15 They have chíldren at | their de- | sire : and leave the rést of their | sub- stance | for their | babes.

16 But as for me * I will behóld thy | presence • in | righteousness : and when I awake up after thy likeness * I° shall be | satis- | -fied | with it.

DAY III. EVENING.

PSALM XVIII.—*Diligam te, Domine.*

F. f 1 I WILL love thee O Lord my strength * the Lord is my stony rock and I my de- I -fence : my Saviour, my God, and my might, in whom I will trust * my buckler, the horn also of my sal- I vation I and my I refuge.

F. 2 I will call upon the Lord, which is worthy I to be I praised : so shall I" be I safe I from mine I enemies.

p 3 The sorrows of death I compassed I me : and the overflowings of ungodliness I made I me a- I -fraid.

4 The pains of hell I came a- I -bout me : the snares of I death I over-I-took me.

5 In my trouble I will call up-I-on the I Lord : and com-I-plain I unto · my I God.

6 So shall he hear my voice out of his I holy I temple : and my complaint shall come before him * it shall enter I even I into · his I ears.

mf 7 The earth I trembled · and I quaked : the very foundations also of the hills shook * and were removed be- I -cause I he was I wroth.

8 There went a smoke out I in his I presence : and a consuming fire out of his mouth * so that I coals were I kindled I at it.

9 He bowed the heavens also and I came I down : and it was I dark I under · his I feet.

10 He rode upon the cherubims I and did I fly : he came flying upon the I wings I of the I wind.

11 He made darkness his I secret I place : his pavilion round about him with dark water * and thick I clouds to I cover I him.

12 At the brightness of his presence his I clouds re- I -moved : hail- I -stones and I coals of I fire.

f 13 The Lord also thundered out of heaven * and the Highest I gave his I thunder : hail- I -stones and I coals of I fire.

14 He sent out his arrows and I scattered I them : he cast forth lightnings I and de- I -stroyed I them.

DAY III. EVENING (continued).

15 The springs of waters were seen, and the foundations of the round world were discovered * at thy | chiding . O | Lord : at the blásting of the | breath of | | thy dis- | -pleasure.

mf 16 He shall send dówn from on | high to | fetch me : and shall táke me | out of | many | waters.

17 He shall deliver me from my strong- est enemy * ánd from | them which | hate me : fôr they | are too | mighty . for | me.

18 They prevented me in the dáy | of my | trouble : bût the | Lord was | my up- | -holder.

19 He brought me forth also ínto a | place of | liberty : he brought me forth * éven because he hád a | favour | unto | me.

20 The Lord shall reward me áfter my | righteous | dealing : according to the cleanness of my hánds | shall he | recom- pense | me.

21 Because I have kept the wáys | of the | Lord : and have not forsaken my Gód | as the | wicked | doth.

22 For I have an éye unto | all his | laws : and will not cást out | his com- | mandments | from me.

23 I was also úncor- | -rupt be- | -fore him : ánd es- | -chewed . mine | own | wickedness.

24 Therefore shall the Lord reward me áfter my | righteous | dealing : and accord- ing unto the cléanness of my | hands | in his | eyesight.

25 With the hóly thou | shalt be | holy : and with a pérfect man | thou | shalt be | perfect.

26 With the cléan thou | shalt be | clean : and with the fróward | thou shalt | learn | frowardness.

27 For thou shalt save the péople that are | in ad- | -versity : and shalt bring dówn the | high looks | of the | proud.

28 Thou álso shalt | light my | candle : the Lord my God shall máke my *f* dark- ness | to be | light.

29 For in thee I shall discómfit an | host of | men : and with the help of my Gód I shall | leap | over . the | wall.

f 30 The way of God is an únde- | -filed | way : the word of the Lord also is tried in the fire * he is the defender of all thém that | put their | trust in | him.

31 For who is Gód | but the | Lord : or whó hath any strength ex- | -cept our God ?

32 It is God that gírdeth me with | strength of | war : ánd | maketh . my | way | perfect.

33 He máketh my | feet like | harts' feet : ánd | setteth . me | up on | high.

34 He téacheth mine | hands to | fight : and mine arms shall bréak | even a | bow of | steel.

35 Thou hast given me the defénce of | thy sal- | -vation : thy right hand also shall hold me up * and thy lóving cor- | -rec- tion . shall | make me | great.

36 Thou shalt make room enough únder me | for to | go : thát my | footsteps | shall not | slide.

37 I will follow upon mine énemies and | over- | -take them : neither will I turn agáin till I | | have de- | -stroyed | them.

38 I will smite them * that they shal nót be | able . to | stand : bút | fall | under . my | feet.

39 Thou hast girded me with stréngth | unto . the | battle : thou shalt throw dówn mine | enemies | under | me.

40 Thou hast made mine enemies also to túrn their | backs up- | -on me : and I' shall de- | -stroy | them that | hate me.

41 They shall cry * but thére shall be i none to | help them : yea even unto the Lord shall they crý | but he | shall not | hear them.

42 I will beat them as small as the dúst be- | -fore the | wind : I will cast them óut as the | clay | in the | streets.

43 Thou shalt deliver me from the strívings | of the | people : and thou shalt máke me the | head | of the | heathen

44 A péople whom I | | have not | known : shall | serve | — | me.

45 As soon as they héar of me they | shall o- | -bey me : but the stránge children | shall dis- | -semble | with me.

46 The stránge | children . shall | fail : ánd be a- | -fraid | out of . their | prisons.

47 The Lord liveth * and blessed bé my | strong | helper : and praised bé the | God of | my sal- | -vation.

48 Even the God that séeth that I | be a- | -venged : and subdúeth the | people | unto | me.

49 It is he that delivereth me from my cruel enemies * and setteth me úp a- | bove mine | adversaries : thou shalt rid me | from the | wicked | man.

50 For this cause will I give thanks unto thee O Lórd a- | -mong the | Gen- tiles : and síng | praises | unto . thy | Name.

51 Great prosperity gíveth he | unto . his | king : and sheweth loving-kindness unto David his Anointed * and únto his | seed for | ever- | -more.

DAY IV. MORNING.

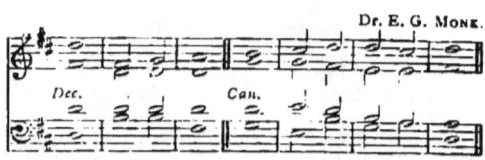

PSALM XIX.—*Cœli enarrant.*

THE heavens declâre the | glory · of | God : and the fírmament | sheweth · his | handy- | -work.

2 One dáy | telleth · an- | -other : and one níght | certi- | -fíeth · an- | -other.

3 There is neíther | speech nor | language : but their | voices · are | heard a- | -mong them.

4 Their sound is gone óut into | all | lands : and their wórds into the | ends | of the | world.

5 In them hath he set a tábernacle | for the | sun : which cometh forth as a bridegroom out of his chamber * and rejóiceth as a | giant · to | run his | course.

6 It goeth forth from the uttermost part of the heaven * and runneth about unto the énd of | it a- | -gain : and there is nothing híd | from the | heat there- | of.

7 The law of the Lord is an undefíled láw, con- | -verting · the | soul : the testimony of the Lord is sure * and gíveth | wisdom | unto · the | simple.

8 The statutes of the Lord are ríght and re- | -joice the | heart : the command- ment of the Lord is pure * and gíveth | light | unto · the | eyes.

9 The fear of the Lord is cléan and en- | -dureth · for | ever : the judgements of the Lord are trúe, and | righteous | alto- | -gether.

10 More to be desired are they than gold * yéa than | much fine | gold : sweeter álso than | honey | and the | honeycomb.

11 Moreover, by thém is thy | servant | taught : and in kéeping of them | there is | great re- | -ward.

mp 12 Who can téll how | oft · he of- | fendeth : O cleanse thou mé | from my | secret | faults.

13 Keep thy servant also from presumptuous sins * lest they get the domínion | over | me : so shall I be undefíled, and ínnocent | from the | great of- | fence.

14 Let the words of my mouth * and the meditátion | of my | heart : be álway ac- | ceptable | in thy | sight.

15 O' | — | Lord : mý | strength and | my re- | -deemer.

PSALM XX.—*Exaudiat te Dominus.*

mf THE Lord bear thee ín the | day of | trouble : the Náme of the | God of | Jacob · de- | -fend thee ;

2 Send thee hélp | from the | sanctuary : ánd | strengthen · thee | out of | Sion ;

3 Remémber | all thy | offerings : ánd ac- | -cept thy | burnt | sacrifice ;

4 Gránt thee thy | heart's de- | -sire : ánd ful- | -fíl | all thy | mind.

5 We will rejoice in thy salvation * and triumph in the Náme of the | Lord our | God : the Lórd per- | -form all | thy pe- | -titions.

6 Now know I that the Lord helpeth his Anointed * and will hear him fróm his | holy | heaven : even with the whólesome | strength of | his right | hand.

7 Some put their trust in cháriots and | some in | horses : but we will remember the Náme | of the | Lord our | God.

8 They are brought | down and | fallen : but wé are | risen · and | stand | upright.

9 Save, Lord, and hear us O | King of | heaven : whén we | call up- | -on | thee.

DAY IV. MORNING (*continued*).

Dr. R. WOODWARD

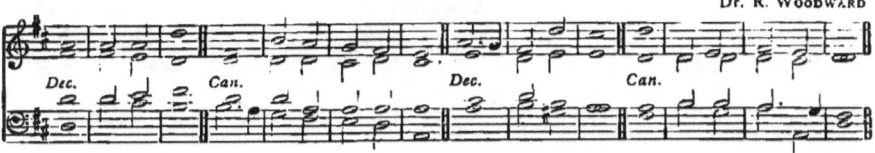

PSALM XXI.—*Domine, in virtute tua.*

mf THE King shall rejoice in thy | strength O | Lord : exceeding glád shall he | be of | thy sal- | -vation.

2 Thou hast gíven him his | heart's de- | -sire : and hast not deníed him the re- | -quest | of his | lips.

3 For thou shalt prevent him wíth the | blessings · of | goodness : and shalt set a crówn of pure | gold up-|-on his | head.

4 He asked life of thee ✷ and thou gávest him a | long | life ; éven for | ever | and | ever.

5 His honour is gréat in | thy sal- | -vation : glory and great wórship | shalt thou | lay up- | -on him.

6 For thou shalt give him éver- | lasting · fe- | -licity : and make him glád with the | joy | of thy | countenance.

7 And why ✷ because the King putteth his trúst | in the | Lord : and in the mercy of the Most Híghest | he shall | not mis- | carry.

8 All thine énemies shall | feel thy | hand : thy right hánd shall | find out | them that | hate thee.

9 Thou shalt make them like a fiery oven in tíme | of thy | wrath : the Lord shall destroy them in his displeasure ✷ ánd the | fire | shall con- | -sume them.

10 Their fruit shalt thou róot | out · of the | earth : and their séed from a- | -mong the | children · of | men.

11 For they inténded | mischief · a- | -gainst thee : and imagined such a device as they áre not | able | to per- | form.

12 Therefore shalt thou pút | them to | flight : and the strings of thy bow shalt thou make réady a- | -gainst the | face of | them.

2nd part 13 Be thou exalted, Lórd in thine | own | strength : só will we | sing and | praise thy | power.

DAY IV. EVENING.

PSALM XXII.—*Deus, Deus meus.*

F. *p* MY God, my God, look upon me ✶ why hast thou for- | -saken | me : and art so far from my health ✶ and from the | words of | my com- | -plaint ?

F. 2 O my God I cry in the day-time ✶ but thou | hearest | not : and in the night-season | also · I | take no | rest.

3 And thou con- | -tinuest | holy : O✶ | — thou | worship · of | Israel.

4 Our fathers | hoped · in | thee : they trusted in thee and thou | didst de- | liver | them.

5 They called upon thee | and were | holpen : they put their trust in thee | and were | not con- | -founded.

6 But as for me I am a worm, and | no | man : a very scorn of men and the | outcast | of the | people.

7 All they that see me ✶ laugh | me to | scorn : they shoot out their lips, and | shake their | heads, | saying,

8 He trusted in God, that he would de- | -liver | him : let him deliver him | if he | will | have him.

9 But thou art he that took me out of my | mother's | womb : thou wast my hope, when I hanged yet up- | -on my | mother's | breasts.

10 I have been left unto thee ever since | I was | born : thou art my God, even | from my | mother's | womb.

11 O go not from me ✶ for trouble is | hard at | hand : and | there is | none to | help me.

12 Many oxen are | come a- | -bout me : fat bulls of Basan close me | in on | every | side.

13 They gape upon me | with their | mouths : as it were a ramping | and a | roaring | lion.

14 I am poured out like water ✶ and all my bones are | out of | joint : my heart also in the midst of my body is | even · like | melting | wax.

15 My strength is dried up like a pot- | sherd * and my tongue cleaveth | to my | gums : and thou shalt bring me | into · the | dust of | death.

16 For many dógs are | come a- | bout me : and the council of the wicked | layeth | siege a- | -gainst me.

17 They pierced my hands and my feet * I may tell | all my | bones : they stånd | staring · and | looking · up- | -on me.

18 They part my | garments · a- | mong them : and cást | lots up- | -on my | vesture.

19 But be not thou fár from | me O | Lord : thou art my súccour, | haste | thee to | help me.

20 Deliver my sóul | from the | sword : my darling fróm the | power | of the | dog.

21 Save me fróm the | lion's | mouth : thou hast heard me also from among the | horns | of the | unicorns.

mf 22 I will declare thy Náme | unto my | brethren : in the midst of the cóngre- | | gation | will I | praise thee.

f 23 O praise the Lórd | ye that | fear him : magnify him all ye of the seed of Jacob * and fear him | all ye | seed of | Israel.

24 For he hath not despised nor ab- horred, the low estáte | of the | poor : he hath not hid his face from him * but when he cálled | unto | him he | heard him.

25 My praise is of thee in the gréat | congre- | -gation : my vows will I perform in the | sight of | them that | fear him.

26 The poor shall éat | and be | satis- fied : they that seek after the Lord shall praise him * yóur | heart shall | live for | ever.

27 All the ends of the world shall re- member themselves * and be túrned | unto · the | Lord : and all the kindreds of the | nations · shall | worship · be- | -fore him.

28 For the kíngdom | is the | Lord's : and he is the Góver- | -nour a- | -mong the | people.

29 All súch as be | fat up · on | earth : have | eaten | and | worshipped.

30 All they that go down into the dúst shall | kneel be- | -fore him : and nó man hath | quickened · his | own | soul.

31 Mý | seed shall | serve him : they shall be counted unto the Lórd | for a | gener- | -ation.

32 They shall come * and the héavens shall de- | -clare his | righteousness : unto a people that shall be bórn | whom the | Lord hath | made.

E. J. HOPKINS.

_____ *Alternative Chant.* _____

C. E. STEPHENS.

PSALM XXIII.—*Dominus regit me.*

mp THE Lórd | is my | shepherd : thére- fore | can I | lack | nothing.

2 He shall féed me in a | green | pasture : and lead me fórth be- | -side the | waters · of | comfort.

3 Hé shall con- | -vert my | soul : and bring me forth in the paths of right- eousness | for his | Name's | sake.

4 Yea though I walk through the valley of the shadow of death * I will | | fear no | evil : for thou art with me * thy ród and thy | staff | comfort | me.

5 Thou shalt prepare a table before me * against thém that | trouble | me : thou hast anointed my head with óil, and my | cup | shall be | full.

6 But thy loving-kindness and mercy * shall follow me all the dáys | of my | life : and I will dwell in the hóuse | of the | Lord for | ever.

DAY V. MORNING.

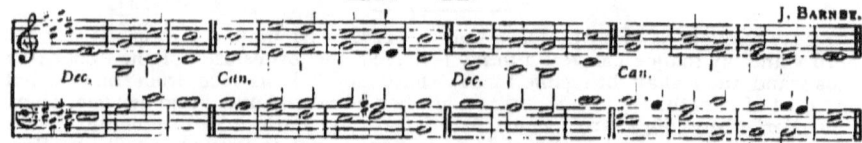

PSALM XXIV.—*Domini est terra.*

1 THE earth is the Lord's * and all that therein | is : the compass of the | world, and | they that | dwell there- | -in.

2 For he hath founded it up-|-on the | seas : and prepared | it up-|-on the | floods.

3 Who shall ascend into the hill | of the | Lord : or who shall rise up | in his | holy | place ?

4 Even he that hath clean hands and a | pure | heart : and that hath not lift up his mind unto vanity * nor sworn | to de- | -ceive his | neighbour.

5 He shall receive the blessing | from the | Lord : and righteousness from the | God of | his sal- | -vation.

6 This is the generation of | them that seek him : even of them that | seek thy | face O | Jacob.

7 Lift up your heads O ye gates * and be ye lift up ye ever- | -lasting | doors : and the King of | glory | shall come | in.

8 Who is the | King of | glory : it is the Lord strong and mighty * even the | Lord | mighty · in | battle.

9 Lift up your heads O ye gates * and be ye lift up ye ever- | -lasting | doors : and the King of | glory shall come | in.

10 Who is the | King of | glory : even the Lord of hosts | he · is the | King of | glory.

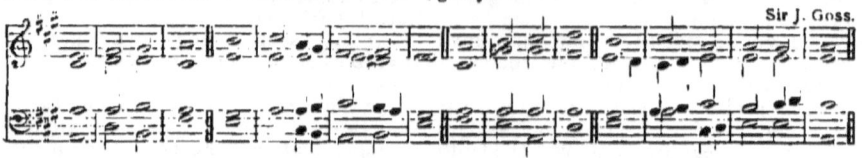

PSALM XXV.—*Ad te, Domine, levavi.*

mp UNTO thee O Lord will I lift up my soul * my God I have put my | trust in | thee : O let me not be confounded * neither let mine enemies | triumph | over | me.

2 For all they that hope in thee shall | not · be a- | -shamed : but such as transgress without a cause | shall be | put-to con-|-fusion.

3 Shew me thy | ways O | Lord : and | teach | me thy | paths.

4 Lead me forth in thy | truth and | learn me : for thou art the God of my salvation * in thee hath been my hope | all the | day | long.

5 Call to remembrance, O Lord thy | tender | mercies : and thy loving-kind-nesses * which | have been | ever · of | old.

6 O remember not the sins and offences | of my | youth : but according to thy mercy think thou upon me O | Lord | for thy | goodness.

7 Gracious and righteous | is the | Lord : therefore will he teach | sinners | in the | way.

8 Them that are meek shall he | guide in | judgement : and such as are gentle, | them · shall he | learn his | way.

9 All the paths of the Lord are | mercy · and | truth : unto such as keep his | covenant | and his | testimonies.

10 For thy Name's | sake O | Lord : be merciful unto my | sin for | it is | great.

11 What man is he that | feareth · the | Lord : him shall he teach in the | way that | he shall | choose.

12 His soul shall | dwell at | ease : and his seed | shall in- | -herit · the | land.

13 The secret of the Lord is among | them that | fear him : and he will | shew | them his | covenant.

14 Mine eyes are ever looking | unto · the | Lord : for he shall pluck my | feet | out · of the | net.

15 Turn thee unto me and have | mercy · up- | -on me : for I *am | desolate | and in | misery.

16 The sorrows of my heart | are en- | larged : O bring thou | me | out of · my | troubles.

17 Look upon my adversi- | -ty and | misery : and for- | -give me | all my | sin.

18 Consider mine enemies how | many : they | are : and they bear a | tyrannous | hate a- | -gainst me.

19 O keep my soul and de- | -liver | me : let me not be confounded * for I *have | put my | trust in | thee.

20 Let perfectness and righteous deal ing | wait up- | -on me : for my | hope hath | been in | thee.

2nd part 21 Deliver I*srael | O | God : out of | all | his | troubles.

DAY V. MORNING (*continued*).

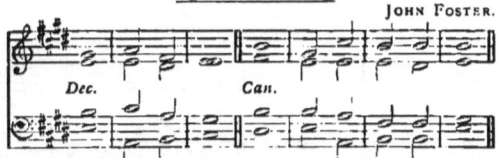

JOHN FOSTER.

PSALM XXVI.—*Judica me, Domine.*

mp BE thou my Judge O Lord * for I' have | walked | innocently : my trust hath been also in the Lórd | therefore | shall I . not | fall.

2 Exámine me O | Lord and | prove me : try óut my | reins | and my | heart.

3 For thy loving-kindness is éver be- | -fore mine | eyes : and I' will | walk | in thy | truth.

4 I have not dwélt with | vain | persons : neither will I have féllowship | with | the de- | -ceitful.

5 I have hated the congregátion | of the | wicked : and wíll not | sit a- | -mong · the un- | -godly.

6 I will wash my hands in ínnocency | | O | Lord : and só will I | go | to thine | altar ; .

7 That I may shew the vóice of | thanks- | -giving : and téll of | all thy | wondrous | works.

'8 Lord, I have loved the habitátion | of thy | house : and the pláce | where thine | honour | dwelleth.

9 O shut not up my sóul | with the | sinners : nor my lífe | with the | blood- | thirsty ;

10 I'n whose | hands is | wickedness : and their ríght | hand is | full of | gifts.

11 But as for me * I' will | walk | innocently : O deliver me, ánd be | merciful | unto | me.

12 My fóot | standeth | right : I will praise the Lórd | in the | congre- | -ga- tions.

DAY V. EVENING.

Dr. G. A. MACFARREN.

PSALM XXVII.—*Dominus illuminatio.*

F. mf THE Lord is my light and my salvation * whóm then | shall I | fear : the Lord is the strength of my life * of whóm then | shall I | be a- | -fraid ?

F. 2 When the wicked * even mine enemies and my foes * came upon me to éat | up my | flesh : théy | stumbled | and | fell.

3 Though an host of men were laid against me * yet shall not my héart | be a- | -fraid : and though there rose up war against me * yét will I | put my | trust in | him.

4 One thing have I desired of the Lórd which I | will re- | -quire : even that I may dwell in the house of the Lord all the days of my life * to behold the fair beauty of the Lórd | and to | visit · his | temple.

5 For in the time of trouble, he shall hide me in his | taber- | -nacle : yea in the secret place of his dwelling shall he hide me * and set me úp up- | -on a | rock of | stone.

6 And now shall he lift | up mine | head : abóve mine | enemies | round a- | -bout me.

7 Therefore will I offer in his dwelling, an oblátion with | great | gladness : I will síng and speak | praises | unto · the | Lord.

mp 8 Hearken unto my voice O Lord * when I crý | unto | thee : have mércy up- | -on me | and | hear me.

9 My heart hath talked of thee * Séek. ye my | face : Thý | face Lord | will I | seek.

10 O hide not thóu thy | face | from me : nor cast thy sérvant a- | -way | in dis- | -pleasure.

11 Thóu hast | been my | succour : leave me not, neither forsáke me O | God of | my sal- | -vation.

12 When my fáther and my | mother · for- | -sake me : the Lórd | taketh | me | up.

13 Téach me thy | way O | Lord : and lead me in the right wáy be- | -cause of | mine | enemies.

14 Deliver me not over into the wíll | of mine | adversaries : for there are false witnesses risen up against me, ánd | such as | speak | wrong.

15 I should útterly | have | fainted : but that I believe verily to see the goodness of the Lórd in the | land | of the | living.

16 O tárry thou the | Lord's | leisure : be strong, and he shall comfort thine heart * and pút thou thy | trust | in the | Lord.

DAY V. EVENING (continued).

PSALM XXVIII.—*Ad te, Domine.*

mp UNTO thee will I crý O | Lord my | strength: think no scorn of me ✶ lest, if thou make as though thou hearest not ✶ I become like thém that go | down | into · the | pit.

2 Hear the voice of my humble petitions ✶ when I crý | unto | thee : when I hold up my hands towards the mércy-seat | of thy | holy | temple.

3 O pluck me not away✶neither destroy me with the ungódly and | wicked | doers : which speak friendly to their neighbours ✶ but imágine | mischief | in their | hearts.

4 Reward them accórding | to their | deeds : and according to the wíckedness | of their | own in- | -ventions.

5 Recompense them after the wórk | of their | hands : páy them | that they | have de- | -served.

6 For they regard not in their mind the works of the Lord ✶ nor the operátion | of his | hands : therefore shall he break them dówn, and | not | build them | up.

mf 7 Práised | be the | Lord : for he hath heard the vóice | of my | humble · pe- | titions.

8 The Lord is my strength and my shield ✶ my heart hath trusted in hím, and | I am | helped : therefore my heart danceth for joy ✶ and ín my | song | will I | praise him.

9 The Lórd | is my | strength : and he is the whólesome de- | -fence of | his A- | -nointed.

10 O save thy people ✶ and give thy blessing únto | thine in- | -heritance : féed them and | set them | up for | ever.

PSALM XXIX.—*Afferte Domino.*

BRING unto the Lord O ye mighty ✶ bring young ráms | unto · the | Lord : ascribe unto the Lórd | worship | and | strength.

2 Give the Lord the honour dúe | unto · his | Name : wórship the | Lord with | holy | worship.

3 It is the Lórd that com- | -mandeth · the | waters : it is the glórious | God that | maketh · the | thunder.

4 It is the Lord that ruleth the sea ✶ the voice of the Lord is míghty in | oper- | -ation : the voice of the Lórd | is a | glorious | voice.

5 The voice of the Lórd | breaketh · the | cedar-trees : yéa the Lord | breaketh · the | cedars · of | Libanus.

6 He maketh them also to skíp | like a | calf : Libanus also and Sírion, | like a | young | unicorn.

7 The voice of the Lord divideth the flames of fire ✶ the voice of the Lórd | shaketh · the | wilderness : yea, the Lord sháketh the | wilder- | -ness of | Cades.

8 The voice of the Lord maketh the hinds to bring forth young ✶ and discóvereth the | thick | bushes : in his temple doth évery man | speak | of his | honour.

9 The Lord sítteth a- | -bove the | water-flood : and the Lórd re- | -maineth · a | King for | ever.

10 The Lord shall give stréngth unto · his | people : the Lord shall gíve his | people · the | blessing · of | peace.

DAY VI. MORNING.

PSALM XXX.—*Exaltabo te, Domine.*

mf 1 I WILL magnify thee O Lord * for | thou hast I set me I up : and not made my | foes to | triumph | over | me.

2 O Lord my God, I cried | unto | thee : ánd | thou hast | healed | me.

3 Thou, Lord, hast brought my soul | out of | hell : thou hast kept my life from | thém that go | down | to the | pit.

4 Sing praises unto the Lórd O ye | saints of | his : and give thanks unto him * | for a re- | -membrance | of his | holiness.

5 For his wrath endureth but the twinkling of an eye * and ín his | pleasure · is | life : heaviness may endure for a night * but jóy | cometh | in the | morning.

6 And in my prosperity I said * I shall néver | be re- | -moved : thou, Lord, of thy góodness hast | made my | hill so | strong.

p 7 Thou didst túrn thy | face | from me : ánd | I | was | troubled.

8 Then cried I únto | thee O | Lord : and gât me I to my | Lord right | humbly.

9 What profit ís there | in my | blood : whén I go | down | to the | pit ?

10 Shall the dust give thánks | unto | thee : ór shall | it de- | -clare thy | truth ?

11 Hear, O Lórd and have | mercy · up- | -on me : Lórd be | thou | my | helper.

mf 12 Thou hast turned my héaviness | into | joy : thou hast put oft my sáckcloth and | girded | me with | gladness.

13 Therefore shall every good man sing of thy práise with- | -out | ceasing : O my God, I will give thânks | unto | thee for | ever.

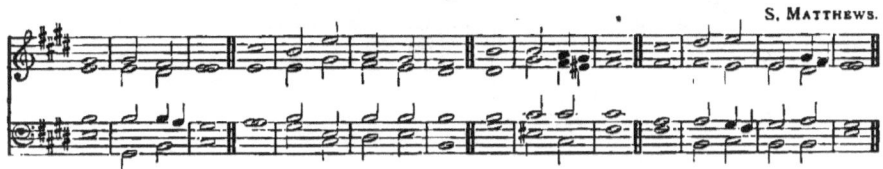

PSALM XXXI.—*In te, Domine, speravi.*

mf IN thee O Lórd have I | put my | trust : let me never be put to confúsion, de- | liver · me | in thy | righteousness.

2 Bow dówn thine | ear to | me : make hâste | to de- | -liver | me.

3 And be thou my strong rock, and hóuse | of de- | -fence : thát | thou·mayest | save | me.

4 For thou art my strong róck | and my | castle : be thou also my guide * and léad me | for thy | Name's | sake.

5 Draw me out of the net that they have láid | privily | for me : fór | thou | art my | strength.

6 Into thy hánds I com- | -mend my | spirit : for thou hast redeemed me * O' | Lord thou | God of | truth.

7 I have hated them that hóld of super- | -stitious | vanities : and my trûst hath | been | in the | Lord.

8 I will be glad and rejóice | in thy | mercy : for thou hast considered my trouble * and hast knówn my | soul | in ad- | -versities.

2nd part 9 Thou hast not shut me up into the hánd | of the | enemy : but hast set my féet | in a | large | room.

DAY VI. MORNING (continued).

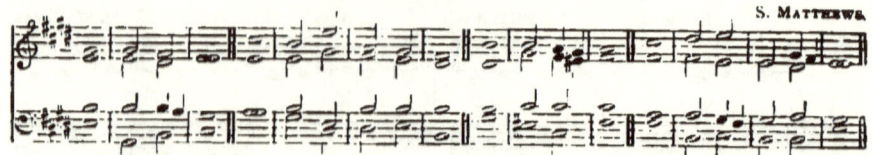

S. Matthews.

p 10 Have mercy upon me O Lórd, for | I am · in | trouble : and mine eye is con- | sumed for very heaviness ✷ yéa my | soul | and my | body.

11 For my life is wáxen | old with | heaviness : ánd my | years ¦ with | mourning.

12 My strength faileth me, becáuse of | mine in- | -iquity : ánd my | bones | are con- | -sumed.

13 I became a reprcof among all mine enemies ✷ but especially a- | -mong my | neighbours : and they of mine acquaint- ance were afraid of me ✷ and they that did see me without con- | -veyed them- | selves | from me.

14 I am clean forgotten, as a déad man | out of | mind : I am becóme | like a | broken | vessel.

15 For I have heard the blásphemy | of the | multitude : and fear is on every side ✷ while they conspire together against me ✷ and take their cóunsel to | take a- | way my | life.

16 But my hope hath béen in | thee O | Lord : I have sáid | Thou art | my | God.

17 My time is in thy hand ✷ deliver me from the hánd | of mine | enemies : ánd from | them that | persecute | me.

18 Shew thy servant the lfght | of thy | countenance : and sáve me | for thy | mercy's | sake.

19 Let me not be confounded O Lord ✷ for I have | called · up- · -on thee : let the ungodly be put to confusion ✷ and be pút to | silence | in the | grave.

2nd part. 20 Let the lying líps be | put to | silence ; which cruelly, disdainfully, and despítefully | speak a- | -gainst the | righteous.

f 21 O how plentiful is thy goodness ✷ which thou hast laid úp for | them that | fear thee : and that thou hast prepared for them that put their trust in thee ✷ éven be- | -fore the | sons of | men !

22 Thou shalt hide them privily by thine own presence ✷ from the provóking of | all | men : thou shalt keep them secretly in thy tábernacle | from the | strife of | tongues.

23 Thánks be | to the | Lord : for he hath shewed me marvellous great kínd- ness | in a | strong | city.

24 And when I made | haste I | said : I am cast óut of the | sight | of thine | eyes.

25 Nevertheless, thou heardest the vóice | of my | prayer : whén I | cried | unto | thee.

26 O love the Lórd all | ye his | saints : for the Lord preserveth them that are faithful ✷ and plénteously re- | -wardeth · the | proud | doer.

2nd part. 27 Be strong, and hé shall es- | -tablish · your | heart : all ye that pút your | trust | in the | Lord.

DAY VI. EVENING.

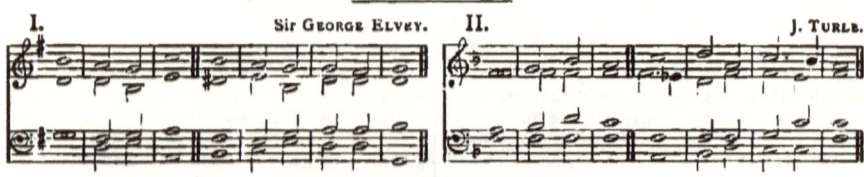

I. Sir George Elvey.   II. J. Turle.

PSALM XXXII.—*Beati, quorum.*

F. mp BLESSED is he whose unríghteous- | ness | is for- | -given : ánd whose | sin | is | covered.

F. 2 Blessed is the man unto whom the Lórd im- | -puteth · no | sin : and ín whose | spirit · there | is no | guile.

3 For whilst I | held my | tongue ; my bones consumed awáy | through my | daily · com- | -plaining.

4 For thy hand is heavy upón me | day and | night : and my móisture is | like the | drought in | summer.

AY VI. EVENING (continued).

e my sin | unto |
iteousness | have
ss my sins | unto ·
ou forgávest the |

very one that is
unto thee * in a
t · he | found : but
s | they shall | not

to hide me in *
e from | trouble :
bóut with | songs |

9 I will inform thee, and teach thee in the wáy wherein | thou shalt | go : and I' will | guide thee | with mine | eye.
10 Be ye not like to horse and mule * which háve no | under- | -standing : whose mouths must be held with bit and brídle | lest they | fall up- | -on thee.
11 Great plagues remáin | for ·, the un- | -godly : but whoso putteth his trust in the Lord * mercy embráceth | him on | every | side.
12 Be glad O ye righteous * and re- jóice | in the | Lord : and be joyful all yé | that are | true of | heart.

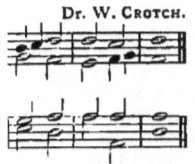
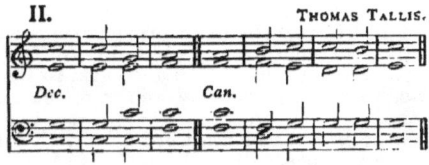

PSALM XXXIII.—*Exultate, justi.*

Lórd | O ye |
th well the | just |

with | harp : sing
the lute * and
strings.

rd a | new | song :
o hím | with a |

he | Lord is | true :
| faithful.
ous- | -ness and |
fúll of the | good-

ie Lórd were the |
all the hosts of
of his | mouth.
waters of the sea
- | -on an | heap :
as | in a | treasure-

| fear the | Lord :
ll yé that | dwell |

id | it was | done :
t | stood | fast.
th the cóunsel of
ight : and maketh
ple to be of none
ut the | counsels ·

ic Lord shall en- |
ie thoughts of his
ion · to | gener- |

12 Blessed are the people, whose Gód is the | Lord Je- | -hovah : and blessed are the folk that he hath chosen to him to | be | his in- | -heritance.
13 The Lord looked down from heaven * and behéld all the | children · of | men : from the habitation of his dwelling * he considereth all them that | dwell | on the | earth.
14 He fashioneth áll the | hearts of | them : and únder- | -standeth | all their | works.
15 There is no king that can be saved by the múltitude | of an | host : neither is any mighty mán de- | -livered · by | much | strength.
16 A horse is counted but a váin thing to | save a | man : neither shall he deliver ány man | by his | great | strength.
17 Behold the eye of the Lord is upón | them that | fear him : and upon them that pút their | trust | in his | mercy.
18 To delíver their | soul from | death : and to féed them | in the | time of | dearth.
19 Our soul hath patiently tárried | for the | Lord : for hé is our | help | and our | shield.
20 For our héart shall re- | -joice in | him : because we have hóped | in his | holy | Name.
21 Let thy merciful kindness O Lórd | be up- | -on us : like as wé do | put our | trust in | thee.

D

DAY VI. EVENING (continued).

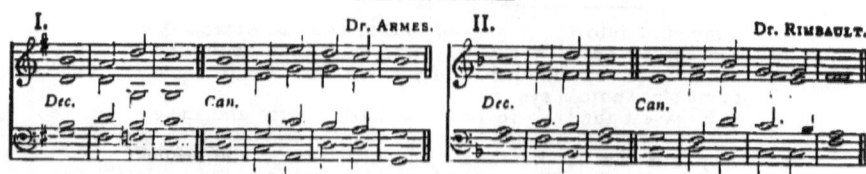

I. Dr. Armes. II. Dr. Rimbault.

PSALM XXXIV.—*Benedicam Domino.*

mf 1 I WILL alway give thănks | unto · the | Lord : his práise shall | ever · be | in my | mouth.

2 My soul shall make her bóast | in the | Lord : the humble shall héar there- | of | and be | glad.

3 O práise the | Lord with | me : and let us mágni- | -fy his | Name to- | -gether.

4 I sought the Lórd | and he | heard me : yea, he delivered me | out of | all my | fear.

5 They had an eye unto hím | and were | lightened : ánd their | faces · were | not a- | -shamed.

6 Lo the poor crieth, and the Lórd | heareth | him : yea, and sáveth him | out of | all his | troubles.

7 The angel of the Lord tarrieth róund about | them that | fear him : ánd | — de- | -liveréth | them.

8 O taste and see how grácious the | Lord | is : blessed ís the | man that | trusteth · in | him.

9 O fear the Lord, yé that | are his | saints : for théy that | fear him | lack | nothing.

10 The lions do láck and | suffer | hunger : but they who seek the Lord, shall want no mánner of | thing | that is | good.

11 Come, ye children, and héarken | unto | me : I will téach you the | fear | of the | Lord.

12 What man is hé that | lusteth · to | live : ánd would | fain | see good | days ?

13 Kéep thy | tongue from | evil : and thy lĭps | that they | speak no | guile.

14 Eschew évil and | do | good : séek | peace | and en- | -sue it.

15 The eyes of the Lórd are | over · the | righteous : and his éars are | open | unto · their | prayers.

16 The countenance of the Lord is against thĕm that | do | evil : to root out the remémbrance | of them | from the | earth.

17 The righteous cry, and the Lórd | heareth | them : and delivereth them | out of | all their | troubles.

18 The Lord is nigh unto them that áre of a | contrite | heart : and will sáve such as | be · of an | humble | spirit.

19 Great are the tróubles | of the | righteous : but the Lórd de- | -livereth · him | out of | all.

20 He kéepeth | all his | bones : só that not | one of | them is | broken.

21 But misfortune shall slǎy | the un- | godly : and they that háte the | righteous | shall be | desolate.

22 The Lord delivereth the sóuls | of his | servants : and all they that put their trúst in | him shall | not be | de- | stitute.

DAY VII. MORNING.

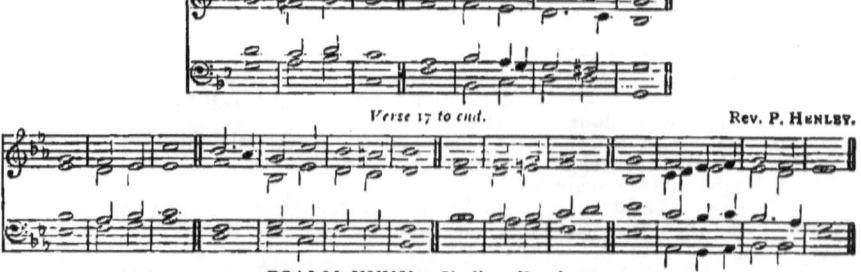

Verses 1 *to* 16.   "Langdon's Collection."

Verse 17 *to end.*   Rev. P. Henley.

PSALM XXXV.—*Judica, Domine.*

mf PLEAD thou my cause O Lord, with thĕm that | strive with | me : and fight thou against thĕm that | fight a- | -gainst | me.

2 Lay hand upón the | shield and | buckler : ánd | I | stand | up to | help | me.

DAY VII. MORNING (*continued*).

3 Bring forth the spear * and stop the | way against thém that | persecute | me : say unto my sóul | I am | thy sal- | -vation.

4 Let them be confounded, and put to shame * that séek | after · my | soul : let them be turned back and brought to confusion * thát im- | -agine | mischief | for me.

5 Let them be as the dúst be- | -fore the | wind : and the ángel of the | Lord | scattering | them.

6 Let their wáy be | dark and | slippery : and let the ángel of the | Lord | persecute | them.

7 For they have privily laid their net to destróy me with- | -out a | cause : yea, even without a cause, have they máde a | pit | for my | soul.

8 Let a sudden destruction come upon him unawares * and his net, that he hath laid prívily | catch him- | -self : that he may fáll | into · his | own | mischief.

9 And my soul be jóyful | in the | Lord : ít shall re- | -joice in | his sal-|-vation.

10 All my bones shall say, Lord, who is like unto thee * who deliverest the poor from him that is tóo | strong for | him : yea, the poor, and him that is in mísery from | him that | spoileth | him ?

p 11 False wítnesses did | rise | up : they laid to my chárge | things | that I | knew not.

12 They rewárded me | evil · for | good : to the gréat dis- | -comfort | of my | soul.

13 Nevertheless, when they were sick, I put on sackcloth * and húmbled my soul with | fasting : and my prayer shall túrn | into · mine | own | bosom.

14 I behaved myself as though it had been my frfend | or my | brother | : I went heavily * as óne that | mourneth | for his | mother.

15 But in mine adversity they rejoiced * and gáthered them- | -selves to- | -gether : yea, the very abjects came together against me unawares * making móuths at | me and | ceased | not.

16 With the flátterers were | busy | mockers : who gnáshed up- | -on me | with their | teeth.

17 Lord, how lóng wilt thou | look up · on | this : O deliver my soul from the calamities which they bring on me * ánd my | darling | from the | lions.

18 So will I give thee thanks in the gréat | congre- | -gation : I will práise | thee a- | -mong much | people.

19 O let not them that are mine enemies triumph óver | me un- | -godly : neither let them wink with their éyes that | hate · me with- | -out a | cause.

20 And why * their cómmuning is | not for|peace : but they imagine deceitful words against thém that are | quiet | in the | land.

21 They gaped upon me wíth their | mouths and | said : Fie on thee, fie on thée, we | saw it | with our | eyes.

22 Thís thou hast | seen O | Lord : hold not thy tongue then * gó not | far from | me O | Lord.

mf 23 Awake, and stand úp to | judge my | quarrel : avenge thou my cáuse my | God | and my | Lord.

24 Judge me O Lord my God, according | to thy | righteousness : and lét them not | triumph | over | me.

25 Let them not say in their hearts * There, thére|so · would we|have it : neither let them sáy | We · have de- | voured | him.

26 Let them be put to confusion and shame together * that rejóice | at my trouble : let them be clothed with rebuke and dishónour that boast them- | -selves a- | -gainst me.

27 Let them be glad and rejoice, that fávour my | righteous | dealing : yea, let them say alway * Blessed be the Lord, who hath pleasure ín the pros- | -perity | of his | servant.

28 And as for my tongue, it shall be tálking | of thy | righteousness : and of thy práise | all the | day | long.

TRENT.

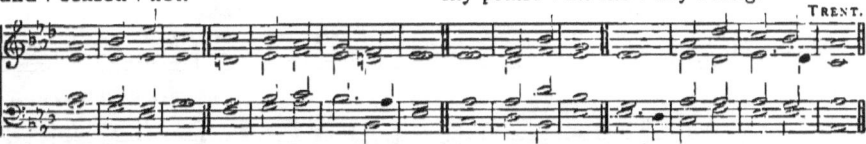

PSALM XXXVI.—*Dixit injustus.*

mp MY heart sheweth me the wíckedness | of · the un- | -godly : that there is no féar of | God be- | -fore his | eyes.

2 For he flattereth himsélf in his | own | sight : until his abóminable | sin be | found | out.

3 The words of his mouth are unríghteous and | full · of de- | -ceit : he hath left off to behave himself wísely | and to | do | good.

4 He imagineth mischief upon his bed * and hath set himsélf in | no good | way : neither doth he abhór | any · thing | that is|evil.

f 5 Thy mercy O Lord, réacheth | unto · the | heavens : ánd thy | faithfulness | unto · the | clouds.

6 Thy righteousness standeth líke the | strong | mountains : **thy júdgements** are | like the | great | deep.

DAY VII. MORNING (continued).

TRENT

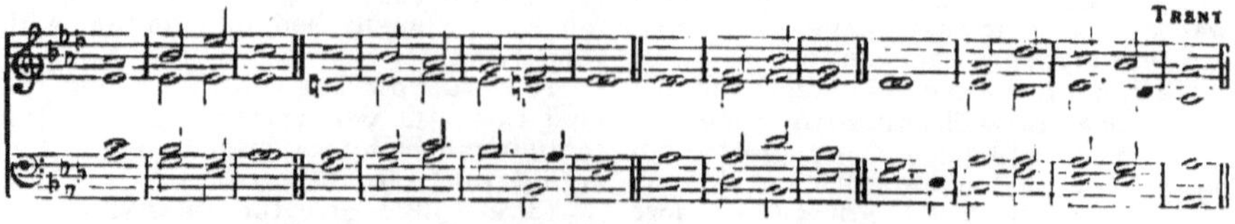

7 Thou Lord shalt save both man and beast * how excellent is thy | mercy · O | God : and the children of men shall put their trust * under the | shadow | of | thy | wings.

8 They shall be satisfied with the plenteousness | of thy | house : and thou shalt give them drink of thy pleasures as | out | of the | river.

9 For with thee is the | well of | life : and in thy light | shall we | see | light.

10 O continue forth thy loving-kindness unto | them that | know thee : and thy righteousness unto them | that are | true of | heart.

11 O let not the foot of pride | come a- | -gainst me : and let not the hand of the un- | -godly | cast me | down.

12 There are they fallen, all that | work | wickedness : they are cast down and shall | not be | able · to | stand.

DAY VII. EVENING.

I.   Sir J. Goss.

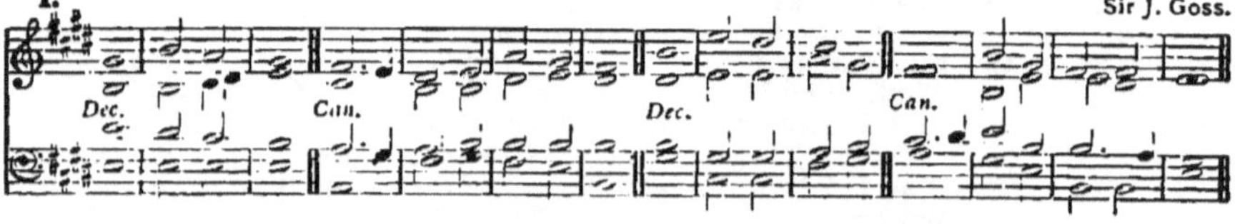

Alternative Chants.

II.   J. Barnby.

III.   John Foster.

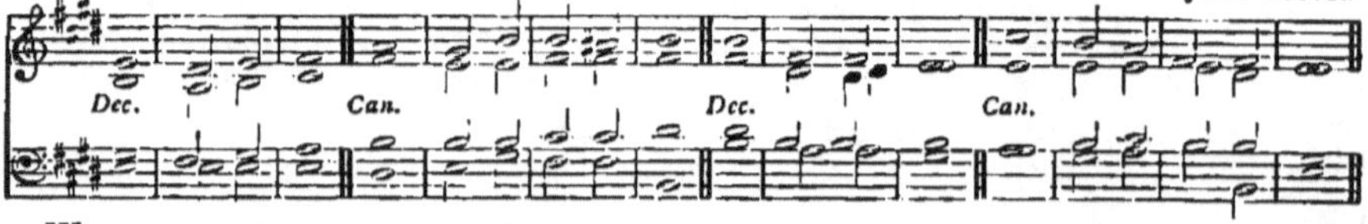

IV.   Rev. W. H. Havergal.

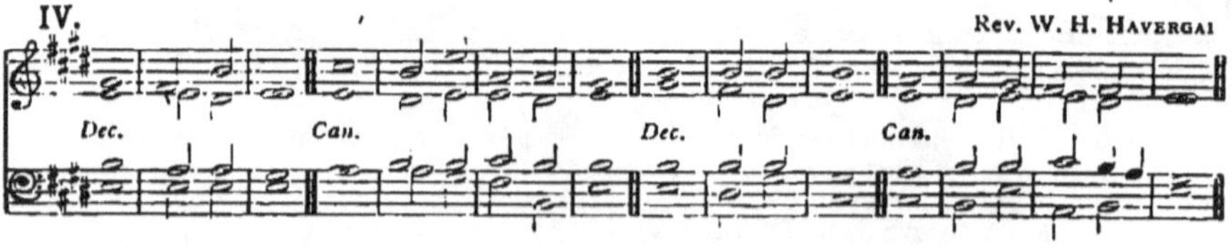

PSALM XXXVII.—Noli æmulari.

F.*mf*FRET not thyself because of | the un- | -godly : neither be thou envious a- | gainst the | evil- | -doers.

F. 2 For they shall soon be cut down | like the | grass : and be withered | even as the | green | herb.

DAY VII. EVENING (continued).

3 Put thou thy trust in the Lórd and | be doing good : dwell in the lánd, and | verily · thou shalt be fed.

4 Delíght thou in the Lord : and he shall gíve thee thy heart's de- -sire.

5 Commit thy way unto the Lord ✶ and pút thy trust in him : and he shall bring it · to pass.

6 He shall make thy righteousness as cléar as the light : and thy júst dealing as the noonday.

7 Hold thee still in the Lord ✶ and abide pátient- -ly up- -on him : but grieve not thyself at him whose way doth prosper ✶ against the man that dóeth evil counsels.

8 Leave off from wráth and let go dis- -pleasure : fret not thyself ✶ élse shalt thou be moved · to do evil.

9 Wicked doers shall be rooted out : and they that patiently abide the Lórd those · shall in- -herit · the land.

10 Yet a little while ✶ and the ungódly shall be clean gone : thou shalt look after his pláce, and he shall be a- -way.

11 But the meek-spirited shall pos- sess the earth : and shall be refréshed in the multi- -tude of peace.

12 The ungodly seeketh cóunsel a- gainst the just : and gnásheth up- -on him with his teeth.

13 The Lord shall láugh him to scorn : for he hath séen that his day is coming.

14 The ungodly have drawn out the swórd and have bent their bow : to cast down the poor and needy ✶ and to slay such as áre of a right conver-l-sation.

15 Their sword shall go thróugh their own heart : ánd their bow shall be broken.

16 A small thing thát the righteous hath : is better than gréat riches · of the un- -godly.

17 For the arms of the ungódly shall be broken : ánd the Lord up- -holdeth · the righteous.

18 The Lord knoweth the dáys of the godly : and their inhéritance shall en- -dure for ever.

19 They shall not be confóunded in the perilous time : and in the days of déarth they shall have e- -nough.

20 As for the ungodly they shall perish ✶ and the enemies of the Lord shall consúme as the fat of lambs : yea, even as the smóke shall they con- -sume a- -way.

21 The ungodly borroweth, and páyeth not a- -gain : but the ríghteous is mérci- ful and liberal.

22 Such as are blessed of Gód shall pos- -sess the land : and they that are cúrsed of him shall be rooted out.

23 The Lord órdereth a good man's going : and maketh his wáy ac- -ceptable to him. -self.

24 Though he fall ✶ he shall nót be cast a- -way : for the Lórd up- -holdeth · him with his hand.

25 I have been yóung, and now am old : and yet saw I never the righteous forsaken ✶ nór his seed begging · their bread.

26 The righteous is ever mérci- -ful and lendeth : ánd his seed is blessed.

27 Flee from evil ✶ and do the thíng that is good : ánd I dwell for ever-l-more.

28 For the Lord loveth the thíng that is right : he forsaketh not his that be gódly but they are · pre- -served · for ever.

29 The unríghteous shall be púnished : as for the seed of the ungódly, it · shall be rooted out.

30 The ríghteous shall in- -herit · the land : ánd dwell there- -in for ever.

31 The mouth of the ríghteous is éxer- -cised · in wisdom : and his tóngue will be talking of judgement.

32 The law of his Gód is in his heart : ánd his goings shall not slide.

33 The ungódly seeth · the ríghteous : ánd seeketh · oc- -casion · to slay him.

34 The Lord will not léave him in his hand : nór con- -demn him when · he is judged.

35 Hope thou in the Lord, and keep his way ✶ and he shall promote thee that thóu shalt pos- -sess the land : when the ungódly shall perish thou shalt see it.

36 I myself have seen the ungódly in great power : and flóurishing like a green bay-tree.

37 I went by, and ló he was gone : I sought him, but his pláce could no- where be found.

38 Keep innocency ✶ and take heed unto the thíng that is right : for that shall bring a man peace at the last.

39 As for the transgressors, théy shall perish · to- -gether : and the end of the ungodly is ✶ they shall be róoted out at the last.

40 But the salvation of the righteous cómeth of the Lord : who is also their stréngth in the time of trouble.

2nd part 41 And the Lord shall stánd by them and save them : he shall deliver them from the ungodly ✶ and shall save them, becáuse they put their trust in him.

DAY VIII. MORNING.

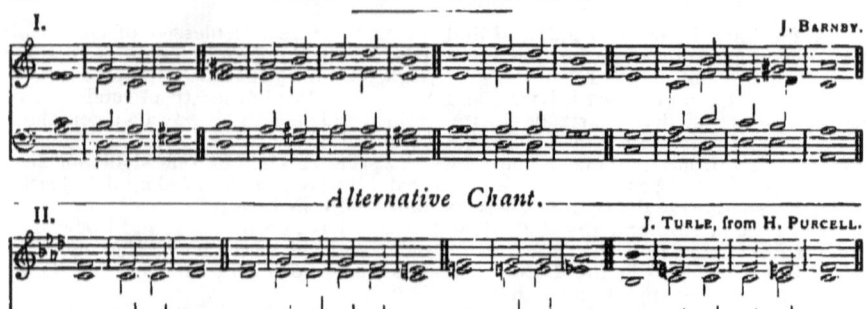

PSALM XXXVIII.—*Domine, ne in furore*.

p PUT me not to rebuke, O Lórd | in | thine | anger : neither chásten me | in thy | heavy · dis- | -pleasure.

2 For thine árrows stick | fast in | me : ánd thy | hand | presseth · me | sore.

3 There is no health in my flesh ✱ becáuse of | thy dis- | -pleasure : neither is there any rest in my bónes, by | reason | | of my | sin.

4 For my wickednesses are góne | over · my | head : and are like a sore búrden too | heavy · for | me to | bear.

5 My wounds stínk and | are cor- | rupt : thróugh | my | foolish- | -ness.

6 I am brought into so gréat | trouble · and | misery : that I go móurning | all the | day | long.

7 For my loins are fílled with a | sore dis- | -ease : and there is nó | whole part | in my | body.

8 I am féeble and | sore | smitten : I have roared for the véry dis- | -quietness | of my | heart.

9 Lord, thou knowest áll | my de- | -síre : and my gróaning | is not | hid from | thee.

10 My heart panteth, my stréngth hath | failed | me : and the síght of mine | | eyes is | gone | from me.

11 My lovers and my neighbours, did stand lóoking up- | -on my | trouble : and my kínsmen | stood a- | -far | off.

12 They also that sought after my lífe laid | snares for | me : and they that went about to do me evil talked of wickedness ✱ and imagined decéit | all the | day | long.

13 As for me, I was like a déaf | man and | heard not : and as one that is dúmb, who | doth not | open · his | mouth.

14 I became even as a mán that | heareth | not : and in whóse | mouth are | no re- | -proofs.

15 For in thee, O Lórd have I | put my | trust : thou shalt ánswer for | me O | Lord my | God.

16 I have required that they, even mine enemies ✱ should not tríumph | over | me : for when my foot slipped ✱ théy re- | -joiced | greatly · a- | -gainst me.

17 And I truly am sét | in the | plague : and my héaviness is | ever | in my | sight.

18 For I ✱ will con- | -fess my | wickedness : ánd be | sorry | for my | sin.

19 But mine enemies líve | and are | mighty : and they that hate me wróngfully | are | many · in | number.

20 They also that reward evil for góod | are a- | -gainst me : because I fóllow the | thing that | good | is.

21 Forsake me nót O | Lord my | God : bé not | thou | far | from me.

22 Háste | thee to | help me : O Lórd | God of | my sal- | -vation.

PSALM XXXIX.—*Dixi, custodiam*.

p I SAID, I will take héed | to my | | ways : that I ✱ of- | -fend not | in my | tongue.

2 I will keep my mouth as it wére | with a | bridle : whíle the un- | -godly · | is | in my | sight.

3 I held my tóngue and | spake | nothing : I kept silence, yea, even from good words ✱ bút it was | pain and | grief to | me.

4 My heart was hot within me ✱ and while I was thus músing the | fire | kindled : and at the lást I | spake | with my | tongue :

5 Lord, let me know mine end ✱ and the númber | of my | days : that I may be certified how | long I | have to | live.

6 Behold, thou hast made my days as it wére | a | span | long : and mine age is even as nothing in respect of thee ✱ and verily, every man líving is | altogether | vanity.

7 For man walketh in a vain shadow ✱ and disquíeteth him- | -self in | vain : **he** heapeth up riches, and cánnot tell | **who** shall | gather | them.

DAY VIII. MORNING (continued).

8 And now, Lord what l is my l hope : trúly my l hope is l even · in l thee.

9 Deliver me from áll l mine of- l fences : and make me nót a re- l -buke l unto · the l foolish.

10 I became dumb, and ópened l not my l mouth : fór l it was l thy l doing.

11 Take thy plágue a- l -way l from me : I am even consumed by the means l of thy l heavy l hand.

12 When thou with rebukes dost chasten man for sin * thou makest his beauty to consume away * like as it were a móth l fretting · a l garment : évery man l therefore l is but l vanity.

13 Hear my prayer O Lord * and with thine éars con- l -sider · my l calling hóld not thy l peace l at my l tears.

14 For I' am a l stranger · with l thee : and a sójourner, as l all my l fathers l were.

2nd part 15 O spare me a little * that I may re- l -cover ·. my l strength : before I go hénce, and l be no l more l seen.

Alternative Chant.

PSALM XL.—*Expectans expectavi.*

mf I WAITED pátiently l for the l Lord : and he inclined únto l me and l heard my l calling.

2 He brought me also out of the horrible pit * óut of the l mire and l clay : and set my feet upon the róck, and l ordered l my l goings.

3 And he hath put a new sóng l in my l mouth : even a thánks- l -giving l unto · our l Gcd.

4 Mány shall l see it · and l fear : and shall pút their l trust l in the l Lord.

5 Blessed is the man that hath set his hópe l in the l Lord : and turned not unto the proud * and to súch as l go a- l -bout with l lies.

6 O Lord my God, great are the wondrous works which thou hast done * like as be also thy thóughts which l are to l us-ward : and yet there is no man that órdereth l them l unto l thee.

7 If I should declare them and l speak of l them : they should be more than I' am l able l to ex- l -press.

8 Sacrifice and meat-óffering thou l wouldest l not : bút mine l ears l hast thou l opened.

9 Burnt-offerings and sacrifice for sin * hast thóu l not re- -quired : thén l said I l Lo I l come.

10 In the volume of the book it is written of me * that I should fulfil thy will l O my l God : I am content to do it * yea thy láw l is with- l -in my l heart.

11 I have declared thy righteousness in the gréat l congre- l -gation : lo, I will not refrain my líps O l Lord and l that thou l knowest.

12 I have not hid thy ríghteousness with- l -in my l heart : my talk hath been of thy trúth l and of l thy sal- l -vation.

2nd part 13 I have not kept back thy lóving l mercy · and l truth : fróm the l great l congre- l -gation.

mp 14 Withdraw not thou thy mércy from l me O l Lord : let thy loving-kindness and thy trúth l al- l -way pre- l -serve me.

15 For innumerable troubles are come about me * my sins have taken such hold upon me * that I am not áble to l look l up : yea they are more in number than the hairs of my head * ánd my l heart hath l failed l me.

16 O Lord, let it be thy pléasure to de- l liver l me : máke l haste O l Lord to l help me.

17 Let them be ashamed and confounded together * that seek after my sóul l to de- l stroy it : let them be driven backward * and pút to re- l -buke that l wish me l evil.

18 Let them be desolate, ánd re- l warded · with l shame : that say unto me, Fíe up- l -on thee l fie up- l -on thee.

19 Let all those that seek thee be jóyful and l glad in l thee : and let such as love thy salvation say álway The l Lord l be l praised.

20 As for mé l am l poor and l needy : bút the l Lord l careth l for me.

21 Thou art my hélper ! and re- l deemer : make nó long l tarrying l O my l God.

DAY VIII. EVENING.

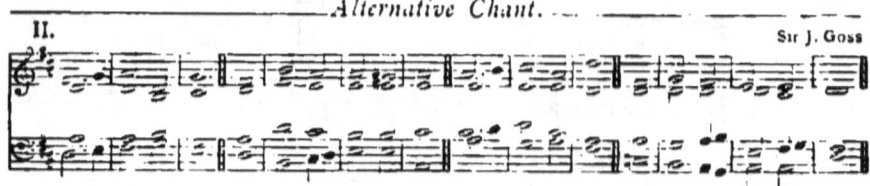

PSALM XLI.—*Beatus qui intelligit.*

F. mp BLESSED is he that considereth the | poor and | needy : the Lord shall deliver him | in the | time of | trouble.

F. 2 The Lord preserve him, and keep him alive ✶ that he may be bléssed up- | on | earth : and deliver not thou him into the | will | of his | enemies.

3 The Lord comfort him, when he lieth sick up- | ·on his | bed : make thou áll his | bed | in his | sickness.

4 I said, Lord, be mérciful | unto | me : heal my sóul, for | I have | sinned · a- | -gainst thee.

5 Mine enemies spéak | evil | of me : When shall he díe | and his | name | perish ?

6 And if he come to sée me he | speaketh | vanity : and his heart conceiveth falsehood within himself ✶ and when he cómeth | forth he | telleth | it.

7 All mine enemies whísper to- | gether · a- | -gainst me : even against mé do | they im- | -agine · this | evil.

8 Let the sentence of gúiltiness pro- | ceed a- | -gainst him : and now that he líeth, | let him · rise | up no | more.

9 Yea, even mine own familiar friend | whom I trusted : who did also eat of my bréad, hath | laid great | wait for | me.

10 But be thou merciful únto | me O | Lord ; raise thou me up agáin | and I | shall re- | -ward them.

11 By this I knów thou | favourest | me : that mine énemy | doth not | triumph · a- | -gainst me.

12 And when I am in my health ✶ thou up- | -holdest | me : and shalt sét me be- -fore thy | face for | ever.

2nd part 13 Blessed be the Lórd | God of | Israel ; wórld without | end. | A- | -men.

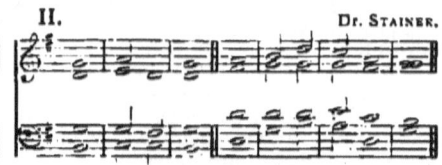

PSALM XLII.—*Quemadmodum.*

mf LIKE as the hárt de- | -sireth · the | water-brooks : so longeth my sóul | after | thee O | God.

2 My soul is athirst for God ✶ yea, éven for the | living | God : when shall I come to appear be- | -fore the presence · of | God ?

3 My tears have been my méat · day and | night : while they daily sáy unto me | Where is | now thy | God ?

4 Now when I think thereupon ✶ I pour out my heart | by my- | -self : for I went with the multitude ✶ and brought them fórth | into · the | house of | God ;

5 In the voice of práise and | thanks- | giving : amóng | such as | keep | holyday.

6 Why art thou so full of héaviness | O my | soul : and why art thou só dis- | quiet- | -ed with- | -in me ?

7 Put thy | trust in God : for I will yet give him thanks for the | help ‚ of his ‧ countenance.

8 My God, **my soul** is | vexed ‧ with‑in me : therefore will I remember thee concerning the land of Jordan ✶ ånd the little hill of Hermon.

9 One deep calleth another ✶ because of the nóise ‖ of the water‑pipes : all thy waves and stórms are gone over me.

10 The Lord hath granted his loving‑kindness ‖ in the | day‑time : and in the night‑season did I sing of him ✶ and made my prayer únto the God of my life.

11 I will say unto the God of my strength ✶ Why hast thou for‑ ‑gotten | me : why go I thus heavily ✶ while the | ene ‧ my op‑ ‑presseth me?

12 My bones are smitten asúnder ‖ as ‧ with a sword : while mine enemies that tróuble me cast me in the ‧ teeth;

13 Namely, while they say daily unto me : Whére ⸺ is now thy God?

14 Why art thou so véxed O my | soul : and why art thou só dis‑ ‑quiet‑ ‑ed with‑ ‑in me?

15 O put thy trust in God : for I will yet thank him ✶ which is the help of my countenance and my God.

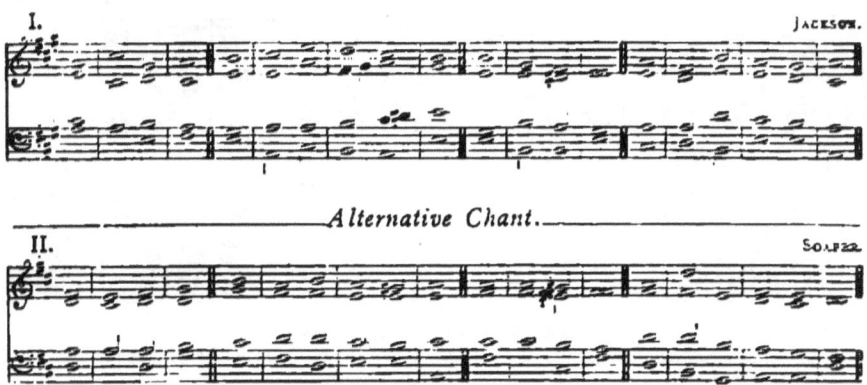

I.   Jackson.

Alternative Chant.

II.   Souza.

PSALM XLIII.—*Judica me, Deus.*

mf GIVE sentence with me O God ✶ and defend my cause agàinst the un‑ ‑godly | people : O deliver me from the de‑ceitful ‧ and wicked man.

2 For thou art the God of my strength ✶ why hast thou ‖ put me from thee : and why go I so heavily ✶ while the | ene ‧ my op‑ ‑presseth me?

3 O send out thy light and thy truth, that | they may ‖ lead me : and bring me unto thy hóly hill and | to thy dwelling.

4 And that I may go unto the altar of God ✶ even unto the Gód of my joy and gladness : and upon the harp will I give thanks unto thee O God ‧ my | God.

5 Why art thou so héavy ‧ O my ‧ soul : and why art thou só dis‑ ‑quiet‑ ‑ed with‑ ‑in me?

6 O put thy trust in God : for I will yet give him thanks ✶ which is the help of my countenance and my | God

DAY IX. MORNING.

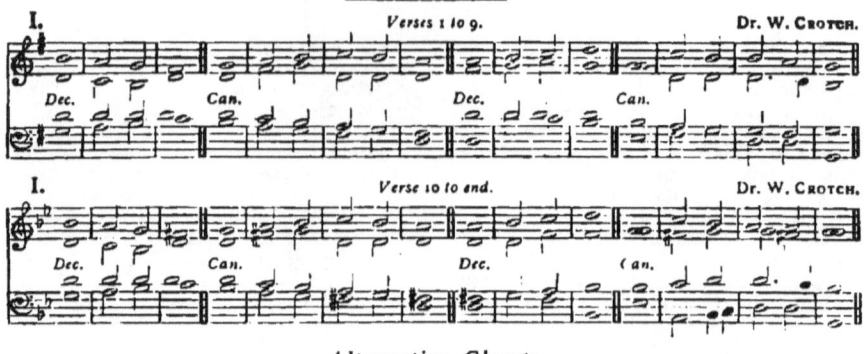

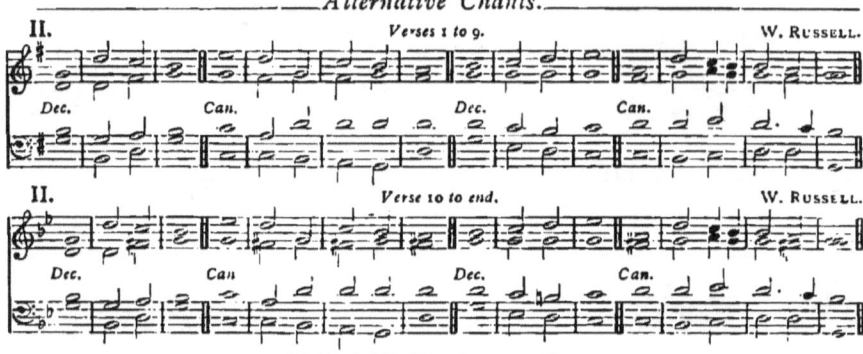

PSALM XLIV.—*Deus, auribus.*

mf WE have heard with our ears O God, our | fathers · have | told us : what thou hast dóne | in their | time of | old;

2 How thou hast driven out the heathen with thy hand * and plánted | them | in : how thou hast destróyed the | nations · and | cast them | out.

3 For they gat not the land in possession * through their | own | sword : neither was it their ówn | arm that | helped | them;

4 But thy right hand and thine arm * and the light | of thy | countenance : because thou hádst a | favour | unto | them.

5 Thóu art my | King O | God : sénd | help | unto | Jacob.

6 Through thee will we óver- | -throw our | enemies : and in thy Name will we tread them únder that | rise | up a- | gainst us.

7 For I will not trúst | in my | bow : it is nót my | sword | that shall | help me;

8 But it is thou that sávest us | from our | enemies : and púttest them | to | con- | -fusion · that | hate us.

^{2nd}_{part.} 9 We make our boast of God | all day | long : ánd will | praise thy | Name for | ever.

p 10 But now thou art far off * and púttest us | to con- | -fusion : and góest not | forth | with our | armies.

11 Thou makest us to turn our bácks up- | -on our | enemies : so that théy which | hate us | spoil our | goods.

12 Thou lettest us be éaten | up like | sheep : and hast scáttered | us a- | -mong the | heathen.

13 Thou séllest thy | people · for | nought : ánd | takest · no | money | for them.

14 Thou makest us to be rebúked | of our | neighbours : to be laughed to scorn * and had in derision of thém | that are | round a- | -bout us.

15 Thou makest us to be a bý-word a- | -mong the | heathen : and that the péople | shake their | heads | at us.

16 My confusion is | daily · be- | -fore me : and the sháme of my | face hath | covered | me.

17 For the voice of the slánderer | and blas- | -phemer : fór the | enemy | and a- | venger.

DAY IX. MORNING (continued).

18 And though all this be come upon us ∗ yět do we I not for- I -get thee : nor behāve ourselves I frowardly I in thy I covenant.

19 Our heart is not I turned I back : neíther our I steps gone I out of · thy I way ;

20 No, not when thou hast smitten us ínto the I place of I dragons : and cóvered us I with the I shadow · of I death.

21 If we have forgotten the Name of our God ∗ and holden up our hånds to any I strange I god : shall not God search it out ∗ for he knoweth the véry I secrets I of the I heart.

22 For thy sake also are we kílled I all the · day I long : and are counted as sheep ap- I -pointed I to be I slain.

mf 23 Up, Lórd, why I sleepest I thou : awake, and bé not I absent · from I us for I ever.

24 Wherefore hídest I thou thy I face : and forgěttest our I mise-I-ry and I trouble ?

25 For our soul is brought lów even I unto · the I dust : our bělly I cleaveth I unto · the I ground.

2nd part 26 Arīse I and I help us : and delíver us I for thy I mercy's I sake.

I.   *Verses 1 to 10* Rev. W. H. HAVERGAL.   I.   *Verse 11 to end.*   Dr. H. HILES.

— *Alternative Chants.* —

II.   *Verses 1 to 10.* Dr. G. A. MACFARREN.   II.   *Verse 11 to end.*   J. TURLE.

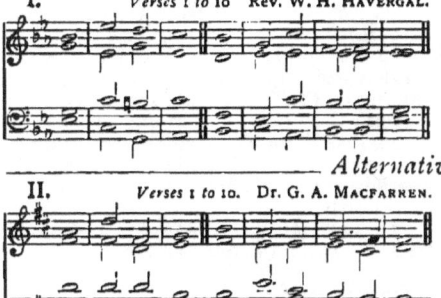

PSALM XLV.—*Eructavit cor meum.*

mf MY heart is indíting of a I good I matter : I speak of the things which I' have I made I unto · the I King.

2 My tôngue I is the I pen : óf I — a I ready I writer.

3 Thou art fairer thán the I children · of I men : full of grace are thy lips ∗ because Gód hath I blessed I thee for I ever.

4 Gird thee with thy sword upon thy thígh O I thou most I Mighty : accórding to thy I worship I and re- I -nown.

5 Good lúck have thou I with thine I honour : ride on because of the word of truth ∗ of meekness and righteousness ∗ and thy right hánd shall I teach thee I terrible I things.

6 Thy arrows are very sharp ∗ and the people shall be subdúed I unto I thee : even in the mídst a-I-mong the King's I enemies.

7 Thy seat, O Gód en- I -dureth · for I ever : the sceptre of thy kíngdom I is a I right I sceptre.

8 Thou hast loved ríghteousness and I hated · in- I -iquity : wherefore God, even thy God ∗ hath anointed thee with the óil of I gladness · a- I -bove thy I fellows.

9 All thy garments smell of mýrrh I aloes · and I cassia : out of the ivory palaces ∗ whereby I they have I made thee I glad.

10 King's daughters were among thy hónour- I -able I women : upon thy right hand did stand the queen in a vesture of gold ∗ wróught a- I -bout with I divers I colours.

11 Hearken, O daughter, and consíder, in- I -cline thine I ear : forget also thine own people I and thy I father's I house.

12 So shall the King have pleasure I in thy I beauty : for he is thy Lord Gód, and I worship I thou I him.

13 And the daughter of Tyre shall be thére I with a I gift : like as the rich also among the people ∗ shall make their I suppli- I -cation · be- I -fore thee.

14 The Kíng's daughter is all glóri- I -ous with- I -in : her clóthing I is of I wrought I gold.

15 She shall be brought unto the Kíng in I raiment · of I needlework : the virgins that be her fellows shall bear her company ∗ and sháll be I brought I unto I thee.

16 With joy and gládness shall I they be I brought : and shall ěnter I into · the I King's I palace.

17 Instead of thy fáthers thou I shalt have I children : whom thou máyest make I princes · in I all I lands.

18 I will remember thy Name from one generátion I to an- I -other : therefore shall the people give thanks unto thée I world with- I -out I end.

DAY IX. MORNING (continued).

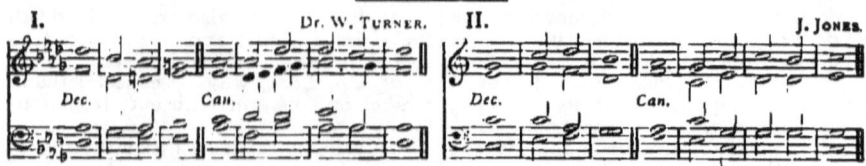

PSALM XLVI.—*Deus noster refugium.*

f GÓD is our | hope and | strength : a vèry | present | help in | trouble.

2 Therefore will we not fear, thóugh the | earth be | moved : and though the hills be carried ínto the | midst | of the | sea.

3 Though the waters theréof | rage and | swell : and though the mountains sháke at the | tempest | of the | same.

4 The rivers of the flood theréof, shall make glád the | city · of | God : the holy place of the tábernacle | of the | most | Highest.

5 God is in the midst of her ∗ therefore shall she nót | be re- | -moved : Gód shall | help her · and | that right | early.

6 The heathen make much adó and the | kingdoms · are | moved : but God hath shewed his vóice and the | earth shall | melt a- | -way.

7 The Lórd of | hosts is | with us : the Gód of | Jacob | is our | refuge.

8 O come hither, and behold the wórks | of the | Lord : what destruction hé hath | brought up- | -on the | earth.

9 He maketh wars to céase in | all the | world : he breaketh the bow, and knappeth the spear in sunder ∗ and búrneth the | chariots | in the | fire.

10 Be still then, and knów that | I am | God : I will be exalted among the heathen ∗ and I′ will be ex- | -alted | in the | earth.

11 The Lórd of | hosts is | with us : the Gód of | Jacob | is our | refuge.

DAY IX. EVENING.

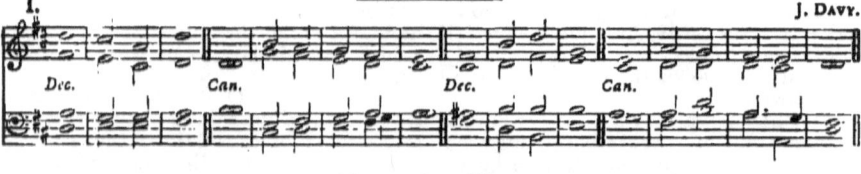

PSALM XLVII.—*Omnes gentes, plaudite.*

F. f O CLAP your hands togéther | all ye | people : O sing unto Gód | with the | voice of | melody.

F. 2 For the Lord is hígh and | to be | feared : he is the great Kíng up- | -on | all the | earth.

3 He shall subdue the péople | under | us : ánd the | nations | under · our | feet.

4 He shall choose óut an | heritage | for us : even the wórship of | Jacob | whom he | loved.

5 God is gone úp with a | merry | noise : and the Lórd with the | sound | of the | trump

6 O sing praises, sing práises | unto | our | God : O sing práises, sing | praises | unto · our | King.

7 For God is the Kíng of | all the | earth : sing ye | praises · with | under- | standing.

8 God régneth | over · the | heathen : God sítteth up- | -on his | holy | seat.

2nd part 9 The princes of the people ∗ are joined unto the péople of the | God of | Abraham : for God which is very high exalted ∗ doth defend the éarth as it | were | with a | shield.

DAY IX. EVENING (*continued*). 33

PSALM XLVIII.—*Magnus Dominus.*

f GREAT is the Lord, and highly | to be | praised : in the city of our God ✶ éven up- | -on his | holy | hill.

2 The hill of Sion is a fair place ✶ and the joy of the | whole | earth : upon the north side lieth the city of the great King ✶ God is well known in her pálaces | as a | sure | refuge.

3 For lo, the kíngs | of the | earth : are gáthered and | gone | by to- | -gether.

4 They márvelled to | see such | things : they were astónished and | sudden-. -iy | cast | down.

5 Fear came thére upon | them and | sorrow : as upón a | woman | in her | travail.

6 Thou shalt break the shíps | of the | sea : through | — the | east- | -wind.

7 Like as we have heard ✶ so have we seen in the city of the Lord of hosts ✶ in the cíty | of our | God : Gód up- | -holdeth . the | same for | ever.

8 We wait for thy lóving- | -kindness . O | God : ín the | midst of | thy | temple.

9 O God according to thy Name ✶ so is thy praise únto the | world's | end : thy right | hand is | full of | righteousness.

10 Let the mount Sion rejoice ✶ and the dáughter of | Judah . be | glad : bé- | -cause of | thy | judgements.

11 Walk about Sion, and gó | round a- | bout her : ánd | tell the | towers there- | -of.

12 Mark well her bulwarks, sét | up her | houses : that ye may téll | them that | come | after.

13 For this God is our Gód for | ever . and | ever : he shall bé our | guide | unto | death.

PSALM XLIX.—*Audite hæc, omnes.*

f O HEAR ye thís | all ye | people : ponder it with your ears ✶ all yé that | dwell | in the | world;

2 High and lów | rich and | poor : óne | with | an- | -other.

mf 3 My móuth shall | speak of | wisdom : and my héart shall | muse of | under- | -standing.

4 I will incline mine éar | to the | parable : and shéw my dark | speech up- | -on the | harp.

5 Wherefore should I féar in the | days of | wickedness : and when the wickedness of my heels cómpasseth | me | round a- | -bout ?

6 There be some that put their trúst | in their | goods : and boast themsélves in the | multi . tude | of their | riches.

7 But no man máy de- | -liver . his | brother : nor make agréement | unto | God | for him.

8 For it cost móre to re- | -deem their | souls : so that he must lét | that a- | -lone for | ever ;

9 Yea, though he | live | long : ánd | see | not the | grave.

10 For he seeth that wise men also díe and | perish . to- | -gether : as well as the ignorant and fóolish and | leave their | riches . for | other.

11 And yet they think that their houses shall con- | -tinue . for | ever : and that their dwelling-places shall endure from one generation to another ✶ and call the lánds | after . their | own | names.

12 Nevertheless, mán will not a- | -bide in | honour : seeing he may be compared unto the beasts that pérish ; | this . is the | way of | them.

13 This | is their | foolishness : and théir pos- | -terity | praise their | saying.

14 They lie in the hell like sheep ✶ death gnaweth upon them ✶ and the righteous shall have dominion óver them | in the | morning : their beauty shall consúme in the | sepulchre | out of . their | dwelling.

15 But God hath delivered my sóul from the | place of | hell : fór | he | shall re- | -ceive me.

16 Be not thou afraid ✶ though one be | made | rich : or if the glóry of his | house | be in- | -creased ;

17 For he shall carry nothing awáy with him | when he | dieth : neither sháll his | pomp | follow | him.

18 For while he lived ✶ he counted himsélf an | happy | man : and so long as thou doest well unto thyself ✶ mén will | speak | good of | thee.

19 He shall follow the generátion | of his | fathers : ánd shall | never | see | light.

20 Man being in honour hath nó | under- | standing : but is compáred | unto . the | beasts that | perish.

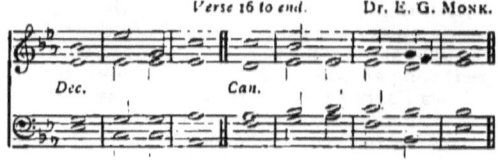

PSALM L.—*Deus deorum.*

f THE Lord, even the most mĭghty |ʹ God hath | spoken : and called the world, from the rising up of the sun ✻ únto the | going | down there- | -of.

2 Out of Síon hath | God ap- | peared : in | per- | -fect | beauty.

3 Our God shall cóme and shall | not keep | silence : there shall go before him a consuming fire ✻ and a mighty tempest sháll be | stirred · up | round a- | -bout him.

4 He shall call the héaven | from a- | -bove : and the éarth, that | he may | judge his | people.

5 Gather my saints togéther | unto | me : those that have made a cóve- | -nant with | me with | sacrifice.

6 And the héavens shall de- | -clare his | righteousness : fór | God is | judge him- | -self.

7 Hear, O my péople and | I will |ʹ speak : I myself will testify against thee O Israel ✻ for I am Gód | even | thy | God.

8 I will not reprove thee because of thy sacrifices ✻ or fór thy | burnt- | -offer- ings : becáuse they | were not | alway · be- | -fore me.

9 I will take no búllock | out of · thine | house : nór | he-goat | out of · thy | folds.

10 For all the béasts of the | forest · are | mine : and so are the cáttle up- | -on a | thousand | hills.

11 I know all the fówls up- | -on the | mountains : and the wild béasts of the | field are | in my | sight.

12 If I be hungry, Iʹ will | not tell | thee ; for the whole world is mine, and | **all that** | is there- | **-in.**

13 Thinkest thou that Í will | eat bulls' | flesh : ánd | drink the | blood of | goats?

14 Offer unto Gód | thanks- | -giving : and pay thy vóws | unto · the | most | Highest.

15 And call upon mé in the | time of |ʹ trouble : so will I héar thee and | thou shalt | praise | me.

16 But unto the ungódly | said God : Why dost thou preach my laws ✻ and tákest my | covenant | in thy | mouth;

17 Whereas thou hátest to | be re- | formed : ánd hast | cast my | words be- | hind thee?

18 When thou sawest a thief ✻ thou consentedst | unto | him : and hast béen par- | -taker | with · the a- | dulterers.

19 Thou hast lét thy | mouth speak | wickedness : and with thy tóngue thou hast | set | forth de- | -ceit.

20 Thou satest, and spákest a- | -gainst thy | brother : yea, and hast slándered thine | own | mother's | son.

21 These things hast thou done, and I held my tongue ✻ and thou thoughtest wickedly that I am even súch a one | as thy- | -self : but I will reprove thee ✻ and set befóre thee the | things that | thou hast | done.

22 O consider this, yé that for- | -get | God : lest I pluck you away ✻ and there be nóne | to de- | -liver | you.

23 Whoso offereth me thanks and práise he | honoureth | me : and to him that ordereth his conversation right will I | shew **the** · **sal-** | -vation · of | **God.**

DAY X. MORNING (*continued*).

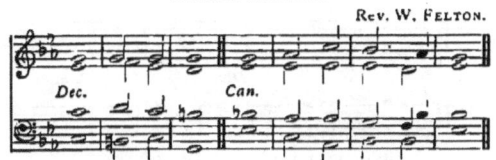

Rev. W. Felton.

PSALM LI.—*Miserere mei, Deus.*

p HAVE mercy upon me O God ✶ áfter thy | great | goodness : according to the multitude of thy mercies, dó a- | -way | mine of- | -fences.

2 Wash me thróughly | from my | wickedness : ánd | cleanse me | from my | sin.

3 For I' ac- | -knowledge · my | faults : ánd my | sin is | ever · be- | -fore me.

4 Against thee only have I sinned ✶ and done this évil | in thy | sight : that thou mightest be justified in thy sáying and | clear when | thou art | judged.

5 Behóld I was | shapen · in | wickedness : and in sín hath my | mother · con- | ceived | me.

6 But lo, thou requirest trúth in the | ir ward | parts : and shalt make me to únder- | stand | wisdom | secretly.

7 Thou shalt purge me with hyssop ✶ ánd I | shall be | clean : thou shalt wash me ✶ ánd I | shall be | whiter · than | snow.

8 Thou shalt make me héar of | joy and | gladness : that the bones which thóu hast | broken | may re- | -joice.

9 Turn thy fáce | from my | sins : and pút out | all | my mis- | -deeds.

10 Make me a cléan | heart O | God : ánd re-|-new a · right | spirit · with-|-in me.

11 Cast me not awáy | from thy | presence : and táke not thy | holy | Spirit | from me.

12 O give me the cómfort of thy | help a- | -gain : and stáblish me | with thy | free | Spirit.

13 Then shall I teach thy wáys | unto · the | wicked : and sinners shall bé con- | verted | unto | thee.

14 Deliver me from blood-guiltiness O God ✶ thou that art the Gód | of my | health : and my tóngue shall | sing | of thy | righteousness.

15 Thou shalt ópen my | lips O | Lord : ánd my | mouth shall | shew thy | praise.

16 For thou desirest no sacrifice ✶ élse would I | give it | thee : but thou de- lightest | not in | burnt- | -offerings.

17 The sacrifice of Gód is a | troubled | spirit : a broken and contrite heart, O Gód | shalt thou | not de- | -spise.

18 O be favourable and grácious | unto | Sion : búild thou the | walls | of Je- | -rusalem.

19 Then shalt thou be pleased with the sacrifice of righteousness ✶ with the burnt-ófferings | and ob- | -lations : then shall they óffer young | bullocks · up- | -on thine | altar.

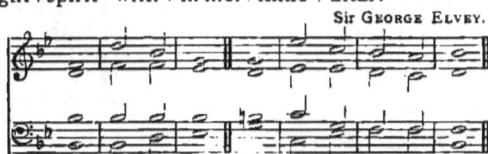

Sir George Elvey.

PSALM LII.—*Quid gloriaris?*

mf WHY bóastest thou thy- | -self thou | tyrant : thát | thou canst | do | mischief; 2 Whereás the | goodness · of | God : én- | -dureth | yet | daily?

3 Thy tóngue im- | -agineth | wickedness : and with lies thou cúttest | like a | sharp | razor.

4 Thou hast loved unríghteousness | more than | goodness : and to tálk of | lies | more than | righteousness.

5 Thou hast loved to speak all wórds that | may do | hurt : O' | — thou | false | tongue.

6 Therefore shall God destróy | thee for | ever : he shall take thee, and pluck thee out of thy dwelling ✶ and root thee óut of the | land | of the | living.

7 The righteous also shall sée | this and | fear : ánd shall | laugh | him to | scorn,

8 Lo, this is the man that took not Gód | for his | strength : but trusted unto the multitude of his riches ✶ and stréngthened him- | -self | in his | wickedness.

9 As for me, I am like a green olivetrée in the | house of | God : my trust is in the tender mércy of | God for | ever · and | ever.

10 I will always give thanks unto thee for thát | thou hast | done : and I will hope in thy Name, fór thy | saints | like it | well,

DAY X. EVENING.

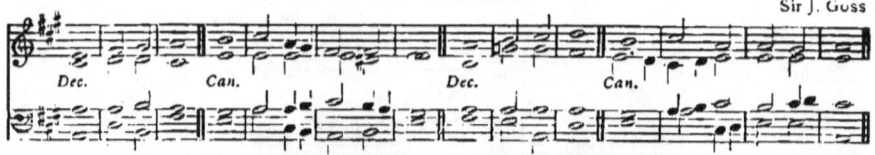

Sir J. Goss

PSALM LIII.—*Dixit insipiens.*

F.mp THE foolish body hath said | in his | heart : Thére | is | no | God.

F. 2 Corrupt are they * and become abóminable | in their | wickedness : thére is | none that | doeth | good.

3 God looked down from heaven upón the | children of | men : to see if there were any that would understánd, and | seek | after | God.

4 But they are all gone out of the way * they are altogéther be- | -come a- | bominable : there is also none that dóeth | good | no not | one.

5 Are not they without understand- ing that | work | wickedness : eating up my people as if they would eat bread * they háve not | called · up- | -on | God.

6 They were afráid where | no fear | was : for God hath broken the bones of him that besieged thee * thou hast put them to confusion * because Gód | hath de- | -spised | them.

f 7 Oh, that the salvation were given unto I'srael | out of | Sion : Oh, that the Lord would deliver his | people | out of · cap- | -tivity !

8 Then should | Jacob · re- | -joice : and I'srael | should be | right | glad.

Rev. C. A. Wickes.

PSALM LIV.—*Deus, in Nomine.*

mp SAVE me O Gód for thy | Name's | sake : and a- | -venge me | in thy | strength.

2 Hear my | prayer O | God : and hearken únto the | words·| of my | mouth.

3 For strangers are rísen | up a- | gainst me : and tyrants, which have not God before their éyes | seek | after · my | soul.

4 Behold, Gód | is my | helper : the Lord is with thém | that up- | -hold my | soul.

5 He shall reward évil | unto · mine | enemies : destróy thou | them | in thy | truth.

6 An offering of a free heart will I give thee * and práise thy | Name O | Lord : be- | -cause it | is so | comfortable.

7 For he hath delivered me óut of | all my | trouble : and mine eye hath séen his de- | -sire up- | -on mine | enemies.

Verses 1 to 8.   Dr. W. Croft.

PSALM LV.—*Exaudi, Deus.*

p HEAR my | prayer O | God : and hide not thy- | -self from | my pe- | -tition.

2 Take héed unto | me and | hear me : how I móurn in my | prayer | and am | vexed.

3 The enemy crieth so * and the ungodly cómeth | on so | fast : for they are minded to do me some mischief * so malíciously | are they | set a- | -gainst me.

4 My heart is disquíet- | -ed with- | in me : and the fear of | death is | fallen · up- | -on me.

5 Fearfulness and trémbling are | come up- | -on me : and an horrible dréad hath | over- | -whelmed | me.

6 And I said, O that I had wíngs | like a | dove : for then would I flée a- | way and | be at | rest.

7 Lo, then would I gét me a- | -way far | off : and re- | -main | in the | wilderness.

8 I would make háste | to es- | -cape · becáuse of the | stormy | wind and | tempest.

DAY X. EVENING (continued).

Verses 9 to 16.   Dr. W. Crotch.

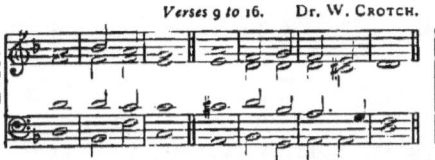

Verse 17 to end.   Rev. G. Heathcote.

9 Destroy their tongues O Lórd | and di- | -vide them : for I have spied unrighteousness and | strife | in the | city.

10 Day and night they go about within the | walls there- | -of : mischief also and sórrow are | in the | midst of | it.

11 Wíckedness | is there- | -in : deceit and gúile | go not | out of · their | streets.

12 For it is not an open enemy that hath dóne me | this dis- | -honour : fór | then I | could have | borne it.

13 Neither was it mine adversary * that did mágnify him- | -self a- | -gainst me : for then, peradventure, I' would have | hid my- | -self | from him.

14 But it was even thóu | my com- | panion : my gúide and mine | own fa- | miliar | friend.

15 We tóok sweet | counsel · to- | gether : and wálked in the | house of | God as | friends.

16 Let death come hastily upon them * and let them go down qúick | into | hell : for wickedness is ín their | dwellings | and a- | -mong them.

mf 17 As for mé I will | call up · on | God : ánd the | Lord | shall | save me.

18 In the evening and morning * and at noonday will I práy, and | that | instantly : ánd | he shall | hear my | voice.

19 It is he that hath delivered my soul in peace * from the báttle that | was a- | gainst me : fór | there were | many | with me.

20 Yea, even God that endureth for ever * shall héar me and | bring them | down : for they wíll not | turn nor | fear | God.

21 He laid his hands upon such as bé at | peace with | him : ánd he | brake | his | covenant.

22 The words of his mouth were softer than butter * having wár | in his | heart : his words were smoother than oil * and yét | be they | very | swords.

23 O cast thy burden upon the Lord * and hé shall | nourish | thee : and shall not súffer the | righteous · to | fall for | ever.

24 Ánd | as for | them : thou, O God, shalt bring them ínto the | pit | of de- | struction.

25 The blood-thirsty and deceitful men * shall not live óut | half their | days : nevertheless, my trúst shall | be in | thee O | Lord.

DAY XI. MORNING.

J. Turle.

PSALM LVI.—*Miserere mei, Deus.*

mp BE merciful unto me, O God * for man goeth abóut | to de- | -vour me : he is dáily | fighting · and | troubling | me.

2 Mine enemies are daily in hánd to | swallow · me | up : for they be many that fíght against | me O | thou most | Highest.

3 Nevertheless, thóugh I am | sometime · a- | -fraid : yĕt put | I my | trust in | thee.

4 I will praise God, becáuse | of his | word : I have put my trust in God * and will not féar what | flesh can | do · unto | me.

5 They dáily mis- | -take my | words : all that they imágine | is to | do me | evil.

6 They hold all togéther and | keep them · selves | close : and mark my steps * whén they lay | wait | for my | soul

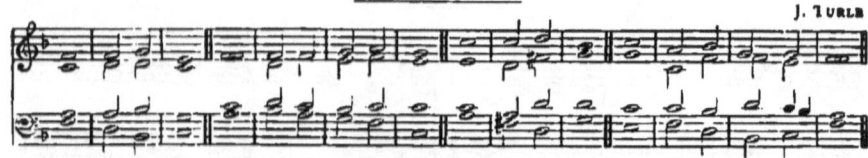

J. TURLE

7 Shall they escape | for their | wickedness : thou O Gód in thy dis- | pleasure · shalt | cast them | down.

8 Thou tellest my wanderings∗put my | tears | into · thy | bottle : are not thése things | noted | in thy | book?

9 Whensoever I call upon thee ∗ then shall mine énemies be | put to | flight : this I know, for | God is | on my | side.

10 In God's wórd will | I re- | -joice :

11 Yea, in Gód have I | put my | trust : I will not be afráid what | man can | do · unto | me.

12 Unto thee, O Gód will I | pay my | vows : unto thée | will I | give | thanks.

2nd 13 For thou hast delivered my soul from déath and my | feet from | falling : that I may walk before Gód in the | light | of the | living.

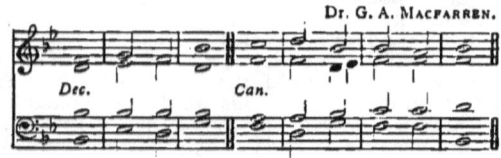

Dr. G. A. MACFARREN.

Dec.   Can.

PSALM LVII.—*Miserere mei, Deus.*

mp BE merciful unto me O God ∗ be merciful unto me, for my sóul | trusteth · in | thee : and under the shadow of thy wings shall be my refuge ∗ untíl this | tyranny · be | over- | -past.

2 I will cáll unto the | most high | God : even unto the God that shall perform the cáuse | which I | have in | hand.

3 Hé shall | send from | heaven : and save me from the reproof of hím | that would | eat me | up.

4 God shall send fórth his | mercy · and | truth ; my sóul | is a- | -mong | lions.

5 And I lie even among the children of mén that are | set on | fire : whose teeth are spears and arrows ∗ ánd their | tongue a | sharp | sword.

6 Set up thyself, O Gód a- | -bove the | heavens : and thy glóry a- | -bove | all the | earth.

7 They have laid a net for my feet ∗ and préssed | down my | soul : they have digged a pit before me ∗ and are fallen into the | midst of | it them- | -selves.

8 My heart is fixed O Gód my | heart is | fixed : I' will | sing and | give | praise.

mf 9 Awake up my glory∗awake lute and | harp : I mysélf | will a- | -wake right | early.

10 I will give thanks unto thee, O Lórd a- | -mong the | people : and I will síng unto | thee a- | -mong the | nations.

11 For the greatness of thy mercy, réacheth | unto · the | heavens : ánd thy | truth | unto · the | clouds.

12 Set up thyself, O Gód a- | -bove the | heavens : and thy glóry a- | -bove | all the | earth.

GREGORY.

PSALM LVIII.—*Si vere utique.*

mf ARE your minds set upon righteousness ∗ O ye | congre- | -gation : and do ye judge the thing that is ríght | O ye | sons of | men?

2 Yea, ye imagine mischief in your héart up- | -on the | earth :

ánd your | hands | deal with | wickedness.

3 The ungodly are froward ∗ even from their | mother's | womb : as soon as they are born ∗ they gó a- | -stray and | speak | lies.

DAY XI. MORNING (continued).

4 They are as venomous as the | poison | of a | serpent : even like the | deaf | adder · that | stoppeth · her | ears ;

5 Which refuseth to hear the vóice | of the | charmer : chárm he | never | so | wisely.

6 Break their teeth O God in their mouths ✶ smite the jaw-bónes of the | lions · O | Lord : let them fall away like water that runneth apace ✶ and when they shoot their árrows | let them · be | rooted | out.

7 Let them consume away like a snail ✶ and be like the untimely frúit | of a | woman : ánd | let them · not | see the | sun.

8 Or ever your póts be made | hot with | thorns : so let indignation vex him ✶ éven as a | thing | that is | raw.

9 The righteous shall rejóice when he | seeth · the | vengeance : he shall wash his footsteps, ín the | blood of | the un-|-godly.

10 So that a man shall say, Verily there is a rewárd | for the | righteous : doubtless, there ís a | God that | judgeth · the | earth.

DAY XI. EVENING.

I.   J. Turle, from Purcell.

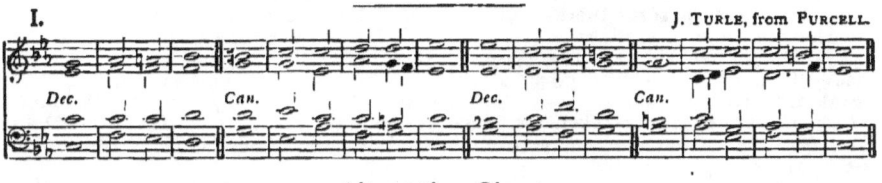

Alternative Chant.

II.   J. Barnby.

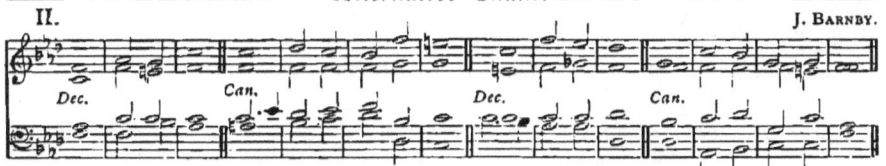

PSALM LIX.—*Eripe me de inimicis.*

*F. mp*DELIVER me from mine énemies | | O | God : defend me from thém that | rise | up a- | -gainst me.

F. 2 O deliver me, fróm the | wicked | doers : and sáve me | from the | bloodthirsty | men.

3 For lo, they lie wáiting | for my | soul : the mighty men are gathered against me ✶ without any offénce or | fault of | me O | Lord.

4 They run and prepare themsélves with- | -out my | fault : arise thou thérefore to | help me | and be- | -hold.

5 Stand up, O Lord God of hosts, thou God of Israel ✶ to vísit | all the | heathen : and be not merciful unto them that offénd | of ma- | -licious | wickedness.

6 They go to and fró | in the | evening : they grin like a dog, and gó a- | bout | through the | city.

7 Behold they speak with their mouth ✶ and swórds are | in their | lips : fór | who | doth | hear ?

8 But thou, O Lord, shalt háve them | in de- | -rision : and thou shalt láugh | all the | heathen · to | scorn.

9 My strength will I ascríbe | unto | thee : for thóu art the | God | of my | refuge.

10 God shéweth me his | goodness | plenteously : and God shall let me sée my de- | -sire up- | -on mine | enemies.

11 Slay them not, lést my | people · for- | -get it : but scatter them abroad among the people ✶ and put them dówn O | Lord | our de- | -fence.

12 For the sin of their mouth, and for the words of their lips ✶ they shall be táken | in their | pride : and why ✶ their preaching | is of | cursing · and | lies.

13 Consume them in thy wrath ✶ consúme them that | they may | perish : and know that it is God that ruleth in Jacob ✶ and únto the | ends | of the | world.

14 And in the évening they | will re- | turn : grin like a dóg and will | go a- | bout the | city.

15 They will rún here and | there for | meat : and grúdge | if they | be not | satisfied.

16 As for me, I will sing of thy power ✶ and will praise thy mercy betímes | in the | morning : for thou hast been my defence and refuge ✶ ín the | day | of my | trouble.

2nd part 17 Unto thee, O my stréngth | will I | sing : for thou, O God, art my réfuge | and my | merciful | God.

DAY XI. EVENING (continued).

PSALM LX.—*Deus, repulisti nos.*

mp O GOD, thou hast cast us out * and scáttered us a- | -broad : thou hast also been displeased * O túrn thee | unto | us a- | -gain.

2 Thou hast moved the lánd and di- | vided | it : heal the sóres there- | -of | for it | shaketh.

3 Thou hast shewed thy péople | heavy | things : thou hast gíven us a | drink of | deadly | wine.

4 Thou hast given a tóken for | such as | fear thee : that they may tríumph be- | -cause | of the | truth.

5 Therefore were thý be- | -loved | de- | -livered : help me with | thy right | hand and | hear me.

6 God hath spoken in his holiness * I will rejóice and di- | -vide | Sichem :

and méte | out the | valley · of | Succoth.

7 Gilead is míne and Ma- | -nasses · is | mine : Ephraim also is the strength of my héad | Judah | is my | lawgiver ;

8 Moab is my wash-pot * over Edom will I cást | out my | shoe : Philístia | be thou | glad of | me.

9 Who will lead me ínto the | strong | city ; whó will | bring me | into | Edom ?

10 Hast not thou cást us | out O | God : wilt not thou, O Gód go | out | with our | hosts ?

11 O be thóu our | help in | trouble : for váin | is the | help of | man.

12 Through Gód will we | do great | acts : for it is hé that shall | tread | down our | enemies.

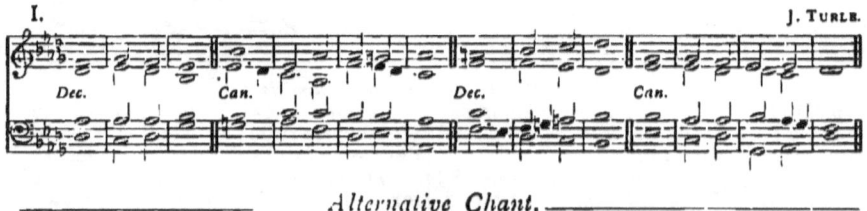

Alternative Chant.

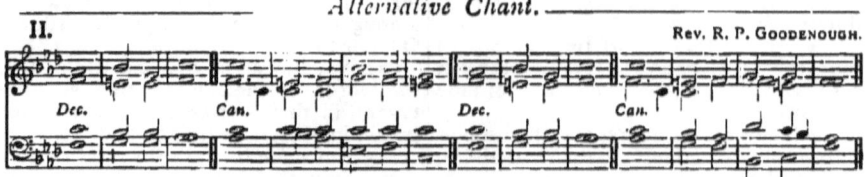

PSALM LXI.—*Exaudi, Deus.*

mf HÉAR my | crying · O | God : gíve | ear | unto · my | prayer.

2 From the ends of the éarth will I | call up · on | thee : whén my | heart | is in | heaviness.

3 O set me up upon the róck that is | higher · than | I : for thou hast been my hope * and a strong tówer for | me a- | gainst the | enemy.

4 I will dwell in thy táber- | -nacle · for | ever : and my trust shall be únder the | covering | of thy | wings.

5 For thou O Lord, hast héard | my de- | -sires : and hast given an heritage únto | those that | fear thy | Name.

6 Thou shalt grant the Kíng a | long | life : that his years may endúre through- out | all | gener- | -ations.

7 He shall dwell before | God for | ever : O prepare thy loving mercy and fáithfulness | that they | may pre- | -serve him.

8 So will I alway sing práise | unto · thy | Name : that I | may | daily per- | form my | vows.

DAY XII. MORNING.

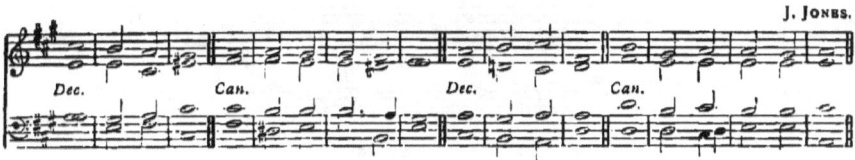

J. JONES.

PSALM LXII.—*Nonne Deo?*

mf MY soul truly wáiteth | still up - on | |
God : for of hím | cometh | my sal- |
vation.

2 He verily is my stréngth and | my
sal- | -vation : he is my defence, só that
I | shall not | greatly | fall.

3 How long will ye imagine mischief
agáinst | every | man : ye shall be slain
all the sort of you ✻ yea as a tottering
wall shall ye bé, and | like a | broken |
hedge.

4 Their device is only how to put
him out whom Gód | will ex- | -alt : their
delight is in lies ✻ they give good words
with their móuth, but | curse | with their |
heart.

5 Nevertheless my soul ✻ wáit thou |
still up - on | God ; fór my | hope | is in | him.

6 He truly is my stréngth and | my
sal- | -vation : he is my defénce | so that ·
I | shall not | fall.

7 In God is my héalth | and my |
glory : the rock of my might ✻ ánd in |
God | is my | trust.

8 O put your trust in hím | alway ·
ye | people : pour out your hearts befóre
him for | God | is our | hope.

9 As for the children of mén | they
are · but | vanity : the children of men
are deceitful upon the weights ✻ they are
altogether lighter than | vani- | -ty it- |
self.

10 O trust not in wrong and robbery ✻
give not yoursélves | unto | vanity : if
riches increase, sét | not your | heart up- |
on them.

11 God spake once, and twice I have
álso | heard the | same : that pówer be- |
longeth | unto | God ;

12 And that thóu | Lord art | merci-
ful : for thou rewardest every mán ac- |
cording | to his | work.

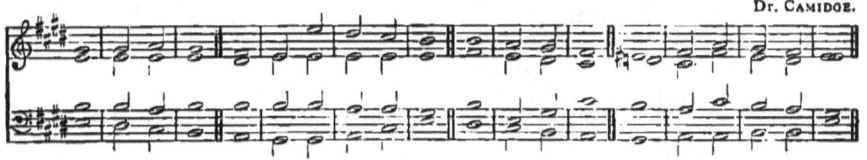

Dr. CAMIDGE.

PSALM LXIII.—*Deus, Deus meus.*

mf O GÓD thou art | my | God : éarly |
will I | seek | thee.

2 My soul thirsteth for thee ✻ my
flesh also lóngeth | after | thee : in a
barren and dry lánd | where no | water | is.

3 Thus have I lóoked for | thee in |
holiness : that I might be- | -hold thy |
power and | glory.

4 For thy loving-kindness is better
thán the | life it- | -self : mý | lips | shall |
praise thee.

5 As long as I live will I mágnify
thee | in this | manner : and lift úp my |
hands in | thy | Name.

6 My soul shall be satisfied ✻ even as
it wére with | marrow · and | fatness :
when my mouth práiseth | thee with |
joyful | lips.

7 Have I not remembered théee | in
my | bed : and thóught upon | thee when |
I was | waking ?

8 Becáuse thou hast | been my |
helper : therefore under the shádow of
thy | wings will | I re- | -joice.

9 My sóul | hangeth · up- | -on thee :
thy right hánd | hath up- | -holden | me.

10 These also that seek the húrt | of
my | soul : théy shall | go | under · the |
earth.

11 Let them fall upon the édge | of
the | sword : that théy may | be a | por-
tion · for | foxes.

12 But the King shall rejoice in God ✻
all they also that swear by hím shall | be
com- | -mended : for the mouth of thém
that speak | lies | shall be | stopped.

DAY XII. MORNING (*continued*).

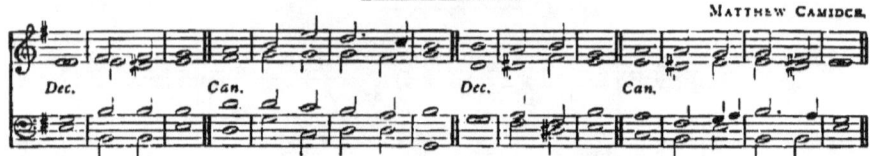

MATTHEW CAMIDGE.

PSALM LXIV.—*Exaudi, Deus.*

mp HEAR my voice, O Gód | in my | prayer : preserve my lífe from | fear | of the | enemy.

2 Hide me from the gathering to-géther | of the | froward : and from the insur- | rection · of | wicked | doers ;

3 Who have whet their tóngue | like a | sword : and shoot out their árrows, | even | bitter | words ;

4 That they may privily shoot at hím | that is | perfect : suddenly dó they | hit him | and | fear not.

5 They encóurage them- | -selves in | mischief : and commune among themselves, how they may lay snares * and sáy that | no | man shall | see them.

6 They imagine wíckedness and | practise | it : that they keep secret among themselves * every man ín the | deep | of his | heart.

7 But God shall suddenly shoot at thém with a | swift | arrow : thát | they | shall be | wounded.

8 Yea, their own tóngues shall | make them | fall : insomuch that whoso séeth them shall | laugh | them to | scorn.

9 And all men that see it shall say, Thís hath | God | done : for they shall percéive that | it is | his | work.

10 The righteous shall rejoice in the Lord * and pút his | trust in | him : and all they that are trúe of | heart | shall be | glad.

DAY XII. EVENING.

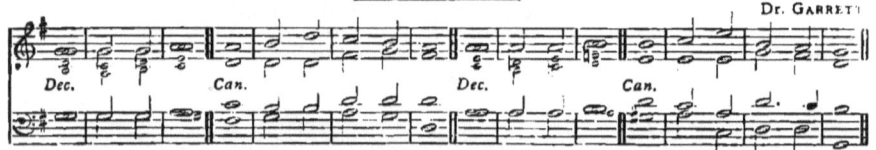

Dr. GARRETT

PSALM LXV.—*Te decet hymnus.*

F. mf THOU, O Gód art | praised · in | Sion : and unto thee shall the vów be per- | -formed | in Je- | -rusalem.

F. 2 Thóu that | hearest · the | prayer : únto | thee shall | all flesh | come.

3 My misdéeds pre- | -vail a- | -gainst me : O be thou | merciful | unto · our | sins.

4 Blessed is the man, whom thou choosest, and recéivest | unto | thee : he shall dwell in thy court * and shall be satisfied with the pleasures of thy house * éven | of thy | holy | temple.

5 Thou shalt shew us wonderful things in thy righteousness * O Gód of | our sal- | -vation : thou that art the hope of all the ends of the earth * and · of them that remáin | in the | broad | sea.

6 Who in his stréngth setteth | fast the | mountains : ánd is | girded · a- | bout with | power.

7 Who stilleth the ráging | of the | sea : and the noise of his wáves and the | madness | of the | people.

8 They also that dwell in the uttermost parts of the earth * shall be afráid | at thy | tokens : thou that makest the outgoings of the mórning and | evening · to | praise | thee.

9 Thou visitest the éarth and | blessest | it : thóu | makest · it | very | plenteous.

10 The river of Gód is | full of | water : thou preparest their corn * for só thou pro- | -videst | for the | earth.

11 Thou waterest her furrows * thou sendest rain into the líttle | valleys · there- | -of : thou makest it soft with the drops of ráin and | blessest · the | in- crease | of it.

12 Thou crownest the yéar | with thy | goodness : ánd thy | clouds | drop | fatness.

13 They shall drop upon the dwéllings | of the | wilderness : and the little hílls shall re- | -joice on | every | side.

14 The fólds shall be | full of | sheep : the valleys also shall stand so thick with córn that | they shall | laugh and | sing.

DAY XII. EVENING (continued).

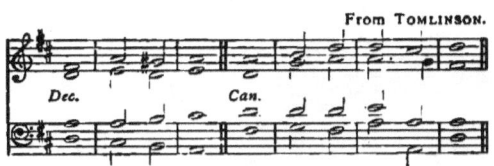

From Tomlinson.

PSALM LXVI.—*Jubilate Deo.*

f O BE joyful in Gód | all ye | lands : | sing praises unto the honour of his Name * máke his | praise | to be | glorious.

2 Say unto God, O how wonderful art thóu | in thy | works : through the greatness of thy power * shall thine enemies be fóund | liars | unto | thee.

3 For all the wórld shall | worship | thee : sing of | thee and | praise thy | Name.

4 O come hither, and behóld the | works of | God : how wonderful he is in his dóing | toward · the | children · of | men.

5 He turned the séa into | dry | land : so that they went through the water on foot * thére did | we re- | ·joice there- | of.

6 He ruleth with his power for ever * his éyes be- | -hold the | people : and such as will not believe, shall not be áble | to ex- | -alt them- | -selves.

7 O práise our | God ye | people : and make the vóice of his | praise | to be | heard ;

8 Who hóldeth our | soul in | life : and súffereth | not our | feet to | slip.

9 For thou O Gód hast ! proved | us : thou also hast tríed us | like as | silver · is | tried.

10 Thou bróughtest us | into · **the** | snare : and láidest | trouble · up- | ·on our | loins.

11 Thou sufferedst men to ríde | over· our | heads : we went through fire and water * and thou broughtest us óut | into · a | wealthy | place.

12 I will go into thine hóuse with | burnt- | ·offerings : and will pay thee my vows * which I promised with my lips, and spake with my móuth | when I | was in | trouble.

13 I will offer unto thee fat burnt-sacrifices * with the | incense · of | rams : I' will | offer | bullocks · and | goats.

14 O come hither, and hearken * all yē that | fear | God : and I will tell you what hē hath | done | for my | soul.

15 I called unto hím | with my | mouth : and gáve him | praises | with my | tongue.

16 If I incline unto wíckedness | with mine | heart : thē | Lord | will not | hear me.

17 Bŭt | God hath | heard me : and considered the | voice | of my | prayer.

18 Praised be God, who hath nót cast | out my | prayer : nór | turned · his | mercy | from me.

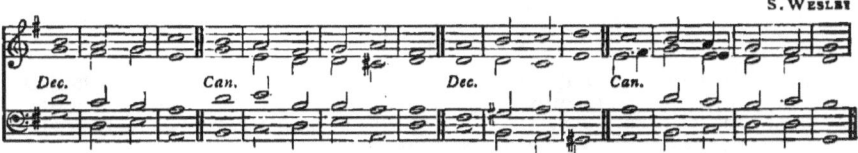

S. Wesley.

PSALM LXVII.—*Deus misereatur.*

mf GOD be merciful únto | us and | bless us : and shew us the light of his counten-ance * ánd be | merciful | unto | us ;

2 That thy way may be knówn up- | on | earth : thy sáving | health a- | ·mong all | nations.

F, 3 Let the people práise | thee O | God : yéa let | all the · | people | praise thee.

4 O let the nations rejóice | and be | glad : for thou shalt judge the folk ríght-eously * and gốvern the | nations · up- | on | earth.

F. 5 Let the people práise | thee O | God ; yéa let | all the | people | praise thee.

6 Then shall the éarth bring | forth her | increase : and God, even our own Gód, shall | give | us his | blessing.

2nd part. 7 Gód | shall | bless us : and all the énds of the | world shall | fear | him.

DAY XIII. MORNING.

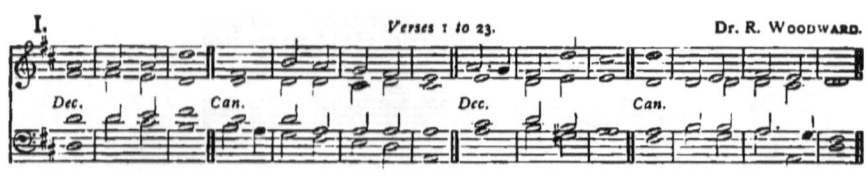

Dr. R. Woodward. — Verses 1 to 23.

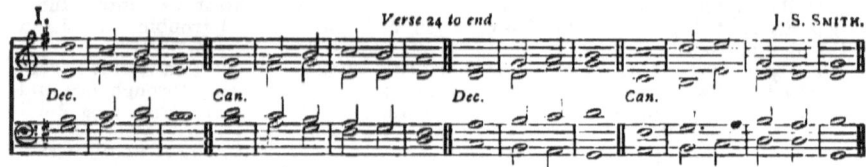

J. S. Smith. — Verse 24 to end.

Alternative Chants.

Dr. W. Crotch. — Verses 1 to 23.

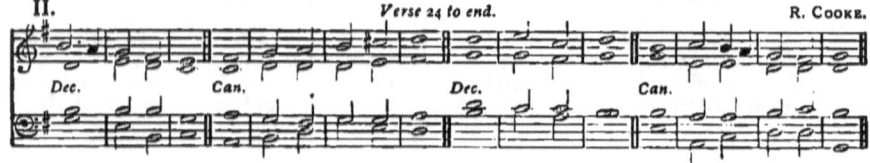

R. Cooke. — Verse 24 to end.

PSALM LXVIII.—*Exurgat Deus.*

f LET God arise, and let his éne- | mies be | scattered : let them álso that | hate him | flee be- | -fore him.

2 Like as the smoke vanisheth, ✶ so shalt thou drive | them a- | -way : and like as wax melteth at the fire ✶ so let the ungodly pérish | at the | presence · of | God.

3 But let the righteous be gláđ and re- | -joice be · fore | God : lét them | also · be | merry · and | joyful.

4 O sing unto God, and sing práises | unto · his | Name : magnify him that rideth upon the heavens as it were upon an horse ✶ praise him in his Name JA'H | and re- | -joice be- | -fore him.

5 He is a Father of the fatherless ✶ and defendeth the cáuse | of the | widows : even Gód in his | holy | habit- | ation.

6 He is the God that maketh men to be of one mind in an house ✶ and bringeth the prísoners | out of · cap- | -tivity : but letteth the runagátes con- | -tinue | in | scarceness.

7 O God when thou wentest fórth be- | -fore the | people : whěn thou | wentest | through the | wilderness,

8 The earth shook, and the heavens dropped át the | presence · of | God : even as Sinai also was moved at the presence of Gód, who | is the | God of | Israel.

DAY XIII. MORNING (continued).

9 Thou, O God, sentest a gracious ráin upon | thine in- | -heritance : and re-fréshedst | it when | it was | weary.

10 Thy congregátion shall | dwell there- | -in : for thou, O God, hast of thy góodness pre- | -pared | for the | poor.

11 The Lórd | gave the | word : gréat was the | company | of the | preachers.

12 Kings with their armies did fléc and | were dis- | -comfited : and théy of the | household · di- | -vided · the | spoil.

13 Though ye have lain among the pots * yet shall ye be as the wíngs | of a | dove : that is covered with silver wíngs | and her | feathers · like | gold.

14 When the Almighty scattered kíngs | for their | sake : thén were they as | white as | snow in | Salmon.

15 As the hill of Basan, só is | God's | hill : even an hígh hill | as the | hill of | Basan.

16 Why hop ye so ye high hills * this is God's hill, in the which it pléaseth | him to | dwell : yea the Lórd will a- | -bide in | it fcr | ever.

17 The chariots of God are twenty thousand * éven | thousands · of | angels : and the Lord is among them * as ín the | holy | place of | Sinai.

18 Thou art gone up on high * thou hast led captivity captive, and recéived | gifts for | men : yea, even for thine enemies * that the Lórd | God might | dwell a- | -mong them.

19 Praised bé the | Lord | daily : even the God who helpeth us, and póureth his | bene- | -fits up- | -on us.

20 He is our God * even the Gód of whom | cometh · sal- | -vation : God is the Lórd by | whom · we es- | -cape | death.

21 God shall wound the héad | of his | enemies : and the hairy scalp of such a one as góeth on | still | in his | wicked-ness.

22 The Lord hath said * I will bring my people agáin as I | did from | Basan : mine own will I bring again * as I did sometime fróm the | deep of the | sea.

2nd part 23 That thy foot may be dipped in the blóod | of thine | enemies ; and that the tongue of thy dógs may be | red | through the | same.

24 It is well seen O Gód | how thou | goest : how thou, my God and Kíng | goest | in the | sanctuary.

25 The singers go before * the mín strels | follow | after : in the midst are the dámsels | playing | with the | tim-brels.

26 Give thanks O Israel, unto God the Lórd in the | congre- | -gations : fróm the | ground | of the | heart.

27 There is little Benjamin their ruler * and the princes of | Judah · their | coun-sel : the princes of Zabúlon | and the | princes · of | Nephthali.

28 Thy God hath sént forth | strength for | thee : stablish the thing, O Gód that | thou hast | wrought in | us,

29 For thy temple's sáke | at Je- | rusalem : so shall kings bring | presents | unto | thee.

30 When the company of the spear-men, and multitude of the mighty * are scattered abroad among the beasts of the people * so that they húmbly bring | pieces · of | silver : and when he hath scattered the péople | that de- | -light in | war ;

31 Then shall the princes cóme | out of | Egypt : the Morians' land shall soon stretch óut her | hands | unto | God.

ff 32 Sing unto God, O ye kíngdoms | of the | earth : O' sing | praises | unto · the | Lord ;

33 Who sitteth in the heavens over áll | from · the be- | -ginning : lo, he doth send out his voice * yéa and | that a | mighty | voice.

34 Ascribe ye the power to Gód | over | Israel : his wórship and | strength is | in the | clouds.

35 O God, wonderful art thóu in thy | holy | places : even the God of Israel * he will give strength and power unto his péople, | blessed | be | God.

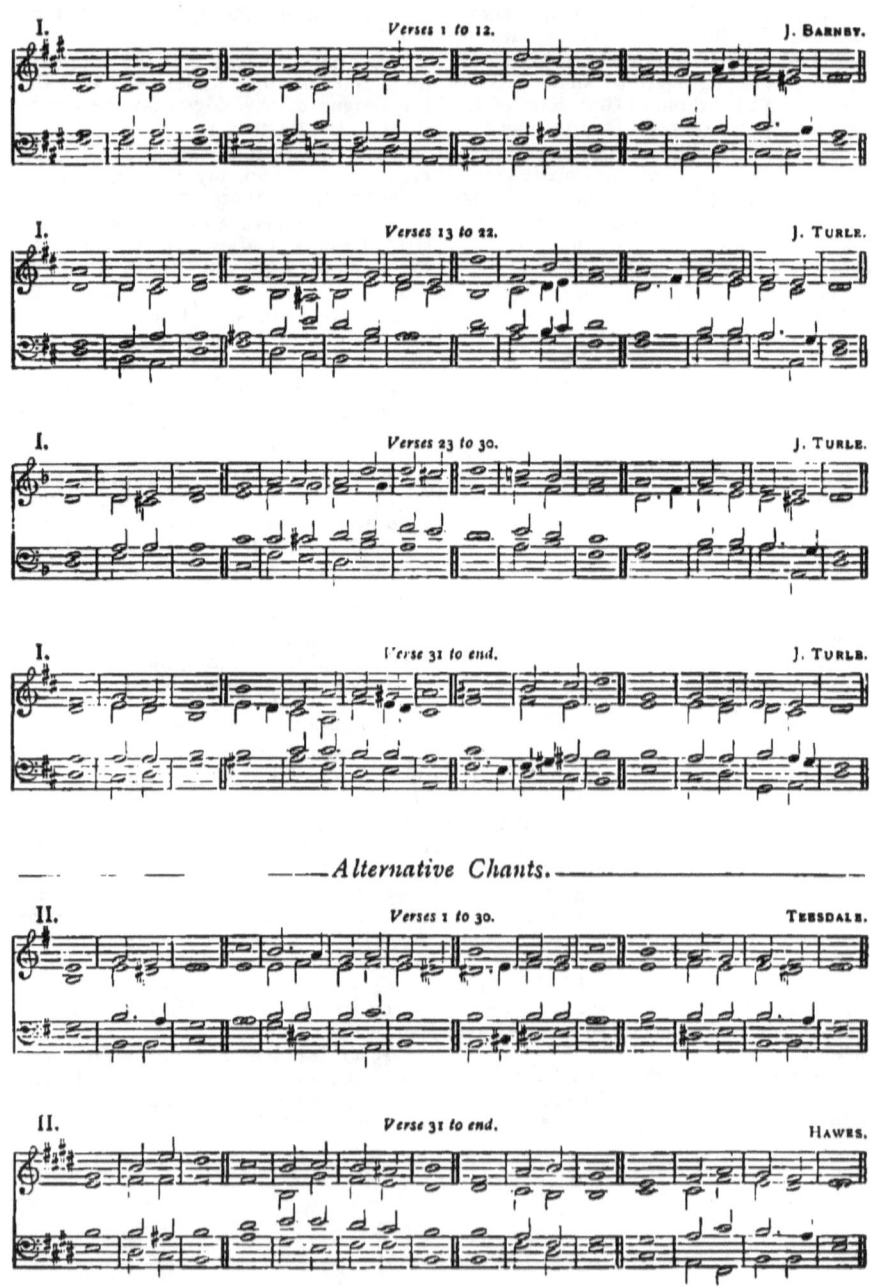

PSALM LXIX.—*Salvum me fac.*

F. mp SAVE | me O | God : for the waters | are come ín | even | unto · my | soul.

F. 2 I stick fast in the deep mire ✶ whére no | ground | is : I am come into deep waters ✶ só that the | floods run | over | me.

3 I am weary of crýing; my | throat is | dry : my sight faileth me for wáiting so | long up- | -on my | God.

4 They that hate me without a cause, are more than the háirs | of my | head : they that are mine enemies, and wóuld de- | -stroy me | guiltless · are | mighty.

5 I paid them the thíngs that I | never | took : God, thou knowest my simpleness ✶ and my fáults | are not | hid from | thee.

6 Let not them that trust in thee, O Lord God of hosts ✶ be ashámed for | my | cause : let not those that seek thee ✶ be confounded through mé O | Lord | God of | Israel.

7 And why ✶ for thy sáke have I | suffered · re- | -proof : sháme hath | covered | my | face.

8 I am become a stránger | unto · my | brethren : even an álien | unto · my | mother's | children.

9 For the zeal of thine house hath éven | eaten | me : and the rebukes of them that rebúked | thee are | fallen · up- | on me.

10 I wept, and chástened my- | -self with | fasting : and thát was | turned · to | my re- | -proof.

11 I pút on | sackcloth | also : ánd they | jested · up- | -on | me.

12 They that sit in the gáte | speak a- | gainst me : ánd the | drunkards · make | songs up- | -on me.

13 But, Lord, I make my práyer | unto | thee : ín | an ac- | -ceptable | time.

14 Hear me, O God, in the múltitude | of thy | mercy : even ín the | truth of | thy sal- | -vation.

15 Take me out of the míre | that I | sink not : O let me be delivered from them that hate me ✶ ánd | out · of the | deep | waters.

16 Let not the water-flood drown me ✶ neither let the déep | swallow · me | up : and let not the pít | shut her | mouth up- | | on me.

17 Hear me O Lord, for thy lóving- | kindness · is | comfortable : turn thee unto me accórding to the | multitude | of thy | mercies.

18 And hide not thy face from thy sérvant for | | I am · in | trouble : O' | | haste | thee and | hear me.

19 Draw nígh unto my | soul and | save it : O delíver me be- | -cause of | mine | enemies.

20 Thou hast known my reproof, my sháme and | my dis- | -honour : mine ádversaries are | all in | thy | sight.

21 Thy rebuke hath broken my heart ✶ I' | am | full of | heaviness : I looked for some to have pity on me, but there was no man ✶ neither fóund I | any · to | comfort | me.

22 They gáve me | gall to | eat : and when I was thirsty they gáve me | vine- | gar to | drink.

23 Let their table be made a snare to táke them- | -selves with- | -al : and le' the things that should have been for their wealth ✶ be unto thém | an oc- | -casion · of | falling.

24 Let their eyes be blínded, | that they | see not : and éver | bow thou | down their | backs.

25 Pour out thine índig- | -nation · up- | -on them : and let thy wráthful dis- | pleasure · take | hold of | them.

26 Let their hábit- | -ation · be | void : and nó man to | dwell | in their | tents.

27 For they persecute hím whom | thou hast | smitten : and they talk how they may véx | them whom | thou hast | wounded.

28 Let them fall from one wíckedness | to an- | -other : ánd | not come | into · thy | righteousness.

29 Let them be wiped out of the bóok | of the | living : and nót be | written · a- | -mong the | righteous.

30 As for me, when I am póor | and in | heaviness : thy hélp O | God shall | lift me | up.

f 31 I will praise the Name of Gód | with a | song : and mágni- | -fy it · with | thanks- | -giving.

32 This álso shall | please the | Lord : better than a búllock | that hath | horns and | hoofs.

33 The humble shall consider thís | and be | glad : seek ye after Gód | and your | soul shall | live.

34 For the Lórd | heareth · the | poor : ánd de- | -spiseth | not his | prisoners.

35 Let héaven and | earth | praise him : the séa, and | all that | moveth · there- | -in.

36 For God will save Sion ✶ and búild the | cities · of | Judah : that men may dwell thére, and | have it | in pos- | session.

2nd part 37 The posterity also of his servants shall ín- | -herit | it : and they that lóve his | Name shall | dwell there- | -in.

DAY XIII. EVENING (continued).

I. W. Beale.

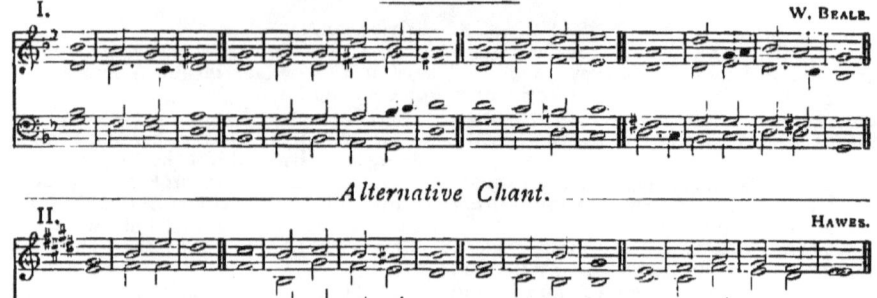

Alternative Chant.

II. Hawes.

PSALM LXX.—*Deus in adjutorium.*

p HASTE thee O Gód to de- | -liver ||
me : make háste to | help | me O | Lord.

2 Let them be ashamed and confounded, that séek | after · my | soul : let them be turned backward ✶ and pút to con- | -fusion · that I wish me | evil.

3 Let them for their reward be sóon | brought to | shame : that crý | over · me | There | there.

4 But let all those that seek thee be jóyful and | glad in | thee : and let all such as delight in thy salvation say álway, The | Lord | be | praised.

5 As for me, I am póor | and in | misery : háste thee | unto | me O | God.

6 Thou art my hélper and | my re- | deemer : O Lórd | make no | long | tarrying.

DAY XIV. MORNING.

Verses 1 to 14. J. Robinson.

Verse 15 to end. Dr. B. Cooke.

PSALM LXXI.—*In te, Domine, speravi.*

mp IN thee O Lord, have I put my trust ✶ let me never be pút | to con- | -fusion : but rid me and deliver me in thy righteousness ✶ incline thine éar | unto | me and | save me.

2 Be thou my stronghold ✶ whereuntó I may | alway · re- | -sort : thou hast promised to help me ✶ for thou art my hóuse of de- | -fence | and my | castle.

3 Deliver me, O my God, out of the hánd of | the un- | -godly : out of the hánd of the un- | -righteous · and | cruel | man.

4 For thou, O Lord God art the thíng | that I | long for : thou art my hópe | even | from my | youth.

5 Through thee have I been holden up ever since | I was | born : thou art he that took me out of my mother's womb ✶ my práise | shall be | always · of | thee.

6 I am become as it were a mónster | unto | many : but my súre | trust | is in | thee.

7 O let my mouth be fílled | with thy | praise : that I may sing of thy glory and hónour | all the | day | long.

8 Cast me not awáy in the | time of | age : forsake me not whén my | strength | faileth | me.

9 For mine enemies speak against me ✶ and they that lay wait for my soul take their cóunsel to- | -gether | saying : God hath forsaken him ✶ persecute him and take him ✶ for there is nóne | to de- | -liver | him.

10 Go not fár from | me O | God : my | Gód | haste | thee to | help me.

11 Let them be confounded and perish that áre a- | -gainst my | soul : let them be covered with shame and dishónour | that | seek to | do me | evil.

12 As for me, I will pátiently a- | bide | alway : ánd will | praise thee | more and | more.

f 13 My mouth shall daily speak of thy righteousness | and sal- | -vation : fór I know no | end there- | -of.

14 I will go forth in the stréngth of the | Lord | God : and will make mén- | tion | of thy | righteousness | only.

mf 15 Thou, O God, hast taught me from my yóuth up | until | now : therefore will I téll | of thy | wondrous | works.

16 Forsake me not O God in mine old age * whén I am | gray- | -headed : until I have shewed thy strength unto this generation * and thy power to all thém that are | yet | for to | come.

17 Thy righteousness O God is | very | high : and great things are they that thou hast done * O Gód | who is | like . unto thee ?

18 O what great troubles and adver- sities hast thou shewed me * and yet didst thou túrn | and re- | -fresh me : yea, and broughtest me from the déep | of the | earth a- | -gain.

19 Thou hast brought me to | great | honour : and cómforted | me on | every | side.

20 Therefore will I praise thee and thy faithfulness O God * playing upon an ínstru- | -ment of | musick : unto thee will I sing upon the harp * O' thou | Holy | One of | Israel.

21 My lips will be fain when I síng | unto | thee : and so will my sóul | whom thou | hast de- | -livered.

22 My tongue also shall talk of thy righteousness | all the . day | long : for they are confounded and brought unto sháme that | seek to | do me | evil.

Dr. T. S. Dupuis.

PSALM LXXII.—*Deus, judicium.*

f GIVE the Kíng thy | judgments . O | God : and thy ríghteousness | unto . the | King's | son.

2 Then shall he judge thy people according | unto | right : ánd de- | -fend | the | poor.

3 The mountains álso shall | bring | peace : and the little hílls | righteousness | unto . the | people.

4 He shall keep the símple folk | by their | right : defend the children of the póor, and | punish . the | wrong | doer.

5 They shall fear thee, as long as the sún and | moon en- | -dureth : from óne gener- | -ation | to an- | -other.

6 He shall come down like the ráin into a | fleece of | wool : éven as the | drops that | water . the | earth.

7 In his tíme shall the | righteous | flourish : yea, and abundance of péace, so | long . as the | moon en- | dureth.

8 His dominion shall be also from the óne sea | to the | other : and from the flóod | unto . the | world's | end.

9 They that dwell in the wílderness shall | kneel be- | -fore him : his éne- | mies shall | lick the | dust.

10 The kings of Tharsis and of the ísles shall | give | presents : the kings of Arábia and | Saba | shall bring | gifts.

11 All kings shall fáll | down be- | -fore him : áll | nations . shall | do him | service.

12 For he shall deliver the póor when he | crieth : the needy álso and | him that | hath no | helper.

13 He shall be favourable tó the | simple . and | needy : and shall presérve the | souls | of the | poor.

14 He shall deliver their sóuls from | falsehood . and | wrong : and déar shall their | blood be | in his | sight.

15 He shall live * and unto him shall be given of the góld | of A- | -rabia : prayer shall be made ever unto hím, and | daily . shall | he be | praised.

16 There shall be an heap of corn in the earth * hígh up- | -on the | hills : his fruit shall shake like Libanus * and shall be green in the cíty | shall | grass up- | -on the | earth.

17 His Name shall endure for ever * his Name shall remain under the sún a- | mongst the . pos- | -terities : which shall be blessed through hím, and | all the | heathen . shall | praise him.

18 Blessed be the Lord God * éven the | God of | Israel : which ónly | doeth | wondrous | things ;

19 And blessed be the Name of his Májes- | -ty for | ever : and all the earth shall be filled with his Májesty. | Amen. | A- | -men.

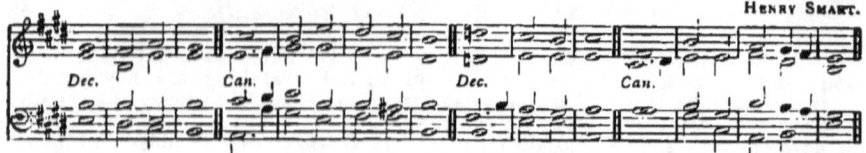

PSALM LXXIII.—*Quam bonus Israel!*

F. mp TRULY God is lóving | unto | Israel : even unto súch as | are · of a | clean | heart.

F. 2 Nevertheless, my féet were | almost | gone : mý | treadings · had | wellnigh | slipt.

3 And why ✻ I was griéved | at the | wicked : I do also sée the un- | -godly · in | such pros- | -perity.

4 For they are ín no | peril · of | death : but are | lusty | and | strong.

5 They come in no misfórtune like | other | folk : neither áre they | plagued · like | other | men.

6 And this is the cause that they áre so | holden · with | pride : ánd | over- | whelmed · with | cruelty.

7 Their éyes | swell with | fatness : and they dó | even | what they | lust.

8 They corrupt other ✻ and speák of | wicked | blasphemy : their talking is a- | gainst the | most | High.

9 For they stretch forth their móuth | unto · the | heaven : and their tóngue | goeth | through the | world.

10 Therefore fall the péople | unto | them : and thereóut suck | they no | small ad- | -vantage.

11 Tush, say they ✻ hów should | God per- | -ceive it : is there knówledge | in the | most | High ?

12 Lo, these are the ungodly, these prosper in the world ✻ and these have ríches | in pos- | -session : and I said, Then have I cleansed my heart in váin, and | washed · mine | hands in | innocency.

13 All the day lóng have | I been | punished : ánd | chastened | every | morning.

14 Yea, and I had almost sáid | even · as | they : but lo, then I should have condemned the géner- | -ation | of thy | children.

15 Then thought I to únder- | -stand | this : bút it | was too | hard for | me,

16 Until I went into the sánctu- | -ary · of | God : then understóod I the | end of | these | men ;

17 Namely, how thou dost sét them in | slippery | places : and castest them dówn | and de- | -stroyest | them.

18 Oh, how súddenly do | they con- | sume : pérish and | come · to a | fearful | end.

19 Yea, even like as a dréam | when · one a- | -waketh : so shalt thou make their ímage to | vanish | out · of the | city.

20 Thús my | heart was | grieved and it wént | even | through my | reins.

2nd part. 21 So fóolish was | I and | ignorant : éven as it | were a | beast be- | -fore thee.

mf 22 Nevertheléss I am | alway · by thee : for thou hast hólden me | by my | right | hand.

23 Thou shalt gúide me | with thy · counsel : and after thát re- | -ceive | me with | glory.

24 Whóm have I in | heaven · but | thee : and there is none upon earth that I desíre in com- | -pari- | -son of | thee.

25 My flésh and my | heart | faileth : but God is the strength of my héart | and my | portion · for | ever.

26 For lo, they that forsáke | thee shall | perish : thou hast destroyed all them that commít | forni- | -cation · a- | gainst thee.

27 But it is good for me to hold me fast by God ✻ to put my trúst in the | Lord | God : and to speak of all thy works in the gátes | of the | daughter · of | Sion.

DAY XIV. EVENING (*continued*).

PSALM LXXIV.—*Ut quid, Deus?*

mf O GOD, wherefore art thou ábsent from | us so | long : why is thy wrath so hot against the | sheep of | thy | pasture?

2 O think upón thy | congre-|-gation : whom thou hast púrchased | and re- | deemed · of | old.

3 Think upon the tríbe of | thine in- | heritance : and Mount Síon where- | -in | thou hast | dwelt.

4 Lift up thy feet ✻ that thou mayest utterly destróy | every | enemy : which hath dóne | evil | in thy | sanctuary.

5 Thine adversaries roar in the mídst of thy | congre- | -gations : and sét | up their | banners · for | tokens.

6 He that hewed timber afore, óut of the | thick | trees : was known to bring it | to an | excellent | work.

mp 7 But now they break down all the cárved | work there- | -of : with | axes | and | hammers.

8 They have set fire upón thy | holy | places : and have defiled the dwelling-place of thy Náme | even | unto · the | ground.

9 Yea, they said in their hearts ✻ Let us make hávock of them | alto- | -gether : thus have they burnt up all the hóuses of | God | in the | land.

10 We see not our tokens ✻ there is not óne | prophet | more : no, not one is there among us ✻ that únder- | -standeth | any | more.

mf 11 O God, how long shall the adversary dó | this dis- | -honour : how long shall the énemy blas- | -pheme thy | Name for | ever?

12 Why withdráwest | thou thy | hand : why pluckest thou not thy right hand out of thy bósom | to con- | -sume the | enemy?

13 For Gód is my | King of | old : the help that is done upon éarth he | doeth | it him- | -self.

14 Thou didst divide the séa | through thy | power : thou brakest the héads of the | dragons | in the | waters.

15 Thou smotest the heads of Levía- | -than in | pieces : and gavest him to be méat for the | people | in the | wilderness.

16 Thou broughtest out fountains and waters, óut of the | hard | rocks : thóu | driedst · up | mighty | waters.

17 The day is thíne and the | night is | thine : thou hast prepáred the | light | and the | sun.

18 Thou hast set all the bórders | of the | earth : thóu hast | made | summer · and | winter

19 Remember this, O Lord ✻ how the énemy | hath re- | -buked : and how the foolish péople | hath blas- | -phemed · thy | Name.

20 O deliver not the soul of thy turtle-dove ✻ unto the múltitude | of the | enemies : and forget not the congregátion | of the | poor for | ever.

21 Lóok up- | -on the | covenant : for all the earth is full of dárkness and | cruel | habit- | -ations.

22 O let not the simple gó a- | -way a- | -shamed : but let the poor and néedy give | praise | unto · thy | Name.

23 Arise, O God, maintáin thine | own | cause : remember how the foolish mán blas- | -phemeth | thee | daily.

24 Forget not the vóice | of thine | enemies : the presumption of them that hate thee, incréaseth | ever | more and | more.

DAY XV. MORNING.

PSALM LXXV.—*Confitebimur tibi.*

mf UNTO thee, O Gód do | we give | thanks : yéa unto | thee do | we give | thanks.

2 Thy Náme also | is so | nigh : and thát do thy | wondrous | works de- | clare.

3 When I recéive the | congre- | -ga- tion : I shall júdge ac- | -cording | unto | right.

4 The earth is weak * and all the inhábit- | -ers there- | -of : I' bear | up the pillars | of it.

5 I said unto the fools, Déal | not so | madly : and to the ungódly, | Set not | up your | horn.

6 Set not úp your | horn on | high : and spéak not | with a | stiff | neck.

7 For promotion cometh neither from the éast nor | from the | west : nór | yet | from the | south.

8 And whý? | God · is the | Judge : he putteth down óne, and | setteth | up an- | -other.

9 For in the hand of the Lord there is a cúp and the | wine is | red : it is full mixt * and he póureth | out | of the | same.

10 Ás for the | dregs there- | -of : all the ungodly of the éarth shall | drink · them and | suck them | out.

f 11 But I will tálk of the | God of | Jacob : ánd | praise · him for | ever.

12 All the horns of the ungodly álso | will I ' break : and the hórns of the | righteous · shall | be ex- | -alted.

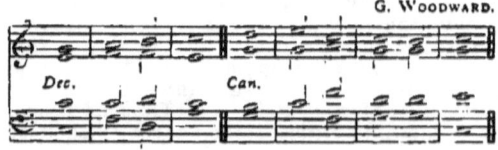

PSALM LXXVI.—*Notus in Judæa.*

mf IN Jéwry is | God | known : his Name is | great in | Israel.

2 At Salem ís his | taber- | -nacle : ánd his | dwelling | in | Sion.

3 There brake he the árrows | of the | bow : the shíeld the | sword | and the | battle.

4 Thou art of móre | honour · and | might : thán the | hills | of the | robbers.

5 The proud are robbed, théy have | slept their | sleep : and all the men whose hánds were | mighty · have | found | nothing.

6 At thy rebúke O | God of | Jacob : bóth the | chariot · and | horse are | fallen.

7 Thou, even thóu art | to be | feared :

and who may stánd in thy | sight when | thou art | angry ?

8 Thou didst cause thy júdgement to be | heard from | heaven : the éarth | trembled | and was | still.

9 When Gód a- | -rose to | judge- ment : and to hélp | all the | meek up- on | earth.

10 The fierceness of man shall túrn | to thy | praise : and the fíerceness of | them shalt | thou re- | -frain.

11 Promise unto the Lord your God * and keep it all yé that are | round a- | bout him : bring presents unto hím that | ought | to be | feared.

12 He shall refráin the | spirit · of | princes : and is wonderful among the kings | of the | earth.

DAY XV. MORNING (continued).

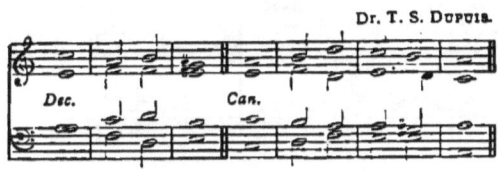

Dr. T. S. Dupuis.

PSALM LXXVII.—*Voce mea ad Dominum.*

mp 1 I WILL cry unto Gód | with my | voice : even unto God will I cry with my rŏice ✶ and hĕ shall | hearken | unto ! me.

2 In the time of my trŏuble I | sought the | Lord : my sore ran, and ceased not in the nightseason ✶ mý | soul re- | -fused | comfort.

3 When I am in heaviness ✶ I' will | think up · on | God : when my héart is | vexed · I | will com- ! plain.

4 Thou hŏldest mine | eyes | waking : I am so féeble | that I | cannot | speak.

5 I have consĭdered the | days of | old : ánd the | years | that are | past.

6 I cáll to re- | -membrance · my | song : and in the night I commune with mine own héart, and | search | out my | spirits.

7 Will the Lord absént him- | -self for | ever : and wíll he | be no | more in- | treated ?

8 Is his mercy cléan | gone for | ever : and is his promise come utterly tŏ an | end for | ever- | -more ?

9 Hath God forgŏtten | to be | gracious : and will he shut up his lóving- | kindness | in dis- | -pleasure ?

10 And I said, It ís mine | own in- | firmity : but I will remember the years of the right hánd | of the | most | Highest.

f 11 I will remember the wŏrks | of the | Lord : and call to mínd thy | wonders · of | old | time.

12 I will think ălso of | all thy | works : and my tálking shall | be of | thy | doings.

13 Thy wáy O | God is | holy : who is so gréat a | God as | our | God ?

14 Thou art the Gód that | doeth | wonders : and hast declăred thy | power a- | -mong the | people.

15 Thou hast mightily de- | -livered · thy | people : even the | sons of | Jacob and | Joseph.

16 The waters saw thee O God ✶ the waters sáw thee and | were a- | -fraid : the depths | also | were | troubled.

17 The clouds poured out water the | air | thundered : ánd thine | arrows | went a- | -broad.

18 The voice of thy thunder was héard | round a- | -bout : the lightnings shone upon the ground ✶ the éarth was | moved · and | shook with- | -al.

19 Thy way is in the sea ✶ and thy páths in the | great | waters : ánd thy | footsteps | are not | known.

20 Thou léddest thy | people · like | sheep : bý the | hand of | Moses and | Aaron.

DAY XV. EVENING

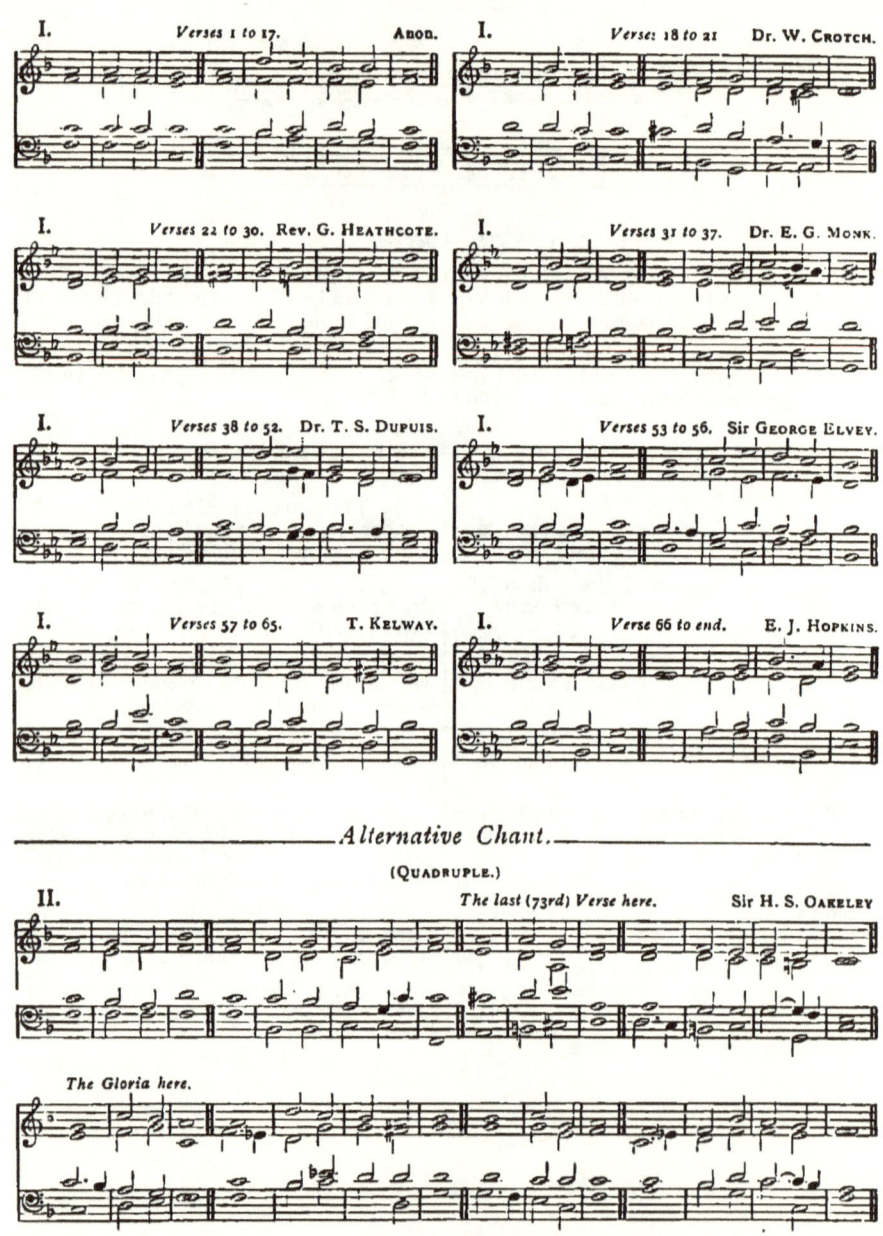

Verses 1 to 4, 13 to 16, 21 to 28, 45 to 52, 73, and the Gloria, to be chanted *in unison*, and full. Verses 5 to 12, 17 to 20, 29 to 44, 53 to 72, *in harmony*, and antiphonally: verses 53 to 56 soft (without organ); verses 66 and 67 loud.

If used for the *Te Deum*, verses 12 and 13 of that Hymn must be chanted as if one verse.

DAY XV. EVENING (*continued*).

PSALM LXXVIII.—*Attendite, popule.*

F. mf HEAR my láw | O my | people :| incline your éars unto the | words | of my | mouth.
F. 2 I will open my móuth | in a | parable : I will decláre hard | senten- | -ces of | old ;
3 Whích we have | heard and | known : and súch | as our | fathers • have | tóld us ;
4 That we should not hide them * from the children of the géner- | -ations • to | come : but to shew to the honour of the Lord * his mighty and wónderful | works that | he hath | done.
5 He made a covenant with Jacob´* and gave I'sra- | -el a | law : which he commanded óur fore- | -fathers • to | teach their | children ;
6 That their postéri- | -ty might | know it : and the chíldren | which were | yet un- | -born ;
7 To the inténi that when | they came | up : théy might | shew their | children • the | same ;
8 That they might pút their | trust in | God : and not to forget the works of Gód but to | keep | his com- | -mandments ;
9 And not to be as their forefathers * a faithless and stúbborn | gener- | -ation : a generation that set not their heart aright * and whose spirit cléaveth not | stedfastly | unto | God ;
10 Líke as the | children • of | Ephraim : who being harnessed and carrying bows * turned themselves báck | in the | day of | battle.
11 They kept not the cóve- | -nant of | God : and wóuld not | walk | in his | law ;
12 But forgát what | he had | done : and the wonderful wórks that | he had | shewed | for them.
f 13 Marvellous things did he in the sight of our forefathers * ín the | land of | Egypt : éven | in the | field of | Zoan.
14 He divided the séa and let | them go | through : he made the wáters to | stand | on an | heap.
15 In the day-time also he léd them | with a | cloud : and all the níght through | with a | light of | fire.
16 He clave the hard rócks | in the | wilderness : and gave them drink thereof * as it had béen | out • of the | great | depth.
17 He brought waters óut of the | stony | rock : so that it gúshed | out | like the | rivers.
p 18 Yet for all this they sínned | more a- | -gainst him : and provóked the most | Highest | in the | wilderness.

19 They tempted Gód | in their | hearts : and reqúired ; meat | for their | lust.
20 They spake against Gód | also | saying : Shall God prepáre a | table | in the | wilderness ?
21 He smote the stony rock indeed * that the water gushed out, and the stréams | flowed • with- | -al : but can he give bread also * or províde | flesh | for his | people ?
mf 22 When the Lord heard thís | he was | wroth : so the fire was kindled in Jacob * and there came up héavy dis- | -pleasure • a- | -gainst | Israel ;
23 Because they belíeved | not in | God : and pút not their | trust | in his | help.
24 So he commánded the | clouds a- | -bove : ánd | opened • the | doors of | heaven.
25 He rained down manna also upón them | for to | eat : ánd | gave them | food from | heaven.
26 So mán did eat | angels' | food : fór he | sent them | meat e- | -nough.
27 He caused the east wind to blów | under | heaven : and through his pówer he brought | in the | south-west | wind.
28 He rained flesh upón them as | thick as | dust : and feathered fowls líke as the | sand | óf the | sea.
29 He let it fáll a- | -mong their | tents : even róund a- | -bout their | habit- | ation.
30 So they did eat, and were well filled * for he gáve them their | own de- | -sire : they were nót disap- | -pointed | of their | lust.
mp 31 But while the meat was yet in their mouths * the heavy wrath of God came upon them, and sléw the | wealthiest | of them : yea, and smote down the chósen | men that | were in | Israel.
32 But for all thís they | sinned • yet | more : and belíeved | not his | wondrous | works.
33 Therefore their dáys did he con- | sume in | vanity : ánd their | years | in | trouble.
34 When he sléw | them they | sought him : and turned them early * ánd en- | quired | after | God.
35 And they remembered that Gód | was their | strength : and that the hígh | God was | their Re- | -deemer.
36 Nevertheless, they did but flátter him | with their | mouth : and dissémbled | with him | in their | tongue.
37 For their héart was not | whole with | him : neither contínued they | stedfast | in his | covenant.

DAY XV. EVENING (continued).

Verses 1 to 4, 13 to 16, 21 to 28, 45 to 52, 73, and the Gloria, to be chanted *in unison*, and full. Verses 5 to 12, 17 to 20, 29 to 44, 53 to 72, *in harmony*, and antiphonally; verses 53 to 56 soft (without organ); verses 66 and 67 loud.

If used for the *Te Deum*, verses 12 and 13 of that Hymn must be chanted as if one verse.

DAY XV. EVENING (continued).

38 But he was so merciful * that he forgáve | their mis- | -deeds : ánd de- | stroyed | them | not.
39 Yea, many a time túrned he his | wrath a- | -way : and would not suffer his | whôle dis- | -pleasure | to a- | -rise.
40 For he considered thát they | were but | flesh : and that they were even a | wind that passeth awáy, and | cometh | not a- | -gain.
41 Many a time did they provôke | him | in the | wilderness : ánd | grieved · him | in the | desert.
42 They turned báck, and | tempted | God : and móved the | Holy | One in | Israel.
43 They thôught not | of his | hand : and of the day when he delivered them | frôm the | hand | of the | enemy ;
44 How he had wrôught his | miracles · in | Egypt : and his wônders | in the | field of | Zoan.
45 He turned their wáters | into | blood : so that they might not | drink | of | the | rivers.
46 He sent lice among them * ánd de- | -voured · them | up : ánd | frogs | to de- | -stroy them.
47 He gave their frúit | unto · the | caterpillar : ánd their | labour | unto · the | grasshopper.
48 He destrôyed their | vines with | hailstones : and their múlberry- | -trees | with the | frost.
49 He smote their cáttle | also · with | hailstones : ánd their | flocks with | hot | thunderbolts.
50 He cast upon them the furiousness of his wrath * ánger. dis- | -pleasure · and | trouble : and sént | evil | angels · a- | -mong them.
51 He made a way to his indignation * and spáred not their | soul from | death : but gáve their life | over | to the | pestilence ;
52 And smôte all the | first-born · in | Egypt : the most principal and míghtiest | in the | dwellings · of | Ham.
mf 53 But as for his own people * he léd them | forth like | sheep : and carried them ín the | wilderness | like a | flock.
54 He brought them out safely * thát they | should not | fear : and overwhélmed their | enemies | with the | sea.
55 And brought them within the bórders | of his | sanctuary : even to his | mountain which he púrchased | with his | right | hand.

56 He cast out the héathen | also · be- | -fore them : caused their land to be divided among them for an heritage * and made the tribes of I'srael to | dwell in | their | tents.
mp 57 So they tempted and displéased the | most high | God : ánd | kept | not his | testimonies ;
58 But turned their backs, and fell awáy | like their | forefathers : starting asíde | like a | broken | bow.
59 For they grieved him wíth their | hill- | -altars : and provoked him tó dis- | pleasure | with their | images.
60 When God heard thís | he was | wroth : and tóok | sore dis- | -pleasure · at | Israel.
61 So that he forsook the tåber- | nacle · in | Silo : even the tént that he had | pitched · a- | -mong | men.
62 He delivered their pówer | into cap- | -tivity : and their béauty | into · the | enemy's | hand.
63 He gave his people óver also | unto · the | sword : ánd was | wroth with | his in- | -heritance.
64 The fire consúmed their | young | men : and their máidens | were not | given - to | marriage.
2nd part 65 Their priests were sláin | with the | sword : and there were no widows to | make | lamen- | -tation.
ff 66 So the Lord awaked as óne | out of | sleep : and líke a | giant · re- | freshed · with | wine.
67 He smote his enemies ín the | hinder | parts : and pút them | to a · per- | petual | shame.
68 He refused the tåber- | -nacle · of | Joseph : and chôse | not the | tribe of | Ephraim ;
69 But chôse the | tribe of | Judah : even the híll of | Sion | which he | loved.
70 And there he búilt his | temple · on | high : and laid the foundation of it * like the gróund which | he hath | made con- | -tinually.
71 He chose Dávid | also · his | servant : and tóok him a- | -way | from the | sheepfolds.
72 As he was following the éwes great with | young ones · he | took him : that he might feed Jacob his péople and | Israel | his in- | -heritance.
73 So he fed them with a fáithful and | true | heart : and ruled them prúdent- | -ly with | all his | power.

DAY XVI. MORNING.

J. Weldon.

PSALM LXXIX.—*Deus, venerunt.*

p O GOD, the heathen are cóme into | thine in- | -heritance : thy holy temple have they defiled ✱ and made Jerúsa- | lem an | heap of | stones.

2 The dead bodies of thy servants ✱ have they given to be meat unto the fówls | of the | air : and the flesh of thy sáints unto the | beasts | of the | land.

3 Their blood have they shed like water on every síde | of Je- | -rusalem : and there was nó | man to | bury | them.

4 We are become an open shâme | to our | enemies : a very scorn and derision unto thém | that are | round a- | -bout us.

mf 5 Lord, how lông wilt | thou be | angry : shall thy jéalousy | burn like | fire for | ever?

6 Pour out thine indignation upon the héathen that | have not | known thee : and upon the kingdoms that háve not | called · up- | -on thy | Name.

7 For théy have de- | -voured | Jacob : ánd | laid | waste his | dwelling-place.

p 8 O remember not our old sins ✱ but have mercy upón us and | that | soon : fór we are | come to | great | misery.

9 Help us, O God of our salvation ✱ for the glóry | of thy | Name : O deliver us ✱ and be mérciful unto our síns | for thy | Name's | sake.

10 Whérefore do the | heathen | say : Where | — is | now their | God?

11 O let the vengeance of thy servants' blóod | that is | shed : be openly shewed upón the | heathen | in our | sight.

12 O let the sorrowful sighing of the prísoners | come be- | -fore thee : according to the greatness of thy power ✱ preserve thou thôse that | are ap- | -pointed · to | die.

mf 13 And for the blasphemy wherewith our neighbours háve blas- | -phemed | thee : reward thou them O Lôrd | sevenfold | into · their | bosom.

f 14 So we that are thy people and sheep of thy pasture ✱ shall gíve thee | thanks for | ever : and will alway be shewing forth thy praise ✱ from gêner- | -ation · to | gener- | -ation.

Dr. Rimbault.

PSALM LXXX.—*Qui regis Israel.*

mf HEAR, O thou Shepherd of Israel ✱ thou that leadest Jóseph | like a | sheep : shew thyself also ✱ thóu that | sittest · up- | -on the | cherubims.

2 Before Ephraim, Béniamin | and Ma- | -nasses : stir úp thy | strength and | come and | help us.

3 Túrn us a- | -gain O | God : shew the light of thy cóuntenance | and we | shall be | whole.

4 O Lórd | God of | hosts : how long wilt thou be ángry | with thy | **people** · that | prayeth?

5 Thou feedest them with the | bread of | tears : and givest them plénteous- | ness of | tears to | drink.

6 Thou hast made us a very strífe | unto · our | neighbours : and our ênemies | laugh | us to | scorn.

7 Turn us agáin thou | God **of** | hosts : shew the light of thy cóuntenance | and we | shall be | whole.

DAY XVI. MORNING (continued).

8 Thou hast brought a víne | out of | | Egypt : thou hast cast óut the | heathen · and | planted | it.

9 Thou mádest | room for | it : and when it had táken | root it | filled · the | land.

10 The hills were covered wíth the | shadow | of it : and the boughs theréof were | like the | goodly | cedar-trees.

11 She stretched out her bránches | unto · the | sea : ánd her | boughs | unto · the | river.

p 12 Why hast thou then bróken | down her | hedge : that all théy that go | by | pluck | off her | grapes ?

13 The wild boar out of the wóod doth | root it | up : and the wild béasts | of the | field de- | -vour it.

14 Turn thee again, thou God of hósts, | look | down from | heaven : behóld and | visit | this | vine ;

15 And the place of the vineyard that thy right | hand hath | planted : and the branch that thou mádest so | strong | for thy- | -self.

16 It is burnt with fíre and | cut | down : and they shall perish át the re- | buke | of thy | countenance.

17 Let thy hand be upon the mán of thy | right | hand : and upon the son of man * whom thou madest so stróng | for thine | own | self.

18 And so will not wé go | back from | thee : O let us live * and wé shall | call up- | -on thy | Name.

mf 19 Turn us again, O Lórd | God of | hosts : shew the light of thy cóuntenance | and we | shall be | whole.

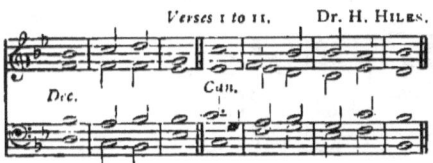

Verses 1 to 11.   Dr. H. HILES.

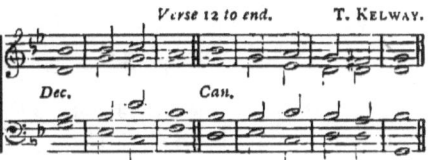

Verse 12 to end.   T. KELWAY.

PSALM LXXXI.—*Exultate Deo.*

f SING we merrily únto | God our | | strength : make a cheerful nóise | unto · the | God of | Jacob.

2 Take the psálm, bring | hither · the | tabret : the mérry | harp | with the | lute.

3 Blow up the trúmpet in the | new | moon : even in the time appointed * ánd up- | -on our | solemn | feast-day.

4 For this was máde a | statute · for | Israel : and a láw | of the | God of | Jacob.

5 This he ordained in Jóseph | for a | testimony : when he came out of the land of Egypt * ánd had | heard a | strange | language.

6 I eased his shóulder | from the | burden : and his hánds were de- | -livered · from | making · the | pots.

7 Thou calledst upon me in troubles * and I' de- | -livered | thee : and heard thee what tíme as the | storm I fell up- | on thee.

8 I' | proved · thee | also : át the | waters | of | strife.

9 Hear, O my people * and I will assure | thee O | Israel : íf thou wilt | hearken | unto | me.

10 There shall no strange gód | be in | thee : neither shalt thou wórship | any | other | god.

11 I am the Lord thy God * who brought thee óut of the | land of | Egypt : open thy móuth | wide and | I shall | fill it.

mf 12 But my people wóuld not | hear my | voice : and I'srael | would | not o- | -bey me.

13 So I gave them up unto their ówn | hearts' | lusts : and let them fóllow their | own im- | -agin- | -ations.

mf 14 O that my people would have héarkened | unto | me : for if I'srael had | walked | in my | ways,

15 I should sóon have put | down their | enemies : and túrned my | hand a- | -gainst their | adversaries.

16 The haters of the Lord shóuld have been | found | liars : but their time | should have · en- | -dured · for | ever.

17 He should have fed them álso with the | finest | wheat-flour : and with honey out of the stony róck should | | I have | satisfied | thee.

DAY XVI. EVENING.

PSALM LXXXII.—*Deus stetit.*

F.mf GOD standeth in the cóngre- | -ga-tion · of | princes : hé is a | Júdge a· | -móng | gods.

F. 2 How lóng will ye | give wrong | judgement : and accépt the | persons | of · the un- | -gódly ?

3 Defénd the | poor and | fátherless : see that such as are in néed and ne-céssity | I have | ríght.

4 Delíver the | outcast · and | poor : save them from the | hand of | the un- | gódly.

5 They will not be learned nor understand * but wálk on | still in | dárkness : all the foundátions of the | earth are | out of | course.

6 I have sáid | Ye are | gods : and ye are all the chíldren | of the | most | Híghest.

7 Bút ye shall | die like | men : ánd | fall like | one · of the | prínces.

8 Arise O God, and júdge | thou the | earth : for thou shalt táke all | heathen · to | thine in- | -héritance.

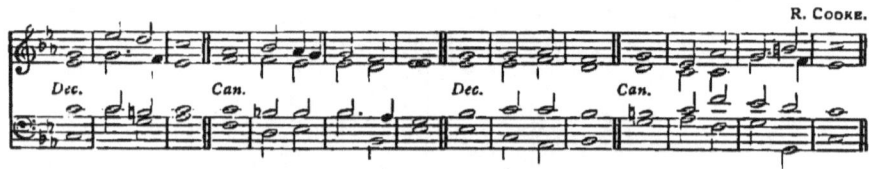

PSALM LXXXIII.—*Deus, quis similis ?*

mf HOLD not thy tongue O God * keep | not still | silence : refráin not thy- | -self O | God.

2 For lo, thine énemies | make a | murmuring : and they that háte thee have | lift | up their | head.

3 They have imagined cráftily a-gainst thy | people : and taken cóunsel a- | -gainst thy | secret | ones.

4 They have said, Come and let us root them out * that they bé no | more a | people : and that the name of Israel may bé no | more | in re- | -mémbrance.

5 For they have cast their heads togéther with | one con- | -sent : and áre con- | -feder- | -ate a- | -gainst thee.

6 The tabernacles of the E'domites | and the | Ismaelites : thé | Moab- | -ites and | Hagarenes ;

7 Gébal and | Ammon · and | Amalek : the Philistines with | them that | dwell at | Tyre.

8 Assur álso is | joined | with them : ánd have | holpen · the | children · of | Lot.

9 But do thou to thém as | unto · the | Madianites : unto Sisera, and unto Jábin | at the | brook of | Kison ;

10 Who pérished | at | Endor : and became as the | dung | of the | earth.

11 Make them and their prínces like | Oreb · and | Zeb : yea, make all their princes like as | Zéba | and Sal- | mana ;

12 Who say, Let us táke | to our- | selves : the hóuses of | God | in pos- | session.

13 O my God, make them líke | unto · a | wheel : and ás the | stubble · be- | -fore the | wind ;

14 Like as the fire that búrneth | up the | wood : and as the fláme | that con- | sumeth · the | mountains.

15 Persecute them even só | with thy | tempest : and máke them a- | -fraid | with thy | storm.

16 Make their fáces a- | -shamed · O | Lord : that | they may | seek thy | Name.

17 Let them be confounded and véxed ever | more and | more : lét them be | put to | shame and | perish.

f 18 And they shall know that thou, whose Náme | is Je- | -hovah : art only the most Híghest ' over | all the | earth.

DAY XVI. EVENING (continued).

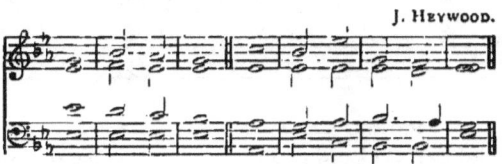

J. HEYWOOD.

PSALM LXXXIV.—*Quam dilecta!*

mf O HOW ámiable | are thy | dwellings : | thóu | Lord | of | hosts !

2 My soul hath a desire and longing * to enter into the cóurts | of the | Lord : my heart and my flesh rejóice | in the | living | God.

3 Yea, the sparrow hath found her an house * and the swallow a nest, where shé may | lay her | young : even thy altars, O Lord of hósts, my | King | and my | God.

4 Blessed are they that dwéll | in thy | house : théy will be | alway | praising | thee.

5 Blessed is the man whose stréngth | is in | thee : ín whose | heart | are thy | ways.

6 Who going through the vale of misery úse it | for a | well : ánd the | pools are | filled · with | water.

7 They will gó from | strength to | strength : and unto the God of gods appeareth évery | one of | them in | Sion.

8 O Lord God of hósts | hear my | prayer : héarken | O | God of | Jacob.

9 Behold, O Gód | our de- | -fender : and look upón the | face of | thine A- | nointed.

10 For one dáy | in thy | courts : ís | better | than a | thousand.

11 I had rather be a door-keeper in the hóuse | of my | God : than to dwéll in the | tents | of un- | -godliness.

12 For the Lord God is a líght | and de- | -fence : the Lord will give grace and worship * and no good thing shall he withhold from thém that | live a | godly | life.

13 O Lórd | God of | hosts : blessed is the mán that | putteth · his | trust in | thee.

E. J. HOPKINS.

PSALM LXXXV.—*Benedixisti, Domine.*

mp LORD, thou art become grácious | | unto · thy | land : thou hast turned awáy the cap- | -tivi- | -ty of | Jacob.

2 Thou hast forgiven the offénce | of thy | people : ánd | covered | all their | sins.

3 Thou hast taken awáy all | thy dis- | -pleasure : and turned thysélf from thy | wrathful | indig- | nation.

4 Turn us thén O | God our | Saviour : and lét thine | anger | cease | from us.

5 Wilt thou be displéased at | us for | ever : and wilt thou stretch out thy wrath from óne gener- | -ation | to an- | -other ?

6 Wilt thou not turn agáin, and | quicken | us : that thy péople | may re- | joice in | thee ?

7 Shéw us thy | mercy · O | Lord : ánd | grant us | thy sal- | -vation.

8 I will hearken what the Lord God will sáy con- | -cerning | me : for he shall speak peace unto his people and to his saints * thát they | turn | not a- | gain.

9 For his salvation is nígh | them that | fear him : that glóry may | dwell | in our | land.

10 Mercy and trúth are | met to- | gether : ríghteousness and | peace have | kissed · each ſ other.

11 Truth shall flóurish | out · of the | earth : and ríghteousness hath | looked | down from | heaven.

12 Yea, the Lord shall shéw | loving- | kindness : ánd our | land shall | give her | increase.

13 Righteousness shall | go be- | -fore him : and he shall diréct his | going | in the | way.

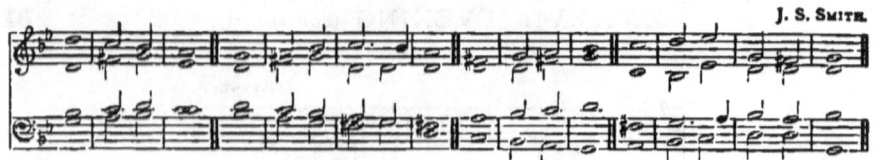

J. S. SMITH.

PSALM LXXXVI.—*Inclina, Domine.*

mp BOW down thine ear O | Lord and || hear me : for I' am | poor | and in | misery.

2 Preserve thou my soul, for | I am | holy : my God, save thy servant that | putteth · his | trust in | thee.

3 Be merciful únto | me O | Lord : for I' will | call | daily up· | ·on thee.

4 Comfort the soul | of thy | servant : for unto thee O Lord do I | lift | up my|soul.

5 For thou, Lórd art | good and | gracious : and of great mercy unto áll | them that | call up· | ·on thee

6 Give ear, Lórd | unto · my | prayer : and ponder the voice | of my | humble · de· | ·sires.

7 In the time of my trouble I' will | call up · on | thee | for | thou | hearest | me.

8 Among the gods there is none like unto | thee O | Lord : there is not óne that can | do as | thou | doest.

9 All nations whom thou hast made * shall come and wórship | thee O | Lord : and shall | glori· | ·fy thy | Name.

10 For thou art great, and dóest | wondrous | things : thóu | — art | God a- | ·lone.

11 Teach me thy way O Lord * and I will wálk | in thy | truth : O knit my heart unto thée, that | I may | fear thy | Name.

12 I will thank thee O Lord my Gód with | all my | heart : and will práise thy | Name for | ever· | ·more.

13 For gréat is thy | mercy | toward me : and thou hast delivered my sóul | from the | nethermost | hell.

14 O God, the próud are | risen · a- | gainst me : and the congregations of naughty men have sought after my soul * and have nót set | thee be· | ·fore their | eyes.

15 But thou O Lord God, art fúll of com· | ·passion · and | mercy : long-súffering | plenteous · in | goodness · and | truth.

16 O turn thee then unto mé and have | mercy · up· | ·on me : give thy strength unto thy servant * and hélp the | son | of thine | handmaid.

2nd part. 17 Shew some token upon me for good * that they who hate me may sée it and | be a· | ·shamed : because thou Lord hast hólpen | me and | comforted | me.

W. V. WALLACE.

PSALM LXXXVII.—*Fundamenta ejus.*

mp HER foundations are upón the | holy | hills : the Lord loveth the gates of Sion, móre than | all the | dwellings · of | Jacob.

2 Very excellent thíngs are | spoken · of | thee : thou | city | of | God.

3 I will thínk upon | Rahab · and | Babylon : with | them that | know | me.

4 Behóld ye the | Philistines | also : and they of Tyre with the Morians * ló | there | was he | born.

5 And of Sion it shall be reported that hé was | born in | her : ánd the most | High shall | stablish | her.

6 The Lord shall rehearse it when he wríteth | up the | people : thát | he was | born | there.

7 The singers also and trúmpeters shall | he re· | ·hearse | A'll my **fresh** | springs shall | be in | thee.

DAY XVII. MORNING (continued).

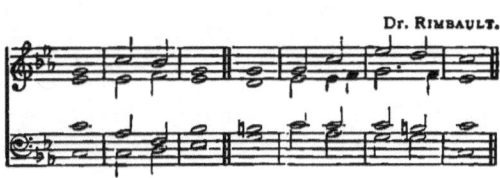
Dr. Rimbault.

PSALM LXXXVIII.—*Domine Deus.*

mp O LORD God of my salvation * I have cried day and | night be- | -fore thee : O let my prayer enter into thy presence * incline thine | ear | unto · my | calling.

2 For my soul is | full of | trouble : and my life draweth | nigh | unto | hell.

3 I am counted as one of them that go down | into · the | pit : and I have been even as a | man that | hath no | strength.

4 Free among the dead * like unto them that are wounded and lie | in the | grave : who are out of remembrance * and are cut a- | -way | from thy | hand.

5 Thou hast laid me in the | lowest | pit : in a place of | darkness · and | in the | deep.

6 Thine indignation lieth | hard up- | on me : and thou hast vexed | me with | all thy | storms.

7 Thou hast put away mine acquaint- ance | far | from me : and made me to | be ab- | -horred | of them.

8 I am so | fast in | prison : that I | cannot | get | forth.

9 My sight faileth for | very | trouble : Lord, I have called daily upon thee * I have stretched forth my | hands | unto | thee.

10 Dost thou shew wonders a- | -mong the | dead : or shall the dead rise | up a- | -gain and | praise thee ?

11 Shall thy loving · kindness be shewed | in the | grave : or thy | faithful- ness | in de- | -struction ?

12 Shall thy wondrous works be known | in the | dark : and thy righteous- ness in the land where | all things | are for- | -gotten ?

13 Unto thee have I | cried O | Lord : and early shall my | prayer | come be- | fore thee.

14 Lord, why abhorrest | thou my | soul : and hidest | thou thy | face | from me ?

15 I am in misery * and like unto him that is at the | point to | die : even from my youth up, thy terrors have I suffered | with a | troubled | mind.

16 Thy wrathful displeasure goeth | over | me : and the fear of | thee | hath un- | -done me.

17 They came round about me | daily · like | water : and compassed me to- | gether · on | every | side.

18 My lovers and friends hast thou put a- | -way | from me : and hid mine ac- | -quaintance | out of · my | sight.

DAY XVII. EVENING.

PSALM LXXXIX.—*Misericordias Domini.*

F. mf MY song shall be alway of the loving-kíndness | of the | Lord : with my mouth will I ever be shewing thy trúth ✱ from óne gener- | -ation | to an- | -other.

F. 2 For I have said, Mercy shall be sét | up for | ever : thy trúth shalt thou | stablish | in the | heavens.

3 I have made a cóvenant | with my | chosen : I have swórn | unto | David · my | servant ;

4 Thy séed will I | stablish · for | ever : and set up thy throne from óne gener- | -ation | to an- | -other.

5 O Lord, the very heavens shall práise thy | wondrous | works : and thy truth in the cóngre- | -gation | of the | saints.

6 For who is hé a- | -mong the | clouds : that sháll be com- | -pared | unto · the | Lord ?

7 And what is hé a- | -mong the | gods : that sháll be | like | unto · the | Lord ?

8 God is very greatly to be feared in the cóuncil | of the | saints : and to be had in reverence of all thém | that are | round a- | -bout him.

9 O Lord God of hosts ✱ who is | like · unto | thee ; thy truth, most mighty Lórd | is on | every | side.

10 Thou rulest the ráging | of the | sea : thou stillest the wáves there- | -of when | they a- | -rise.

11 Thou hast subdued Egypt ✱ ánd de- | -stroyed | it : thou hast scattered thine enemies abróad | with thy | mighty | arm.

12 The heavens are thine, the éarth | also · is | thine : thou hast laid the foundation of the round wórld, and | all that | therein | is.

13 Thou hast made the nórth | and the | south : Tabor and Hermon sháll re- | -joice | in thy | Name.

14 Thou hást a | mighty | arm : strong is thy hánd, and | high is | thy right | hand.

DAY XVII. EVENING (continued).

15 Righteousness and equity are the | habitátion | of thy | seat : mercy and trúth shall | go be- | -fore thy | face.

16 Blessed is the people O Lord ✱ that cân re- | -joice in | thee : they shall wâlk in the | líght | of thy | countenance.

17 Their delight shall be dáily | in thy | Name : and in thy ríghteousness | shall they | make their | boast.

18 For thou art the glóry | of their | strength : and in thy lóving-kindness, thôu shalt | lift | up our | horns.

19 For the Lórd is | our de- | -fence : the Hóly One of | Israel | is our | King.

20 Thou spakest sometime in visions ûnto thy | saints and | saidst : I have laid help upon one that is mighty ✱ I have exálted one | chosen | out · of the | people.

21 I have fôund | David · my | servant : with my holy ôil have | | I a- | -nointed | him.

22 My hând shall | hold him | fast : ând my | arm shall | strengthen | him.

23 The enemy shall not be áble to | do him | violence : the sôn of | wickedness | shall not | hurt him.

24 I will smite down his fóes be- | -fore his | face : ând | plague | them that | hate him.

25 My truth also and my mércy | shall be | with him : and in my Náme shall his | horn | be ex- | -alted.

26 I will set his dominion álso | in the | sea : ând his | right hand | in the | floods.

27 He shall call me, Thóu | art my | Father : my Gód | and my | strong sal- | -vation.

28 And I will máke | him my | first-born : hígher than the | kings | of the | earth.

29 My mercy will I kéep for him for | ever- | -more : and my cóvenant shall | stand | fast | with him.

30 His seed also will I máke to en- | -dure for | ever : and his thróne | as the | days of | heaven.

mf 31 But if his chíldren for- | -sake my | law : ând | walk not | in my | judgements ;

32 If they break my statutes ✱ and kéep not | my com- | -mandments : I will visit their offences with the ród | and their | sin with | scourges.

33 Nevertheless, my loving-kindness will I not útterly | take | from him : nôr | suffer · my | truth to | fail.

34 My covenant will I nct break ✱ nor alter the thing that is góne | out of · my | lips : I have sworn once by my holiness ✱ that I' | will not | fail | David.

35 His séed shall en- | -dure for | ever : and his séat is | like · as the | sun be- | fore me.

36 He shall stand fast for evermóre | as the | moon : and âs the | faithful | witness · in | heaven.

p 37 But thou hast abhorred and forsáken | thine A- | -nointed : ând | art dis- | pleased | at him.

38 Thou hast broken the cóvenant | of thy | servant : and câst his | crown | to the | ground.

39 Thou hast overthrówn | all his | hedges : ând | broken | down his | strongholds.

40 All théy that go | by | spoil him : and he is becôme a re- | -proach | to his | neighbours.

41 Thou hast set up the right hând | of his | enemies : and máde all his | adversaries | to re- | -joice.

42 Thou hast taken away the édge | of his | sword : and givest him nót | victory | in the | battle.

43 Thôu hast put | out his | glory : and câst his | throne | down · to the | ground.

44 The days of his yôuth | hast thou | shortened : ând | covered · him | with dis- | -honour.

45 Lord, how long wilt thou híde thy- | self for | ever : and shâll thy | wrath | burn like | fire ?

46 O remember how shórt my | time | is : wherefore hast thou máde | all | men for | nought ?

47 What man is he that líveth and shall | not see | death : and shall he deliver his sóul | from the | hand of | hell ?

48 Lord, where are thy óld | loving- | kindnesses : which thou swárest unto | David | in thy | truth ?

49 Remember Lord, the rebúke that thy | servants | have : and how I do bear in my bósom the re- | -bukes of | many | people ;

50 Wherewith thine enemies have blasphemed thee ✱ and slandered the fóotsteps of | thine A- | -nointed : Praised be the Lord for evermóre. | A---men **and** | A- | -men.

DAY XVIII. MORNING.

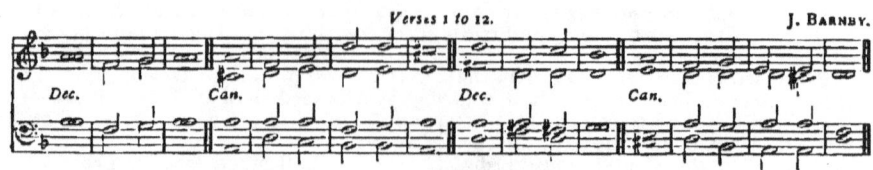

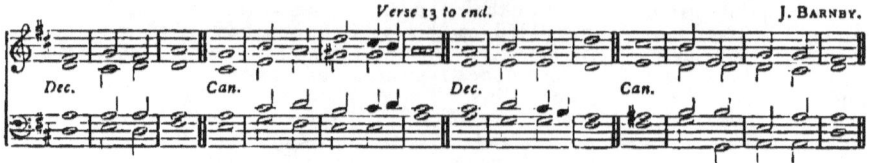

PSALM XC.—*Domine, refugium.*

p LÓRD thou hast | been our | refuge from óne gener- | -ation | to an- | -other.

2 Before the mountains were brought forth * or ever the éarth and the | world were | made : thou art God from ever- lásting and | world with- | -out | end.

3 Thou turnest mán | to de- | -struc- tion : again thou sayest, Cóme a- | -gain ye | children · of | men.

4 For a thousand years in thý sight | are but · as | yesterday : seeing that is pást as a | watch | in the | night.

5 As soon as thou scatterest them * they are éven | as a | sleep : and fáde away | suddenly | like the | grass.

6 In the morning it is gréen and | groweth | up : but in the evening it is cut dówn | dried | up and | withered.

7 For we consume awáy in | thy dis- | pleasure : and are afráid at thy | wrath- ful | indig- | -nation.

8 Thou hast sét our mis- | -deeds be- fore thee : and our secret síns in the | light | of thy | countenance.

9 For when thou art angry, áll our | days are | gone : we bring our years to an end * as it wére a | tale | that is | told.

10 The days of our age are three-score years and ten * and though men be so strong that they cóme to | four-score | years : yet is their strength then but labour and sorrow * so soon pásseth it a- | way and | we are | gone.

11 But who regardeth the pówer | of thy | wrath : for even thereafter as a man féareth | so is | thy dis- | -pleasure.

12 So téach us to | number · our | days : that we may applý our | hearts | unto | wisdom.

13 Turn thee again, O Lórd|at the|last : ánd be | gracious | unto · thy | servants.

14 O satisfy us with thy mércy and | that | soon : so shall we rejoice and be glád all the | days | of our | life.

15 Comfort us again * now after the tíme that thou hast | plagued | us : and for the years wherein | we have | suffered · ad- | -versity.

16 Shéw thy | servants · thy | work : ánd their | children | thy | glory.

2nd part. 17 And the glorious Majesty of the Lord our Gód | be up- | -on us : prosper thou the work of our hands upon us * O prósper | thou our | handy- | -work.

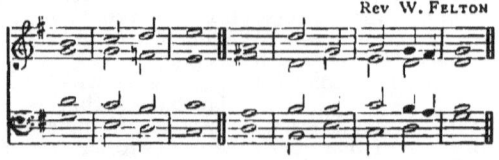

PSALM XCI.—*Qui habitat.*

mf WHOSO dwelleth under the defénce of the | most | High : shall abíde under the | shadow · of | the Al- | -mighty.

2 I will say unto the Lord * Thou art my hópe | and my | stronghold : my Gód, in | him I will | I | trust.

DAY XVIII. MORNING (continued).

3 For he shall deliver thee from the snáre | of the | hunter : ánd | from the | noisome | pestilence.

4 He shall defend thee under his wiugs * and thou shalt be sáfe | under · his | feathers : his faithfulness and trúth shall | be thy | shield and | buckler.

5 Thou shalt not be afráid for any | terror · by | night : nór for the | arrow · that | flieth · by | day ;

6 For the pêstilence that | walketh · in | darkness : nor for the síckness that de- | -stroyeth | in the | noonday.

7 A thóusand shall fall beside thee * and ten thóusand at | thy right | hand : bût it shall | not come | nigh | thee.

8 Yea, with thine éyes shalt | thou be- | -hold : and sée the re- | -ward of | the un- | -godly.

9 For thou, Lórd | art my | hope : thou hast set thine hóuse of de- | fence | very | high.

10 There shall no evil háppen | unto | thee : neither shall ány | plague come | nigh thy | dwelling.

11 For he shall give his angels chárge | over | thee : to kéep | thee in | all thy | ways.

12 They shall béar thee | in their | hands : that thou hûrt not thy | foot a- | gainst a | stone.

13 Thou shalt go upón the | lion and | adder : the young lion and the dragon shált thou | tread | under · thy | feet.

14 Because he hath set his love upon me * therefore will I' de- | -liver | him : I will set him up * becáuse | he hath | known my | Name.

15 He shall call upon mé, and | I will | hear him : yea, I am with him in trouble * I will delíver him and | bring | him to | honour.

16 With long lífe will I | satisfy | him : ánd | shew him | my sal- | -vation.

Right Hon. G. C. BENTINCK.

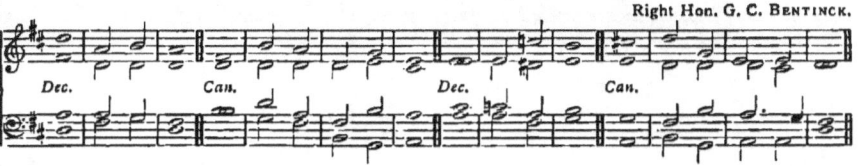

PSALM XCII.—*Bonum est confiteri.*

1 IT is a good thing to give thánks | | unto · the | Lord : and to sing praises únto thy | Name | O most | Highest ;

2 To tell of thy loving-kindness éarly | in the | morning : and of thy trúth | in the | night- | -season ;

3 Upon an instrument of ten strings * ánd up- | -on the | lute : upon a loud ín- strument | and up- | -on the | harp.

4 For thou, Lord, hast made me glád | through thy | works : and I will rejoice in giving praise, for the óper- | ations | of thy | hands.

5 O Lord, how glórious | are thy | works : thý | thoughts are | very | deep.

6 An unwise man doth not wéll con- | sider | this : and a fóol | doth not | under- | -stand it.

7 When the ungodly are green as the grass * and when all the workers of wícked- | -ness do | flourish : then shall they be destroyed for ever * but thou, Lord, árt the most | Highest · for | ever- | more.

8 For lo, thine enemies O Lord * lo, thine éne- | -mies shall | perish : and all the workers of wícked- | -ness shall | be de- | -stroyed.

9 But mine horn shall be exalted like the hórn | of an | unicorn : for I' am a- | nointed · with | fresh | oil.

10 Mine eye also shall see his lúst | of mine | enemies : and mine ear shall hear his desire of the wícked that a- | -rise | up a- | -gainst me.

11 The righteous shall flóurish | like a | palm-tree : and shall spread abróad | like a | cedar · in | Libanus.

12 Such as are planted in the hóuse | of the | Lord : shall flourish in the cóurts of the | house of | our | God.

13 They also shall bring forth more frúit | in their | age : and shâll be | fat and | well- | -liking.

14 That they may shew how true the Lórd my | strength | is : and that there is nó un- | -righteous- | -ness in | him.

PSALM XCIII.—*Dominus regnavit.*

F. f THE Lord is King * and hath put on glóri- | -ous ap- | -parel : the Lord hath put on his appárel and | girded · him- | -self with | strength.

F. 2 He hath máde the round | world so | sure : thát it | cannot | be | moved.

3 Ever since the world began hath thy séat | been pre- | -pared : thóu | art from | ever- | -lasting.

4 The floods are risen O Lord * the floods have lift | up their | voice : thé | floods lift | up their | waves.

5 The waves of the sea are mighty and | rage | horribly : but yet the Lórd who | dwelleth · on | high is | mightier.

6 Thy testimonies O Lórd are | very | sure : hóliness be- | -cometh · thine | house for | ever.

Alternative Chant.

PSALM XCIV.—*Deus ultionum.*

mf O LORD Gód to whom | vengeance · be- | -longeth : thou God, to whom véngeance be- | -longeth | shew thý- | self.

2 Arise thou Júdge | of the | world : and reward the próud | after | their de- | serving.

3 Lord, how lóng | shall · the un- | godly : how lóng | shall · the un- | -godly | triumph?

4 How long shall all wicked doers spéak | so dis- | -dainfully : ánd | make such | proud | boasting?

5 They smite dówn thy | people · O | Lord : ánd | trouble | thine | heritage.

6 They murder the wídow | and the | stranger : and pút the | father- | -less to | death.

2nd part. 7 And yet they say, Tush, the Lórd | shall not | see : neither sháll the | God of | Jacob · re- | -gard it.

8 Take heed ye unwíse a- | -mong the | people : O ye fóols | when · will ye | under- | -stand?

9 He that planted the éar, shall | he not | hear : or he that máde the | eye shall | he not | see?

10 Or he that núrtur- | -eth the | heathen : it is he that teacheth man knówledge, | shall not | he | punish?

DAY XVIII. EVENING (*continued*).

11 The Lord knóweth the | thoughts of | man : thát | they | are but | vain.

12 Blessed is the man whom thou chástenest | O | Lord : ánd | teachest · him | in thy | law ;

13 That thou mayest give him patience in time | of ad- | -versity : until the pit be dígged | up for | the un- | -godly.

14 For the Lórd will not | fail his | people : neither wíll he for- | -sake | his in- | -heritance ;

15 Until righteousness túrn again | unto | judgement : all such as are trúe in | heart shall | follow | it.

16 Who will rise up with mé a- | -gainst the | wicked : or who will take my párt a- | -gainst the | evil- | -doers ?

17 If the Lórd had not | helped | me :

it had not failed but my sóul | had been | put to | silence.

18 But when I sáid My | foot hath | slipt : thy mércy O | Lord | held me | up.

19 In the multitude of the sorrows that I hád | in my | heart : thy cómforts | have re- | -freshed · my | soul.

20 Wilt thou have anything to dó with the | stool of | wickedness : which imágineth | mischief | as a | law ?

21 They gather them together against the sóul | of the | righteous : ánd con- | demn the | innocent | blood.

22 But the Lórd | is my | refuge : and my Gód is the | strength | of my | confidence.

23 He shall recompense them their wickedness * and destroy them ín their | own | malice : yea, the Lórd our | God | shall de- | -stroy them.

DAY XIX. MORNING.

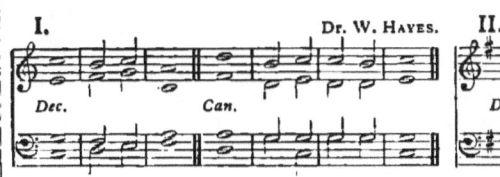
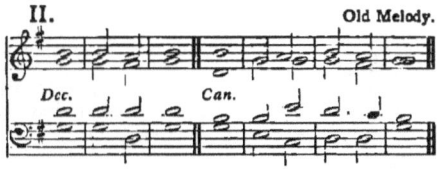

PSALM XCV.—*Venite, exultemus Domino.*

F. f O COME, let us síng | unto · the | Lord : let us heartily rejóice in the | strength of | our sal- | -vation.

F. 2 Let us come before his présence with | thanks- | -giving : and shéw ourselves | glad in | him with | psalms.

3 For the Lórd is a | great | God : and a gréat | King a- | -bove all | gods.

4 In his hand are all the córners | of the | earth : and the stréngth of the | hills is | his | also.

5 The séa is his | and he | made it : and his hánds pre- | -pared · the | dry | land.

mf 6 O come, let us wórship and | fall | down : and knéel be- | -fore the | Lord our | Maker

7 For hé is the | Lord our | God : and we are the people of his pasture * ánd the | sheep of | his | hand.

8 To-day if ye will hear his voice * hárden | not your | hearts : as in the provocation * and as in the dáy of tempt- | ation | in the | wilderness ;

9 When your fáthers | tempted | me : próved | me and | saw my | works.

10 Forty years long was I grieved with thís gener- | -ation and | said : It is a people that do err in their hearts * fór they | have not | known my | ways;

11 Unto whom I swáre | in my | wrath : that they shóuld not | enter | into · my | rest.

DAY XIX. MORNING (continued).

PSALM XCVI.—*Cantate Domino.*

f O SING unto the Lórd a | new |
song : sing unto the Lórd | all the |
whole | earth.

2 Sing unto the Lórd and | praise
his | Name : be telling of hís sal- | ·vation ·
from | day to | day.

3 Declare his hónour | unto · the |
heathen : and his wónders | unto | all |
people.

4 For the Lord is great ✶ and cannot
wórthi- | ·ly be | praised : he is móre to be |
feared · than | all | gods.

5 As for all the gods of the héathen, |
they are · but | idols : but it ís the | Lórd
that | made the | heavens.

6 Glory and wórship | are be- | ·fore
him : pówer and | honour · are | in his |
sanctuary.

7 Ascribe unto the Lord ✶ O ye
kíndreds | of the | people : ascribe unto
the Lórd | worship | and | power.

8 Ascribe unto the Lord the honour
dúe | unto · his | Name : bring présents
and | come | into · his | courts.

9 O worship the Lórd in the | beauty ·
of | holiness : let the whole éarth | stand
in | awe of | him.

10 Tell it ·out among the héathen that
the | Lord is | King : and that it is who
hath made the round world so fast ✶ that
it cannot be moved ✶ and how that hé
shall | judge the | people | righteously.

11 Let the heavens rejóice and let
the | earth be | glad : let the sea make a
nóise, and | all that | therein | is.

12 Let the field be jóyful and | all
that · is | in it : then shall all the trees of
the wóod re- | ·joice be- | ·fore the | Lord.

2nd part. 13 For he cometh, for he cómeth to |
judge the | earth : and with righteousness
to judge the wórld and the | people | with
his | truth.

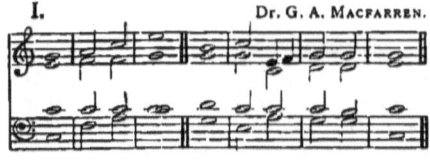

PSALM XCVII.—*Dominus regnavit.*

f THE Lord is King ✶ the éarth may
be | glad there- | ·of : yea, the multitude
of the ísles | may be | glad there- | ·of.

2 Clouds and dárkness are | round
a- | ·bout him : righteousness and judge-
ment are the hábit- | ·ation | of his |
seat.

3 There shall gó a | fire be- | ·fore
him : and burn úp his | ene · mies on |
every | side.

4 His lightnings gave shíne | unto ·

the | world : the éarth | saw it · and | was
a- | ·fraid.

5 The hills melted like wax ✶ at the
présence | of the | Lord : at the presence
of the Lórd | of the | whole | earth.

6 The héavens have de- | ·clared ·
his | righteousness : and áll the | people ·
have | seen his | glory.

7 Confounded be all they that wor-
ship carved images ✶ and that delíght in |
vain | gods : wórship | him | all ye | gods.

DAY XIX. MORNING (*continued*).

8 Sion héard of it | and re- | -joiced : | and the daughters of Judah were glad * becáuse of thy | judgements | O | Lord.

9 For thou Lord, art higher than áll that are | in the | earth : thou art exálted | far a- | -bove all | gods.

10 O ye that love the Lord * see that ye hate the thíng | which is | evil : the Lord preserveth the souls of his saints * he shall deliver them fróm the | hand of | the un- | -godly.

11 There is sprung up a líght | for the | righteous : and joyful gládness for | such as | are true- | -hearted.

12 Rejóice in the | Lord ye | righteous : and give thanks * fór a re- | -membrance | of his | holiness.

DAY XIX. EVENING.

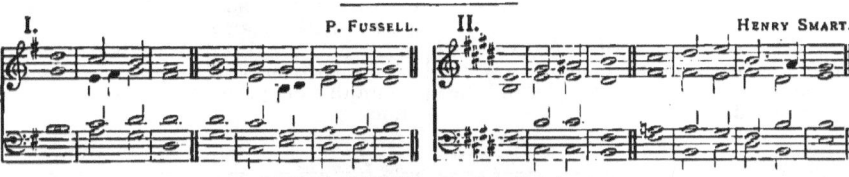

PSALM XCVIII.—*Cantate Domino*.

F *f* O SING unto the Lórd a | new | song : for hé hath | done | marvellous | things.

F. 2 With his own right hand * and wíth his | holy | arm : háth he | gotten . him- | self the | victory.

3 The Lord declared | his sal- | -vation : his righteousness hath he openly shéwed in the | sight | of the | heathen.

4 He hath remembered his mercy and truth tóward the | house of | Israel : and all the ends of the world have séen the sal- | -vation | of our | God.

5 Shew yourselves joyful unto the Lórd | all ye | lands : síng, re- | -joice and | give | thanks.

6 Praise the Lórd up- | -on the | harp : sing to the hárp with a | psalm of | thanks- | giving.

7 With trúmpets | also and | shawms : O shew yourselves jóyful be- | -fore the | Lord the | King.

8 Let the sea make a noise, * and áll that | therein | is : the round wórld, and | they that | dwell there- | -in.

9 Let the floods clap their hands, * and let the hills be joyful together be- | fore the | Lord : for he is | come to | judge the | earth.

10 With righteousness sháll he | judge the | world : ánd the | people | with | equity.

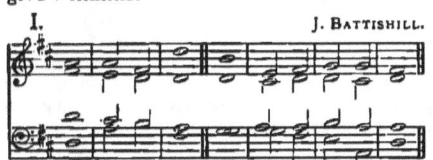 

PSALM XCIX.—*Dominus regnavit*.

f THE Lord is King * be the people néver | so im- | -patient : he sitteth between the cherubims * be the éarth | never | so un- | -quiet.

2 The Lórd is | great in | Sion : ánd | high a- | -bove all | people.

3 They shall give thánks | unto . thy | Name : which is gréat | wonder- | -ful and | holy.

4 The king's power loveth judgement * thóu hast pre- | -pared | equity : thou hast executed júdgement and | righteous- | -ness in | Jacob.

5 O mágnify the | Lord our | God : and fall down before his fóotstool, | for | he is | holy.

6 Moses and Aaron among his priests * and Samuel among such as cáll up- | -on his | Name : these called upón the | Lord | and he | heard them.

7 He spake unto them óut of the | cloudy | pillar : for they kept his testimonies * ánd the | law | that he | gave them.

8 Thou héardest them O | Lord our | God : thou forgavest them O God * and púnish- | -edst their | own in- | ventions.

9 O magnify the Lord our God * and worship him upón his | holy | hill : fór the | Lord our | God is | holy.

DAY XIX. EVENING (continued).

PSALM C.—*Jubilate Deo.*

f O BE joyful in the Lórd | all ye | lands : serve the Lord with gladness ✷ and come befóre his | presence | with a | song.

2 Be ye sure that the Lórd | he is | God : it is he that hath made us and not we ourselves ✷ we are his people, ánd the | sheep of | his | pasture.

3 O go your way into his gates with thanksgiving ✷ and ínto his | courts with | praise : be thankful unto him, and | speak good | of his | Name.

mf 4 For the Lord is gracious ✷ his mércy is | ever- | -lasting : and his truth endureth from géner- | -ation · to | gener- | ation.

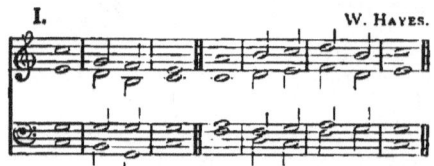 

PSALM CI.—*Misericordiam et judicium.*

mf MY sóng shall be of | mercy · and | judgement : unto theé O | Lord | will I | sing.

2 O lét me have | under- | -standing : in the | way of | godli- | -ness.

3 When wilt thou cóme | unto | me : I will walk in my hóuse | with a | perfect | heart.

4 I will take no wicked thing in hand ✷ I hate the síns | of un- | -faithfulness : there shall nó such | cleave | unto | me.

5 A fróward héart shall de- | -part from | me : I wíll not | know a | wicked | person.

6 Whoso privily slánder- | -eth his | neighbour : hím | — will | I de- | -stroy.

7 Whoso hath also a proud lóok and | high | stomach : I' | will not | suffer | him.

8 Mine eyes look upon such as are fáithful | in the | land : thát | they may | dwell with | me.

9 Whoso léadeth a | godly | life : hé | — shall | be my | servant.

10 There shall no deceitful person dwéll | in my | house : he that telleth lies, sháll not | tarry | in my | sight.

11 I shall soon destroy all the ungódly that are | in the | land : that I may root out all wicked doers, fróm the | city | of the | Lord.

DAY XX. MORNING.

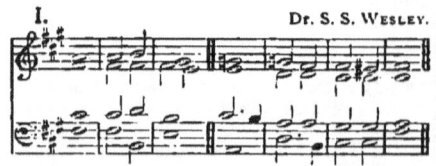 

PSALM CII.—*Domine, exaudi.*

F.mp HÉAR my | prayer O | Lord : and let my crýing | come | unto | thee.

F. 2 Hide not thy face from me in the tíme | of my | trouble : incline thine ear unto me when I call ✷ O héar | me and | that right | soon.

3 For my days are consúmed a- | -way like | smoke : and my bones are burnt úp | as it | were a | firebrand.

4 My heart is smitten dówn and | withered · like | grass : so that I' **for-** | get to | eat my | bread.

DAY XX. MORNING (continued).

5 For the vóice | of my | groaning : | my bones will scárce | cleave | to my | flesh.

6 I am become like a pélican | in the | wilderness : and like an ówl | that is | in the | desert.

7 I have watched * and am éven as it | were a | sparrow : that sítteth a- | -lone up- | -on the | house-top.

8 Mine enemies revíle me | all the · day | long ; and they that are mad upón me are | sworn to- | -gether · a- | -gainst me.

9 For I have eaten áshes | as it · were | bread : ánd | mingled · my | drink with | weeping ;

10 And that because of thine índig- | -nation · and | wrath : for thou hast táken me | up and | cast me | down.

11 My days are góne | like a | shadow : and I' am | withered | like | grass.

12 But thou, O Lórd shalt en- | -dure for | ever : and thy remembrance through- óut | all | gener- | -ations.

13 Thou shalt arise, and have mércy up- | -on | Sion : for it is time that thou have mercy upón her, | yea the | time is | come.

14 And why * thy servants thínk up- | -on her | stones : and it pitieth thém to | see her | in the | dust.

15 The heathen shall féar thy | Name O | Lord ; and all the kíngs | of the | earth thy | Majesty ;

16 When the Lórd shall | build up | Sion : and whén his | glory|shall ap-|-pear ;

17 When he turneth him unto the prayer of the | poor | destitute : ánd de- | -spiseth · not | their de- | -sire.

18 This shall be written for thóse that | come | after : and the people which shall be | born shall | praise the | Lord.

19 For he hath looked dówn | from his | sanctuary : out of the héaven did the | Lord be- | -hold the | earth ;

20 That he might hear the mourning of súch as are | in cap- | -tivity : and deliver the chíldren ap- | -pointed | unto | death ;

21 That they may declare the Náme of the | Lord in | Sion : ánd his | wor- ship | at Je- | -rusalem ;

22 When the péople are | gathered · to- | -gether : and the kíngdoms | also · to | serve the | Lord.

23 He brought down my stréngth | in my | journey : ánd | shortened | my | days.

24 But I said * O my God, take me not away in the mídst | of mine | age : as for thy years, they endure throughóut | all | gener- | -ations.

mf 25 Thou, Lord, in the beginning * hast laid the foundation | of the | earth : and the héavens are the | work of | thy | hands.

26 They shall perish, but thóu | shalt en- | -dure : they áll shall wax | old as | doth a | garment ;

27 And as a vesture shalt thou change them * ánd they | shall be | changed : but thou art the same, ánd thy | years | shall not | fail.

28 The children of thy sérvants | shall con- | -tinue : and their séed shall stand | fast | in thy | sight.

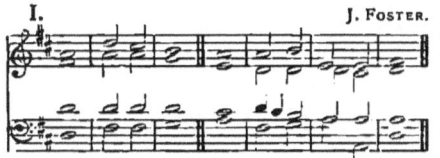

I. J. Foster.

II. Rev. Sir Fred. A. G. Ouseley.

PSALM CIII.—*Benedic, anima mea.*

f PRAISE the Lórd | O my | soul : | and all that is withín me | praise his | holy | Name.

2 Praise the Lórd | O my | soul : ánd for- | -get not | all his | benefits ;

3 Who forgíveth | all thy | sin : and héaleth | all | thine in- | -firmities ;

4 Who saveth thy lífe | from de- | -struction : and crowneth thée with | mercy · and | loving- | -kindness ;

5 Who satisfieth thy móuth with | good | things : making thee yóung and | lusty | as an | eagle.

6 The Lórd executeth ríghteous- | -ness and | judgement : for all thém that | are op- | -pressed · with | wrong.

7 He shewed his wáys | unto | Moses ; his wórks | unto · the | children · of | Israel.

8 The Lord is fúll of com- | -passion · and | mercy : long-súffering, | and of | great | mercy.

9 He wíll not | alway · be | chiding : neither kéepeth | he his | anger · for | ever.

10 He hath not déalt with us | after · our | sins : nor rewárded us ac- | -cording | to our | wickednesses.

11 For look how high the heaven is in compárison | of the | earth : so great is his mercy álso|toward|them that|fear him.

12 Look how wide also the éast is | from the | west : so fár hath he | set our | sins | from us.

DAY XX. MORNING (continued).

I. J. FOSTER.
II. Rev. Sir FRED. A. G. OUSELEY.

13 Yea, like as a father pítieth his | own | children : even so is the Lord mérciful | unto | them that | fear him.

14 For he knoweth whereóf | we are | made : he remémbereth | that we | are but | dust.

mp 15 The days of mán are | but as | grass : for he flourisheth ás a | flower | of the | field.

16 For as soon as the wind goeth óver it | it is | gone : and the place theréof shall | know it | no | more.

mf 17 But the merciful goodness of the Lord ✽ endureth for ever and éver upon | them that | fear him : and his righteousness up- | -on | children's | children ;

18 Even upon súch as | keep his | covenant : and thínk upon | his commandments · to | do them.

f 19 The Lord hath prepáred his | seat in | heaven : and his kíngdom | ruleth | over | all.

20 O praise the Lord, ye angels of his ✽ yé that ex- | -cel in | strength : ye that fulfil his commandment ✽ and hearken únto the | voice | of his | word.

21 O praise the Lórd, all | ye his | hosts : ye sérvants of | his that | do his | pleasure.

22 O speak good of the Lord, all ye works of his ✽ in all pláces of | his dominion : práise thou the | Lord | O my | soul.

DAY XX. EVENING.

I. Verses 1 to 13. HENRY SMART.

I. Verses 14 to 23. Right Rev. Bishop TURTON.
I. Verses 24 to 26. HENRY SMART.

I. Verses 27 to 30. E. J. HOPKINS.
I. Verse 31 to end. HENRY SMART.

DAY XX EVENING (*continued*). 75

Alternative Chants.

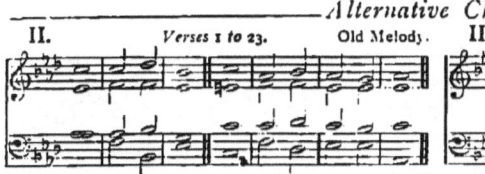

PSALM CIV.—*Benedic, anima mea.*

F. ⨍ PRAISE the Lórd | O my | soul : O Lord my God, thou art become exceed- ing glorious ✶ thou art clóthed with | majes- | -ty and | honour.

F. 2 Thou deckest thyself with light as it wére | with a | garment : and spreadest óut the | heavens | like a | curtain.

3 Who layeth the beams of his chám- bers | in the | waters : and maketh the clouds his chariot ✶ and walketh upón the | wings | of the | wind.

4 He máketh his | angels | spirits : | and his mínis- | -ters a | flaming | fire.

5 He laid the foundátions | of the | earth : that it néver should | move at | any | time.

6 Thou coveredst it with the deep, líke as | with a | garment : the wáters | stand | in the | hills.

7 At thý re- | -buke they | flee : at the vóice of thy | thunder · they | are a- | -fraid.

8 They go up as high as the hills ✶ and dówn to the | valleys · be- | -neath : even unto the pláce which | thou · hast ap- | -pointed | for them.

9 Thou hast set them their bóunds which they | shall not | pass : neither túrn a- | -gain to | cover · the | earth.

10 He sendeth the springs | into · the | rivers : whích | run a- | -mong the | hills.

11 All beasts of the fíeld | drink there- | -of : ánd the wild | asses | quench their | thirst.

12 Beside them shall the fowls of the áir have their | habit- | -ation : ánd | sing a- | -mong the | branches.

13 He watereth the hílls | from a- | bove : the earth is fílled with the | fruit | of thy | works.

14 He bringeth forth gráss | for the | cattle : and green hérb | for the | service · of | men ;

15 That he may bring food out of the earth ✶ and wine that maketh glád the | heart of | man : and oil to make him a cheerful countenance ✶ and bréad to | strengthen | man's | heart.

16 The trees of the Lord álso are | full of | sap : even the cedars of Líban- | us which | he hath | planted ;

17 Wherein the bírds | make their | nests : and the fir-trees áre a | dwelling | for the | stork.

18 The high hills are a refuge fór the | wild | goats : and so are the stóny | rocks | for the | conies.

19 He appointed the móon for | cer- tain | seasons : and the sún | knoweth · his | going | down.

20 Thou makest darkness ✶ that it | may be | night : wherein all the béasts | of the | forest · do | move.

21 The lions róaring | after · their | prey : dó | seek their | meat from | God.

22 The sun ariseth ✶ and they gét them a- | -way to- | -gether : and láy them | down | in their | dens.

23 Man goeth forth to his wórk and | to his | labour : ún- | -til the | even- | -ing.

24 O Lord, how mánifold | are thy | works : in wisdom hast thou made them all ✶ the éarth is | full | of thy | riches.

25 So is the great and | wide sea | also : wherein are things creeping innu- merable ✶ bóth | small and | great | beasts.

⨍ 26 There go the ships ✶ and thére is | that Le- | -viathan : whom thou hast made to | take his | pastime · there- | -in.

27 These wáit | all up- · -on | thee : that thou mayest gíve them | meat in | due | season.

28 When thou givest it thém they | gather | it : and when thou openest thy hánd | they are | filled · with | good.

mp 29 When thou hidest thy fáce | they are | troubled : when thou takest away their breath they die ✶ and are túrned a- | -gain | to their | dust.

mf 30 When thou lettest thy breath go fórth they | shall be | made : and thou shalt renéw the | face | of the | earth.

⨍ 31 The glorious Majesty of the Lórd shall en- | -dure for | ever : the Lórd shall re- | -joice | in his | works.

32 The earth shall trémble at the | look of | him : if he do but tóuch the | hills | they shall | smoke.

33 I will sing unto the Lórd as | long as · I | live : I will praise my Gód | while I | have my | being.

34 And só shall my | words | please him : my jóy shall | be | in the | Lord.

35 As for sinners, they shall be con- sumed out of the earth ✶ and the ungódly shall | come · to an | end : praise thou the Lord, O my sóul, | praise | — the | Lord.

DAY XXI. MORNING.

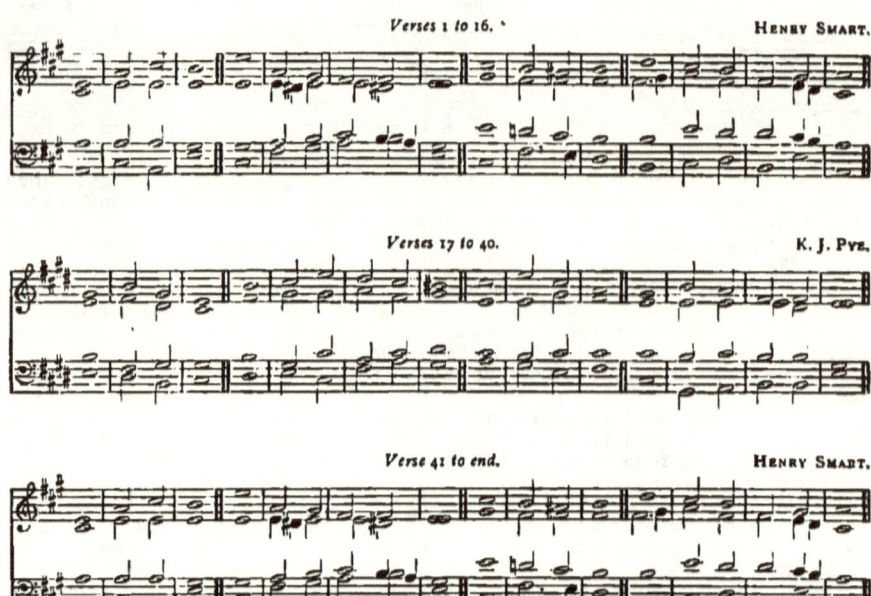

PSALM CV.—*Confitemini Domino.*

mf O GIVE thanks unto the Lord * and cáll up- | -on his | Name : tell the people what | things | he hath | done.

2 O let your sóngs be of | him and | praise him : and let your talking bé of | all his | wondrous | works.

3 Rejóice in his | holy | Name : let the heart of thêm re- | -joice that | seek the | Lord.

4 Seek the Lórd | and his | strength : séek his | face | ever- | -more.

5 Remember the marvellous wórks that | he hath | done : his wonders, ánd the | judgements | of his | mouth.

6 O ye seed of A´bra- | -ham his | servant : yé | children · of | Jacob · his | chosen.

7 Hé is the | Lord our | God : his júdgements | are in | all the | world.

8 He hath been alway mindful of his cóve- | -nant and | promise : that he máde to a | thousand | gener- | ations :

9 Even the covenant that he máde with | Abra- | -ham : and the óath that he | sware | unto | Isaac ;

10 And appointed the same unto Jácob | for a | law : and to Israel fór an | ever- | -lasting | testament ;

11 Saying, Unto thee will I gíve the | land of | Canaan : thé | lot of | your in- | heritance ;

12 When there were yêt but a | few of | them : and théy | strangers | in the | land ;

13 What time as they went from óne nation | to an- | -other : from one kíngdom | to an- | -other | people ;

14 He suffered nó man to | do them | wrong : but repróved even | kings for | their | sakes ;

15 Tóuch not | mine A- | -nointed : ánd I do my | prophets · no | harm.

16 Moreover, he called for a déarth up- | -on the | land : and destróyed | all the · pro- | -vision · of | bread.

17 But he had sént a | man be- | -fore them : even Joseph, who was sóld to | be a | bond- | -servant;

18 Whose feet they húrt | in the | stocks : the íron | entered | into · his | soul;

19 Until the time cáme that his | cause was | known : the wórd | of the | Lord | tried him.

20 The king sént, and de- | -livered | him : the prince of the péople | let him | go | free.

21 He made him lórd also | of his | house : ánd | ruler · of | all his | substance;

22 That he might inform his prínces | after · his | will : ánd | teach his | senators | wisdom.

23 Israel also cáme | into | Egypt : and Jacob was a stránger | in the | land of | Ham.

24 And he incréased his | people · ex- | ceedingly : and máde them | stronger | than their | enemies;

25 Whose heart turned só that they | hated · his | people : and déalt un- | -truly | with his | servants.

26 Thén sent he | Moses · his | servant : ánd | Aaron · whom | he had | chosen.

27 And these shéwed his | tokens · a- | mong them : and wónders | in the | land of | Ham.

28 He sent dárkness, and | it was | dark : and they were nót o- | -bedient | unto · his | word.

29 He turned their wáters | into | blood : ánd | slew | their | fish.

30 Their lánd | brought forth | frogs : yea, éven | in their | kings' | chambers.

31 He spake the word ✶ and there cáme all | manner · of | flies : ánd | lice in | all their | quarters.

32 He gave them háil- | -stones for | rain : and flámes of | fire | in their | land.

33 He smote their vínes | also · and | fig-trees : and destroyed the trées | that were | in their | coasts.

34 He spake the word, and the grasshoppers came ✶ and cáter- | -pillars · in- | numerable : and did eat up all the grass in their land ✶ and devóured the | fruit | of their | ground.

35 He smote all the fírst-born | in their | land : éven the | chief of | all their | strength.

36 He brought them forth álso with | silver · and | gold : there was not óne feeble | person · a- | -mong their | tribes.

37 Egypt was glád at | their de- | -parting : fór they | were a- | -fraid of | them.

38 He spread out a clóud to | be a | covering : and fire to give líght | in the | night- | -season.

39 At their desíre he | brought | quails : and he fílled them | with the | bread of | heaven.

40 He opened the rock of stone ✶ and the wáters | flowed | out : so that rivers rán | in the | dry | places.

41 For why, he remémbered his | holy | promise : ánd | Abra- | -ham his | servant.

42 And he brought fórth his | people · with | joy : ánd his | chosen | with | gladness;

43 And gave them the lánds | of the | heathen : and they took the lábours of the | people | in pos- | -session ;

44 That théy might | keep his | statutes: ánd ob- | -serve | his | laws.

DAY XXI. EVENING.

PSALM CVI.—*Confitemini Domino.*

P. m/O GIVE thanks unto the Lórd, for | he is | gracious : ánd his | mercy - en- | dureth - for | ever.

F. 2 Who can express the noble ácts | of the | Lord : ór | shew forth | all his | praise ?

3 Blessed are théy that | alway . keep | judgement : ánd | do | righteous- | ness.

4 Remember me O Lord ⁕ according to the favour that thou béarest | unto . thy | people : O vísit | me with | thy sal- | vation ;

5 That I may see the felícity | of thy | chosen : and rejoice in the gladness of thy people ⁕ ánd give | thanks with | thine in- | -heritance.

6 We have sínned | with our | fathers : | we have dóne a- | -miss and dealt | wickedly.

7 Our fathers regarded not thy wonders in Egypt ⁕ neither kept they thy great goodness | in re- | -membrance : but |

were disobedient at the sea ⁕ éven | at the | Red | Sea.

8 Nevertheless, he helped them fór his | Name's | sake : that he might máke his | power | to be | known.

9 He rebuked the Red Sea also ⁕ ánd it was | dried | up : so he led them through the | deep as | through a | wilderness.

10 And he saved them from the ádver- | -sary's | hand : and delivered them fróm the | hand | of the | enemy.

11 As for those that troubled them ⁕ the waters óver- | -whelmed | them : there wás not | one of | them | left.

12 Then believed | they his | words : and sáng | praise | unto | him.

13 But within a while they for- | -gat his | works : ánd would | not a- | -bide his | counsel.

14 But lust came upón them | in the | wilderness : and they témpted | God | in the | desert

DAY XXI. EVENING (continued).

15 And he gáve them | their de- | -sire : and sent léanness with- | -al | into · their | soul.

16 They angered Moses álso | in the | tents : and Aáron the | saint | of the | Lord.

17 So the earth ópened, and | swallowed · up | Dathan : and covered the cóngre- | -gation | of A· | -biram.

18 And the fire was kíndled | in their | company : the fláme | burnt up | the un- | godly.

19 They máde a | calf in | Horeb : ánd | worshipped · the | molten | image.

20 Thús they | turned · their | glory : into the similitude óf a | calf that | eateth | | hay.

21 And they forgát | God their | Saviour : who had dóne so | great | things in | Egypt ;

22 Wondrous wórks in the | land of | Ham : and fearful thíngs | by the | Red | Sea.

23 So he said, he would have destroyed them * had not Moses his chosen stood befóre him | in the | gap : to turn away his wrathful indignátion, | lest he | should de- | -stroy them.

24 Yea, they thought scórn of that | pleasant | land : and gáve no | credence | unto · his | word ;

25 But múrmured | in their | tents : and hearkened not únto the | voice | of the | Lord.

26 Then lift he úp his | hand a-|-gaiust them : to óver- | -throw them | in the | wilderness ;

27 To cast out their séed a- | -mong the | nations : ánd to | scatter · them | in the | lands.

28 They joined themsélves unto | Baal- | -peor : and áte the | offerings | of the | dead.

29 Thus they provoked him to anger wíth their | own in- | -ventions : ánd the | plague was | great a- | -mong them.

30 Thén stood up | Phinees · and | prayed : ánd | so the | plague | ceased.

31 And that was cóunted unto | him for | righteousness : among áll pos- | -teri · ties for | ever- | -more.

32 They angered him also át the | waters · of | strife : so that he púnished | Moses · for | their | sakes ;

33 Becáuse they pro- | -voked · his | spirit : so that he spáke unad- | -visedly | with his | lips.

34 Neither destróyed | they the | heathen : ás the | Lord com- | -manded | them ;

35 But were míngled a- | -mong the | heathen : ánd | learned | their | works.

36 Insomuch that they worshipped their idols * which túrned to their | own de- | -cay : yea, they offered their sóns and their | daughters | unto | devils ;

37 And shed innocent blood * even the blood of their sóns and | of their | daughters : whom they offered unto the idols of Canaan * and the lánd | was de- | filed · with | blood.

38 Thus were they stained wíth their | own | works : and went a whóring | with their | own in- | -ventions.

39 Therefore was the wrath of the Lord kíndled a- | -gainst his | people : insomúch that he ab- | -horred · his | own in- | -heritance.

40 And he gave them over into the hánd | of the | heathen : and they that háted them were | lords | over | them.

41 Their énemies op- | -pressed | them : ánd | had them | in sub- | -jection.

42 Many a tíme did he de- | -liver | them : but they rebelled against him with their own inventions * and were brought | down | in their | wickedness.

43 Nevertheless when he sáw | their ad- | -versity : hé | heard | their com- | plaint.

44 He thought upon his covenant, and pitied them * according unto the múltitude | of his | mercies : yea, he made all those that led them awáy | captive · to | pity | them.

45 Deliver us, O Lord our God * and gather us fróm a- | -mong the | heathen : that we may give thanks unto thy holy Name * and máke our | boast | of thy | praise.

46 Blessed be the Lord God of Israel from everlásting, and | world with · out | end : and let áll the | people | say A-|-men.

DAY XXII. MORNING.

Alternative Chants.

PSALM CVII.—*Confitemini Domino.*

mf O GIVE thanks unto the Lórd, for | he is | gracious : ánd his | mercy · en- | dureth · for | ever.

2 Let them give thanks whom the Lórd | hath re- | -deemed : and delivered from the | hand | of the | enemy ;

3 And gathered them out of the lands * from the éast and | from the | west : fróm the | north and | from the | south.

4 They went astray in the wilderness | out · of the | way : ánd | found no | city · to | dwell in ;

DAY XXII. MORNING (continued).

5 Húngry | and | thirsty : théir | soul | | fainted | in them.

6 So they cried unto the Lórd | in their | trouble : and he delívered them | from | their dis- | -tress.

2nd part 7 He led them fórth by the | right | way : that they might gó to the | city | where they | dwelt.

F. 8 O that men would therefore praise the | Lórd | for his | goodness : and declare the wonders that he dóeth | for the | children · of | men !

9 For he satisfíeth the | empty | soul : and fílleth the | hungry | soul with | goodness.

10 Such as sit in darkness ✳ and in the | shadow · of | death : being fast bóund in | mise- | -ry and | iron ;

11 Because they rebelled against the wórds | of the | Lord : and lightly regarded the cóunsel | of the | most | Highest ;

12 He also brought dówn their | heart through | heaviness : they fell dówn, and | there was | none to | help them.

13 So when they cried unto the Lórd | in their | trouble : he delívered them | out of | their dis- | -tress.

2nd part 14 For he brought them out of darkness ✳ and óut of the | shadow · of | death : ánd | brake their | bonds in | sunder.

F. 15 O that men would therefore praise the | Lórd | for his | goodness | and declare the wonders that he dóeth | for the | children · of | men !

16 For he hath brόken the | gates of | brass : and smítten the | bars of | iron · in | sunder.

17 Foolish men are plágued for | their of- | -fence : ánd be- | -cause of | their | wickedness.

18 Their soul abhórred all | manner · of | meat : and they were éven | hard at | death's | door.

19 So when they cried unto the Lórd | in their | trouble : he delívered them | out of | their dis- | -tress.

20 He sent his wórd, and | healed | them : and théy were | saved · from | their de- | -struction.

F. 21 O that men would therefore praise the | Lórd | for his | goodness : and declare the wonders that he dóeth | for the | children · of | men !

22 That they would offer unto him the sácrifice of | thanks- | -giving : and téll | out his | works with | gladness !

23 They that go dówn to the | sea in | ships : and óccupy their | business · in | great | waters ;

24 These men see the wόrks | of the | Lord : ánd his | wonders | in the | deep.

25 For at his word the stórmy | wind a- | -riseth : which lífteth | up the | waves there- | -of.

26 They are carried up to the heaven ✳ and dόwn again | to the | deep : their soul melteth awáy be- | -cause | of the | trouble.

27 They reel to and fro ✳ and stagger líke a | drunken | man : ánd are | at their | wits' | end.

28 So when they cry unto the Lórd | in their | trouble : he delivereth them | out of | their dis- | -tress.

29 For he máketh the | storm to | cease : só that the | waves there- | -of are | still.

30 Then are they glad, becáuse they | are at | rest : and so he bringeth them unto the háven | where they | would | be.

F. 31 O that men would therefore praise the Lόrd | for his | goodness : and declare the wonders that he dóeth | for the | children · of | men !

32 That they would exalt him also in the congregátion | of the | people : and práise him in the | seat | of the | elders !

33 Who turneth the flóods | into · a | wilderness : ánd | drieth | up the | watersprings.

34 A fruitful lánd | maketh · he | barren : for the wíckedness of | them that | dwell there- | -in.

35 Again, he maketh the wílderness a | standing | water : and wáter-springs | of a | dry | ground.

36 And thére he | setteth · the | hungry : that théy may | build · them a | city · to | dwell in ;

37 That they may sow their lánd, and | plant | vineyards : tό | yield them | fruits of | increase.

38 He blesseth them ✳ so that they múlti- | -ply ex- | -ceedingly : and suffereth nót their | cattle | to de- | -crease.

39 And again ✳ when they are mínished and | brought | low : through oppréssion, through | any | plague or | trouble ;

40 Though he suffer them to be évil in- | treated · through | tyrants : and let them wander óut of the | way | in the | wilderness ;

41 Yet helpeth he the pόor | out of | misery : and maketh him hóuseholds | like a | flock of | sheep.

42 The ríghteous will consider thís | and re- | -joice : and the móuth cf all | wickedness | shall be | stopped.

2nd part 43 Whoso is wíse will | ponder · these | things : and they shall understánd the lόving- | -kindness | of the | Lord.

DAY XXII. EVENING.

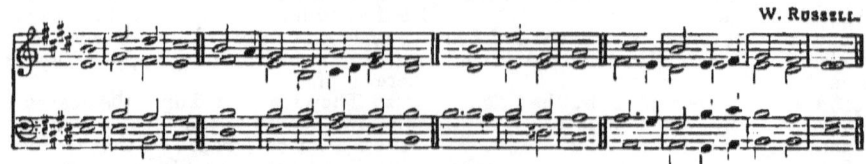
W. Russell.

PSALM CVIII.—*Paratum cor meum.*

F.mf O GOD my heart is | ready, my | heart is | ready : I will sing and give praise with the best | member | that I | have.

F. 2 Awake, thou | lute and | harp : I myself | will a- | -wake right | early.

3 I will give thanks unto thee, O Lord, a- | -mong the | people : I will sing praises unto | thee a- | -mong the | nations.

4 For thy mercy is greater | than the | heavens : and thy truth | reacheth | unto · the | clouds.

5 Set up thyself O God, a- | -bove the | heavens : and thy glory a- | -bove | all the | earth.

6 That thy beloved may | be de- | livered : let thy right hand save | them, and | hear thou | me.

7 God hath spoken | in his | holiness : I will rejoice therefore, and divide Sichem * and mete | out the | valley · of | Succoth.

8 Gilead is mine, and Ma- | -nasses · is | mine : Ephraim also is the | strength | of my | head.

2nd part 9 Judah is my law-giver * Moab | is my | washpot : over Edom will I cast out my shoe * upon Phi- | -listia | will I | triumph.

10 Who will lead me into the | strong | city : and who will | bring me | into | Edom ?

11 Hast not thou forsaken | us O | God : and wilt not thou, O God, go | forth | with our | hosts ?

12 O help us a- | -gainst the | enemy : for vain | is the | help of | man.

13 Through God we shall | do great | acts : and it is he that shall | tread | down our | enemies.

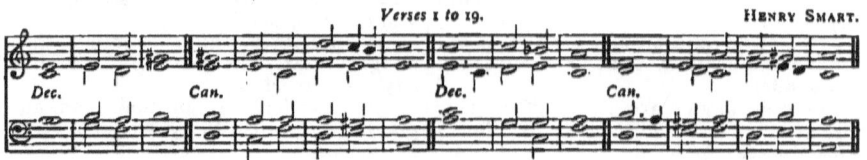
Verses 1 to 19.   Henry Smart.
Dec.   Can.   Dec.   Can.

PSALM CIX.—*Deus laudum.*

mp HOLD not thy tongue O God | of my | praise : for the mouth of the ungodly * yea the mouth of the de- | -ceitful · is | opened · up- | -on me.

2 And they have spoken against me with | false | tongues : they compassed me about also with words of hatred * and fought against | me with- | -out a | cause.

3 For the love that I had unto them * lo, they take now my | contrary | part : but I | give my---self | unto | prayer.

4 Thus have they rewarded me | evil · for | good : and | hatred · for | my good | will.

5 Set thou an ungodly man to be ruler | over | him : and let Satan stand | at his | right | hand.

6 When sentence is given upon him * let him | be con- | -demned : and let his prayer be | turned | into | sin.

7 Let his | days be | few : and let an- | -other | take his | office.

8 Let his | children · be | fatherless : and | — his | wife a | widow.

9 Let his children be vagabonds, and | beg their | bread : let them seek it also | out of | desolate | places.

DAY XXII. EVENING (*continued*).

10 Let the extortioner consúme | all that · he | hath : and lét the | stranger | spoil his | labour.

11 Let there be nó man to | pity | him : nor to have compássion up-|-on his | fatherless | children.

12 Let his postérity | be de- | -stroyed : and in the next generation lét his | name be | clean put | out.

13 Let the wickedness of his fathers be had in remembrance * in the síght | of the | Lord : and let not the sín of his | mother · be | done a- | -way.

14 Let them alway bé be- | -fore the | Lord : that he may root out the memórial of | them from | off the | earth ;

15 And that, because his mínd was | not to · do | good : but persecuted the poor helpless man * that he might slay hím that was | vexed | at the | heart.

16 His delight was in cursing * and it shall háppen | unto | him : he loved not blessing * thérefore shall | it be | far from | him.

17 He clothed himself with cursing * líke as | with a | raiment : and it shall come into his bowels like water * ánd like | oil | into · his | bones.

18 Let it be unto him as the clóke that he | hath up- | -on him : and as the girdle that hé is | alway | girded · with- | -al.

2nd part. 19 Let it thus happen from the Lórd | unto · mine | enemies : and to thóse that speak | evil · a- | -gainst my | soul.

Verse 20 to end.   Rev. R. P. GOODENOUGH.

20 But deal thou with me, O Lord God * accórding | unto · thy | Name : fór | sweet | is thy | mercy.

21 O deliver me * for I' am | helpless | and | poor : ánd my | heart is | wounded · with- | -in me.

22 I go hence like the shádow | that de- | -parteth : and am dríven a- | -way | as the | grasshopper.

23 My knées are | weak through | fasting : my flésh is dried | up for | want of | fatness.

24 I became also a repróach | unto | them : they that lóoked up- | -on me | shaked · their | heads.

25 Hélp me, O | Lord my | God : O sáve me ac- | -córding | to thy | mercy ;

26 And they shall know * how that thís is | thy | hand : ánd that | thou | Lord hast | done it.

27 Though they cúrse, yet | bless | thou : and let them be confounded that rise up against me * bút | let thy | ser- vant · re- | -joice.

28 Let mine ádversaries be | clothed · with | shame : and let them cover them- selves with their ówn con- | -fusion · as | with a | cloke.

29 As for me * I will give great thanks unto the Lórd | with my | mouth : and práise | him a- | -mong the | multitude ;

2nd part. 30 For he shall stand at the right hánd | of the | poor : to save his sóul | from un- | -righteous | judges.

DAY XXIII. MORNING.

Rev. Sir Fred. A. G. Ouseley

PSALM CX.—*Dixit Dominus.*

mf THE Lord said unto | my | Lord : Sit thou on my right hand * until I make thine | ene- | -mies thy | footstool.

2 The Lord shall send the rod of thy power | out of | Sion : be thou ruler * even in the | midst a- | -mong thine | enemies.

3 In the day of thy power shall the people offer thee free-will-offerings * with an | holy | worship : the dew of thy birth is of the | womb | of the | morning.

4 The Lord sware, and will | not re- | pent : Thou art a Priest for ever * after the | order | of Mel- | -chisedech.

5 The Lord upon | thy right | hand : shall wound even kings in the | day | of his | wrath.

6 He shall judge among the heathen * he shall fill the places with the | dead | bodies : and smite in sunder the heads | over | divers | countries.

7 He shall drink of the brook | in the | way : therefore shall he | lift | up his | head.

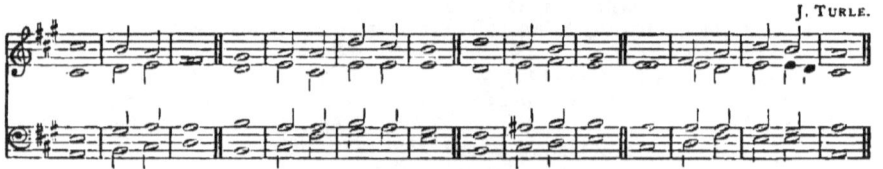

J. Turle.

PSALM CXI.—*Confitebor tibi.*

mf I WILL give thanks unto the Lord with my | whole | heart : secretly among the faithful and | in the | congre- | gation.

2 The works of the | Lord are | great : sought out of all them | that have | pleasure · there- | -in.

3 His work is worthy to be praised, and | had in | honour : and his righteous- | ness en- | -dureth · for | ever.

4 The merciful and gracious Lord hath so done his | marvellous | works : that they ought to be | had | in re- | membrance.

5 He hath given meat unto | them that | fear him : he shall ever be | mind- | ful | of his | covenant.

6 He hath shewed his people the power | of his | works : that he may give them the | heritage | of the | heathen.

7 The works of his hands are verity | and | judgement : all | his com- | -mand- | ments · are | true.

8 They stand fast for | ever · and | ever : and are | done in | truth and | equity.

9 He sent redemption | unto · his | people : he hath commanded his covenant for ever * holy and | reverend | is his | Name.

10 The fear of the Lord is the be- | ginning · of | wisdom : a good under- standing have all they that do thereafter * the praise of | it en- | -dureth · for | ever.

DAY XXIII. MORNING (*continued*).

Sir George Elvey.

PSALM CXII.—*Beatus vir.*

mf BLESSED is the man that | feareth ·| the | Lord : he hath great de- | -light in | his com- | -mandments.

2 His seed shall be mighty up- | -on | earth : the generation of the | faithful | shall be | blessed.

3 Riches and plenteousness shall be | in his | house : and his righteous- | -ness en- | -dureth · for | ever.

4 Unto the godly there ariseth up light | in the | darkness : he is | merciful | loving · and | righteous.

5 A good man is merci- | -ful and | lendeth : and will guide his | words | with dis- | -cretion.

6 For he shall | never · be | moved :

and the righteous shall be had in | ever- | lasting · re- | -membrance.

7 He will not be afraid of any | evil | tidings : for his heart standeth fast, and be- | -lieveth | in the | Lord.

8 His heart is stablished, and | will not | shrink : until he see his de- | -sire up- | -on his | enemies.

9 He hath dispersed abroad ✳ and given | to the | poor : and his righteousness remaineth for ever ✳ his horn shall | be ex- | -alted · with | honour.

10 The ungodly shall see it, and | it shall | grieve him : he shall gnash with his teeth, and consume away ✳ the desire of the un- | -godly | shall | perish.

Henry Smart.

PSALM CXIII.—*Laudate, pueri.*

f PRAISE the | Lord ye | servants : O praise the | Name | of the | Lord.

2 Blessed be the Name | of the | Lord : from this time | forth for | ever- | more.

3 The Lord's | Name is | praised : from the rising up of the sun, unto the going | down | of the | same.

4 The Lord is high a- | -bove all | heathen : and his | glory · a- | -bove the | heavens.

5 Who is like unto the Lord our

God ✳ that hath his | dwelling · so | high : and yet humbleth himself to behold the things that | are in | heaven and | earth ?

6 He taketh up the simple | out · of the | dust : and lifteth the | poor | out · of the | mire ;

7 That he may set him | with the | princes : even with the | princes | of his people.

8 He maketh the barren woman to keep | house : and to be a | joyful mother · of | children.

DAY XXIII. EVENING.

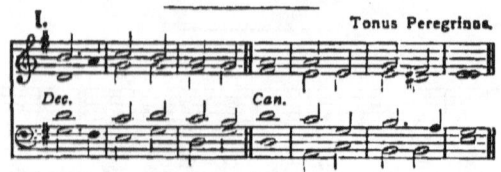

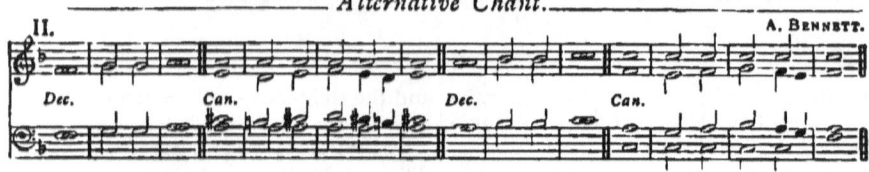

PSALM CXIV.—*In exitu Israel.*

mf F. WHEN Israel cáme | out of | Egypt : | and the house of Jacob fròm a- | -mong the | strange | people.

F. 2 Júdah | was his | sanctuary : ánd | Israel | his do- | -minion.

3 The séa saw | that, and | fled : Jór- | -dan was | driven | back.

4 The móuntains | skipped . like | rams : and the líttle | hills like | young | sheep.

5 What aileth thee, O thou séa | that thou | fleddest : and thou Jórdan that | thou wast | driven | back ?

6 Ye mountains, thát ye | skipped . like | rams : and ye líttle | hills like | young | sheep ?

7 Tremble thou earth, at the présence | of the | Lord : at the présence | of the | God of | Jacob ;

8 Who turned the hard róck into a | standing | water : and the flínt-stone | into . a | springing | well.

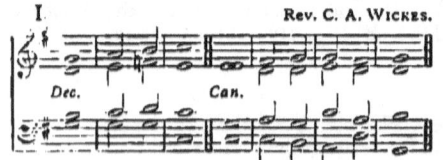

PSALM CXV.—*Non nobis, Domine.*

mf NOT unto us O Lord, not unto us ✱ but unto thy Náme | give the | praise : for thy loving mércy, and | for thy | truth's | sake.

2 Wherefore shàll the | heathen | say : Whére | — is | now their | God ?

3 As for óur God | he is . in | heaven : he hath dóne whatso- | -ever | pleased | him.

4 Their ídols are | silver . and | gold : éven the | work of | men's | hands.

5 They have | mouths and | speak not : éyes | have | they and | see not.

6 They have | ears and | hear not : nóses | have | they and | smell not.

7 They have hands and handle not ✱ féet have | they and | walk not : neíther | speak they | through their | throat.

8 They that make them are líke | unto | them : and so are all súch as | put their | trust in | them.

9 But thou house of Israel ✱ trúst thou | in the | Lord : hé is their | succour | and de- | -fence.

10 Ye house of Aaron ✱ put your trúst | in the | Lord : hé is their | helper | and de- | -fender.

11 Ye that fear the Lord ✱ put your trúst | in the | Lord : hé is their | helper | and de- | -fender.

12 The Lord hath been mindful of ús, and | he shall | bless us : even he shall bless the house of Israel ✱ hé shall | bless the | house of | Aaron.

13 He shall bless thém that | fear the | Lord : bóth | small | and | great.

14 The Lord shall incréase you | more and | more : yóu | and | your | children.

15 Ye are the bléssed | of the | Lord : whó | made | heaven and | earth.

16 All the whole héavens | are the | Lord's : the earth hath he gíven | to the | children . of | men.

17 The dead práise not | thee O | Lord : neither all théy that go | down | into | silence.

18 But wé will | praise the | Lord : from this time forth for evermóre | Praise | — the | Lord.

DAY XXIV. MORNING.

Dr. Camidge.

PSALM CXVI.—*Dilexi, quoniam.*

mf I′ AM | well | pleased : that the Lord hath héard the | voice of | my | prayer;

2 That he hath inclined his éar | unto | me : therefore will I call upon hím as | long | as I | live.

3 The snares of death cómpassed me | round a- | -bout : and the páins of | hell gat | hold up- | -on me.

4 I shall find trouble and heaviness * and I will call upon the Náme | of the | Lord : O Lord, I beséech | thee de- | -liver • my | soul.

5 Gracious ís the | Lord and | righteous : yéa, our | God is | mercí- | -ful.

6 The Lórd pre- | -serveth • the | simple : I was in mísery | and he | helped | me.

7 Turn again then unto thy rêst | O my | soul : for the Lórd | hath re- | warded | thee.

8 And why ? thou hast delivered my | soul from | death : mine eyes from téars | and my | feet from | falling.

9 I will wálk be- | -fore the | Lord : in the | land | of the | living.

10 I believed, and therefore will I speak * but I′ was | sore | troubled : I said in my háste | All | men are | liars.

11 What reward shall I gíve | unto • the | Lord : for all the benefits that hê hath | done | unto | me ?

12 I will receive the cúp | of sal- | -vation : and cáll upon the | Name | of the | Lord.

13 I will pay my vows now in the présence of | all his | people : right dear in the sight of the Lórd is the | death | of his | saints.

14 Behold, O Lord, hów that | I am • thy | servant : I am thy servant and the son of thine handmaid * thóu hast | broken • my | bonds in | sunder.

15 I will offer to thee the sácrifice of | thanks- | -giving : and will call upón the | Name | of the | Lord.

16 I will pay my vows unto the Lord * in the síght of | all his | people : in the courts of the Lord's house * even in the midst of thee O Jerúsalem | Praise | — the | Lord.

PSALM CXVII.—*Laudate Dominum.*

f O PRAISE the Lórd | all ye | heathen: práise | — him | all ye | nations.

2 For his merciful kindness is ever more and móre | towards | us : and the truth of the Lord endureth for éver | Praise | — the | Lord.

Verses 1 to 14. F. Kinke
Dec. Can.

PSALM CXVIII.—*Confitemini Domino.*

f O GIVE thanks unto the Lórd, for | he is | gracious : becáuse his | mercy • en- | -dureth • for | ever.

2 Let Israel now confèss that | he is | gracious : and thát his | mercy • en- | dureth • for | ever.

3 Let the house of Aáron | now con- | fess : thát his | mercy • en- | -dureth • for | ever.

4 Yea, let them now that fêar the | Lord con- | -fess : thát his | mercy • en- | dureth • for | ever.

mf 5 I called upón the | Lord in | trouble : and the Lórd | heard | me at | large.

6 The Lórd is | on my | side : I will not féar what | man • doeth | unto | me.

7 The Lord taketh my párt with | them that | help me : therefore shall I sêe my de- | -sire up, | -on mine | enemies.

8 It is better to trúst | in the | Lord : than to pút any | confi- | -dence in | man.

9 It is better to trúst | in the | Lord : than to pút any | confi- | -dence in | princes.

DAY XXIV. MORNING (continued).

Verses 1 to 14. F. KINKEE. *Verse 15 to end.* TRAVERS.

10 All nations compassed me | round a- | -bout : but in the Náme of the | Lord will | I de- | -stroy them.

11 They kept me in on every side * they kept me in | sáy on | every | side : but in the Náme of the | Lord will | I de- | -stroy them.

12 They came about me like bees * and are extinct even as the fire a- | -mong the | thorns : for in the Náme of the | Lord I | will de- | -stroy them.

13 Thou hast thrust sore at mé, that | I might | fall : but the | Lord | was my | help.

14 The Lord is my strength | and my | song : and is be- | -come | my sal- | -vation.

15 The voice of joy and health is in the dwéllings | of the | righteous : the right hand of the Lórd bringeth | mighty | things to | pass.

16 The right hand of the Lórd | hath . the pre- | -eminence : the right hand of the Lórd bringeth | mighty | things to | pass.

17 I shall not | die but | live : and declare the | works | of the | Lord.

18 The Lord hath chástened and cor- | rected | me : but he hath not gíven me | over | unto | death.

19 O'pen me the | gates of | righteous-

ness : that I may go into them * ánd give | thanks | unto · the | Lord.

20 This is the gáte | of the | Lord : the righteous shall | enter | into | it.

21 I will thánk thee for | thou hast | heard me : and árt be- | -come | my sal- | vation.

22 The same stóne which the | builders · re- | -fused : is become the | head-stone | in the | corner.

23 This is the | Lord's | doing : and it is | marvellous | in our | eyes.

24 This is the dáy which the | Lord hath | made : we will rejóice | and be | glad in | it.

25 Hélp me | now O | Lord : O Lórd | send us | now pros- | -perity.

26 Blessed be he that cometh in the Náme | of the | Lord : we have wished you good luck * ye that áre of the | house | of the | Lord.

27 God is the Lórd who hath | shewed · us | light : bind the sacrifice with cords * yea, even únto the | horns | of the | altar.

28 Thou art my Gód, and | I will | thank thee : thóu art my | God, and | I will | praise thee.

29 O gíve thanks unto the Lórd, for | he is | gracious : ánd his | mercy · en- | dureth · for | ever.

DAY XXIV. EVENING.

Verses 1 to 8. FITZHERBERT.

PSALM CXIX.—*Beati immaculati.*

F. mf BLESSED are those that are un- defíled | in the | way : and wálk in the | law | of the | Lord.

F. 2 Blessed are théy that | keep his | testimonies : and séek him | with their | whole | heart.

3 For théy who | do no | wickedness : walk | — in | his | ways.

4 Thóu | hast | charged : that we shall díligently | keep | thy com- | -mand- ments.

5 O that my ways were máde | so di- | -rect : thát | I might | keep thy | statutes !

6 So shall I nót | be con- | -founded : while I have respéct unto | all | thy com- | mandments.

7 I will thank thee with an un- | feigned | heart : when I shall have léarned the | judgements | of thy | righteousness.

8 I will | keep thy | ceremonies : O' for- | -sake me | not | utterly.

DAY XXIV. EVENING (continued).

Verses 9 to 16.   Dr. J. Nares.

In quo corriget?

WHEREWITHAL shall a yóung man | cleanse his | way : even by rúling him- | -self | after . thy | word.

10 With my whole héart | have I | sought thee : O let me not go wróng | out of | thy com- | -mandments.

11 Thy words have I híd with- | -in my | heart : thát I | should not | sin a- | gainst thee.

12 Bléssed art | thou O | Lord : O* | teach | me thy | statutes.

13 With my líps have | I been | telling : of áll the | judgements | of thy | mouth.

14 I have had as great delight in the wáy | of thy | testimonies : ás in | all | manner . of | riches.

15 I will tálk of | thy com- | -mandments : and háve re- | -spect | unto . thy | ways.

16 My delight shall bé | in thy | statutes : and I* will|not for-|-get thy|word.

Verses 17 to 24.   Dr. Rimbault.

Retribue servo tuo.

O DO wéll | unto . thy | servant : that I* may | live and | keep thy | word.

18 O*pen | thou mine | eyes : that I may sée the wondrous | things | of thy | law.

19 I am a stránger up- | -on | earth : O híde not | thy com- | -mandments | from me.

20 My soul breakéth out for the véry | fervent . de- | -sire : that it háth | alway | unto . thy | judgements.

21 Thóu hast re- | -buked . the | proud : and cursed are théy that do | err from | thy com- | -mandments.

22 O turn from me the sháme | and re- | buke | fór | I have | kept thy | testimonies

23 Princes also did sít and | speak a- | -gainst me : but thy sérvant is | occu- pied | in thy | statutes.

24 For thy téstimonies are | my de- | light : ánd | — | my | counsellors.

Verses 25 to 32.   Hindle.

Adhæsit pavimento.

MY soul cléaveth | to the | dust : O quicken thou mé ac- | -cording | to thy | word.

26 I have acknowledged my wáys and thou | heardest | me ; O* | teach | me thy | statutes.

27 Make me to understand the wáy of | thy com- | -mandments : and so shall I tálk | of thy | wondrous | works.

28 My soul melteth awáy for | very | heaviness : comfort thou mé ac- | -cording | unto . thy | word.

29 Take from mé the | way of | lying : and cause thou me to máke | much | of thy | law.

30 I have chósen the | way of | truth : and thy júdgements I have I | laid be- | fore me.

31 I have stúck | unto . thy | testimonies : O* | Lord con- | -found me | not.

32 I will run the wáy of | thy com- | mandments : when thou hast | set **my** | heart at | liberty.

DAY XXV. MORNING.

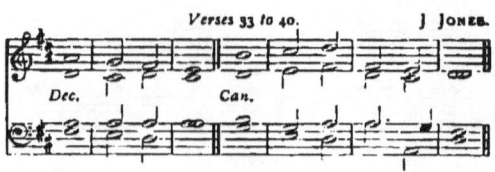

Verses 33 to 40.   J JONES.

PSALM CXIX.—*Legem pone.*

mf TEACH me O Lord, the wáy | of thy | statutes : and I° shall | keep it | unto · the | end.

34 Give me understanding, and I° shall | keep thy | law : yea I shall kéep it | with my | whole | heart.

35 Make me to go in the páth of | thy com- | -mandments : fór there- | -in is | my de- | -sire.

36 Incline my héart | unto · thy | testimonies : ánd | not to | covetous- | -ness.

37 O turn away mine eyes * lést they be- | hold | vanity : and qúicken thou | me in | thy | way.

38 O stablish thy wórd | in thy | servant : thát | I may | fear | thee.

39 Take away the rebúke that | I am · a- | -fraid of : fór thy | judgements | are | good.

40 Behold, my delight is in | thy com- | mandments : O° | quicken · me | in thy | righteousness.

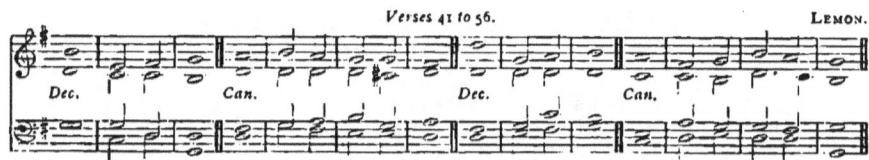

Verses 41 to 56.   LEMON.

Et veniat super me.

LET thy loving mercy come also únto | me O | Lord : even thy salvátion, ac- | -cording | unto · thy | word.

42 So shall I make answer únto | my blas- | -phemers : fór my | trust is | in thy | word.

43 O take not the word of thy truth útterly | out of · my | mouth : fór my | hope is | in thy | judgements.

44 So shall I álway | keep thy | law : yéa, for | ever | and | ever.

45 And I° will | walk at | liberty : fór I | seek | thy com- | -mandments.

46 I will speak of thy testimonies also * éven be- | -fore | kings : ánd | will not | be a- | -shamed.

47 And my delight shall bé in | thy com- | -mandments : which | I | haveIloved.

48 My hands also will I lift up unto thy commándments which | I have | loved : and my stúdy shall | be in | thy | statutes

Memor esto servi tui.

O THINK upon thy servant, ás con- | cerning · thy | word : wherein thou hast cáused | me to | put my | trust.

50 The same is my cómfort | in my | trouble : fór thy|word hath | quickened|me.

51 The proud have had me excéedingly | in de- | -rision : yet háve | I not | shrinked | from thy | law.

52 For I remembered thine everlásting | judgements · O | Lord : ánd | — re- | -ceived | comfort.

53 I am hórri- | -bly a- | -fraid : for the ungódly | that for- | -sake thy | law.

54 Thy státutes have | been my | songs : ín the | house | of my | pilgrimage.

55 I have thought upon thy Name, O Lórd, in the | night- | -season : ánd have | kept | thy | law.

56 Thís | I | had · : becáuse I | kept | thy com- | -mandments.

DAY XXV. MORNING (continued).

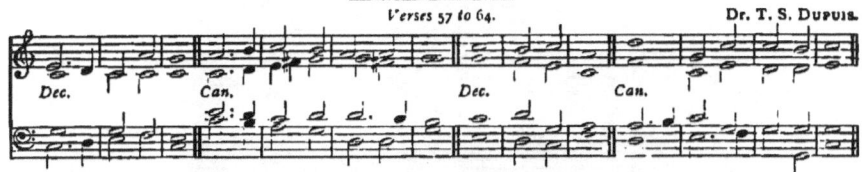

Verses 57 to 64.   Dr. T. S. Dupuis.

Portio mea, Domine.

THŌU art my | portion · O | Lord : I have prómised to | keep | thy | law.

58 I made my humble petition in thy presence * wíth my | whole | heart : O be mercifulunto mé, ac-|-cording|to thy|word.

59 I called mine own wáys | to re-| membrance : and túrned my | feet | unto · thy | testimonies.

60 I made haste, and prolónged | not the | time : tó | keep|thy com-|-mandments.

61 The congregations of the ungódly have | robbed | me : but I' have | not for- | -gotten · thy | law.

62 At midnight I will rise to give thánks | unto | thee : because | of thy | righteous | judgements.

63 I am a companion of áll | them that | fear thee : ánd| keep|thy com-|-mandments.

64 The earth, O Lord, is fúll | of thy | mercy : O' | teach | me thy | statutes.

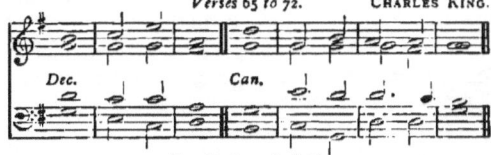

Verses 65 to 72.   CHARLES KING.

Bonitatem fecisti.

O LORD, thou hast dealt gráciously | with thy | servant : ác- | -cording | unto · thy | word.

66 O learn me trúe under- | -standing · and | knowledge : for I' have be- | -lieved | thy com- | -mandments.

67 Before I was tróubled, I | went | wrong : but nów | have I | kept thy | word.

68 Thóu art | good and | gracious : O' | teach | me thy | statutes.

69 The proud have imágined a | lie a- | gainst me : but I will keep thy commánd- ments | with my | whole | heart.

70 Their héart is as | fat as | brawn : but my delíght hath | been in | thy | law.

71 It is good for me that I' have | been in|trouble : thát|I may | learn thy|statutes.

72 The law of thy mouth is déarer | unto | me : thán | thousands · of | gold and | silver.

DAY XXV. EVENING.

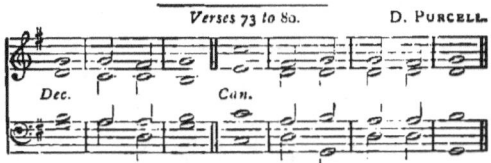

Verses 73 to 80.   D. PURCELL.

Manus tuæ fecerunt me.

F.mf THY hands have máde me and | fash- ioned | me : O give me understanding * that I' may | learn | thy com- | -mandments.

F. 74 They that fear thee will be glád | when they | see me : because I have pút my | trust | in thy | word.

75 I know, O Lórd, that thy | judge- ments · are | right : ard that thou of very fáithfulness hast | caused · me | to be | troubled.

76 O let thy merciful kíndness | be my | comfort : accórding to thy | word | unto · thy | servant.

77 O let thy loving mercies come unto mé, that | I may | live : fór thy | law is | my de- | -light.

78 Let the proud be confounded * for they go wickedly abóut | to de- | -stroy me : but I will be óccu- | -pied in | thy com- | -mandments.

79 Let such as fear thee * ánd have | known thy | testimonies : bé | turned | unto | me.

80 O let my heart be sóund | in thy | statutes : thát I | be | not a- | shamed.

DAY XXV. EVENING (continued).

Verses 81 to 88.   Dr. GARRETT.

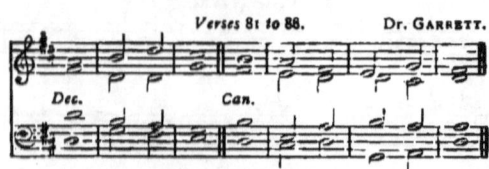

PSALM CXIX.—*Defecit anima mea.*

MY soul hath lónged for | thy sal- | vation : and I have a good hópe be- | cause of | thy | word.

82 Mine eyes long sóre | for thy | word : saying, O when | wilt thou | comfort | me ?

83 For I am become like a bóttle | in the | smoke : yet do I | not for- | -get thy | statutes.

84 How many are the dáys | of thy | servant : when wilt thou be avénged of | them that | persecute | me ?

85 The proud have dígged | pits for | me : which | are not | after · thy | law.

86 A'll thy com- | -mandments · are | true : they persecute me fálsely, | O be | thou my | help.

87 They had almost made an end of me up- | -on | earth : but I* for- | -sook not | thy com- | -mandments.

88 O quicken me áfter thy | loving- | kindness : and so shall I keep the | testi- monies | of thy | mouth.

Verses 89 to 96.   Dr. T. A. WALMISLEY.

In æternum, Domine.

O LÓRD | thy | word : én- | -dureth · | for | ever · in | heaven.

90 Thy truth also remaineth from one generation | to an- | -other : thou hast laid the foundátion of the | earth and | it a- | -bideth.

91 They continue this day accórding | to thine | ordinance : for | all things | serve | thee.

92 If my delight had nót been | in thy | law : I* should have | perished | in my | trouble.

93 I will never forgét | thy com- | mandments : for with thém | thou hast | quickened | me.

94 I* am | thine O | save me : for I* have | sought | thy com- | -mandments.

95 The ungodly laid wáit for me | to de- | -stroy me : but I* will con- | -sider | thy | testimonies.

96 I see that áll things | come · to an | end : but thy commándment | is ex- | ceeding | broad.

Verses 97 to 104.   J. TURLE.

Quomodo dilexi !

LORD, what lóve have I | unto · thy | law : all the day lóng | is my | study | in it.

98 Thou through thy commandments * hast made me wíser | than mine enemies : for | they are | ever | with me.

99 I have more understánding | than my | teachers : for thy | testimonies | are my | study.

100 I am wíser | than the | aged : becáuse I | keep | thy com- | -mandments.

101 I have refrained my feet from évery | evil | way : that I | may | keep thy | word.

102 I have not shrúnk | from thy | judgements : for | thou | teachest | me.

103 O how sweet are thy wórds | unto : my | throat : yea swéeter than | honey | unto · my | mouth.

104 Through thy commandments I gét | under- | -standing : thérefore I | hate all | evil | ways.

DAY XXVI. MORNING.

Verses 105 to 112.   H. BAKER.

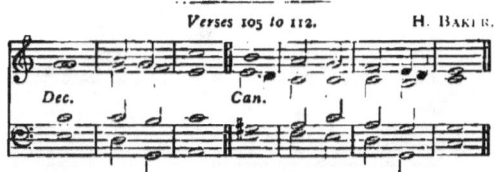

Lucerna pedibus meis.

mf THY word is a lántern | unto · my | | feet : ånd a | light | unto · my | paths.

106 I have swórn, and am | stedfastly | purposed : tó | keep thy | righteous | judgements.

107 I am tróubled a- | -bove | measure : quicken me, O Lórd, ac- | -cording | to thy | word.

108 Let the free-will-offerings of my mouth pléase | thee O | Lord : ånd | teach | me thy | judgements.

109 My soul is álway | in my | hand : yêt do I | not for- | -get thy | law.

110 The ungodly have láid a | snare for | me : but yet I swérved | not from | thy com- | -mandments.

111 Thy testimonies have I claimed as mine hérit- | -age for | ever : and why ? they are the véry | joy | of my | heart.

112 I have applied my heart to fulfíl thy | statutes | alway : éven | un- | -to the | end.

Verses 113 to 120.   Dr. ARMES.

Iniquos odio habui.

I HATE them that imágine | evil | things : bût thy | law | do I | love.

114 Thou art mý de- | -fence and | shield : ånd my | trust is | in thy | word.

115 Awáy from | me ye | wicked : I will kéep the com- | -mandments | of my | God.

116 O stablish me according to thy wórd, that I | I may | live : and let me not be dísap- | -pointed | of my | hope.

117 Hold thou me úp, and I | shall be |

safe : yea, my delíght shall be | ever | in thy | statutes.

118 Thou hast trodden down all them that depárt | from thy | statutes : for théy im- | -agine | but de- | -ceit.

119 Thou puttest away all the ungódly of the | earth like | dross : therefore I | love | thy | testimonies.

120 My flesh trémbleth for | fear of | thee : and I* am a- | -fraid of | thy | judgements.

Verses 121 to 128.   Dr. GREENE.

Feci judicium.

I DEAL with the thing that is | lawful · | and | right : O give me not óver | unto | mine op- | -pressors.

122 Make thou thy servant to delíght in | that which · is | good : that the próud | do me | no | wrong.

123 Mine eyes are wasted away with lóoking | for thy | health : and fôr the | word | of thy | righteousness.

124 O deal with thy servant according únto thy | loving | mercy : ånd | teach | me thy | statutes.

125 I am thy servant, O gránt me | under- | -standing : thát | I may | know thy | testimonies.

126 It is time for thee Lórd to lay | to thine | hand : fôr they | have de- | -stroyed · thy | law.

127 For I lóve | thy com- | -mandments : abóve | gold and | precious | stone.

128 Therefore hold I stráight all | thy com- | -mandments : and all false wáys I | utter- | -ly ab- | -hor.

DAY XXVI. MORNING (*continued*).

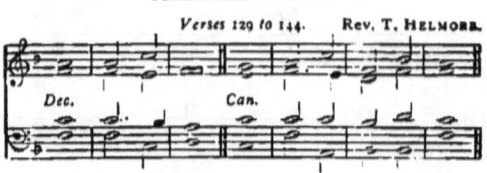

PSALM CXIX.—*Mirabilia*.

THY téstimonies | are | wonderful : thérefore | doth my | soul | keep them.

130 When thy wórd | goeth | forth : it giveth light and únder· | ·standing | unto · the | simple.

131 I opened my móuth, and drew | in my | breath : for my delíght | was in | thy com· | ·mandments.

132 O look thou upon me * and be mérciful | unto | me : as thou usest to dó unto | those that | love thy | Name.

133 Order my stéps | in thy | word and so shall no wickedness háve do· | minion | over | me.

134 O deliver me from the wrôngful | dealings · of | men : and so shall I | keep | thy com· | ·mandments.

135 Shew the light of thy cóuntenance up· | ·on thy | servant : ánd | teach | me thy | statutes.

136 Mine éyes gush | out with | water : because men | keep | not thy | law.

Justus es, Domine.

RÍGHTEOUS art | thou O | Lord : ánd | true | is thy | judgement.

138 The testimonies that thóu | hast com· | ·manded ; áre ex· | ·ceeding | righteous · and | true.

139 My zeal hath éven con· | ·sumed me : because mine énemies | have for· | gotten · thy | words.

140 Thy word is tríed | to the | uttermost : ánd thy | servant | loveth | it.

141 I am small, and of nó | repu· | tation : yet do I nót for· | ·get | thy com· | mandments.

142 Thy righteousness is an éver· | lasting | righteousness : ánd thy | law | is the | truth.

143 Trouble and heaviness have táken | hold up· | ·on me ; yet is mý de· | ·light in | thy com· | ·mandments.

144 The righteousness of thy téstimonies is | ever· | ·lasting : O gránt me únder· | ·standing · and I | shall | live.

DAY XXVI. EVENING.

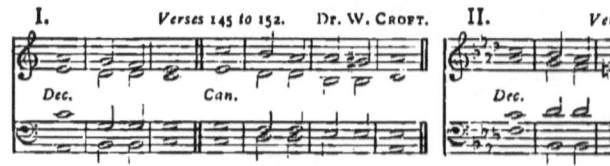

Clamavi in toto corde meo.

F. mf I CÁLL with my | whole | heart : hear me, O Lórd | I will | keep thy | statutes.

F. 146 Yea, even unto thée | do I | call : help me, and | I shall | keep thy | testimonies.

147 Early in the morning do I crý | unto | thee : for ín thy | word | is my | trust.

148 Mine eyes prevént the | night· | watches : that I míght be | occupied | in thy | words.

149 Hear my voice, O Lord * according únto thy | loving· | ·kindness : qúicken me ac· | ·cording · as | thou art | wont.

150 They draw nigh that of málice | persecute | me : ánd are | far | from thy | law.

151 Be thou nígh at | hand O | Lord : for áll | thy com· | ·mandments · are | true.

152 As concerning thy testimonies * I' have | known long | since : that thóu hast | grounded | them for | ever.

DAY XXVI. EVENING (*continued*).

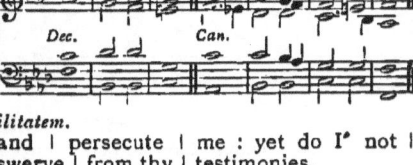

Vide humilitatem.

O CONSIDER mine adversity ✱ ánd | de- | -liver | me : for I' do | not for- | -get thy | law.

154 Avenge thou my cáuse, and de- | liver | me : qúicken me, ac- | -cording | to thy | word.

155 Health is fár from | the un- | -godly : for théy re- | -gárd | not thy | statutes.

156 Gréat is thy | mercy ● O | Lord : qúicken | me as | thou art | wont.

157 Many there are that tróuble me, and | persecute | me : yet do I' not | swerve | from thy | testimonies.

158 It grieveth me whén I | see the ● trans- | -gressors : becáuse they | keep | not thy | law.

159 Consider O Lord, how I lóve | thy com- | -mandments : O quicken me, according | to thy | loving- | -kindness.

160 Thy word is trúe from | ever- | -lasting : all the judgements of thy righteousness ✱ en- | -dure for | ever- | -more.

Principes persecuti sunt.

PRINCES have persecuted mé with- | out a | cause : but my heart stándeth in | awe | of thy | word.

162 I am as glád | of thy | word : as óne that | findeth | great | spoils.

163 As for lies, I háte | and ab- | -hor them : bút thy | law | do I | love.

164 Seven times a dáy do I | praise | thee : becáuse | of thy | righteous | judgements.

165 Great is the peace that théy have who | love thy | law : ánd they are | not of- | -fended | at it.

166 Lord, I have lóoked for thy | saving | health : and dóne | after | thy com- | -mandments.

167 My sóul hath | kept thy | testimonies : ánd | loved | them ex- | -ceedingly.

168 I have képt thy com- | -mandments ● and | testimonies : for áll my | ways | are be- | -fore thee.

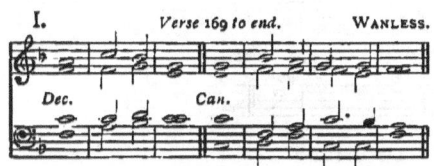
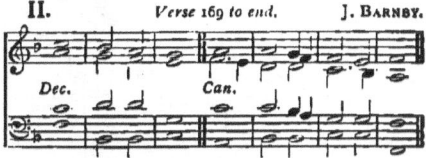

Appropinquet deprecatio.

LET my complaint cóme before | thee O | Lord : give me understánding, ac- | -cording | to thy | word.

170 Let my supplicátion | come be- | fore thee ● deliver me, ac- | -cording | to thy | word.

171 My lips shall spéak | of thy | praise : when thóu hast | taught | me thy | statutes.

172 Yea, my tongue shall síng | of thy | word : for áll thy com- | -mandments ● are | righteous.

173 Lét thine | hand | help me : for I' have | chosen | thy com- | -mandments.

174 I have longed for thy sáving | health O | Lord : and ín thy | law is | my de- | -light.

175 O let my soul líve, and | it shall | praise thee : ánd thy | judgements | shall | help me.

176 I have gone astray like a shéep | that is | lost : O seek thy servant ✱ for I do nót for- | -get | thy com- | -mandments.

DAY XXVII. MORNING.

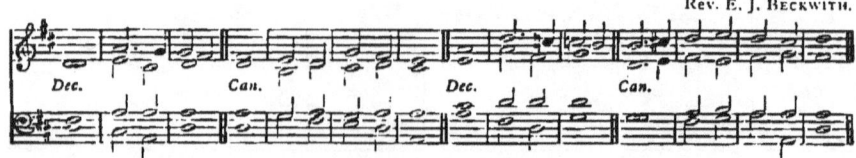

Rev. E. J. BECKWITH.

PSALM CXX.—*Ad Dominum.*

mp WHEN I was in trouble I called up-| on the | Lord : and I — he | heard | me.

2 Deliver my soul, O Lord, from | lying | lips : and | from · a de- | -ceitful | tongue.

3 What reward shall be given or done unto thee, thou | false | tongue : even mighty and sharp arrows, with | hot | burning | coals.

4 Woe is me, that I am constrained to | dwell with | Mesech : and to have my habitation a- | -mong the | tents of | Kedar.

5 My soul hath long | dwelt a · mong | them : that are | enemies | unto | peace.

6 I labour for peace ✶ but when I speak unto | them there- | -of : they | make them | ready · to | battle.

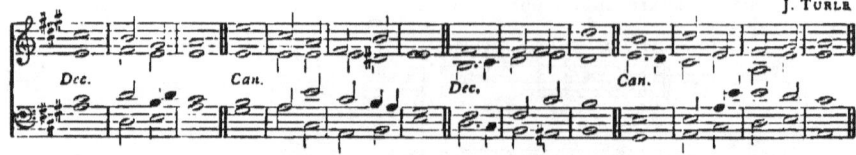

J. TURLE.

PSALM CXXI.—*Levavi oculos.*

mf I WILL lift up mine eyes | unto · the | hills : from | whence | cometh · my | help.

2 My help cometh even | from the | Lord : who hath | made | heaven and | earth.

3 He will not suffer thy foot | to be | moved : and he that | keepeth · thee | will not | sleep.

4 Behold, he that | keepeth | Israel : shall | neither | slumber · nor | sleep.

5 The Lord himself | is thy | keeper : the Lord is thy defence up- | -on thy | right | hand ;

6 So that the sun shall not burn | thee by | day : neither the | moon|by|night.

7 The Lord shall preserve thee from | all | evil : yea, it is even he | that shall | keep thy | soul.

8 The Lord shall preserve thy going out ✶ and thy | coming | in : from this time | forth for | ever- | -more.

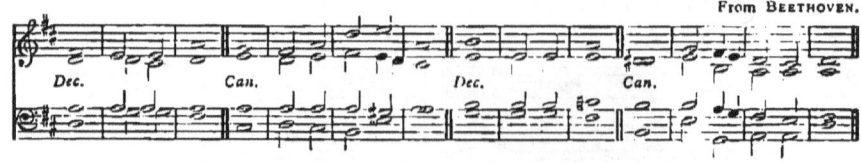

From BEETHOVEN.

PSALM CXXII.—*Lætatus sum.*

mf I WAS glad when they said | unto | me : We will go into the|house|of the|Lord.

2 Our feet shall stand | in thy | gates : O° | — Je- | -rusa- | -lem.

3 Jerusalem is built | as a | city : that is at | unity | in it- | -self.

4 For thither the tribes go up ✶ even the tribes | of the | Lord : to testify unto Israel ✶ to give thanks unto the | Name | of the | Lord.

5 For there is the | seat of | judgement : even the seat|of the|house of|David.

6 O pray for the peace | of Je- | rusalem : they shall | prosper · that | love | thee.

7 Peace be with- | -in thy | walls : and plenteous- | -ness with- | -in thy | palaces.

8 For my brethren and com- | panions' | sakes : I° will | wish | thee pros- | -perity.

part 9 Yea, because of the house of the | Lord our | God : I° will | seek to | do thee | good.

DAY XXVII. MORNING (*continued*). 97

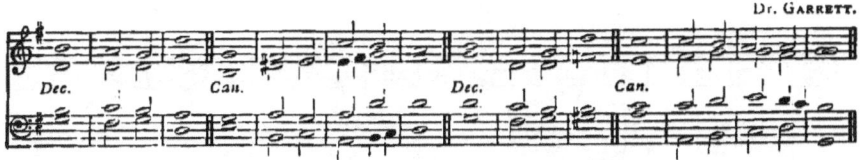
Dr. GARRETT.

PSALM CXXIII.—*Ad te levavi oculos meos.*

mp UNTO thée lift I | up mine | eyes : O thóu that | dwellest | in the | heavens.

2 Behold, even as the eyes of servants look unto the hand of their masters ✱ and as the eyes of a maiden unto the hánd | of her | mistress : even so our eyes wait upon the Lord our God ✱ untíl | he have | mercy · up- | -on us.

3 Have mercy upon us, O Lórd, have | mercy · up- | -on us : for wé are | utter- | -ly de- | -spised.

4 Our soul is filled with the scornful repróof | of the | wealthy : and with the de- | -spiteful · ness | of the proud.

PSALM CXXIV.—*Nisi quia Dominus.*

mp IF the Lord himself had not been on our side ✱ nów may | Israel | say : If the Lord himself had not been on our síde, when | men rose | up a- | -gainst us ;

2 They had swállowed | us up | quick : when they were so wráthful- | -ly dis- | -pleased | at us.

3 Yea, the wáters had | drowned | us : and the stream had | gone | over · our | soul.

4 The déep waters | of the | proud : had góne | even | over · our | soul.

mf 5 But práised | be the | Lord : who hath not given us over fór a | prey | unto · their | teeth.

6 Our soul is escaped ✱ even as a bird out of the snáre | of the | fowler : the snare is bróken, | and we | are de- | -livered.

2nd part 7 Our help standeth in the Náme | of the | Lord : whó hath | made | heaven and | earth.

Rev. J. TROUTBECK.

PSALM CXXV.—*Qui confidunt.*

mf THEY that put their trust in the Lord shall be éven as the | mount | Sion : which may not be remóved, but | standeth | fast for | ever.

2 The hills stánd a- | -bout Je- | rusalem : even so standeth the Lord round about his people ✱ from thís time | forth for | ever- | -more.

3 For the rod of the ungodly cometh not into the lót | of the | righteous : lest the righteous pút their | hand | unto | wickedness.

4 Do | well O | Lord : unto thóse that are | good and | true of | heart.

5 As for such as turn báck unto their | own | wickedness : the Lord shall lead them forth with the evil-doers ✱ but péace shall | be up- | -on | Israel.

DAY XXVII. EVENING.

J. Turle.

PSALM CXXVI.—*In convertendo.*

F. mf WHEN the Lord turned again the captívi- | -ty of | Sion : then were we líke | unto | them that | dream.

F. 2 Then was our móuth | filled · with | laughter : ánd our | tongue | with | joy.

3 Then sáid they a- | -mong the | heathen : The Lórd hath | done great | things for | them.

4 Yea, the Lord hath done great things for | us al- | -ready : whére- | -of | we re- | -joice.

5 Turn our captívity | O | Lord : ás the | rivers | in the | south.

6 Théy that | sow in | tears : sháll | reap | in | joy.

2nd part 7 He that now goeth on his way weeping ✶ and béareth | forth good | seed : shall doubtless come again with jóy, and | bring his | sheaves | with him.

Sir J. Goss.

PSALM CXXVII.—*Nisi Dominus.*

mf EXCEPT the Lórd | build the | house : their lábour | is but | lost that | build it.

2 Except the Lórd | keep the | city : the wátchman | waketh | but in | vain.

3 It is but lost labour that ye haste to rise up early ✶ and so late take rest, and éat the | bread of | carefulness : for so he gíveth | his be- | -loved | sleep.

4 Lo, children and the frúit | of the | womb : are an heritage and gíft that | cometh | of the | Lord.

5 Like as the arrows in the hánd | of the | giant : even só | are the | young | children.

6 Happy is the man that hath his qúiver | full of | them : they shall not be ashamed when they spéak with their | enemies | in the | gate.

PSALM CXXVIII.—*Beati omnes.*

mf BLESSED are all théy that | fear the | Lord : ánd | walk | in his | ways.

2 For thou shalt eat the lábours | of thine | hands : O well is thée, and | happy | shalt thou | be.

3 Thy wife shall bé as the | fruitful | vine : upón the | walls | of thine | house.

4 Thy children líke the | olive- | branches : róund | — a- | -bout thy | table.

5 Lo, thús shall the | man be | blessed : thát | fear- | -eth the | Lord.

6 The Lord from out of Síon shall | so | bless thee : that thou shalt see Jerusalem in prospérity | all thy | life | long.

2nd part 7 Yea, that thou shalt sée thy | children's | children : ánd | peace up- | on | Israel.

DAY XXVII. EVENING (*continued*).

J. TURLE.

PSALM CXXIX.—*Sæpe expugnaverunt.*

mp MANY a time have they fought against me fróm my | youth | up : máy | Israel | now | say.

2 Yea, many a time have they vexed me fróm my | youth | up : bút they have | not pre- | -vailed - a- | -gainst me.

3 The plowers plówed up- | -on my | back : ánd | made | long | furrows.

4 Bút the | righteous | Lord : hath hewn the snáres of the un- | -godly | in | pieces.

5 Let them be confóunded and | turned | backward : as many as háve | evil | will at | Sion.

6 Let them be even as the grass grówing up- | -on the | house-tops : which withereth afóre | it be | plucked | up.

7 Whereof the mower fílleth | not his | hand : neither he that bíndeth | up the | sheaves his | bosom.

8 So that they who go by ✱ say not so much as, The Lórd | prosper | you : we wish you good lúck in the | Name | of the | Lord.

J. TURLE, from PURCELL.

PSALM CXXX.—*De profundis.*

p OUT of the deep have I called únto | thee, O | Lord : Lórd | hear | my | voice.

2 O let thine éars con- | -sider | well : thé | voice of | my com- | -plaint.

3 If thou, Lord, wilt be extreme to márk what is | done a- | -miss : O Lórd | who | may a- | -bide it ?

4 Fór there is | mercy · with | thee : thérefore | shalt | thou be | feared.

5 I look for the Lord; my sóul doth | wait for | him : ín his | word | is my | trust.

6 My soul fléeth | unto · the | Lord : before the morning watch, I sáy, be | fore the | morning | watch.

7 O Israel, trust in the Lord ✱ for with the Lórd | there is | mercy : ánd with | him is | plenteous · re- | -demption.

8 And hé shall re- | -deem | Israel : fróm | all | his | sins.

PSALM CXXXI.—*Domine, non est.*

p LÓRD, I am | not high- | -minded : I° have | no | proud | looks.

2 I do not exercise mysélf in | great | matters : whích | are too | high for | me.

3 But I refrain my soul, and keep it | low ✱ like as a child that is wéaned | from his | mother : yea, my soul is éven | as a | weaned | child.

4 O Israel, trúst | in the | Lord : from thís time | forth for | ever- | -more.

DAY XXVIII. MORNING

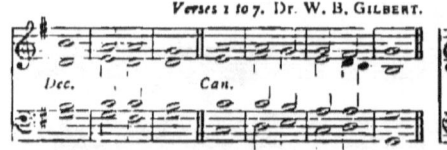
Verses 1 to 7. Dr. W. B. Gilbert.

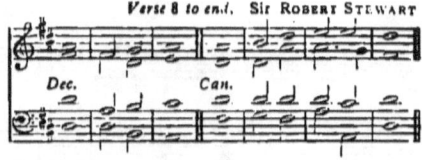
Verse 8 to end. Sir Robert Stewart.

PSALM CXXXII.—*Memento, Domine.*

mf LORD, re- | -member | David : ánd | all | his | trouble ;

2 How he swáre | unto ‧ the | Lord : and vowed a vow únto the Al- | -mighty | God of | Jacob ;

3 I will not come within the tábernacle | of mine | house : nór | climb up | into ‧ my | bed ;

4 I will not suffer mine eyes to sléep, nor mine | eye-lids ‧ to | slumber : neither the temples of my héad to | take | any | rest ;

5 Until I find out a place for the témple | of the | Lord : an habitation fór the | mighty | God of | Jacob.

6 Lo, we héard of the | same at | Ephrata : ánd | found it | in the | wood.

7 We will gó into his | taber- | -nacle : and fall lów on our | knees be- | -fore his | footstool.

8 Arise, O Lórd | into ‧ thy | resting-place : thóu and the | ark | of thy | strength.

9 Let thy priests be | clothed ‧ with | righteousness : and lét thy | saints | sing with | joyfulness.

10 For thy sérvant | David's | sake : turn not awáy the | presence ‧ of | thine A- | -nointed.

11 The Lord hath made a faithful óath | unto | David : ánd he | shall not | shrink | from it.

12 Of the frúit | of thy | body : sháll I | set up- | -on thy | seat.

13 If thy children will keep my covenant ✶ and my téstimonies that | I shall | learn them : their children also shall sit upon thy | seat for | ever- | -more.

14 For the Lord hath chosen Sion to be an habitátion | for him- | -self : hé hath | longed | for | her.

15 This shall bé my | rest for | ever : here will I dwell ✶ fór I | have ‧ a de- | light there- | -in.

16 I will bléss her | victuals ‧ with | increase : and will sátis- | -fy her | poor with | bread.

17 I will déck her | priests with | health : and her sáints | shall re- | -joice and | sing.

18 There shall I make the hórn of | David ‧ to | flourish : I have ordáined a | lantern ‧ for | mine A- | -nointed.

19 As for his enemies ✶ I shall clóthe them with | shame : but upon himsélf I shall his | crown | flourish.

Dr. R. Woodward.

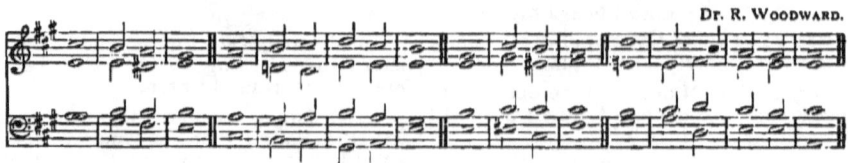

PSALM CXXXIII.—*Ecce, quam bonum!*

mf BEHOLD, how good and jóyful a | thing it | is : bréthren, to | dwell to- | gether ‧ in | unity !

2 It is like the precious ointment upon the head ✶ that ran dówn | unto ‧ the | beard : even unto Aaron's beard ✶ and went dówn to the | skirts | of his | clothing.

3 Like as the | dew of | Hermon : which féll up- | -on the | hill of | Sion.

4 For there the Lórd | promised ‧ his | blessing : ánd | life for | ever- | -more.

PSALM CXXXIV.—*Ecce nunc.*

mf BEHÓLD, now | praise the | Lord : áll ye | servants | of the | Lord ;

2 Ye that by night stand in the hóuse | of the | Lord : even in the cóurts of the | house of | our ' God.

3 Lift up your hánds | in the | sanctuary : ánd | praise | — the | Lord.

4 The Lórd that made | heaven and | earth : give thee | blessing | out of ‧ | Sion.

DAY XXVIII. MORNING (continued).

Lord MORNINGTON.

PSALM CXXXV.—*Laudate Nomen*

f O PRAISE the Lord * laud ye the Náme | of the | Lord : praise it, O' ye | servants | of the | Lord ;

2 Ye that stand in the hóuse | of the | Lord : in the cóurts of the | house of | our | God.

3 O praise the Lórd, for the | Lord is | gracious : O sing praises únto his | Name for | it is | lovely.

4 For why? the Lord hath chosen Jácob | unto · him· | -self : and I'srael | for his | own pos- | -session.

5 For I knów that the | Lord is | great : and that our Lórd | is a- | -bove all | gods.

6 Whatsoever the Lord pleased * that did he in héaven | and in | earth : and in the séa | and in | all deep | places.

7 He bringeth forth the clouds from the énds | of the | world : and sendeth forth lightnings with the rain * brínging the | winds | out of · his | treasures.

8 He smóte the | first-born · of | Egypt : bóth of | man | and | beast.

9 He hath sent tokens and wonders into the midst of thee, O' thou | land of | Egypt : upón | Pharaoh · and | all his | servants.

10 He smóte | divers | nations : ánd | slew | mighty | kings;

11 Sehon king of the Amorites * and O'g the | king of | Basan : ánd | all the | kingdoms · of | Canaan.

12 And gave their lánd to | be an | heritage : even an heritage únto | Isra- | el his | people.

13 Thy Name, O Lórd, en- | -dureth for | ever : so doth thy memorial, O Lord * from óne gener- | -ation | to an- | -other.

14 For the Lórd will a- | -venge his | people : ánd be | gracious | unto · his | servants.

15 As for the images of the heathen * théy are but | silver · and | gold : thé | work of | men's | hands.

16 They have | mouths and | speak not : éyes | have they | but they | see not.

17 They have éars, and | yet they | hear not : neither is there ány | breath | in their | mouths.

18 They that make them are lfke | unto | them : and so are all théy that | put their | trust in | them.

19 Praise the Lórd, ye | house of | Israel : práise the | Lord ye | house of | Aaron.

20 Praise the Lórd, ye | house of | Levi : ye that féar the | Lord | praise the | Lord.

2nd part. 21 Praised be the Lórd | out of | Sion : whó | dwelleth | at Je- | -rusalem.

PSALM CXXXVI.—*Confitemini.*

F. f O GIVE thanks unto the Lórd, for | he is | gracious : ánd his | mercy · en- | -dureth · for | ever.*

F 2 O give thanks unto the Gód of | all | gods : fór his|mercy·en-|-dureth ·forever.

3 O thank the Lórd of | all | lords : fór his | mercy · en- | -dureth · for | ever.

4 Who ónly | doeth · great | wonders :| fór his | mercy · en- | -dureth · for | ever.

5 Who by his excellent wísdom | made the | heavens : fór his | mercy · en- | dureth · for | ever.

6 Who laid out the éarth a- | -bove the | waters : fór his | mercy · en- | -dureth · for | ever.

7 Who hath máde | great | lights : fór his | mercy · en- | -dureth · for | ever.

8 The sún to | rule the | day : fór his | mercy · en- | dureth · for | ever.

9 The moon and the stárs to | govern · the | night : fór his | mercy · en- | -dureth · for | ever.

10 Who smote E´gypt | with their| first-born : fór his|mercy·en-|-dureth·forever.

11 And brought out I´srael | from a- | -mong them : fór his | mercy · en- | dureth · for | ever.

12 With a mighty hánd, and | stretch-ed-out | arm : fór his | mercy · en- | dureth · for | ever.

13 Who divided the Red Séa in | two | parts : fór his|mercy · en-|dureth·forlever;

14 And made Israel to gó through the | midst of | it : fór his | mercy · en- | dureth · for | ever.

15 But as for Pharaoh and his host | he overthréw them in the | Red | Sea fór his | mercy · en- | -dureth · for | ever.

16 Who led his péople | through the wilderness : fór his | mercy · en- | -dureth for | ever.

17 Who smóte | great | kings : fó his | mercy · en- | -dureth · for | ever·

18 Yea, and sléw | mighty | kings : fó his | mercy · en- | -dureth · for | ever ;

19 Sehon king | of the | Amorites : fó his | mercy · en- | -dureth · for | ever ;

20 And O´g the | king of | Basan fór his | mercy · en- | -dureth · for | ever

21 And gave away their lánd | for an heritage : fór his | mercy · en- | dureth for | ever.

22 Even for an heritage unto I´sra- | -e his | servant : fór his | mercy·en- | -dureth for | ever.

23 Who remembered us whén we were in | trouble : fór his | mercy · en-dureth · for | ever·

24 And hath delívered us | from our enemies : fór his | mercy · en- | -dureth for | ever.

25 Who giveth fóod to | all | flesh fór his | mercy · en- | -dureth · for | ever

26 O give thánks unto the | God of heaven : fór his | mercy · en- | -dureth for | ever.

27 O give thánks unto the | Lord of lords : fór his | mercy · en- | -dureth · for | ever.

* The second part of each verse to be sung *full*.

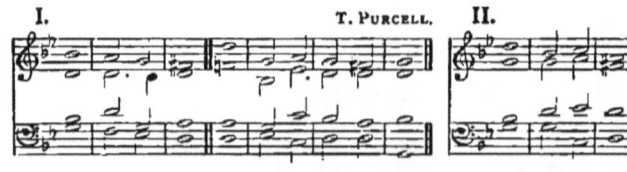

PSALM CXXXVII.—*Super flumina.*

p BY the waters of Babylon we sát | down and | wept : whén we re- | -membered| thee O | Sion.

2 As for our hárps, we | hanged · them | up : upón the | trees that | are there- | -in.

3 For they that led us away captive * required of us then a song and mélody |

in our | heaviness : Síng us | one · of the songs of | Sion.

4 How shall we síng the | Lord's song : ín | — a | strange | land ?

5 If I forget thée | O Je- | -rusalem let my right | hand for- | -get her cunning.

DAY XXVIII. EVENING (continued).

6 If I do not remember thee * let my
tongue cleave to the róof | of my | mouth :
yea, if I prefer not Je- | -rusalem | in my |
mirth.

7 Remember the children of Edom, O
Lord * in the dáy | of Je- | -rusalem ; how
they said, Down with it, dówn with it |
even | to the | ground.

8 O daughter of Bábylon | wasted ·
with | misery : yea, happy shall he be
that rewardeth thée, as | thou hast |
served | us.

9 Blessed shall he bé that | taketh ·
thy | children : and thróweth | them
a- | -gainst the | stones.

I. T. PURCELL.   II. J. TURLE.

PSALM CXXXVIII.—*Confitebor tibi.*

mf 1 WILL give thanks unto thee O
Lórd, with my | whole | heart : even
before the gods will I síng | praise | unto |
thee.

2 I will worship toward thy holy
temple, and praise thy Náme * because
of thy lóving- | -kindness · and | truth : for
thou hast magnified thy Náme, and thy |
Word a- | -bove | all things.

3 When I called upon thée, thou |
heardest | me : and endúedst my | soul
with | much | strength.

4 All the kings of the earth shall
práise | thee O | Lord : for they have
heard the | words | of thy | mouth.

5 Yea, they shall sing in the wáys | |
of the | Lord : that gréat is the | glory |
of the | Lord.

6 For though the Lord be high * yet
hath he respéct | unto · the | lowly : as
for the proud, he behóldeth | them a- |
far | off.

7 Though I walk in the midst of
trouble * yét shalt | thou re- | -fresh me :
thou shalt stretch forth thy hand upon
the furiousness of mine enemies * ánd
thy | right | hand shall | save me.

8 The Lord shall make good his
loving-kíndness | toward | me : yea, thy
mercy, O Lord endureth for ever *
despise not then the wórks | of thine |
own | hands.

DAY XXIX. MORNING.

Right Rev. Bishop TURTON.

Dec.   Can.

PSALM CXXXIX.—*Domine, probasti.*

mf O LORD, thou hast séarched me | |
out and | known me : thou knowest my
down-sitting and mine uprising * thou
understándest my| thoughts|long be-|-fore.

2 Thou art about my páth, and a- |
bout my | bed : ánd | spiest · out | all
my | ways.

3 For lo, there is not a wórd | in my |
tongue : but thou, O Lórd | knowest it |
alto- | -gether.

4 Thou hast fashioned me behínd |
and be- | -fore : ánd | laid thine | hand
up- | -on me.

5 Such knowledge is too wónderful
and | excellent | for me : I cánnot at- |
tain | unto | it.

6 Whither shall I gó then | from
thy | Spirit : or whither shall I | go then |
from thy | presence?

7 If I climb up into héaven | thou
art | there : if I go down to héll | thou
art | there | also.

8 If I take the wíngs | of the |
morning : and remain in the úttermost |
parts | of the | sea ;

9 Even there álso shall | thy hand |
lead me : ánd | thy right | hand shall |
hold me.

DAY XXIX. MORNING (continued).

Right Rev. Bishop Turton.

10 If I say, Peradventure the dárk-ness shall | cover | me : thén shall my | night be | turned · to | day.

11 Yea, the darkness is no darkness with thee * but the night is as cleár | as the | day : the darkness and líght to | thee are | both a- | -like.

12 Fór my | reins are | thine : thou hast cóvered me | in my | mother's | womb.

13 I will give thanks unto thee * for I am fearfully and wónder- | -fully | made : marvellous are thy works * and thát my | soul | knoweth · right | well.

14 My bónes are not | hid from | thee : though I be made secretly * and fáshioned be- | -neath | in the | earth.

15 Thine eyes did see my súbstance, yet | being · im- | perfect : and in thy bóok were | all my | members | written ;

16 Which dáy by | day were | fash-ioned : when as yét | there was | none of | them.

17 How dear are thy counsels únto me O | God : O how gréat | is the | sum of | them !

18 If I tell them * they are more in númber | than the | sand : when I wake úp | I am | present · with | thee.

19 Wilt thou not sláy the | wicked O | God : depart from mé, ye | blood-thirsty | men.

20 For they speak unrighteous- | -ly a- | -gainst thee : and thine énemies take thy | Name in | vain.

21 Do not I hate them, O Lórd, that hate | thee : and am not I grieved with thóse that | rise | up a- | -gainst thee ?

22 Yea, I háte | them right | sore : even as | though they | were mine | enemies.

23 Try me O God, and seek the ground | of my | heart : próve me, | and ex- | -amine · my | thoughts.

24 Look well if there be any wáy of wickedness | in me : and léad me in the way | ever- | -lasting.

J. Barnby

PSALM CXL.—*Eripe me, Domine.*

mp DELIVER me O Lórd, from the | evil | man : and presérve me | from the | wicked | man.

2 Who imagine míschief | in their | hearts : and stir up strífe | all the | day | long.

3 They have sharpened their tóngues | like a | serpent : ádder's | poison · is | under · their | lips.

4 Keep me O Lord, from the hánds of | the un- | -godly : preserve me from the wicked men * who are púrposed to | over- | -throw my | goings.

5 The proud have laid a snare for me * and spread a nét a- | -broad with | cords : yéa, and set | traps | in my | way.

6 I said unto the Lord, Thóu | art my | God : hear the vóice | of my | prayers O | Lord.

7 O Lord God, thou stréngth | of my | health : thou hast covered my héad | in the | day of | battle.

8 Let not the ungodly háve his de-sire O | Lord : let not his mischievous imagination prósper, | lest they | be too | proud.

9 Let the mischief of their own líps fall upón the | head of | them : thát compass | me a- | -bout.

10 Let hot burning cóals | fall up-on them : let them be cast into the fire and into the pit * that they néver | rise up a- | -gain.

11 A man full of words shall no prósper up- | -on the | earth : evil shall húnt the wicked | person · to | over-throw him.

12 Sure I am that the Lórd will a-venge the | poor : and maintáin the cause | of the | helpless.

mp 13 The righteous also shall give thánks | unto · thy | Name : and the júst shall con- | -tinue | in thy | sight.

DAY XXIX. EVENING.

PSALM CXLI.—*Domine, clamavi.*

mp LORD, I call upon thee * háste thee | ínto | me : and consider my vóice when | I cry | unto | thee.

F. 2 Let my prayer be set forth in thy sight | as the | incense : and let the lifting up of my hánds | be an | evening | sacrifice.

3 Set a watch, O Lórd, be- | -fore my | mouth : and kéep the | door | of my | lips.

4 O let not mine heart be inclined to any | evil | thing : let me not be occupied in ungodly works with the men that work wickedness * lest I éat of such | things as | please | them.

5 Let the righteous ráther | smite me | friendly : ánd | — re- | -prove | me.

6 But let not their precious bálms | break my | head : yea, I will práy | yet a- | -gainst their | wickedness.

7 Let their judges be overthrówn in | stony | places : that they may héar my | words for | they are | sweet.

8 Our bones lie scáttered be- | -fore the | pit : like as when one breaketh and héweth | wood up- | -on the | earth.

9 But mine eyes look unto thée, O | Lord | God : in thee is my trúst, O | cast not | out my | soul.

10 Keep me from the snare that théy have | laid for | me : and from the tráps | of the | wicked | doers.

11 Let the ungodly fall into their ówn | nets to- | -gether : ánd let | me | ever · es- | -cape them.

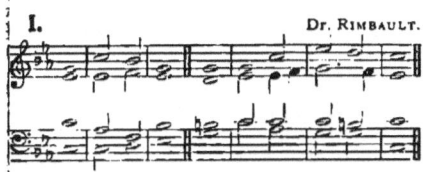 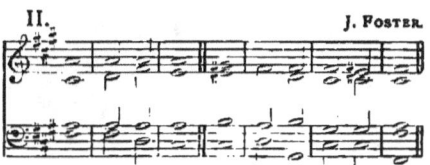

PSALM CXLII.—*Voce mea ad Dominum.*

mf I CRIED unto the Lórd | with my | voice : yea, even unto the Lórd did | I | make my | suppli- | -cation.

2 I poured out mý com- | -plaints be- | -fore him : ánd I shewed · him | of my | trouble.

3 When my spirit was in héaviness thou | knewest · my | path : in the way wherein I walked have they prívily | laid a | snare for | me.

4 I looked also upón my | right | hand : and sáw there was | no man | that would | know me.

5 I had no pláce to | flee | unto : and nó man | cared | for my | soul.

6 I cried unto thée, O | Lord and | said : Thou art my hope * and my portion in the | land | of the | living.

7 Consíder | my com- | -plaint : for I' am | brought | very | low.

8 O delíver me | from my | persecutors : fór they | are too | strong for | me.

9 Bring my soul out of prison * that I may give thánks | unto · thy | Name : which thing if thou wilt grant me * then shall the ríghteous re- | -sort | unto · my | company.

DAY XXIX. EVENING (continued).

I.

Dr. Stainer

Alternative Chant.

II.
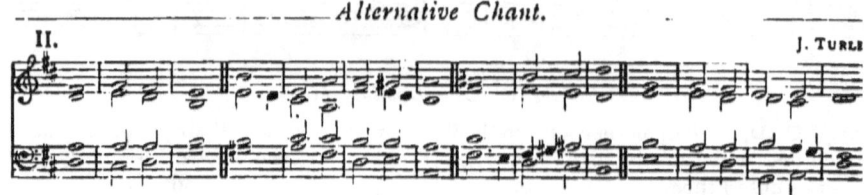
J. Turle

PSALM CXLIII.—*Domine, exaudi.*

mp HEAR my prayer O Lord * and con-sider | my de- | -sire : hearken unto me for thy | truth and | righteousness' | sake.

2 And enter not into júdgement | with thy | servant : for in thy sight shall | no man | living · be | justified.

3 For the enemy hath persecuted my soul * he hath smitten my life | down · to the | ground : he hath laid me in the dark-ness, * as the mén that | have been | long | dead.

4 Therefore is my spírit | vexed · with· | -in me : ánd my | heart with- | -in me · is | desolate.

5 Yet do I remember the time past * I múse upon | all thy | works : yea, I exer-cise myself in the | works | of thy | hands.

6 I stretch forth my hánds | unto | thee : my soul gaspeth unto thée | as a | thirsty | land.

7 Hear me O Lord, and that soon *

for my spírit | waxeth | faint : hide not thy face from me * lest I be like unto thém that go | down | into · the | pit.

8 O let me hear thy loving-kindness betimes in the morning * for in thée | i my | trust : shew thou me the way that should walk in * for I lift úp my | soul unto | thee.

9 Deliver me, O Lórd | from mine enemies : for I flée | unto | thee to | hide me.

10 Teach me to do the thing that pleaseth thee * for thóu | art my | God let thy loving Spirit lead me fórth | into the | land of | righteousness.

11 Quicken me O Lórd, for thy Name's | sake : and for thy righteousness sake bring my | soul | out of | trouble.

12 And of thy góodness | slay mine enemies : and destroy all them that vex my sóul, for | I am | thy | servant

---

DAY XXX. MORNING.

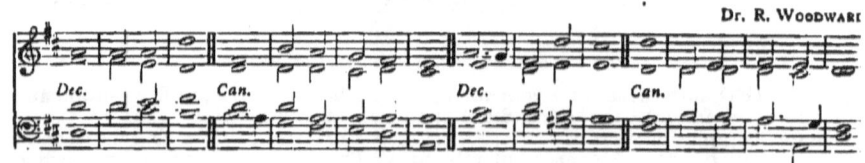
Dr. R. Woodward

PSALM CXLIV.—*Benedictus Dominus.*

mf BLESSED bé the | Lord my | strength : who teacheth my hands to wár | and my | fingers · to | fight;

2 My hope and my fortress, my castle and deliverer * my defénder in | whom I | trust : who subdueth my péople | that is | under | me.

3 Lord, what is man * that thou hast such respéct | unto | him : or the son of man * thát thou | so re- | -gardest | him

4 Man is like a | thing of | nought his time pásseth a- | -way | like a | shadow.

DAY XXX. MORNING (continued).

5 Bow thy heavens O Lórd, and I come I down : tóuch the I mountains · and I they shall I smoke.

6 Cast fórth thy I lightning · and I tear them : shoot óut thine I arrows I and con- I -sume them.

7 Send down thine hánd I from a- I bove : deliver me, and take me out of the great waters * fróm the I hand of I strange I children ;

8 Whose móuth I talketh · of I vanity : and their right hánd is a I right I hand of I wickedness.

9 I will sing a new sóng unto I thee O I God : and sing praises unto thée upon a I ten- I -stringed I lute.

10 Thou hast given víctory I unto I kings : and hast delivered David thy servant fróm the I peril I of the I sword.

11 Save me, and deliver me from the hánd I of strange I children : whose mouth talketh of vanity * and their right hánd is a I right I hand · of in- I -iquity.

12 That our sons may grow úp as the I young I plants : and that our daughters may be as the pólished I corners I of the I temple.

13 That our garners may be full and plenteous with áll I manner · of I store : that our sheep may bring forth thousands * and tén I thousands I in our I streets.

14 That our oxen may be strong to labour * that thére be I no de- I -cay : no leading into captivity * and nó com- I plaining I in our I streets.

2nd part 15 Happy are the people that áre in I such a I case : yea, blessed are the people who háve the I Lord I for their I God.

Dr. W. CROTCH.

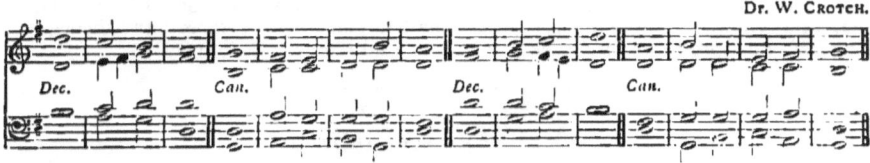

PSALM CXLV.—*Exaltabo te, Deus.*

mf I WILL magnify thée O I God my I King : and I will práise thy I Name for I ever · and I ever.

2 Every day will I give thánks I unto I thee : and práise thy I Name for I ever · and I ever.

3 Great is the Lord, and marvellous * wórthy I to be I praised : there ís no I end I of his I greatness.

4 One generation shall praise thy wórks I unto · an- I -other : ánd de- I clare I thy I power.

5 As for me, I will be tálking I of thy I worship : thy glóry, thy I praise and I wondrous I works;

6 So that men shall speak of the míght of thy I marvellous I acts : and I will álso I tell I of thy I greatness.

7 The memorial of thine abundant kíndness I shall be I shewed : and mén shall I sing I of thy I righteousness.

8 The Lórd is I gracious · and I merciful : long-súffering, I and of I great I goodness.

9 The Lord is loving únto I every I man : and his mércy is I over I all his I works.

10 All thy works práise I thee O I Lord : and thy sáints give I thanks I unto I thee.

11 They shew the glóry I of thy I kingdom : ánd I talk I of thy I power ;

12 That thy power, thy glory, and míghtiness I of thy I kingdom : míght be I known I unto I men.

13 Thy kingdom is an éver- I -lasting I kingdom : and thy domínion en- I -dureth · through- I -out all I ages.

14 The Lord uphóldeth all I such as I fall : and lifteth úp all I those I that are I down.

15 The eyes of all wáit upon I thee O I Lord : and thou gívest them their I meat in I due I season.

16 Thou ópenest I thine I hand : and fíllest I all things I living · with I plenteousness.

17 The Lord is ríghteous in I all his I ways : ánd I holy · in I all his I works.

18 The Lord is nigh unto all thém that I call up- I -on him : yea áll such as I call up- I -on him I faithfully.

19 He will fulfil the desíre of I them that I fear him : he also will héar their I cry I and will I help them.

20 The Lord presérveth all I them that I love him : but scáttereth a- I -broad I all · the un- I -godly.

2nd part 21 My mouth shall speak the práise I of the I Lord : and let all flesh give thanks unto his hóly I Name for I ever · and I ever.

DAY XXX. MORNING (*continued*).

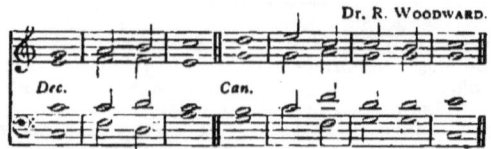
Dr. R. Woodward.

PSALM CXLVI.—*Lauda, anima mea.*

mf PRAISE the Lord, O my soul * while I lĭve will I I praise the I Lord : yea, as long as I have any being * I will sĭng I praises I unto · my I God.

2 O put not your trust in princes * nor in áný I child of I man : fŏr there is I no I help in I them.

3 For when the breath of man goeth forth * he shall túrn again I to his I earth : and thĕn I all his I thoughts I perish.

4 Blessed is he that hath the God of Jácob I for his I help : and whose hópe is I in the I Lord his I God ;

5 Who made heaven and earth * the sea, and áll that I therein I is : whŏ I keepeth · his I promise · for I ever ;

6 Who helpeth them to rĭght that I suffer I wrong : whŏ I feed- I -eth the I hungry.

7 The Lord looseth mĕn I out of I prison : the Lŏrd giveth I sight I to the I blind.

8 The Lord helpeth thĕm I that are I fallen : the Lŏrd I careth I for the I righteous.

9 The Lord careth for the strangers * he defendeth the fáther- I -less and I widow : as for the way of the ungódly, he I turneth · it I upside I down.

10 The Lord thy God O Sion, shall be Kĭng for I ever- I -more : ănd through- out I all I gener- I -ations.

DAY XXX. EVENING.

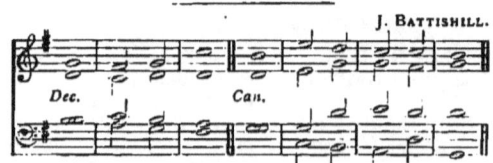
J. Battishill.

PSALM CXLVII.—*Laudate Dominum.*

F.f O PRAISE the Lord * for it is a good thing to sing práises I unto · our I God : yea, a joyful and pleasant thĭng it I is to I be I thankful.

F. 2 The Lord doth búild I up Je- I rusalem : and gather togéther the I out- I casts of I Israel.

3 He healeth thóse that are I broken · in I heart : and gĭveth I medicine · to I heal their I sickness.

4 He telleth the nŭmber I of the I stars : and cálleth them I all I by their I names.

5 Great is our Lord * and gréat I is I his I power : yea, and his I wisdom I is I infinite.

6 The Lŏrd setteth I up the I meek I and bringeth the ungódly I down I to the I ground.

7 O sing unto the Lŏrd with I thanks- I giving : sing praises upŏn the I harp I ŭnto · our I God.

8 Who covereth the heaven with clouds * and prepareth ráin I for the I earth : and maketh the grass to grow upon the mountains * and hérb I for the I use of I men.

9 Who giveth fŏdder I unto · the cattle : and feedeth the yŏung I ravens · that I call up- I -on him.

10 He hath no pleasure in the strĕngth I of an I horse : neither delĭghteth I he in I any · man's I legs.

11 But the Lord's delĭght is in I them that I fear him : and pŭt their I trust I in his I mercy.

12 Praise the Lŏrd I O Je- I -rusalem : práise thy I God I O I Sion.

13 For he hath made fast the bǎrs I of thy I gates : ănd hath I blessed · thy I children · with- I -in thee.

14 He maketh pĕace I in thy I borders : and fílleth thee I with the I flour of I wheat.

DAY XXX. EVENING (continued). 109

15 He sendeth forth his command‐ | ment up‐ | ‐on | earth : and his wórd | runneth | very | swiftly.
16 He gíveth | snow like | wool : and scáttereth the | hoar‐ | ‐frost like | ashes.
17 He casteth fórth his | ice like | morsels : who is áble | to a‐ | ‐bide his | frost ?

18 He sendeth out his wórd, and | melteth | them : he bloweth with his | wínd | and the | waters | flow.
19 He sheweth his wórd | unto | Jacob : his statutes and órdinances | unto | Isra‐ | ‐el.
20 He hath not dealt só with | any | nation : neither have the héathen | knowledge | of his | laws.

J. BATTISHILL.

PSALM CXLVIII.—*Laudate Dominum.*

O PRÁISE the | Lord of | heaven : práise | — him | in the | height.
2 Praise him, áll ye | angels · of | his : práise | — him | all his | host.
3 Práise him, | sun and | moon : práise him, | all ye | stars and | light.
4 Práise him, | all ye | heavens : and ye wáters that | are a‐ | ‐bove the | heavens.
5 Let them praise the Náme | of the | Lord : for he spake the word, and they were made ✻ he commánded, | and they | were cre‐ | ‐ated.
6 He hath made them fást for | ever · and | ever : he hath given them a láw | which shall | not be | broken.
7 Praise the Lórd up‐ | ‐on | earth : yé | dragons · and | all | deeps ;

8 Fire and háil | snow and | vapours : wínd and | storm ful‐ | ‐filling · his | word ;
9 Móuntains and | all | hills : frúitful | trees and | all | cedars ;
10 Béasts and all | cattle : wórms | — and | feathered | fowls ;
11 Kings of the éarth and | all | people : princes and áll | judges | of the | world ;
12 Young men and maidens, old men and children ✻ praise the Náme | of the | Lord : for his Name only is excellent ✻ and his práise a‐ | ‐bove | heaven and | earth.
13 He shall exalt the horn of his people ✻ áll his | saints shall | praise him | even the children of Israel ✻ éven the | people · that | serveth | him.

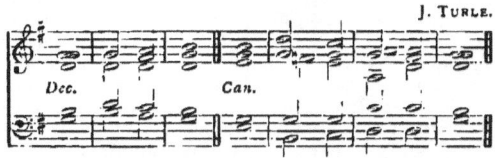
J. TURLE.

PSALM CXLIX.—*Cantate Domino.*

ƒ O SING unto the Lórd a | new | song : let the cóngre‐ | ‐gation · of | saints | praise him.
2 Let Israel rejóice in | him that | made him : and let the children of Síon be | joyful | in their | King.
3 Let them praise his Náme | in the | dance : let them sing praises únto | him with | tabret · and | harp.
4 For the Lord hath pléasure | in his | people : ánd | helpeth · the | meek‐ | hearted.

5 Let the sáints be | joyful · with | glory : lét them re‐ | ‐joice | in their | beds.
6 Let the praises of Gód be | in their | mouth : and a twó‐edged | sword | in their | hands ;
7 To be avénged | of the | heathen · ánd | to re‐ | ‐buke the | people ;
8 To bínd their | kings in | chains : ánd their | nobles · with | links of | iron.
9 That they may be avenged of thém | as it · is | written : Súch | honour · have | all his | saints

DAY XXX. EVENING (continued).

PSALM CL.—*Laudate Dominum.*

ff O PRAISE Gód | in his | 'holiness : práise him in the | firmament | of his | power.

2 Práise him in his | noble | acts : praise him according | to his | excellent | greatness.

3 Praise him in the sóund | of the | trumpet : práise him up· | ·on the | lute and | harp.

4 Práise him in the | cymbals · and | dances : praise him up· | ·on the | strings and | pipe.

5 Praise him upon the wéll- | ·tuned | cymbals : práise him up· | ·on the | loud | cymbals.

F. 6 Let évery thing | that hath | breath· práise | — — | — the | Lord.

DAY XXXI. MORNING.

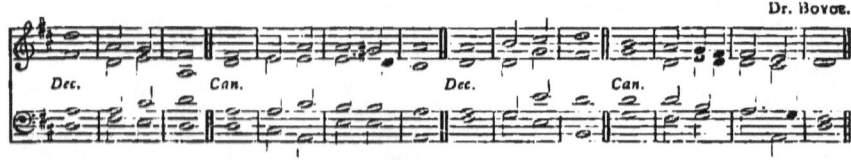

PSALM CXLIV.—*Benedictus Dominus.*

mf BLESSED bé the | Lord my | strength : who teacheth my hands to wár | and my | fingers · to | fight ;

2 My hope and my fortress, my castle and deliverer * my defénder in | whom I | trust : who subdueth my péople | that is | under | me.

3 Lord, what is man * that thou hast such respéct unto | him : or the son of man * thát thou | so re- | ·gardest | him ?

4 Man is líke a | thing of | nought : his time pásseth a- | ·way | like a | shadow.

5 Bow thy heavens O Lórd, and | come | down : tóuch the | mountains · and | they shall | smoke.

6 Cast fórth thy | lightning · and | tear them : shoot óut thine | arrows | and con· | ·sume them.

7 Send down thine hánd | from a- | bove : deliver me, and take me out of the great waters * from the | hand of | strange | children ;

8 Whose móuth | talketh · of | vanity : and their right hánd is a | right | hand of | wickedness.

9 I will sing a new sóng unto | thee O | God : and sing praises unto théc upon a | ten- | ·stringed | lute.

10 Thou hast given víctory | unto kings : and hast delivered David thy servant fróm the | peril | of the | sword.

11 Save me, and deliver me from the hánd of | strange | children : whose mouth talketh of vanity * and their right hánd is a | right | hand · of in· | ·iquity.

12 That our sons may grow úp as the | young | plants : and that our daughters may be as the pólished | corners | of the | temple.

13 That our garners may be full and plénteous with áll | manner · | of | store : that our sheep may bring forth thousands * and tén | thousands | in our | streets.

14 That our oxen may be strong to labour * that thére be | no de· | ·cay : no leading into captivity * and nó com- | plaining | in our | streets.

Dul pour. 15 Happy are the people that áre in | such a | case : yea, blessed are the people who háve the | Lord | for their | God.

DAY XXXI. MORNING (continued).

J. Battishill.

PSALM CXLV.—*Exaltabo te, Deus.*

mf I WILL magnify thée O | God my | King : and I will práise thy | Name for | ever · and | ever.

2 Every day will I give thánks | unto | thee : and práise thy | Name for | ever · and | ever.

3 Great is the Lord, and marvellous * wórthy | to be | praised : there ís no | end | of his | greatness.

4 One generation shall praise thy wórks | unto · an- | -other : ánd de- | clare | thy | power.

5 As for me, I will be tálking | of thy | worship : thy glóry, thy | praise and | wondrous | works;

6 So that men shall speak of the míght of thy | marvellous | acts : and I will álso | tell | of thy | greatness.

7 The memorial of thine abundant kíndness | shall be | shewed : and mén shall | sing | of thy | righteousness.

8 The Lórd is | gracious · and | merciful : long-súffering, | and of | great | goodness.

9 The Lord is loving únto | every | man : and his mércy is | over | all his|works.

10 All thy works práise | thee O | Lord : and thy sáints give | thanks | unto | thee.

11 They shew the glóry | of thy | kingdom : ánd | talk | of thy | power;

12 That thy power, thy glory, and míghtiness | of thy | kingdom : míght be | known | unto | men.

13 Thy kingdom is an éver- | -lasting | kingdom : and thy domínion en- | -dureth · through- | -out all | ages.

14 The Lord uphóldeth all | such as | fall : and lífteth úp all | those | that are | down.

15 The eyes of all wáit upon | thee O | Lord : and thou gívest them their | meat in | due | season.

16 Thou ópenest | thine | hand : and fíllest | all things | living · with | plenteousness.

17 The Lord is ríghteous in | all his | ways : ánd | holy · in | all his | works.

18 The Lord is nigh unto all thém that | call up- | -on him : yea áll such as | call up- | -on him | faithfully.

19 He will fulfil the desíre of | them that | fear him : he also will héar their | cry | and will | help them.

20 The Lord presérveth all | them that | love him : but scáttereth a- | -broad | all · the un- | -godly.

21 My mouth shall speak the práise | of the | Lord : and let all flesh give thanks unto his hóly | Name for | ever · and | ever.

Dr. W. Turner.

PSALM CXLVI.—*Lauda, anima mea.*

mf PRAISE the Lord, O my soul * while I live will I | praise the | Lord : yea, as long as I have any being * I will síng | praises | unto · my | God.

2 O put not your trust in princes * nor in ány | child of | man : fór there is | no | help in | them.

3 For when the breath of man goeth forth * he shall túrn again | to his | earth : and thén | all his | thoughts | perish.

4 Blessed is he that hath the God of Jácob | for his | help : and whose hópe is | in the | Lord his | God ;

5 Who made heaven and earth * the sea, and áll that | therein | is : whó | keepeth · his | promise · for | ever ;

6 Who helpeth them to ríght that | suffer | wrong : whó | feed- | -eth the | hungry.

7 The Lord loosenth mén | out of | prison : the Lórd giveth | sight | to the | blind.

8 The Lord helpeth thém | that are | fallen : the Lórd | careth | for the | righteous.

9 The Lord careth for the strangers * he defendeth the fáther- | -less and | widow : as for the way of the ungódly, he | turneth · it | upside | down.

10 The Lord thy God O Sion, shall be Kíng for | ever- | -more : ánd through- | -out | all | gener- | -ations.

DAY XXXI. EVENING.

PSALM CXLVII.—*Laudate Dominum.*

F. ƒ O PRAISE the Lord ✻ for it is a good thing to sing práises | unto · our | God : yea, a joyful and pleasant thing it | is to | be | thankful.

F. 2 The Lord doth búild | up Je- | rusalem : and gather togéther the | out- casts of | Israel.

3 He healeth thóse that are | broken · in | heart : and gíveth | medicine · to | heal their | sickness.

4 He telleth the númber | of the | stars : and cálleth them | all | by their | names.

5 Great is our Lord ✻ and gréat | is his | power : yéa, and his | wisdom | is | infinite.

6 The Lórd setteth | up the | meek : and bringeth the ungódly | down | to the | ground.

7 O sing unto the Lórd with | thanks- | -giving : sing praises upón the | harp | unto · our | God.

8 Who covereth the heaven with clouds ✻ and prepareth ráin | for the | earth : and maketh the grass to grow upon the mountains ✻ and hérb | for the | use of | men.

9 Who giveth fódder | unto · the | cattle : and feedeth the yóung | ravens · that | call up- | -on him.

10 He hath no pleasure in the stréngth | of an | horse : neither delíghteth | he in | any · man's | legs.

11 But the Lord's delíght is in | them that | fear him : and pút their | trust | in his | mercy.

12 Praise the Lórd | O Je- | -rusalem : práise thy | God | O | Sion.

13 For he hath made fast the bárs | of thy | gates : ánd hath | blessed · thy | children · with- | -in thee.

14 He maketh péace | in thy | borders : and fílleth thee | with the | flour of | wheat.

15 He sendeth forth his commánd- ment up- | -on | earth : and his wórd | runneth | very | swiftly.

16 He gíveth | snow like | wool : and scáttereth the | hoar- | -frost like | ashes.

17 He casteth fórth his | ice like | morsels : who is áble | to a- | -bide his | frost ?

18 He sendeth out his wórd, and | melteth | them : he bloweth with his wind | and the | waters | flow.

19 He sheweth his wórd | unto | Jacob : his statutes and órdinances | unto | Isra- | -el.

20 He hath not dealt só with | any | nation : neither have the héathen | know- ledge | of his | laws.

PSALM CXLVIII.—*Laudate Dominum.*

ƒ O PRÁISE the | Lord of | heaven : práise | — him | in the | height.

2 Praise him, áll ye | angels · of | his : práise | — him | all his | host.

3 Práise him, | sun and | moon : práise him, | all ye | stars and | light.

4 Práise him, | all ye | heavens : and ye wáters that | are a- | -bove the | heavens.

5 Let them praise the Náme | of the | Lord : for he spake the word, and they were made ✻ he commánded, | and they | were cre- | -ated.

6 He hath made them fást for | ever · and ever : he hath given them a láw | which shall | not be | broken.

7 Praise the Lórd up- | -on | **earth :** yé | dragons · and | all | deeps ;

DAY XXXI. EVENING *(continued).* 113

8 Fire and háil | snow and | vapours :|
wínd and | storm ful- | -filling . his | word ;|
9 Móuntains and | all | hills : frúitful |
trees and | all | cedars ;
10 Béasts and | all | cattle : wórms | |
— and | feathered | fowls ;
11 Kings of the éarth and | all |
people : princes and áll | judges | of the |
world ;

12 Young men and maidens, old men
and children ✶ praise the Náme | of the |
Lord : for his Name only is excellent ✶
and his práise a- | -bove | heaven and |
earth.
^{2nd}_{part} 13 He shall exalt the horn of his
people ✶ áll his | saints shall | praise him :
even the children of Israel ✶ éven the |
people . that | serveth | him.

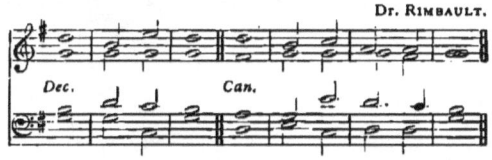

Dr. RIMBAULT.

PSALM CXLIX.—*Cantate Domino.*

f O SING unto the Lórd a | new |
song : let the cóngre- | -gation . of | saints |
praise him.
2 Let Israel rejóice in | him that |
made him : and let the children of Síon
be | joyful | in their | King.
3 Let them praise his Náme | in the |
dance : let them sing praises únto | him
with | tabret . and | harp.
4 For the Lord hath pléasure | in
his | people : ánd | helpeth . the | meek- |
hearted.

5 Let the sáints be | joyful . with |
glory : lét them re- | -joice | in their | beds.
6 Let the praises of Gód be | in their |
mouth : and a twó-edged | sword | in
their | hands ;
7 To be avénged | of the | heathen :
ánd | to re- | -buke the | people ;
8 To bínd their | kings in | chains :
ánd their | nobles . with | links of | iron.
9 That they may be avenged of thém |
as it . is | written : Súch | honour . have |
all his | saints.

P. HUMPHREYS.

PSALM CL.—*Laudate Dominum.*

ff O PRAISE Gód | in his | holiness :
práise him in the | firmament | of his |
power.
2 Práise him in his | noble | acts :
praise him accórding | to his | excellent |
greatness.
3 Praise him in the sóund | of the |
trumpet : práise him up- | -on the | lute
and | harp.

4 Práise him in the | cymbals . and |
dances : práise him up- | -on the | strings
and | pipe.
5 Praise him upon the wéll- | -tuned |
cymbals : práise him up- | -on the | loud |
cymbals.
F. 6 Let évery thing | that hath | breath :
práise | — — | — the | Lord.

PROPER PSALMS

ON CERTAIN DAYS.

FIRST SUNDAY IN ADVENT. MORNING.

Rev. W. Tucker.

PSALM VIII.—*Domine, Dominus noster.*

f O LORD our Governour ✷ how excel- | lent is thy Náme in | all the | world : thou that hast sét thy | glory · a- | -bove the | heavens.

2 Out of the mouth of very babes and sucklings hast thou ordained strength ✷ becáuse | of thine | enemies : that thou mightest stíll the | enemy | and · the a- | -venger.

3 For I will consider thy heavens ✷ even the wórks | of thy | fingers : the moon and the stárs | which thou | hast or- | -dained.

4 What is man, that thóu art | mind- ful · of | him : and the són of man | that thou | visitest | him?

5 Thou madest him lówer | than the | angels : to crówn | him with | glory · and | worship.

6 Thou makest him to have dominion of the wórks | of thy | hands : and thou hast put all things ín sub- | -jection | under · his | feet;

7 A´ll | sheep and | oxen : yéa and the | beasts | of the | field;

8 The fowls of the air, and the físhes | of the | sea : and whatsoever walketh throúgh the | paths | of the | seas.

9 O´ | Lord our | Governour : how excellent ís thy | Name in | all the | world |

FIRST SUNDAY IN ADVENT. MORNING (*continued*). 115

PSALM L.—*Deus deorum.*

f THE Lord, even the most mighty | God hath | spoken : and called the world, from the rising up of the sun * únto the | going | down there- | -of.

2 Out of Síon hath | God ap- | peared : ín | per- | -fect | beauty.

3 Our God shall cóme and shall | not keep | silence : there shall go before him a consuming fire * and a mighty tempest shall be | stirred . up | round a- | -bout him.

4 He shall call the héaven | from a- | -bove : and the éarth, that | he may | judge his | people.

5 Gather my saints togéther | unto | me : those that have made a cóve- | -nant with | me with | sacrifice.

6 And the héavens shall de- | -clare his | righteousness : fór | God is | judge him- | -self.

7 Hear, O my péople and | I will | speak : I myself will testify against thee O Israel * for I am Gód | even | thy | God.

8 I will not reprove thee because of thy sacrifices * or fór thy | burnt- | -offerings : becáuse they | were not ! alway . be- | -fore me.

9 I will take no búllock | out of . thine | house : nór | he-goat | out of . thy | folds.

10 For all the béasts of the | forest . are | mine : and so are the cáttle up- | -on a | thousand | hills.

11 I know all the fówls up- | -on the | mountains : and the wild béasts of the | field are | in my | sight.

12 If I be hungry, I° will | not tell | thee : for the whole world is míne, and | all that | is there- | -in.

13 Thinkest thou that Í will | eat bulls' | flesh : ánd | drink the | blood of | goats ?

14 Offer unto Gód | thanks- | -giving : and pay thy vóws | unto . the | most | Highest.

15 And call upon mé in the | time of | trouble : so will I héar thee and | thou shalt | praise | me.

16 But unto the ungódly | said | God : Why dost thou preach my laws * and tákest my | covenant | in thy | mouth ;

17 Whereas thou hátest to | be re- | formed : ánd hast | cast my | words behind thee ?

18 When thou sawest a thief * thou conséntedst | unto | him : and hast béen par- | -taker | with . the a- | -dulterers.

19 Thou hast lét thy | mouth speak | wickedness : and with thy tóngue thou hast | set | forth de- | -ceit.

20 Thou satest, and spákest a- | -gainst thy | brother : yea, and hast slándered thine | own | mother's | son.

21 These things hast thou done, and I held my tongue * and thou thoughtest wickedly that I am even súch a one | as thy- | -self : but I will reprove thee * and set befóre thee the | things that | thou hast | done.

22 O consider this, yé that for- | -get | God : lest I pluck you away * and there be nóne | to de- | -líver | you.

23 Whoso offereth me thanks and praise he | honoureth | me : and to him that ordereth his conversation ríght will I | shew the . sal- | -vation . of | God.

FIRST SUNDAY IN ADVENT. EVENING.

I.

W. RUSSELL.

Alternative Chant.

II.
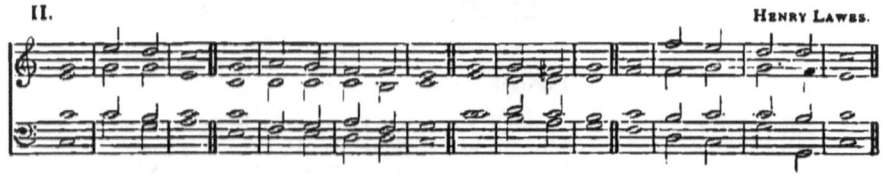
HENRY LAWES.

PSALM XCVI.—*Cantate Domino.*

ƒ O SING unto the Lórd a | new | song : sing unto the Lórd | all the | whole | earth.

2 Sing unto the Lórd and | praise his | Name : be telling of his sal- | -vation · from | day to | day.

3 Declare his hónour | unto · the | heathen : and his wónders | unto | all | people.

4 For the Lord is great ✱ and cannot wórthi- | -ly be | praised : he is móre to be | feared · than | all | gods.

5 As for all the gods of the héathen, | they are · but | idols : but it ís the | Lord that | made the | heavens.

6 Glory and wórship | are be- | -fore him : power and | honour · are | in his | sanctuary.

7 Ascribe unto the Lord ✱ O ye kindreds | of the | people : ascribe unto the Lórd | worship | and | power.

8 Ascribe unto the Lord the honour dúe | unto · his | Name : bring présents and | come | into · his | courts.

9 O worship the Lórd in the | beauty · of | holiness : let the whole éarth | stand in | awe of | him.

10 Tell it out among the héathen that the | Lord is | King : and that it is he who hath made the round world so fast ✱ that it cannot be moved ✱ and how that hé shall | judge the | people | righteously.

11 Let the heavens rejóice and let the | earth be | glad : let the sea make a nóise, and | all that | therein | is.

12 Let the field be jóyful and | all that · is | in it : then shall all the trees of the wóod re- | -joice be- | -fore the | Lord.

2nd part 13 For he cometh, for he cómeth to | judge the | earth : and with righteousness to judge the wórld and the | people | with his | truth.

FIRST SUNDAY IN ADVENT. EVENING (*continued*). 117

I. Sir G. A. Macfarren.   II. Charles King.

PSALM XCVII.—*Dominus regnavit.*

f THE Lord is King * the éarth may be | glad there- | -of: yea, the multitude of the ísles | may be | glad there- | -of.

2 Clouds and dárkness are | round a- | -bout him: righteousness and judgement are the hábit- | -ation | of his | seat.

3 There shall gó a | fire be- | -fore him: and burn úp his | ene · mies on | every | side.

4 His lightnings gave shíne | unto · the | world: the earth I saw it · and I was a- | -fraid.

5 The hills melted like wax * at the présence | of the | Lord: at the presence of the Lórd | of the | whole | earth.

6 The héavens have de- | -clared · his | righteousness: and áll the | people · have | seen his | glory.

7 Confounded be all they that wor- ship carved images * and that delíght in | vain | gods: wórship | him | all ye | gods.

8 Sion héard of it | and re- | -joiced: and the daughters of Judah were glad * becáuse of thy | judgements | O | Lord.

9 For thou Lord, art higher than áll that are | in the | earth: thou art exálted | far a- | -bove all | gods.

10 O ye that love the Lord * see that ye hate the thíng | which is | evil: the Lord preserveth the souls of his saints * he shall deliver them fróm the | hand of | the un- | -godly.

11 There is sprung up a líght | for the | righteous: and joyful gládness for | such as | are true- | -hearted.

12 Rejóice in the | Lord ye | righteous: and give thanks * fór a re- | -membrance | of his | holiness.

K

CHRISTMAS DAY. MORNING

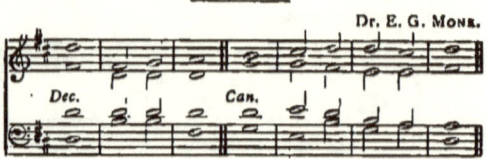
Dr. E. G. Monk.

PSALM XIX.—*Cœli enarrant.*

THE heavens decláre the | glory · of | | God : and the fírmament' | sheweth · his | handy- | -work.

2 One dáy | telleth · an- | -other : and one níght | certi- | -fíeth · an- | -other.

3 There is neíther | speech nor | language : but their | voices · are | heard a- | -mong them.

4 Their sound is gone óut into | all | lands : and their wórds into the | ends | of the | world.

5 In them hath he set a tábernacle | for the | sun : which cometh forth as a bridegroom out of his chamber * and re- jóiceth as a | giant · to | run his | course.

6 It goeth forth from the uttermost part of the heaven * and runneth about unto the énd of | it a- | -gain : and there is nothing híd | from the | heat there- | -of.

7 The law of the Lord is an undefiled láw, con- | -verting · the | soul ; the testimony of the Lord is sure * and gíveth | wisdom | unto · the | simple.

8 The statutes of the Lord are right and re- | -joice the | heart : the command-ment of the Lord is pure * and gíveth | light | unto · the | eyes.

9 The fear of the Lord is cléan and en- | -dureth · for | ever : the judgements of the Lord are trúe, and | rightéous | alto- | -gether.

10 More to be desired are they than gold * yéa than | much fine | gold : sweeter also than | honey | and the | honey-comb.

11 Moreover, by thém is thy | servant | taught : and in keéping of them | there is | great re- | -ward.

mp 12 Who can téll how | oft · he of- | -fendeth : O cleanse thou mé | from my | secret | faults.

13 Keep thy servant also from presumptuous sins * lest they get the do-mínion | over | me : so shall | be unde-filed, and ínnocent | from the | great of- | -fence.

14 Let the words of my mouth * and the meditátion | of my | heart : be álway ac- | -ceptable | in thy | sight,

15 O' | — | Lord : my | strength and | my re- | -deemer.

Verses 1 to 10. Rev. Sir F. Ouseley.

Verse 11 to end. Sir G. A. Macfarren.

PSALM XLV.—*Eructavit cor meum.*

mf MY heart is indíting of a | good | | matter : I speak of the things which I' have | made | unto · the | King.

2 My tóngue | is the | pen : óf | — a | ready | writer.

3 Thou art faírer thán the | children · of | men : ful' of grace are thy lips * because Gód hath | blessed | thee for | ever.

4 Gird thee with thy sword upon thy thígh O | thou most | Mighty : accórding to thy | worsnip | and re- | -nown.

5 Good lúck have thou | with thine | honour : ride on, because of the word of truth * of meekness and righteousness * and thy right hánd shall | teach thee | terrible | things.

CHRISTMAS DAY. MORNING (*continued*). 119

6 Thy arrows are very sharp ∗ and the people shall be subdúed | unto | thee : even in the mídst a-|-mong the | King's|enemies.

7 Thy seat, O Gód en- | -dureth · for | ever : the sceptre of thy kíngdom | is a | right | sceptre.

8 Thou hast loved ríghteousness and | hated · in- | -iquity : wherefore God, even thy God ∗ hath anointed thee with the óil of | gladness · a- | -bove thy | fellows.

9 All thy garments smell of mýrrh | aloes · and | cassia : out of the ivory palaces ∗ wherebý | they have | made thee | glad.

10 Kings' daughters were among thy hónour- | -able | women : upon thy right hand did stand the queen in a vesture of gold ∗ wróught a- | -bout with | divers | colours.

11 Hearken, O daughter, and con-síder, in- | -cline thine | ear : forget also thine own péople | and thy | father's | house.

12 So shall the King have pleasure | in thy | beauty : for he is thy Lord Gód, and | worship | thou | him.

13 And the daughter of Tyre shall be thére | with a | gift : like as the rich also among the people ∗ shall máke their | suppli- | -cation · be- | -fore thee.

14 The King's daughter is all glóri- | ous with- | -in : her clóthing | is of | wrought | gold.

15 She shall be brought unto the Kíng in | raiment · of | needlework : the virgins that be her fellows shall bear her company ∗ and shall be | brought | unto | thee.

16 With joy and gládness shall | they be | brought : and shall énter | into · the | King's | palace.

17 Instead of thy fáthers thou | shalt have | children : whom thou máyest make | princes · in | all | lands.

18 I will remember thy Name from one generátion | to an- | -other : therefore shall the people give thanks unto thée | world with- | -out | end.

J. TURLE.

Dec.   Can.

PSALM LXXXV.—*Benedixisti, Domine.*

mp LORD, thou art become grácious | unto · thy | land : thou hast turned awáy the cap- | -tivi- | -ty of | Jacob.

2 Thou hast forgiven the offénce | of thy | people : ánd | covered | all their | sins.

3 Thou hast taken awáy all | thy dis- | -pleasure : and turned thysélf from thy | wrathful | indig- | -nation.

4 Turn us thén O | God our | Saviour : and lét thine | anger | cease | from us.

5 Wilt thou be displéased at | us for | ever : and wilt thou stretch out thy wrath from óne gener- | -ation | to an- | -other ?

6 Wilt thou not turn agáin, and | quicken | us : that thy péople | may re- | joice in | thee ?

7 Shéw us thy | mercy · O | Lord : ánd | grant us | thy sal- | -vation.

8 I will hearken what the Lord God will sáy con- | -cerning | me : for he shall speak peace unto his people and to his saints ∗ thát they | turn | not a- | gain.

9 For his salvation is nígh | them that | fear him : that glóry may | dwell | in our | land.

10 Mercy and trúth are | met to- | gether : righteousness and | peace have | kissed · each | other.

11 Truth shall flóurish | out · of the | earth : and ríghteousness hath | looked | down from | heaven.

12 Yea, the Lord shall shéw | loving- | kindness : ánd our | land shall | give her | increase.

13 Ríghteousness shall | go be- | -fore him : and he shall diréct his | going | in the | way.

CHRISTMAS DAY. EVENING.

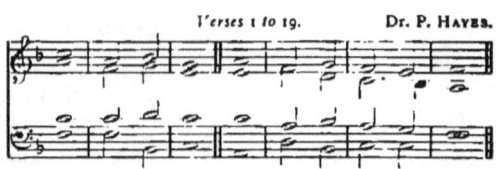

PSALM LXXXIX.—*Misericordias Domini.*

F.mf MY song shall be alway of the loving-kindness | of the | Lord : with my mouth will I ever be shewing thy truth ∗ from óne gener- | -ation | to an- | -other.

F. 2 For I have said, Mercy shall be sét | up for | ever : thy trúth shalt thou | stablish | in the | heavens.

3 I have made a cóvenant | with my | chosen : I have swórn | unto | David · my | servant ;

4 Thy séed will I ! stablish · for | ever : and set up thy throne from óne gener- | -ation | to an- | -other.

5 O Lord, the very heavens shall práise thy | wondrous | works : and thy truth in the cóngre- | -gation | of the | saints.

6 For who is hé a- | -mong the | clouds : that sháll be com- | -pared | unto · the | Lord ?

7 And what is hé a- | -mong the | gods : that sháll be | like | unto · the | Lord ?

8 God is very greatly to be feared in the cóuncil | of the | saints : and to be had in reverence of all thém | that are | round a- | -bout him.

9 O Lord God of hosts ∗ whó is | like · unto | thee : thy truth, most mighty Lórd | is on | every | side.

10 Thou rulest the ráging | of the | sea : thou stillest the wáves there- | -of when | they a- | -rise.

11 Thou hast subdued Egypt ∗ ánd de- | -stroyed | it : thou hast scattered thine enemies abróad | with thy | mighty | arm.

12 The heavens are thine, the éarth also · is | thine : thou hast laid the foundation of the round wórld, and | all that | therein | is.

13 Thou hast made the nórth | and | the | south : Tabor and Hermon shall re- | -joice | in thy | Name.

14 Thou hást a | mighty | arm : strong is thy hánd, and | high is | thy right | hand.

15 Righteousness and equity are the habitátion | of thy | seat : mercy and trúth shall | go be- | -fore thy | face.

16 Blessed is the people O Lord ∗ that cán re- | -joice in | thee : they shall wálk in the | light | of thy | countenance.

17 Their delight shall be dáily | in thy | Name : and in thy ríghteousness | shall they | make their | boast.

18 For thou art the glóry | of their | strength : and in thy loving-kindness. thóu shalt | lift | up our | horns.

19 For the Lórd is | our de- | -fence : the Hóly One of | Israel | is our | King.

20 Thou spakest sometime in visions únto thy | saints and | saidst : I have laid help upon one that is mighty ∗ I have exálted one | chosen | out · of the | people.

21 I have fóund | David · my | servant : with my holy óil have | I a- | -nointed | him.

22 My hánd shall | hold him | fast : ánd my | arm shall | strengthen | him.

23 The enemy shall not be áble to | do him | violence : the són of | wickedness | shall not | hurt him.

24 I will smite down his fóes be- | -fore his | face : ánd I | plague | them that | hate him.

25 My truth also and my mércy | shall be | with him : and in my Náme shall his | horn | be ex- | -alted.

26 I will set his dominion álso | in the | sea : ánd his | right hand | in the | floods

27 He shall call me, Thóu | art my | Father : my Gód | and my | strong sal- | vation.

CHRISTMAS DAY. EVENING (continued).

28 And I will máke | him my | first-| born : hígher than the | kings | of the | earth.

29 My mercy will I kéep for him for | ever- | -more : and my cóvenant shall | stand | fast | with him.

30 His seed also will I máke to en- | dure for | ever : and his thróne | as the | days of | heaven.

mf 31 But if his chíldren for- | -sake my | law : ánd | walk not | in my | judgements;

32 If they break my statutes * and kéep not | my com- | -mandments : I will visit their offences with the ród | and their | sin with | scourges.

33 Nevertheless, my loving-kindness will I not útterly | take | from him : nór | suffer · my | truth to | fail.

34 My covenant will I not break * nor alter the thing that is góne | out of · my | lips : I have sworn once by my holiness * that I' | will not | fail | David.

35 His séed shall en- | -dure for | ever : and his séat is | like · as the | sun be- | fore me.

36 He shall stand fast for evermóre | as the | moon : and ás the | faithful | wit- ness · in | heaven.

p 37 But thou hast abhorred and for- sáken | thine A- | -nointed : ánd | art dis- | pleased | at him.

38 Thou hast broken the cóvenant | of thy | servant : and cást his | crown | to the | ground.

39 Thou hast overthrówn | all his | hedges : ánd | broken | down his | strong- holds.

40 All théy that go | by | spoil him : and he is becóme a re- | -proach | to his | neighbours.

41 Thou hast set up the right hánd | of his | enemies : and máde all his | ad- versaries | to re- | -joice.

42 Thou hast taken away the édge | of his | sword : and givest him nót ' victory | in the | battle.

43 Thóu hast put | out his | glory : and cást his | throne | down · to the | ground.

44 The days of his yóuth | hast thou | shortened : ánd | covered · him | with dis- | -honour.

45 Lord, how long wilt thou híde thy- | self for | ever : and shált thy | wrath | burn like | fire ?

46 O remember how shórt my | time | is : wherefore hast thou máde | all | men for | nought ?

47 What man is he that líveth and shall | not see | death : and shall he de- liver his sóul | from the | hand of hell ?

48 Lord, where are thy óld | loving- | kindnesses : which thou swárest unto | David | in thy | truth ?

49 Remember Lord, the rebúke that thy | servants | have : and how I do bear in my bósom the re- | -bukes of | many | people,

50 Wherewith thine enemies have blasphemed thee * and slandered the fóotsteps of | thine A- | -nointed : Praised be the Lord for evermóre. | A-..-men and | A- | -men.

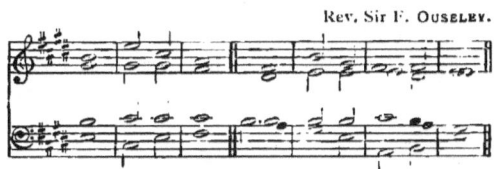

Rev. Sir F. OUSELEY.

PSALM CX.—*Dixit Dominus.*

mf THE Lord sáid unto | my | Lord : Sit thou on my right hand * until I máke thine | ene- | -mies thy | footstool

2 The Lord shall send the rod of thy pówer | out of | Sion : be thou ruler * éven in the | midst a- | -mong thine | ene- mies.

3 In the day of thy power shall the people offer thee free-will-offerings * with an | holy | worship : the dew of thy birth is óf the | womb | of the | morning.

4 The Lord swáre, and will | not re- | pent : Thou art a Priest for ever * áfter the | order ' of Mel- | -chisedech.

5 The Lórd upon | thy right | hand : shall wound even kíngs in the | day | of his | wrath.

6 He shall judge among the heathen * he shall fill the pláces with the | dead | bodies : and smite in sunder the héads | over | divers | countries.

7 He shall drink of the bróok | in the | way : therefore shall he | lift | up his | head.

CHRISTMAS DAY. EVENING (*continued*).

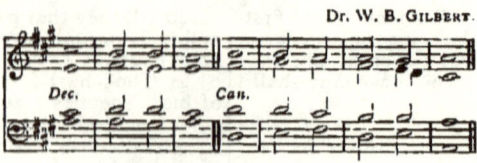
Dr. W. B. Gilbert.

PSALM CXXXII.—*Memento, Domine.*

mf LORD, re- | -member | David : ánd | |
all | his | trouble ;

2 How he swáre | unto · the | Lord : and vowed a vow únto the Al- | -mighty | God of | Jacob ;

3 I will not come within the táber-nacle | of mine | house : nôr | climb up | into · my | bed ;

4 I will not suffer mine eyes to sléep, nor mine | eyelids · to | slumber : neither the temples of my héad to | take | any | rest ;

5 Until I find out a place for the témple | of the | Lord : an habitation fôr the | mighty | God of | Jacob.

6 Lo, we héard of the | same at | Ephrata : ánd | found it | in the | wood.

7 We will gó into his | taber- | -nacle : and fall lów on our | knees be- | -fore his | footstool.

8 Arise, O Lórd | into · thy | resting-place : thóu and the | ark | of thy | strength.

9 Let thy príests be | clothed · with | ríghteousness : and lét thy | saints | sing with | joyfulness.

10 For thy sérvant | David's | sake : turn not awáy the | presence · of | thine A- | -nointed

11 The Lord hath made a faithful óath | unto | David : ánd he | shall not | shrink | from it.

12 Of the frúit | of thy | body : sháll I | set up- | -on thy | seat.

13 If thy children will keep my cove-nant ✱ and my téstimonies that | I shall | learn them : their children also shall sit upón thy | seat for · | ever- | more.

14 For the Lord hath chosen Sion to be an habitátion | for him- | -self : hé hath | longed | for | her.

15 This shall bé my | rest for | ever : here will I dwell ✱ fôr I | have · a de- | light there- | -in.

16 I will bléss her | victuals · with | increase : and will sátis- | -fy her | poor with | bread.

17 I will déck her | priests with | health : and her sáints | shall re- | -joice and | sing.

18 There shall I make the hórn of | David · to | flourish : I have ordáined a | lantern · for | mine A- | -nointed.

19 As for his enemies ✱ I shall clóthe | them with | shame : but upon himsélf | shall his | crown | flourish.

PSALM XL.—*Expectans expectavi.*

mf I WAITED pátiently | for the | Lord : and he inclined únto | me and | heard my | calling.

2 He brought me also out of the horrible pit * óut of the | mire and | clay : and set my feet upon the róck, and | ordered | my | goings.

3 And he hath put a new sóng | in my | mouth : even a thánks- | -giving | unto · our | God.

4 Mány shall | see it · and | fear : and shall pút their | trust | in the | Lord.

5 Blessed is the man that hath set his hópe | in the | Lord : and turned not unto the proud * and to súch as | go a- | -bout with | lies.

6 O Lord my God, great are the wondrous works which thou hast done * like as be also thy thóughts which | are to | us-ward : and yet there is no man that órdereth | them | unto | thee.

7 If I should decláre them and | speak of | them : they should be more than I° am | able | to ex- | -press.

8 Sacrifice and meat-óffering thou | wouldest | not : bût mine | ears | hast thou | opened.

9 Burnt-offerings and sacrifice for sin * hast thóu | not re- | -quired : thén | said I | Lo I | come.

10 In the volume of the book it is written of me * that I should fulfil thy wíll | O my | God : I am content to do it * yea thy láw | is with- | -in my | heart.

11 I have declared thy righteousness in the gréat | congre- | -gation : lo, I will not refrain my líps O | Lord and | that thou | knowest.

12 I have not hid thy righteousness with- | -in my | heart : my talk hath been of thy trúth | and of | thy sal- | -vation.

2nd part 13 I have not kept back thy lóving- | mercy · and | truth : fróm the | great | congre- | -gation.

mp 14 Withdraw not thou thy mércy from | me O | Lord : let thy loving-kindness and thy trúth | al- | -way pre- | -serve me.

15 For innumerable troubles are come about me * my sins have taken such hold upon me * that I am not áble to | look | up : yea, they are more in number than the hairs of my head * ánd my | heart hath | failed | me.

16 O Lord, let it be thy pléasure to de- | liver | me : máke ! haste O | Lord to | help me.

17 Let them be ashamed and confounded together * that seek after my sóul | to de- | -stroy it : let them be driven backward * and pút to re- | -buke that | wish me | evil.

18 Let them be desolate, and re- | warded · with | shame : that say unto me, Fíe up- | -on thee | fie up- | -on thee.

19 Let all those that seek thee be jóyful and | glad in | thee : and let such as love thy salvation say álway The | Lord | be | praised.

20 As for mé I am , poor and | needy : bût the | Lord | careth | for me.

21 Thou art my hélper | and re- | deemer : make nó long | tarrying | O my | God.

124 THE CIRCUMCISION. MORNING (*continued*).

I.

T. PURCELL.

———————— *Alternative Chant.* ————————

II.

Rev. F. A. J. HERVEY.

PSALM XC.—*Domine, refugium.*

p LÔRD thou hast | been our | refuge : from ône gener- | -ation | to an- | -other.

2 Before the mountains were brought forth ✻ or ever the éarth and the | world were | made : thou art God from ever-lâsting and | world with- | -out | end.

3 Thou turnest mân | to de- | -struction : again thou sayest, Côme a- | -gain ye | children · of | men.

4 For a thousand years in thý sight | are but · as | yesterday : seeing that is pást as a | watch | in the | night.

5 As soon as thou scatterest them ✻ they are éven | as a | sleep : and fáde away | suddenly | like the | grass.

6 In the morning it is gréen and | groweth | up : but in the evening it is cut dówn | dried | up and | withered.

7 For we consume awáy in | thy dis- | pleasure : and are afráid at thy | wrath-ful | indig- | -nation.

8 Thou hast sét our mis- | -deeds be- | fore thee : and our secret síns in the | light | of thy | countenance.

9 For when thou art angry, áll our | days are | gone : we bring our years to an end ✻ as it wére a | tale | that is | told.

10 The days of our age are three-score years and ten ✻ and though men be so strong that they cóme to | four-score | years : yet is their strength then but labour and sorrow ✻ so soon pásseth it a- | -way and | we are | gone.

11 But who regardeth the pówer | of thy | wrath : for even thereafter as a man féareth | so is | thy dis- | -pleasure.

12 So téach us to | number · our | days : that we may applý our | hearts | unto | wisdom.

13 Turn thee again, O Lôrd | at the | last : ánd be | gracious | unto · thy | servants.

14 O satisfy us with thy mércy and | that | soon : so shall we rejoice and be glád all the | days | of our | life.

15 Comfort us again ✻ now after the tîme that thou hast | plagued | us : and for the years wherein | we have | suffered · ad- | -versity.

16 Shéw thy | servants · thy | work : ánd their | children | thy | glory.

2nd part 17 And the glorious Majesty of the Lord our Gôd | be up- | -on us : prosper thou the work of our hands upon us ✻ O prósper | thou our | handy- | -work.

THE CIRCUMCISION. EVENING.

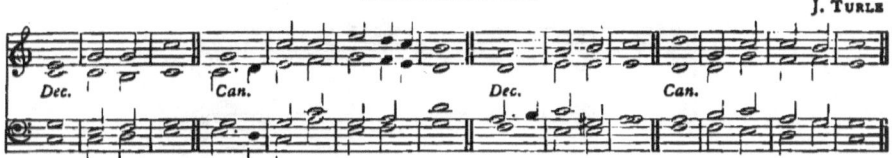

J. TURLE

PSALM LXV.—*Te decet hymnus.*

F.mf THOU, O Gód art | praised · in | Sion : and unto thee the vów be per- | -formed | in Je- | -rusalem.

F. 2 Thóu that | hearest · the | prayer : únto | thee shall | all flesh | come.

3 My misdéeds pre- | -vail a- | -gainst me : O° be thou | merciful | unto · our | sins.

4 Blessed is the man, whom thou choosest, and recéivest | unto | thee : he shall dwell in thy court ✶ and shall be satisfied with the pleasures of thy house ✶ éven | of thy | holy | temple.

5 Thou shalt shew us wonderful things in thy righteousness ✶ O Gód of | our sal- | -vation : thou that art the hope of all the ends of the earth ✶ and of them that remáin | in the | broad | sea.

6 Who in his stréngth setteth | fast the | mountains : ánd is | girded · a- | bout with | power.

7 Who stilleth the ráging | of the | sea : and the noise of his wáves and the | madness | of the | people.

8 They also that dwell in the utter- most parts of the earth ✶ shall be afráid | at thy | tokens : thou that makest the out-goings of the mórning and | evening · to | praise | thee.

9 Thou visitest the éarth and | blessest | it : thóu | makest · it | very | plenteous.

10 The river of Gód is | full of | water : thou preparest their corn ✶ for só thou pro- | -videst | for the | earth.

11 Thou waterest her furrows ✶ thou sendest rain into the líttle | valleys · there- | -of : thou makest it soft with the drops of ráin and | blessest · the | in-crease | of it.

12 Thou crownest the yéar | with thy | goodness : ánd thy | clouds | drop | fat-ness.

13 They shall drop upon the dwéllings | of the | wilderness : and the little hílls shall re- | -joice on | every | side.

14 The fólds shall be | full of | sheep : the valleys also shall stand so thick with córn that | they shall | laugh and | sing.

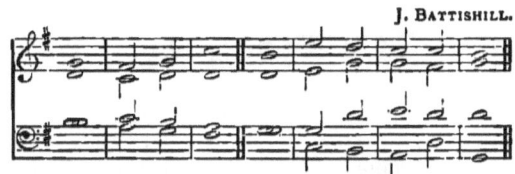

J. BATTISHILL.

PSALM CIII.—*Benedic, anima mea.*

f PRAISE the Lórd | O my | soul : and all that is withín me | praise his | holy | Name.

2 Praise the Lórd | O my | soul : ánd for- | -get not | all his | benefits ;

3 Who forgíveth | all thy | sin : and héaleth | all | thine in- | -firmities ;

4 Who saveth thy lífe | from de- | struction : and crowneth thée with | mercy · and | loving- | -kindness ;

5 Who satisfieth thy móuth with | good | things : making thee yóung and | lusty | as an | eagle.

6 The Lord executeth ríghteous- | ness and | judgement : for all thém that | are op- | -pressed · with | wrong.

7 He shewed his wáys | unto | Moses : his wórks | unto · the | children · of | Israel.

8 The Lord is fúll of com- | passion · and | mercy : long-súffering, | and of | great | goodness.

9 He wíll not | alway · be | chiding : neither kéepeth | he his | anger · for | ever.

10 He hath not déalt with us | after · our | sins : nor rewárded us ac- | -cording | to our | wickednesses.

THE CIRCUMCISION. EVENING (continued).

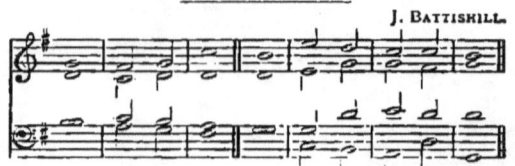
J. BATTISHILL.

11 For look how high the heaven is in compárison | of the | earth : so great is his mercy álso |toward|them that | fear him.

12 Look how wide also the east is | from the | west : so fár hath he | set our | sins | from us.

13 Yea, like as a father pítieth his | own | children : even so is the Lord mérciful | unto | them that | fear him.

14 For he knoweth whereóf | we are | made ; he remémbereth | that we | are but | dust.

mp 15 The days of mán are | but as | grass : for he flourisheth ás a | flower | of the | field.

16 For as soon as the wind goeth óver it | it is | gone : and the place thereóf | shall | know it | no | more.

mf 17 But the merciful goodness of the Lord * endureth for ever and éver

upon | them that | fear him : and his righteousness up- | -on | children's | children ;

18 Even upon súch as | keep his | covenant: and thínk upon | his com- | mandments · to | do them.

f 19 The Lord hath prepáred his | seat in | heaven : and his kíngdom | ruleth | over | all.

20 O praise the Lord, ye angels of his * ye that ex- | -cel in | strength : ye that fulfil his commandment * and hearken únto the | voice | of his | word.

21 O praise the Lórd, all | ye his | hosts : ye sérvants of | his that | do his | pleasure.

22 O speak good of the Lord, all ye works of his * in all pláces of | his do- | minion : práise thou the | Lord | O my | soul.

THE EPIPHANY. MORNING.

From LUTHER.

PSALM XLVI.—*Deus noster refugium.*

f GÓD is our | hope and | strength : a véry | present | help in | trouble.

2 Therefore will we not fear, though the | earth be | moved : and though the hills be carried ínto the | midst | of the | sea.

3 Though the waters thereóf | rage and | swell : and though the mountains sháke at the | tempest | of the | same.

4 The rivers of the flood thereof, shall make glád the | city . of | God : the holy place of the tábernacle | of the | most | Highest.

5 God is in the midst of her * therefore shall she nót | be re- | -moved : Gód shall | help her · and | that right | early.

6 The heathen make much adó and the | kingdoms · are | moved : but God

hath shewed his vóice and the | earth shall | melt a- | -way.

2nd part 7 The Lórd of | hosts is | with us : the Gód of | Jacob | is our | refuge.

8 O come hither, and behold the wórks | of the | Lord : what destruction he hath | brought up- | -on the | earth.

9 He maketh wars to céase in | all the | world : he breaketh the bow, and knappeth the spear in sunder * and búrneth the | chariots | in the | fire.

10 Be still then, and know that | I am | God : I will be exalted among the heathen * and I˚ will be ex- | -alted | in the | earth.

11 The Lórd of | hosts is | with us : the Gód of | Jacob | is our | refuge.

THE EPIPHANY. MORNING (continued).

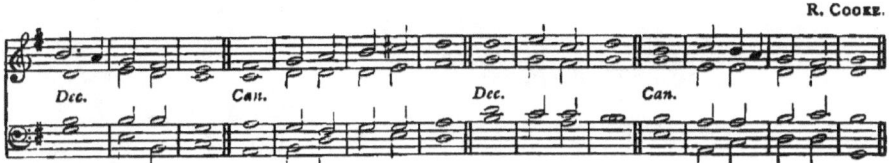
R. COOKE.

PSALM XLVII.—*Omnes gentes, plaudite.*

F. ƒ O CLAP your hands togéther | all ye | people : O sing unto Gód | with the | voice of | melody.

F. 2 For the Lord is hígh and | to be | feared : he is the great Kíng up- | -on | all the | earth.

3 He shall subdue the péople | under | us : ánd the | nations | under . our | feet.

4 He shall choose óut an | heritage | for us : even the wórship of | Jacob | whom he | loved.

5 God is gone úp with a | merry | noise : and the Lórd with the | sound | of the | trump.

6 O sing praises, sing práises | unto . our | God : O sing práises, sing | praises | unto . our | King.

7 For God is the Kíng of | all the | earth : síng ye | praises . with | under- | standing.

8 God réigneth | over . the | hea‑ then : God sítteth up- | -on his | holy | seat.

2nd part. 9 The princes of the people * are joined unto the péople of the | God of | Abraham : for God which is very high exalted * doth defend the éarth as it | were | with a | shield.

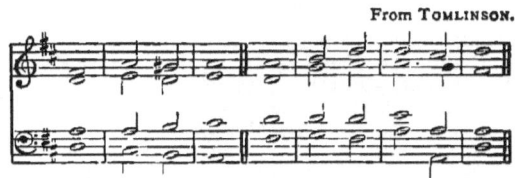
From TOMLINSON.

PSALM XLVIII.—*Magnus Dominus.*

ƒ GREAT is the Lord, and híghly | to | be | praised : in the city of our God * éven up- | -on his | holy | hill.

2 The hill of Sion is a fair place * and the jóy of the | whole | earth : upon the north side lieth the city of the great King * God is well known in her pálaces | as a | sure | refuge.

3 For lo, the kíngs | of the | earth : are gáthered and | gone | by to- | -gether.

4 They márvelled to | see such | things : they were astónished and|sudden‑‑ ly | cast | down.

5 Fear came thére upon | them and | sorrow : as upón a | woman | in her | travail.

6 Thou shalt break the shíps | of the | sea : thróugh | — the | east- | -wind.

7 Like as we have heard * so have we seen in the city of the Lord of hosts * in the cíty | of our | God : Gód up-|-holdeth . the | same for | ever.

8 We wait for thy lóving- | -kindness . O | God : ín the | midst of | thy | temple.

9 O God according to thy Name * so is thy praise únto the | world's | end : thy right | hand is | full of | righteousness.

10 Let the mount Sion rejoice * and the dáughter of | Judah . be | glad : bé- | cause of | thy | judgements.

11 Walk about Sion, and gó | round a-| bout her : ánd | tell the | towers there- | -of.

12 Mark well her bulwarks, sét | up her| houses : that ye may téll ! them that | come | after.

13 For this God is our Gód for | ever . and | ever : he shall bé our | guide | unto | death.

THE EPIPHANY. EVENING.

Sir GEORGE ELVEY.

PSALM LXXII.—*Deus, judicium.*

f GIVE the Kíng thy | judgements • O | God: and thy ríghteousness | unto • the | King's | son.

2 Then shall he judge thy people accórding | unto | right : ánd de- | -fend | the | poor.

3 The mountains álso shall | bring | peace : and the little hílls | righteousness | unto • the | people.

4 He shall keep the símple folk | by their | right : defend the children of the póor, and | punish • the | wrong | doer.

5 They shall fear thee, as long as the sún and | moon en- | -dureth : from óne gener- | -ation | to an- | -other.

6 He shall come down like the ráin into a | fleece of | wool : éven as the | drops that | water • the | earth.

7 In his tíme shall the | righteous | flourish : yea, and abundance of péace, so | long • as the | moon en- | -dureth.

8 His dominion shall be also from the óne sea | to the | other : and from the flóod | unto • the | world's | end.

9 They that dwell in the wilderness shall | kneel be- | -fore him : his éne- | mies shall | lick the | dust.

10 The kings of Tharsis and of the ísles shall | give | presents : the kings of Arábia and | Saba | shall bring | gifts.

11 All kings shall fáll | down be- | -fore him : áll | nations shall | do him service.

12 For he shall eliver the póor when he | crieth : t e needy álso an | him that | hath no | helper.

13 He shall be favourable tó the simple • and | needy : and shall presérve the | souls | of the | poor.

14 He shall deliver their sóuls from | falsehood • and | wrong : and déar shall their | blood be | in his | sight.

15 He shall live ✶ and unto him shall be given of the góld | of A- | -rabia : prayer shall be made ever unto hím, and | daily • shall | he be | praised.

16 There shall be an heap of corn in the earth ✶ hígh up- | -on the | hills : his fruit shall shake like Libanus ✶ and shall be green in the cíty like | grass up- | -on the | earth.

17 His Name shall endure for ever ✶ his Name shall remain under the sún a- | mongst the • pos- -terities : which shall be blessed through hím, and | all the | heathen • shall | praise him.

18 Blessed be the Lord God ✶ éven the | God of | Israel : which ónly | doeth | wondrous | things ;

19 And blessed be the Name of his Májes- | -ty for | ever : and all the earth shall be filled with his Májesty. | Amen. | A- | -men.

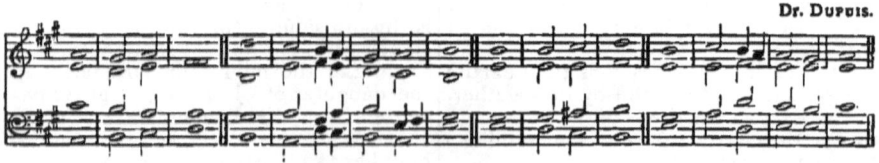
Dr. DUPUIS.

PSALM CXVII.—*Laudate Dominum.*

f O PRAISE the Lórd | all ye | heathen ; práise | — him | all ye | nations.

2 For his merciful kindness is ever more and móre | towards | us : and the truth of the Lord endureth for éver. | Praise | — the | Lord.

THE EPIPHANY. EVENING (continued).

Dr. Dupuis.

PSALM CXXXV.—*Laudate Nomen.*

f O PRAISE the Lord * laud ye the Náme | of the | Lord : praise it, O' ye | servants | of the | Lord ;

2 Ye that stand in the hóuse | of the | Lord : in the cóurts of the | house of | our | God.

3 O praise the Lórd, for the | Lord is | gracious : O sing praises únto his | Name for | it is | lovely.

4 For why? the Lord hath chosen Jácob | unto · him- | -self : and I'srael | for his | own pos- | -session.

5 For I knów that the | Lord is | great : and that our Lórd | is a- | -bove all | gods.

6 Whatsoever the Lord pleased * that did he in héaven | and in | earth : and in the séa | and in | all deep | places.

7 He bringeth forth the clouds from the énds | of the | world : and sendeth forth lightnings with the rain * brínging the | winds | out of · his | treasures.

8 He smóte the | first-born . of | Egypt : bóth of | man | and | beast.

9 He hath sent tokens and wonders into the midst of thee, O' thou | land of | Egypt : upón | Pharaoh · and | all his | servants.

10 He smóte | divers | nations : ánd | slew | mighty | kings ;

11 Sehon king of the Amorites * and O'g the | king of | Basan : ánd | all the | kingdoms . of | Canaan.

12 And gave their lánd to | be an | heritage : even an heritage únto | Isra- | el his | people.

13 Thy Name, O Lórd, en- | -dureth for | ever : so doth thy memorial, O Lord * from óne gener- | -ation | to an- | -other.

14 For the Lórd will a- | -venge his people : ánd be | gracious | unto · his | servants.

15 As for the images of the heathen * théy are but | silver · and | gold : thé | work of | men's | hands.

16 Théy have | mouths and | speak not : éyes | have they | but they | see not.

17 They have éars, and | yet they | hear not : neither is there ány | breath | in their | mouths.

18 They that make them are líke | unto | them : and so are all théy that | put their | trust in | them.

19 Praise the Lórd, ye | house of | Israel : práise the | Lord ye | house of | Aaron.

20 Praise the Lórd, ye | house of | Levi : ye that féar the | Lord | praise the | Lord.

2nd part 21 Praised be the Lórd | out of | **Sion** : whó | dwelleth | at Je- | -rusalem.

THE PURIFICATION. MORNING.

T. KELWAY.

PSALM XX.—*Exaudiat te Dominus.*

mf THE Lord hear thee ín the | day of | trouble : the Náme of the | God of | Jacob . de- | -fend thee ;

2 Send thee hélp | from the | sanc-tuary : ánd | strengthen . thee | out of | Sion ;

3 Remember | all thy | offerings : ánd ac- | -cept thy | burnt | sacrifice ;

4 Gránt thee thy | heart's de- | -sire : ánd ful- | -fil | all thy | mind.

5 We will rejoice in thy salvation ✶ and triumph in the Náme of the | Lord our | God : the Lórd per- | -form all | thy pe- | -titions.

6 Now know I that the Lord helpeth his Anointed ✶ and will hear him from his | holy | heaven : even with the whole-some | strength of | his right | hand.

7 Some put their trust in cháriots and | some in | horses : but we will re-member the Náme | of the | Lord our | God.

8 Théy are brought | down and | fallen : but wé are | risen . and | stand | upright.

9 Save, Lord, and héar us O | King of | heaven : whén we | call up- | -on | thee.

S. WESLEY.

PSALM LXXXVI.—*Inclina, Domine.*

mp BOW down thine éar O | Lord and | hear me : for I˘ am | poor | and in | misery.

2 Preserve thou my sóul, for | I am | holy : my God, save thy sérvant that | putteth . his | trust in | thee.

3 Be merciful únto | me O | Lord : for I˘ will | call | daily up- | -on thee.

4 Comfort the sóul | of thy | servant : for unto thee O Lórd do I | lift | up my | soul.

5 For thou, Lórd art | good and | gracious : and of great mercy unto áll | them that | call up- | -on thee.

6 Give ear, Lórd | unto . my | prayer : and ponder the vóice | of my | humble . de- | -sires.

7 In the time of my trouble I˘ will | call up- | on | thee : fór | thou | hearest | me.

8 Among the gods there is none líke unto | thee Ó | Lord : there is not óne that can | do as | thou | doest.

9 All nations whom thou hast made ✶ shall come and wórship | thee O | Lord : ánd shall | glori- | -fy thy | Name.

10 For thou art great, and dóest | wondrous | things : thóu | — art | God a- | -lone.

11 Teach me thy way O Lord ✶ and I will wálk | in thy | truth : O knit my heart unto thêe, that | I may | fear thy | Name.

12 I will thank thee O Lord my Gód with | all my | heart : and will práise thy | Name for | ever- | -more.

13 For gréat is thy | mercy | toward me : and thou hast delivered my sóul from the | nethermost | hell.

14 O God, the próud are | risen . a- | gainst me : and the congregations of

THE PURIFICATION. MORNING (*continued*).

naughty men have sought after my soul * and have nót set | thee be- | -fore their | eyes.
15 But thou O Lord God, art fúll of com- | -passion . and | mercy : long-súffering | plenteous . in | goodness . and | truth.
16 O turn thee then unto mé and have | mercy . up- | -on me : give thy strength unto thy servant * and hélp the | son | of thine | handmaid.
2nd part 17 Shew some token upon me for good * that they who hate me may sée it and | be a- | -shamed : because thou Lord hast hólpen | me and | comforted | me.

PSALM LXXXVII.—*Fundamenta ejus.*

mp HER foundations are upón the | holy | hills : the Lord loveth the gates of Sion, móre than | all the | dwellings . of | Jacob.
2 Very excellent thíngs are | spoken . of | thee : thóu | city | of | God.
3 I will thínk upon | Rahab . and | Babylon : wíth | them that | know | me.
4 Behóld ye the | Philistines | also : and they of Tyre with the Morians * ló | there | was he | born.

5 And of Sion it shall be reported that hé was | born in | her : ánd the most | High shall | stablish | her.
6 The Lord shall rehearse it when he wríteth | up the | people : thát | he was | born | there.
2nd part 7 The singers also and trúmpeters shall | he re- | -hearse : A'll my fresh | springs shall | be in | thee.

THE PURIFICATION. EVENING.

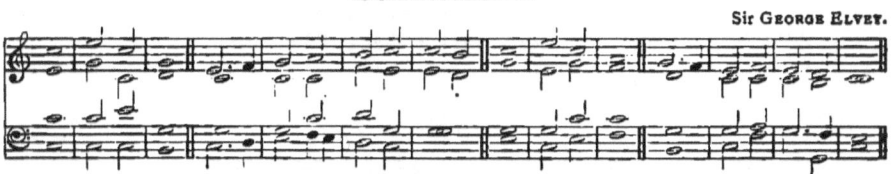
Sir George Elvey.

PSALM LXXXIV.—*Quam dilecta!*

mf O HOW ámiable | are thy | dwellings : thóu | Lord | of | hosts!
2 My soul hath a desire and longing * to enter into the cóurts | of the | Lord : my heart and my flesh rejóice | in the | living | God.
3 Yea, the sparrow hath found her an house * and the swallow a nest, where shé may | lay her | young : even thy altars, O Lord of hósts, my | King | and my | God.
4 Blessed are they that dwéll | in thy | house : théy will be | alway | prais-ing | thee.
5 Blessed is the man whose stréngth | is in | thee : ín whose | heart | are thy | ways.
6 Who, going through the vale of misery úse it | for a | well : ánd the | pools are | filled . with | water.

2nd part 7 They will gó from | strength to | strength : and unto the God of gods ap-peareth évery | one of | them in | Sion.
8 O Lord God of hósts | hear my | prayer : héarken | O | God of | Jacob.
9 Behold, O Gód | our de- | -fender : and look upón the | face of | thine A- | nointed.
10 For one dáy | in thy | courts : ís | better | than a | thousand.
11 I had rather be a door-keeper in the hóuse | of my | God : than to dwéll in the | tents | of un- | -godliness.
12 For the Lord God is a líght | and de- | -fence : the Lord will give grace and worship * and no good thing shall he withhold from thém that | live a | godly | life.
13 O Lórd | God of | hosts : blessed is the mán that | putteth . his | trust in | thee.

THE PURIFICATION. EVENING (continued).

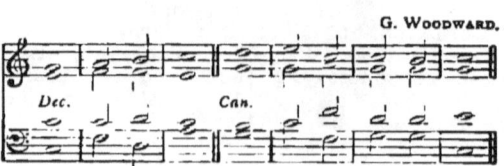

PSALM CXIII.—*Laudate, pueri.*

f PRAISE the | Lord ye | servants : O | God * that hâth his | dwelling · so | high : práise the | Name | of the | Lord.

2 Blessed be the Náme | of the | Lord : from thís time | forth for | ever- | more.

3 The Lórd's | Name is | praised : from the rising up of the sun, unto the góing | down | of the | same.

4 The Lord is hígh a- | -bove all | heathen : ánd his | glory · a- | -bove the | heavens.

5 Who is like unto the Lord our God * that hâth his | dwelling · so | high : and yet humbleth himself to behold the thíngs that | are in | heaven and | earth?

6 He taketh up the símple | out · of the | dust : and lífteth the | poor | out · of the | mire ;

7 That he may sét him | with the | princes : even wíth the | princes | of his | people.

8 He maketh the barren wóman to | keep | house : and to bé a | joyful | mother · of | children.

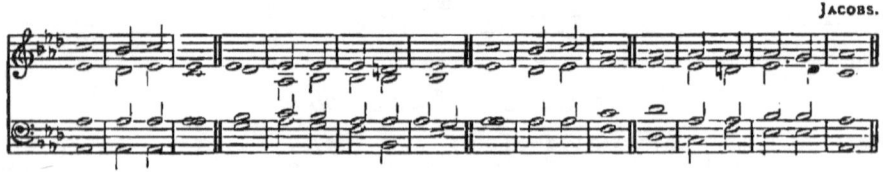

PSALM CXXXIV.—*Ecce nunc.*

mf BEHÓLD, now | praise the | Lord : áll ye | servants | of the | Lord;

2 Ye that by night stand in the hóuse | of the | Lord : even in the cóurts of the | house of | our | God.

3 Lift up your hánds | in the | sanctuary : ánd | praise | — the | Lord.

4 The Lórd that made | heaven and | earth : gíve thee | blessing | out of | Sion.

ASH WEDNESDAY. MORNING. 133

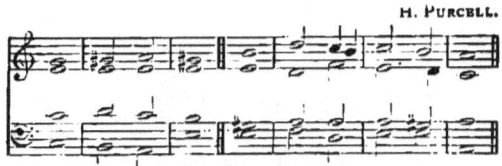

H. PURCELL.

PSALM VI.—*Domine, ne in furore.*

F. mp O LORD rebuke me nót in thine | indig- | -nation : neither chásten | me in | thy dis- | -pleasure.

F. 2 Have mercy upon me O Lórd, for | I am | weak : O Lord héal me | for my | bones are | vexed.

3 My soul álso is | sore | troubled : but Lord, how lóng | wilt thou | punish | me?

4 Turn thee O Lórd and de- | -liver · my | soul : O sáve me | for thy | mercy's | sake.

5 For in death nó man re- | -membereth | thee : and who will gíve thee | thanks | in the | pit?

6 I am weary of my groaning * every night wásh | I my | bed : and wáter my | couch | with my | tears.

7 My beauty is góne for | very | trouble : and worn awáy be- | -cause of | all mine | enemies.

8 Away from me, all yé that | work | vanity : for the Lord hath héard the | voice | of my | weeping.

9 The Lord hath héard | my pe- | tition : the Lórd | will re- | -ceive my | prayer.

10 All mine enemies shall be confóunded and | sore | vexed : they shall be turned báck, and | put to | shame | suddenly.

J. TURLE.

PSALM XXXII.—*Beati, quorum.*

F. mp BLESSED is he whose unrighteousness | is for- | -given : ánd whose | sin | is | covered.

F. 2 Blessed is the man unto whom the Lórd im- | -puteth · no | sin : and ín whose | spirit · there | is no | guile.

3 For whílst I | held my | tongue : my bones consumed awáy | through my | daily · com- | -plaining.

4 For thy hand is heavy upón me | day and | night : and my móisture is | like the | drought in | summer.

5 I will acknowledge my sín unto | thee : and mine unrighteousness | have I | not | hid.

6 I said ⁷ ill confess my síns | unto · the | Lord : and so thou forgávest the | wickedness | of my | sin.

7 For this shall every one that is godly make his prayer unto thee * in a time when thou mayest · be | found : but

in the great wáter-floods | they shall | not come | nigh him.

8 Thou art a place to hide me in * thou shalt presérve | me from | trouble : thou shalt compass me abóut with | songs | of de- | -liverance.

9 I will inform thee, and teach thee in the wáy wherein | thou shalt | go : and I′ will | guide thee | with mine | eye.

10 Be ye not like to horse and mule * which háve no | under- | -standing : whose mouths must be held with bit and brídle | lest they | fall up- | -on thee.

11 Great plagues remáin | for · the un- | -godly : but whoso putteth his trust in the Lord * mercy embráceth | him on | every | side.

12 Be glad, O ye righteous * and rejóice | in the | Lord : and be joyful all yé | that are | true of | heart.

ASH WEDNESDAY. MORNING (continued).

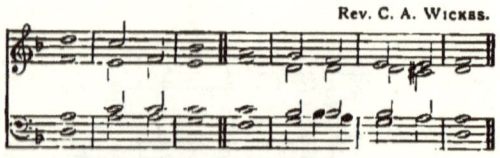
Rev. C. A. Wickes.

PSALM XXXVIII.—*Domine, ne in furore.*

p PUT me not to rebuke, O Lórd | in thine | anger : neither chásten me | in thy | heavy · dis- | -pleasure.

2 For thine árrows stick | fast in | me : ánd thy | hand | presseth · me | sore.

3 There is no health in my flesh ∗ becáuse of | thy dis- | -pleasure : neither is there any rest in my bónes, by | reason | of my | sin.

4 For my wickednesses are góne | over · my | head : and are like a sore búrden too | heavy · for | me to | bear.

5 My wounds stínk and | are cor- | rupt : thróugh | my | foolish- | -ness.

6 I am brought into so gréat | trouble · and | misery : that I go móurning | all the | day | long.

7 For my loins are filled with a | sore dis- | -case : and there is nó | whole part | in my | body.

8 I am féeble and | sore | smitten : I have roared for the véry dis- | -quietness | of my | heart.

9 Lord, thou knowest áll|my de-|-sire : and my gróaning | is not | hid from | thee.

10 My heart panteth, my stréngth hath | failed | me : and the sight of mine | eyes is | gone | from me.

11 My lovers and my neighbours, did stand lóoking up- | -on my | trouble : and my kínsmen | stood a- | -far | off.

12 They also that sought after my lífe laid | snares for | me : and they that went about to do me evil talked of wickedness ∗ and imagined decéit | all the | day | long.

13 As for me, I was like a déaf | man and | heard not : and as one that is dúmb, who | doth not | open · his | mouth.

14 I became even as a mán that | heareth | not : and in whóse | mouth are | no re- | -proofs.

15 For in thee, O Lórd have I | put my | trust : thou shalt ánswer for | me O | Lord my | God.

16 I have required that they, even mine enemies ∗ should not tríumph | over | me : for when my foot slipped ∗ théy re- | -joiced | greatly · a- | -gainst me.

17 And I truly am sét | in the | plague : and my héaviness is | ever | in my | sight.

18 For I' will con- | -fess my | wickedness : ánd be | sorry | for my | sin.

19 But mine enemies live | and are | mighty : and they that hate me wróngfully | are | many · in | number.

20 They also that reward evil for góod | are a- | -gainst me : because I fóllow the | thing that | good | is.

21 Forsake me nót O | Lord my | God : bé not | thou | far | from me.

22 Háste | thee to | help me : O Lórd God of | my sal- | -vation.

ASH WEDNESDAY. EVENING.

Dr. S. S. Wesley.

PSALM CII.—*Domine, exaudi.*

F. mp HÉAR my | prayer O | Lord : and let my crýing | come | unto | thee.

F. 2 Hide not thy face from me in the tíme | of my | trouble : incline thine ear unto me when I call ∗ O héar | me and | that right | soon.

3 For my days are consúmed a- | -way like | smoke : and my bones are burnt úp | as it | were a | fire-brand.

4 My heart is smitten dówn and | withered · like | grass · so that I' for- | get to | eat my | bread.

ASH WEDNESDAY. EVENING (continued).

5 For the vóice | of my | groaning : my bones will scárce | cleave | to my | flesh.

6 I am become like a pélican | in the | wilderness : and like an ówl | that is | in the | desert.

7 I have watched * and am éven as it | were a | sparrow : that sítteth a- | lone up- | -on the | house-top.

8 Mine enemies revíle me | all the · day | long : and they that are mad upón me are | sworn to- | -gether · a- | -gainst me.

9 For I have eaten áshes | as it · were | bread : ánd | mingled · my | drink with | weeping;

10 And that because of thine índig- | nation and | wrath : for thou hast táken me | up and | cast me | down.

11 My days are góne | like a | shadow : and I' am | withered | like | grass.

12 But thou, O Lórd shalt en- | -dure for | ever : and thy remembrance throughóut ' all | gener- | -ations.

13 Thou shalt arise, and have mércy up- | -on | Sion : for it is time that thou have mercy upón her, | yea the | time is | come.

14 And why * thy servants thínk up- | on her | stones : and it pitieth thém to | see her | in the | dust.

15 The heathen shall féar thy | Name O | Lord : and all the kíngs | of the | earth thy | Majesty;

16 When the Lórd shall | build up | Sion : and whén his | glory | shall ap- | pear;

17 When he turneth him unto the prayer of the | poor | destitute : ánd de- | spiseth · not | their de- | -sire.

18 This shall be written for thóse that | come | after : and the people which sháll be | born shall | praise the | Lord.

19 For he hath looked dówn | from his | sanctuary : out of the héaven did the | Lord be- | -hold the | earth;

20 That he might hear the mournings of súch as are | in cap- | -tivity : and deliver the chíldren ap- | -pointed | unto | death;

21 That they may declare the Náme of the | Lord in | Sion : ánd his | worship | at Je- | -rusalem ;

22 When the péople are | gathered · to- | -gether : and the kíngdoms also · to | serve the | Lord.

23 He brought down my stréngth | in my | journey : ánd | shortened | my | days.

24 But I said * O my God, take me not away in the mídst | of mine | age : as for thy years, they endure throughóut | all | gener- | -ations.

mf 25 Thou, Lord, in the beginning * hast laid the foundátion | of the | earth : and the héavens are the | work of | thy | hands.

26 They shall perish, but thóu | shalt en- | -dure : they áll shall wax | old as | doth a | garment;

27 And as a vesture shalt thou change them * ánd they | shall be | changed : but thou art the same, ánd thy | years | shall not | fail.

28 The children of thy sérvants | shall con- | -tinue : and their séed shall stand | fast | in thy | sight.

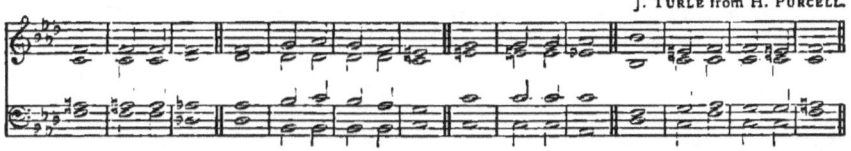

J. Turle from H. Purcell.

PSALM CXXX.—*De profundis.*

p OUT of the deep have I called únto | thee, O | Lord : Lórd | hear | my | voice.

2 O let thine éars con- | -sider | well : thé | voice of | my com- | -plaint.

3 If thou, Lord, wilt be extreme to márk what is | done a- | -miss : O Lórd | | who | may a- | -bide it ?

4 Fór there is | mercy · with | thee : thérefore | shalt | thou be | feared.

5 I look for the Lord ; my sóul doth | wait for | him : ín his | word | is my | trust.

6 My soul fléeth | unto · the | Lord : before the morning watch, I sáy, be- | -fore the | morning | watch.

7 O Israel, trust in the Lord * for with the Lórd | there is | mercy : ánd with | him is | plenteous · re- | -demption.

8 And hé shall re- | -deem | Israel : fróm | all | his | sins.

ASH WEDNESDAY. EVENING (*continued*).

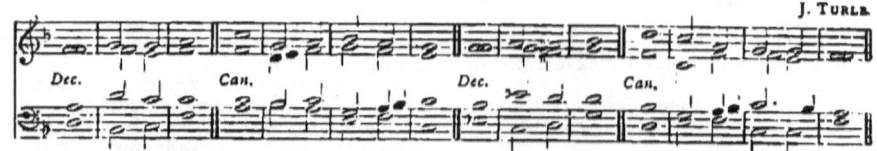

J. TURLE.

PSALM CXLIII.—*Domine, exaudi.*

mp HEAR my prayer O Lord * and con- sider | my de- | -sire : hearken unto me for thy | truth and | righteousness' | sake.

2 And enter not into júdgement | with thy | servant : for in thy sight shall | no man | living • be | justified.

3 For the enemy hath persecuted my soul * he hath smitten my life | down • to the | ground : he hath laid me in the darkness * as the men that | have been | long | dead.

4 Therefore is my spírit | vexed • with- | -in me : ánd my | heart with- | -in me • is | desolate.

5 Yet do I remember the time past * I múse upon | all thy | works : yea, I exercise mysélf in the | works | of thy | hands.

6 I stretch forth my hánds | unto | thee : my soul gaspeth unto theé ! as a | thirsty | land.

7 Hear me O Lord, and that soon * for my spírit | waxeth | faint : hide not thy face from me * lest I be like unto them that go | down ǀ into • the | pit.

8 O let me hear thy loving-kindness betimes in the morning * for in theé | is my | trust : shew thou me the way that I should walk in * for I lift úp my | soul ' unto | thee.

9 Deliver me, O Lórd | from mine | enemies : for I fleé | unto | thee to | hide me.

10 Teach me to do the thing that pleaseth thee * for thóu | art my | God : let thy loving Spirit lead me fórth | into • the | land of | righteousness.

11 Quicken me O Lórd, for thy | Name's | sake : and for thy righteous- ness' sake bring my | soul | out of | trouble.

12 And of thy góodness | slay mine | enemies : and destroy all them that vex my sóul, for | I am | thy | servant.

THE ANNUNCIATION. MORNING.

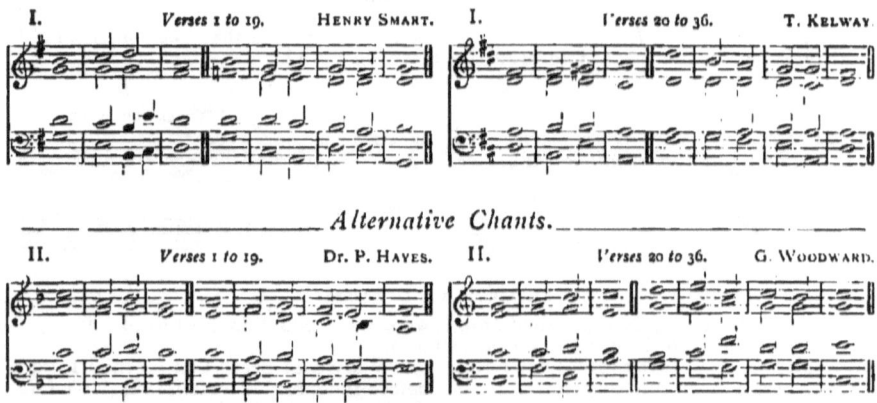

PSALM LXXXIX.—*Misericordias Domini.*

P. m MY song shall be alway of the loving- kindness | of the | Lord : with my mouth will I ever be shewing thy truth * from óne gener- | -ation | to an- | -other.

F. 2 For I have said, Mercy shall be sét | up for | ever : thy trúth shalt thou | stablish | in the | heavens.

3 I have made a cóvenant | with my | chosen : I have swórn ǀ unto | David • my | servant ;

4 Thy seéd will I | stablish • for | ever : and set up thy throne from óne gener- | -ation | to an- | -other.

5 O Lord, the very heavens shall

THE ANNUNCIATION. MORNING (continued).

práise thy | wondrous | works : and thy truth in the cóngre- | -gation | of the | saints.

6 For who is hé a- | -moug the | clouds : that sháll be com- | -pared | unto · the | Lord ?

7 And what is hé a- | -mong the | gods : that sháll be | like | unto · the | Lord ?

8 God is very greatly to be feared in the cóuncil | of the | saints : and to be had in reverence of all thém | that are | round a- | -bout him.

9 O Lord God of hosts * whó is | like · unto | thee : thy truth, most mighty Lórd | is on | every | side.

10 Thou rulest the ráging | of the | sea : thou stillest the wáves there- | -of when | they a- | -rise.

11 Thou hast subdued Egypt * ánd de- | -stroyed | it : thou hast scattered thine enemies abróad | with thy | mighty | arm.

12 The heavens are thine, the éarth | also · is | thine : thou hast laid the foundation of the round wórld, and | all that | therein | is.

13 Thou hast made the nórth | and the | south : Tabor and Hermon sháll re- | -joice | in thy | Name.

14 Thou hást a | mighty | arm : strong is thy hánd, and | high is | thy right | hand.

15 Righteousness and equity are the habitátion | of thy | seat : mercy and trúth shall | go be- | -fore thy | face.

16 Blessed is the people O Lord * that cán re- | -joice in | thee : they shall wálk in the | light | of thy | countenance.

17 Their delight shall be dáily | in thy | | Name : and in thy rígteousness | shall they | make their | boast.

18 For thou art the glóry | of their | strength : and in thy loving-kindness, thóu shalt | lift | up our | horns.

19 For the Lórd is | our de- | -fence : the Hóly One of | Israel | is our | King.

20 Thou spakest sometime in visions únto thy | saints and | saidst : I have laid help upon one that is mighty * I have ex- álted one | chosen | out · of the | people.

21 I have fóund | David · my | servant : with my holy óil have | | I a- | -nointed | him.

22 My hánd shall | hold him | fast : ánd my | arm shall | strengthen | him.

23 The enemy shall not be áble to | do him | violence : the són of | wickedness | shall not | hurt him.

24 I will smite down his fóes be- | -fore his | face : ánd | plague | them that | hate him.

25 My truth also and my mércy | shall be | with him : and in my Náme shall his | horn | be ex- | -alted.

26 I will set his dominion álso | in the | sea : ánd his | right hand | in the | floods.

27 He shall call me, Thóu | art my | Father : my Gód | and my | strong sal- | vation.

28 And I will máke | him my | firstborn : hígher than the | kings | of the | earth.

29 My mercy will I kéep for him for | ever- | -more : and my cóvenant shall | stand | fast | with him.

30 His seed also will I máke to en- | dure for | ever : and his thróne | as the | days of | heaven.

mf 31 But if his chíldren for- | -sake my | law : ánd | walk not | in my | judgements;

32 If they break my statutes * and kéep not | my com- | -mandments : I will visit their offences with the ród | and their | sin with | scourges.

33 Nevertheless, my loving-kindness will I not útterly | take | from him : nór | suffer · my | truth to | fail.

34 My covenant will I not break * nor alter the thing that is góne | out of · my | lips : I have sworn once by my holiness * that I* | will not | fail | David.

35 His séed shall en- | -dure for | ever : and his séat is | like · as the | sun be- | fore me,

36 He shall stand fast for evermóre | as the | moon : and ás the | faithful | witness · in heaven.

THE ANNUNCIATION. MORNING (continued).

I. *Verse 37 to end.* Sir W. Sterndale Bennett.

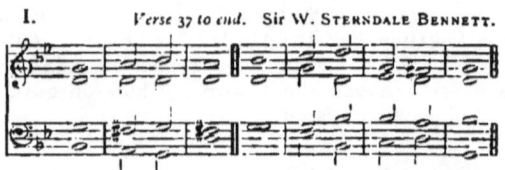

_____ *Alternative Chant.* _____

II. *Verse 37 to end.* Dr. E. G. Monk.

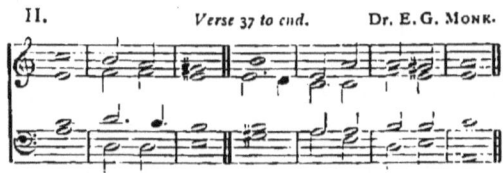

p 37 But thou hast abhorred and for-sáken | thine A- | -noínted : ánd | art dis- | pleased ! at him.

38 Thou hast broken the cóvenant | of thy | servant : and cást his | crown | to the | ground.

39 Thou hast overthrówn | all his | hedges : ánd | broken | down his | strongholds.

40 All théy that go | by | spoil him : and he is becóme a re- | -proach | to his | neighbours.

41 Thou hast set up the right hánd | of his | enemies : and máde all his | ad- versaries | to re- | -joice.

42 Thou hast taken away the édge | of his | sword : and givest him nót | victory | in the | battle.

43 Thóu hast put | out his | glory : and cást his | throne | down · to the | ground.

44 The days of his yóuth | hast thou | shortened : ánd | covered · him | with dis- | -honour.

45 Lord, how long wilt thou hîde thy- | self for | ever : and shált thy | wrath | burn like | fire ?

46 O remember how shórt my | time | is : wherefore hast thou máde | all | men for | nought ?

47 What man is he that líveth and shall | not see | death : and shall he de- liver his sóul | from the | hand of | hell ?

48 Lord, where are thy óld | loving- | kindnesses : which thou swárest unto | David | in thy | truth ?

49 Remember Lord, the rebúke that thy | servants | have : and how I do bear in my bósom the re- | -bukes of | many | people ;

50 Wherewith thine enemies have blasphemed thee * and slandered the fóotsteps of | thine A- | -nointed : Praised be the Lord for evermóre. | A- · · -men and | A- | -men.

THE ANNUNCIATION. EVENING.

Dr. STAINER.

PSALM CXXXI.—*Domine, non est.*

p LÓRD, I am | not high- | -minded :
I' have | no | proud | looks.
  2 I do not exercise mysélf in | great | matters : whích | are too | high for | me.
  3 But I refrain my soul, and keep it low ∗ like as a child that is wéaned | from his | mother : yea, my soul is éven | as a | weaned | child.
  4 O Israel, trúst | in the | Lord : from thís time | forth for | ever- | -more.

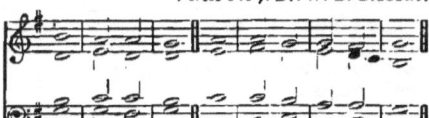
Verses 1 to 7. Dr. W. B. GILBERT.

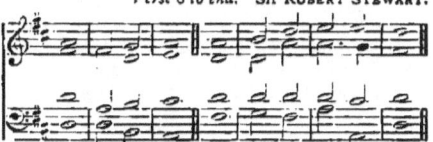
Verse 8 to end. Sir ROBERT STEWART.

PSALM CXXXII.—*Memento, Domine.*

mf LÓRD, re- | -member | David : ánd | all | his | trouble ;
  2 How he swáre | unto · the | Lord : and vowed a vow únto the Al- | -mighty | God of | Jacob ;
  3 I will not come within the táber- nacle | of mine | house : nór | climb up | into · my | bed ;
  4 I will not suffer mine eyes to sléep, nor mine | eye-lids · to | slumber : neither the temples of my héad to | take | any | rest ;
  5 Until I find out a place for the témple | of the | Lord: an habitation fór the | mighty | God of | Jacob.
  6 Lo, we héard of the | same at | Ephrata : ánd | found it | in the | wood.
  7 We will gó into his | taber- | -nacle : and fall lów on our | knees be- | -fore his | footstool.
  8 Arise, O Lórd | into · thy | resting- place : thóu and the | ark | of thy | strength.
  9 Let thy príests be | clothed · with | righteousness : and lét thy | saints ǀ sing with | joyfulness.
  10 For thy sérvant | David's | sake : turn not awáy the | presence · of | thine A- | -nointed.

  11 The Lord hath made a faithful óath | unto | David : ánd he | shall not | shrink | from it.
  12 Of the frúit | of thy | body : sháll I | set up- |-on thy | seat.
  13 If thy children will keep my cóve- nant ∗ and my téstimonies that | I shall | learn them : their children also shall sit upón thy | seat for | ever- | -more.
  14 For the Lord hath chosen Sion to be an habitátion | for him- | -self : hé hath | longed | for | her.
  15 This shall bé my | rest for | ever : here will I dwell ∗ fór I | have · a de- | light there- | -in.
  16 I will bléss her | victuals · with | increase : and will sátis- | -fy her | poor with | bread.
  17 I will déck her | priests with | health : and her sáints | shall re- | -joice and | sing.
  18 There shall I make the hórn of | David · to | flourish : I have ordáined a | lantern · for | mine A- | -nointed.
  19 As for his enemies ∗ I shall clóthe | them with | shame . but upon himsélf . shall his | crown | flourish.

THE ANNUNCIATION. EVENING (continued).

J. TURLE.

PSALM CXXXVIII.—*Confitebor tibi.*

mf I WILL give thanks unto thee O | Lórd, with my | whole | heart : even before the gods will I sing | praise | unto | thee.

2 I will worship toward thy holy temple, and praise thy Name ✷ because of thy lóving- | -kindness · and | truth : for thou hast magnified thy Náme, and thy | Word a- | -bove | all things.

3 When I called upon thée, thou | heardest | me : and endúedst my | soul with | much | strength.

4 All the kings of the earth shall práise | thee O | Lord : for they have héard the | words | of thy | mouth.

5 Yea, they shall sing in the wáys | of the | Lord : that gréat is the | glory | of the | Lord.

6 For though the Lord be high ✷ yet hath he respéct | unto · the | lowly : as for the proud, he behóldeth | them a- | far | off.

7 Though I walk in the midst of trouble ✷ yét shalt | thou re- | -fresh me : thou shalt stretch forth thy hand upon the furiousness of mine enemies ✷ ánd thy | right | hand shall | save me.

8 The Lord shall make good his loving-kíndness | toward | me : yea, thy mercy, O Lord endureth for ever ✷ despise not then the wórks | of thine | own | hands.

GOOD FRIDAY. MORNING.

J. BATTISHILL.

PSALM XXII.—*Deus, Deus meus.*

F. p MY God, my God, look upon me ✷ whý hast thou for- | -saken | me : and art so far from my health ✷ and fróm the | words of | my com- | -plaint ?

F. 2 O my God, I cry in the day-time ✷ bút thou | hearest | not : and in the nîght-season | also · I | take no | rest.

3 And thóu con- | -tinuest | holy : O° | — thou | worship · of | Israel.

4 Our fáthers | hoped · in | thee : they trusted in thée and thou | didst de- | liver | them.

5 They called upon thée | and were | holpen : they put their trust in thée | and were | not con- | -founded.

6 But as for me, I am a wórm, and | no | man : a very scorn of mén and the | outcast | of the | people.

7 All they that see me ✷ láugh | me to | scorn : they shoot out their lîps, and | shake their | heads, | saying,

8 He trusted in God, that hé would de- | -liver | him : let him delíver him | if he | will | have him.

9 But thou art he that took me óut of my | mother's | womb : thou wast my hope, when I hanged yét up | -on my | mother's | breasts.

10 I have been left unto thee ever sínce | I was | born : thou art my God, éven | from my | mother's | womb.

11 O go not from me ✷ for tróuble is | hard at | hand : ánd | there is | none to | help me.

12 Many óxen are | come a- | -bout me : fat bulls of Basan clóse me | in on | every | side

GOOD FRIDAY. MORNING (continued). 141

13 They gape upón me | with their | mouths : as it were a rámping | and a | roaring | lion.

14 I am poured out like water * and all my bónes are | out of | joint : my heart also in the midst of my bódy is | even · like | melting | wax.

15 My strength is dried up like a potsherd * and my tongue cléaveth | to my | gums : and thou shalt bring me | into · the | dust of | death.

16 For many dógs are | come a- | bout me : and the council of the wicked | layeth | siege a- | -gainst me.

17 They pierced my hands and my feet * I may téll | all my | bones : they stánd | staring · and | looking · up- | -on me.

18 They párt my | garments · a- | mong them : and cást | lots up- | -on my | vesture.

19 But be not thou fár from | me O | Lord : thou art my súccour, | haste | thee to | help me.

20 Deliver my sóul | from the | sword : my darling fróm the | power | of the | dog.

21 Save me fróm the | lion's | mouth : thou hast heard me also from amóng the | horns | of the | unicorns.

mf 22 I will declare thy Náme | unto my | brethren : in the midst of the cóngre- | gation | will I | praise thee.

f 23 O praise the Lórd | ye that | fear him : magnify him all ye of the seed of Jacob * and féar him | all ye | seed of | Israel;

24 For he hath not despised nor abhorred, the low estáte | of the | poor : he hath not hid his face from him * but when he cálled | unto | him he | heard him.

25 My praise is of thee in the gréat | congre- | -gation : my vows will I perfórm in the | sight of | them that | fear him.

26 The poor shall éat | and be | satisfied : they that seek after the Lord shall praise him * yóur | heart shall | live forĺever.

27 All the ends of the world shall remember themselves * and be túrned | unto · the | Lord : and all the kíndreds of the | nations · shall | worship · be-|-fore him.

28 For the kíngdom | is the | Lord's : and he is the Góver- | -nour a- | -mong the | people.

29 All súch as be | fat up- · -on | earth : háve | eaten | and | worshipped.

30 All they that go down into the dúst shall | kneel be- | -fore him ; and nó man hath | quickened · his | own | soul.

31 Mý | seed shall | serve him : they shall be counted unto the Lórd | for a | gener- | -ation.

32 They shall come * and the héavens shall de- | -clare his | righteousness : unto a people that shall be bórn | whom the | Lord hath | made.

Sir J. Goss.

PSALM XL.—*Expectans expectavi.*

mf I WAITED pátiently | for the | Lord : and he inclined únto | me and | heard my | calling.

2 He brought me also out of the horrible pit * óut of the | mire and | clay : and set my feet upon the róck, and | ordered | my | goings.

3 And he hath put a new sóng | in my | mouth : even a thánks- | -giving | unto · our | God.

4 Mány shall | see it · and | fear : and shall pút their | trust | in the | Lord.

5 Blessed is the man that hath set his hópe | in the | Lord : and turned not unto the proud * and to súch as | go a- | -bout | with | lies.

6 O Lord my God, great are the wondrous works which thou hast done * like as be also thy thóughts which | are to | us-ward : and yet there is no man that órdereth | them | unto | thee.

7 If I should declare them and | speak of | them : they should be more than I' am | able | to ex- | -press.

8 Sacrifice and meat-óffering thou | wouldest | not : but mine | ears | hast thou | opened.

9 Burnt-offerings and sacrifice for sin * hast thóu | not re- | -quired : thén | said I | Lo I | come,

10 In the volume of the book it is written of me * that I should fulfil thy will | O my | God : I am content to do it * yea thy láw | is with- | -in my | heart.

11 I have declared thy righteousness in the gréat | congre- | -gation : lo, I will not refrain my lips O | Lord and | that thou | knowest.

12 I have not hid thy ríghteousness with- | -in my | heart : my talk hath been of thy trúth | and of | thy sal- | -vation.

GOOD FRIDAY. MORNING (continued).

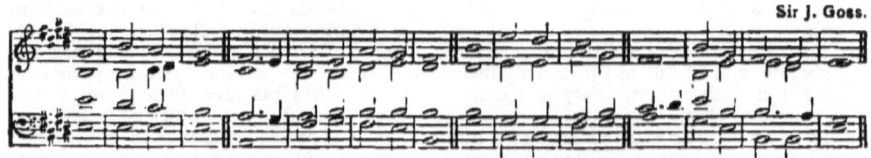
Sir J. Goss.

2nd part. 13 I have not kept back thy lóving | mercy · and | truth : fróm the | great | congre- | -gation.

mp 14 Withdraw not thou thy mércy from | me O | Lord : let thy loving-kindness and thy trúth | al- | -way pre- | -serve me.

15 For innumerable troubles are come about me ✱ my sins have taken such hold upon me ✱ that I am not áble to | look | up : yea, they are more in number than the hairs of my head ✱ ánd my | heart hath | failed | me.

16 O Lord, let it be thy pléasure to de- | liver | me : máke | haste O | Lord to | help me.

17 Let them be ashamed and confounded together ✱ that seek after my sóul | to de- | -stroy it : let them be driven backward ✱ and pút to re- | -buke that | wish me | evil.

18 Let them be desolate, ánd re- | warded · with | shame : that say unto me, Fíe up- | -on thee | fie up- | -on thee.

19 Let all those that seek thee be jóy- | ful and | glad in | thee : and let such as love thy salvation say álway The | Lord | be | praised.

20 As for mé I am | poor and | needy : bút the | Lord | careth | for me.

21 Thou art my hélper | and re- | deemer : make nó long | tarrying | O my | God.

Dr. Croft.

PSALM LIV.—*Deus, in Nomine.*

mp SAVE me, O Gód for thy | Name's | sake : ánd a- | -venge me | in thy | strength.

2 Héar my | prayer O | God : and hearken únto the | words | of my | mouth.

3 For strangers are rísen | up a- | gainst me : and tyrants, which have not God before their éyes | seek | after · my | soul.

4 Behold, Gód | is my | helper : the Lord is with thém | that up- | -hold my | soul.

5 He shall reward évil | unto · mine | enemies : destróy thou | them | in thy | truth.

6 An offering of a free heart will I give thee ✱ and práise thy | Name O Lord : bé- | -cause it | is so | comfortable.

7 For he hath delivered me óut of | all my | trouble : and mine eye hath séen his de- | -sire up- | -on mine enemies.

GOOD FRIDAY. EVENING. 143

Verses 1 to 12.   J. BARNBY.

Verses 13 to 22.   J. TURLE.

PSALM LXIX.—*Salvum me fac.*

F. mp SÁVE | me O | God : for the waters are come ín | even | unto · my | soul.

F. 2 I stick fast in the deep mire ✶ whêre no | ground | is : I am come into deep waters ✶ só that the | floods run | over | me.

3 I am weary of crýing ; my | throat is | dry : my sight faileth me for wáiting so | long up- | -on my | God.

4 They that hate me without a cause, are more than the háirs | of my | head : they that are mine enemies, and would de- | -stroy me | guiltless · are | mighty.

5 I paid them the thíngs that I | never | took : God, thou knowest my simpleness ✶ and my fáults | are not | hid from | thee.

6 Let not them that trust in thee, O Lord God of hosts ✶ be ashámed for | my | cause : let not those that seek thee ✶ be confounded through mê O | Lord | God of | Israel.

7 And why ✶ for thy sáke have I | suffered · re- | -proof : sháme hath | covered | my | face.

8 I am become a stránger | unto · my | brethren : even an álien | unto · my | mother's | children.

9 For the zeal of thine house hath éven | eaten | me : and the rebukes of them that rebúked | thee are | fallen · up- | on me.

10 I wept, and chástened my- | -self with | fasting : and thát was | turned · to | my re- | -proof.

11 I pût on | sackcloth | also : and they | jested · up- | -on | me.

12 They that sit in the gáte | speak a- | gainst me : ánd the | drunkards · make | songs up- | -on me.

13 But, Lord, I make my práyer | unto | thee : ín | an ac- | -ceptable | time.

14 Hear me, O God, in the múltitude | of thy | mercy : even ín the | truth of | thy sal- | -vation.

15 Take me out of the míre | that I | sink not : O let me be delivered from them that hate me ✶ ánd | out · of the | deep | waters.

16 Let not the water-flood drown me ✶ neither let the déep | swallow · me | up : and let not the pít | shut her | mouth up- | -on me.

17 Hear me O Lord, for thy lóving- | kindness · is | comfortable : turn thee unto me according to the | multitude | of thy | mercies.

18 And hide not thy face from thy sérvant for | I am · in | trouble : O° | haste | thee and | hear me.

19 Draw nígh unto my | soul and | save it : O deliver me be- | -cause of | mine | enemies.

20 Thou hast known my reproof, my sháme and | my dis- | -honour : mine ádversaries are | all in | thy | sight.

21 Thy rebuke hath broken my heart ✶ I° am | full of | heaviness : I looked for some to have pity on me, but there was no man ✶ neither fóund I | any · to | com- fort | me.

22 They gáve me | gall to | eat : and when I was thirsty they gáve me | vine- | gar to | drink.

GOOD FRIDAY. EVENING (continued).

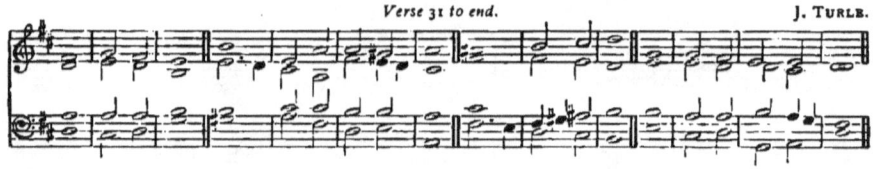

23 Let their table be made a snare to | take them- | -selves with- | -al : and let the things that should have been for their wealth * be unto thém | an oc- | -casion · of | falling.

24 Let their eyes be blínded, | that they | see not : and éver | bow thou | down their | backs.

25 Pour out thine índig- | -nation · up- | -on them : and let thy wráthful dis- | pleasure · take | hold of | them.

26 Let their hábit- | -ation · be | void : and nó man to | dwell | in their | tents.

27 For they persecute hím whom | thou hast | smitten : and they talk how they may véx | them whom | thou hast | wounded.

28 Let them fall from one wíckedness | to an- | -other : ánd | not come | into · thy | righteousness.

29 Let them be wiped out of the book | of the | living : and nót be | written · a- | -mong the | righteous.

30 As for me, when I am poor | and in | heaviness : thy help O | God shall | lift me | up.

f 31 I will praise the Name of Gód | with a | song : and mágni- | -fy it · with | thanks- | -giving.

32 This álso shall | please the | Lord : better than a búllock | that hath | horns and | hoofs.

33 The humble shall consider thís | and be | glad : seek ye after Gód | and your | soul shall | live.

34 For the Lórd | heareth · the | poor : ánd de- | -spiseth | not his | prisoners.

35 Let héaven and | earth | praise him : the séa, and | all that | moveth · there- | -in.

36 For God will save Sion * and build the | cities · of | Judah : that men may dwell thére, and | have it | in pos-|-session.

2nd part 37 The posterity also of his servants shall in- | -herit | it : and they that lóve his | Name shall | dwell there- | -in.

THOMAS TALLIS.

PSALM LXXXVIII.—*Domine Deus.*

mp O LORD God of my salvation * I have crîed day and | night be- | -fore thee : O let my prayer enter into thy presence * incline thine | ear | unto · **my** | calling.

2 For my sóul is | full of | trouble : and my lífe draweth | nigh | unto | hell.

3 I am counted as one of them that go dówn | into · the | pit : and I have been éven as a | man that | hath no | strength.

GOOD FRIDAY. EVENING (continued).

4 Free among the dead * like unto them that are wounded and lie | in the | grave : who are out of remembrance * and are cút a- | -way | from thy | hand.

5 Thou hast láid me in the | lowest | pit : in a pláce of | darkness . and | in the | deep.

6 Thine indignation lieth | hard up- | on me : and thou hast véxed | me with | all thy | storms.

7 Thou hast put away mine acquaint- ance | far | from me : and máde me to | be ab- | -horred | of them.

8 I' am so | fast in. | prison : thát I | cannot | get | forth.

9 My sight fáileth for | very | trouble : Lord, I have called daily upon thee * I have stretched fórth my | hands | unto | thee.

10 Dost thou shew wónders a- | -mong the | dead : or shall the déad rise | up a- | -gain and | praise thee ?

11 Shall thy loving - kindness be shéwed | in the | grave : ór thy | faithful- ness | in de- | -struction ?

12 Shall thy wondrous works be knówn | in the | dark : and thy righteous- ness in the lánd where | all things | are for- | -gotten ?

13 Unto thée have I | cried O | Lord : and early sháll my | prayer | come be- | fore thee.

14 Lord, why abhórrest | thou my | soul : and hídest | thou thy | face | from me ?

15 I am in misery * and like unto him that is át the | point to | die : even from my youth up, thy terrors have I súffered | with a | troubled | mind.

16 Thy wrathful displeasure góeth | over | me : and the féar of | thee | hath un- | -done me.

17 They came round about me | daily . like | water : and cómpassed me to- | gether . on | every | side.

18 My lovers and friends hast thou pút a- | -way | from me : and híd mine ac- | -quaintance | out of . my | sight.

EASTER EVEN. MORNING.

Dr. E. G. Monk.

PSALM IV.—*Cum invocarem.*

mf HEAR me when I call, O Gód | of my | righteousness : thou hast set me at liberty when I was in trouble * have mercy upon mé, and | hearken | unto . my | prayer.

2 O ye sons of men * how lóng will ye blas- | -pheme mine | honour : and have such pleasure in vánity and I seek | after | falsehood ?

3 Know this also * that the Lord hath chosen to himself the mán | that is | godly : when I cáll upon the | Lord | he will | hear me.

4 Stánd in | awe and | sin not : com- mune with your own heart * and ín your | chamber | and be | still.

5 Offer the sácri- | -fice of | righteous- ness : and pút your | trust | in the | Lord.

6 Thére be | many . that | say : Whó will | shew us | any | good ?

7 Lórd | lift thou | up : the light of thy | counte- | -nance up- | -on us.

8 Thou hast put gládness | in my | heart : since the time that their córn and | wine and | oil in- | -creased.

9 I will lay me down in péace, and | take my | rest : for it is thou, Lord, ónly that | makest . me | dwell in | safety.

EASTER EVEN. MORNING (continued).

PSALM XVI.—*Conserva me, Domine.*

mf PRESÉRVE | me O | God : for in | thée | have I | put my | trust.

2 O my soul, thou hast sáid | unto · the | Lord : Thou art my God * my góods are | nothing | unto | thee.

3 All my delight is upon the sáints that are | in the | earth : ánd upon | such as · ex- | -cel in | virtue.

4 But they that run áfter an- | -other | god : shåll | have | great | trouble.

5 Their drink-offerings of blóod will | I not | offer : neither make méntion of their | names with- | -in my | lips.

6 The Lord himself is the portion of mine inhéritance and | of my | cup : thóu | shalt main- | -tain my | lot.

7 The lot is fallen unto mé in a | fair | ground : yéa I | have a | goodly | heritage.

8 I will thank the Lórd for | giving · me | warning : my reins also chásten me | in the | night- | -season.

9 I have set Gód | always · be- | -fore me : for he is on my right hånd | there-fore · I | shall not | fall.

10 Wherefore my heart was glád and my | glory · re- | -joiced : my flésh | also · shall | rest in | hope.

11 For why * thou shalt not léave my | soul in | hell : neither shalt thou suffer thy Hóly | One to | see cor- | -ruption.

12 Thou shalt shew me the path of life * in thy presence ís the | fulness · of | joy : and at thy right hånd there is | pleasure · for | ever- | -more.

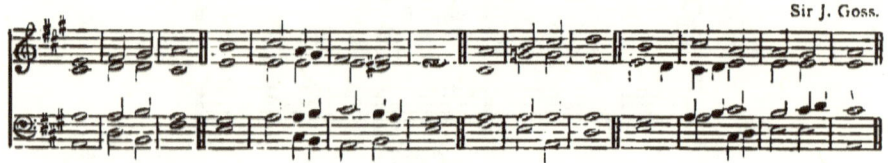

PSALM XVII.—*Exaudi, Domine.*

mp HEAR the right O Lord * consíder | my com- | -plaint : and hearken unto my | prayer * that góeth not | out of | feigned | lips.

2 Let my sentence come fórth | from thy | presence : and let thine eyes look upón the | thing | that is | equal.

3 Thou hast proved and visited mine heart in the night-season * thou hast tried me, and shall fínd no | wickedness | in me : for I am utterly purposed thát my | mouth shall | not of- | -fend.

4 Because of men's works that are done against the wórds | of thy | lips : I have kept me fróm the | ways of | the de- | -stroyer.

5 O hold thou up my góings | in thy | paths : thát my | footsteps | slip | not.

EASTER EVEN. MORNING (continued). 147

6 I have called upon thee O Gód, for I thou shalt I hear me : incline thine ear to mé, and I hearken I unto · my I words.

mf 7 Shew thy marvellous loving-kindness * thou that art the Saviour of them which pút their I trust in I thee : from súch as re- I -sist thy I right I hand.

8 Keep me as the ápple I of an I eye : hide me únder the I shadow I of thy I wings.

9 From the ungódly that I trouble I me : mine enemies compass me round abóut to I take a- I -way my I soul.

10 They are enclósed in their I own I fat : and their móuth I speaketh I proud I things.

11 They lie waiting in our wáy on I every I side : turning their éyes I down I to the I ground ;

12 Like as a lion that is gréedy I of his I prey : and as it were a lion's whélp I lurking · in I secret I places.

13 Up, Lord, disappóint him and ' cast him I down : deliver my soul from the ungódly which I is a I sword of I thine ;

14 From the men of thy hand, O Lord * from the men I say, and fróm the I evil I world : which have their portion in this life * whose bellies thou fíllest I with thy I hid I treasure.

15 They have chíldren at I their desire : and leave the rést of their I substance I for their I babes.

16 But as for me * I will behóld thy I presence · in I righteousness : and when I awake up after thy likeness * I' shall be I satis- I -fied I with it.

EASTER EVEN. EVENING.

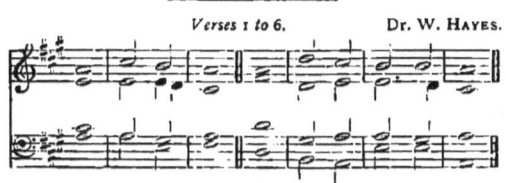

Verses 1 to 6.   Dr. W. HAYES.

PSALM XXX.—*Exaltabo te, Domine.*

mf I WILL magnify thee O Lord * for thóu hast I set me I up : and not made my fóes to I triumph I over I me.

2 O Lord my God, I crîed I unto I thee : ánd I thou hast I healed I me.

3 Thou, Lord, hast brought my sóul I out of I hell : thou hast kept my life from thém that go I down I to the I pit.

4 Sing praises unto the Lórd O ye I sáints of I his : and give thanks unto him *

fór a re- I -membrance I of his I holiness.

5 For his wrath endureth but the twinkling of an eye * and ín his I pleasure · is I life : heaviness may endure for a night * but jóy I cometh I in the I morning.

6 And in my prosperity I said * I shall néver I be re- I -moved : thou, Lord, of thy góodness hast I made my I hill so I strong.

p 7 Thou didst túrn thy | face | from me : ánd I I | was | troubled.

8 Then cried I únto | thee O | Lord : and gát me | to my | Lord right | humbly.

9 What profit ís there | in my | blood : when I go | down | to the | pit ?

10 Shall the dust give thánks | unto | thee : ór shall | it de- | -clare thy | truth ?

11 Hear, O Lórd, and have | mercy · up- | -on me : Lórd be | thou | my | helper.

mf 12 Thou hast turned my héaviness | into | joy : thou hast put off my sáckcloth and | girded | me with | gladness.

13 Therefore shall every good man sing of thy práise with- | -out | ceasing : O my God, I will give thánks | unto | thee for | ever.

S. MATTHEWS.

PSALM XXXI.—*In te, Domine, speravi.*

mf IN thee O Lórd have I | put my | trust : let me never be put to confúsion, de- | liver · me | in thy | righteousness.

2 Bow dówn thine | ear to | me : make háste | to de- | -liver | me.

3 And be thou my strong rock, and hóuse | of de- | -fence : thát | thou · mayest | save | me.

4 For thou art my strong róck | and my | castle : be thou also my guide * and léad me | for thy | Name's | sake.

5 Draw me out of the net that they have láid | privily | for me : fór | thou | art my | strength.

6 Into thy hánds I com- | -mend my | spirit : for thou hast redeemed me * O' | Lord thou | God of | truth.

7 I have hated them that hóld of super- | -stitious | vanities : and my trúst hath | been | in the | Lord.

8 I will be glad and rejóice | in thy | mercy : for thou hast considered my trouble * and hast knówn my | soul | in ad- | -versities.

2nd part. 9 Thou hast not shut me up into the hánd | of the | enemy : but hast set my féet | in a | large | room.

p 10 Have mercy upon me O Lórd, for I am · in | trouble : and mine eye is consumed for very heaviness * yéa my | soul | and my | body.

11 For my life is wáxen | old with | heaviness : and my | years | with | mourning.

12 My strength faileth me, becáuse of | mine in- | -iquity : and my | bones | are con- | -sumed.

EASTER EVEN. EVENING (continued).

13 I became a reproof among all mine enemies * but especially a- | -mong my | neighbours : and they of mine acquaintance were afraid of me * and they that did see me without con- | -veyed · them- | selves | from me.

14 I am clean forgotten, as a dead man | out of | mind : I am become | like a | broken | vessel.

15 For I have heard the blasphemy | of the | multitude : and fear is on every side * while they conspire together against me * and take their counsel to | take a- | way my | life.

16 But my hope hath been in | thee O | Lord : I have said | Thou art | my | God.

17 My time is in thy hand * deliver me from the hand | of mine | enemies : and from | them that | persecute | me.

18 Shew thy servant the light | of thy | countenance : and save me | for thy | mercy's | sake.

19 Let me not be confounded O Lord * for I have | called up- | -on thee : let the ungodly be put to confusion * and be put to | silence | in the | grave.

2nd part. 20 Let the lying lips be | put to | silence : which cruelly, disdainfully, and despitefully | speak a- | -gainst the | righteous.

f 21 O how plentiful is thy goodness * which thou hast laid up for | them that | fear thee : and that thou hast prepared for them that put their trust in thee * even be- | -fore the | sons of | men !

22 Thou shalt hide them privily by thine own presence * from the provoking of | all | men : thou shalt keep them secretly in thy tabernacle | from the | strife of | tongues.

23 Thanks be | to the | Lord : for he hath shewed me marvellous great kindness | in a | strong | city.

24 And when I made | haste I | said: I am cast out of the | sight | of thine | eyes.

25 Nevertheless, thou heardest the voice | of my | prayer : when I | cried | unto | thee

26 O love the Lord all | ye his | saints : for the Lord preserveth them that are faithful * and plenteously re- | -wardeth · the | proud | doer.

2nd part. 27 Be strong, and he shall es- | tablish · your | heart : all ye that put your | trust | in the | Lord.

EASTER DAY. MORNING.

ANTHEMS TO BE USED INSTEAD OF THE VENITE.

P. HUMPHREYS.

F. f CHRIST our passover is sacri- | ficed · for | us : therefore | let us | keep the | feast.

F. 2 Not with the old leaven * nor with the leaven of | malice · and | wickedness : but with the unleavened bread of sin- | -ceri- | -ty and | truth. 1 *Cor.* v. 7.

3 CHRIST being raised from the dead | dieth · no | more : death hath no more do- | -minion | over | him.

p 4 For in that he died * he died unto | sin | once : *f* but in that he liveth he | liveth | unto | God.

5 Likewise reckon ye also yourselves to be dead indeed | unto | sin : but alive unto God through | Jesus | Christ our | Lord. *Rom.* vi. 9.

6 CHRIST is risen | from the | dead : and become the first- | -fruits of | them that | slept.

7 For since by | man came | death : by man came also the resur- | -rection | of the | dead.

p 8 For as in A'dam | all | die : even so in Christ *f* shall | all be | made a- | -live. 1 *Cor.* xv. 20.

F. f Glory be to the Father, | and · to the | Son : and | to the | Holy | Ghost ;

F. As it was in the beginning * is now, and | ever | shall be : world without | end. | A- | -men.

EASTER DAY. MORNING (*continued*).

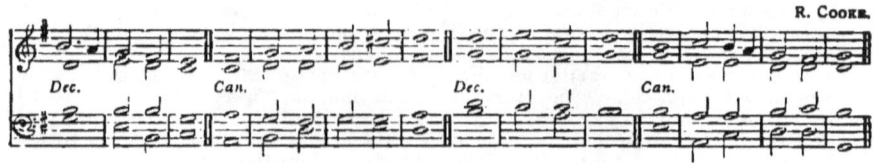

R. COOKE.

PSALM II.—*Quare fremuerunt gentes?*

f WHY do the heathen so fúriously | rage to- | -gether : and why do the péople im- | -agine · a | vain | thing ?

2 The kings of the earth stand up ✶ and the rúlers take | counsel · to- | -gether : against the Lórd and a- | -gainst | his A- | nointed.

3 Let us bréak their | bonds a- | -sunder : and cást a- | -way their | cords | from us.

4 He that dwelleth in héaven shall | laugh them · to | scorn : the Lórd shall | have them | in de- | -rision.

5 Then shall he speak unto thém | in his | wrath : and véx them | in his | sore dis- | -pleasure.

6 Yét have I | set my | King : upón my | hóly | hill of | Sion.

7 I will preach the law ✶ whereof the Lord hath sáid | unto | me : Thou art my | Son ✶ this dáy have | I be- | -gotten | thee.

8 Desire of me ✶ and I shall give thee the héathen for | thine in- | -heritance : and the utmost párts of the | earth for | thy pos- | -session.

9 Thou shalt brúise them with a | rod of | iron : and break them in pièces | like a | potter's | vessel.

10 Be wise now thérefore | O ye | kings : be learned, yé that are | judges of the | earth.

11 Sérve the | Lord in | fear : and rejóice | unto | him with | reverence.

12 Kiss the Son lest he be angry, and so ye pérish from the | right | way : if his wrath be kindled, (yea but a little), ✶ blessed are all théy that | put their | trust in | him.

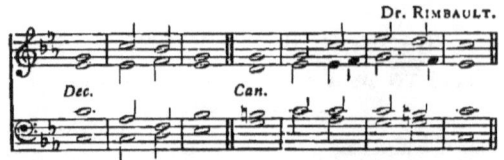

Dr. RIMBAULT.

PSALM LVII.—*Miserere mei, Deus.*

mp BE merciful unto me O God ✶ be merciful unto me, for my sóul | trusteth · in | thee : and under the shadow of thy wings shall be my refuge ✶ untíl this | tyranny · be | over- | -past.

2 I will cáll unto the | most high | God : even unto the God that shall perform the cáuse | which I | have in | hand.

3 Hé shall | send from | heaven : and save me from the reproof of hím | that would | eat me | up.

4 God shall send fórth his | mercy · and | truth : my sóul | is a- | -mong | lions.

5 And I lie even among the children of mén that are | set on | fire : whose teeth are spears and arrows ✶ ánd their | tongue a | sharp | sword.

6 Set up thyself, O Gód a- | -bove the | heavens : and thy glóry a- | -bove | all the | earth.

7 They have laid a net for my feet ✶ and préssed | down my | soul : they have digged a pit before me ✶ and are fallen into the | midst of | it them- | -selves.

8 My heart is fixed O Gód my | heart is | fixed : I' will | sing and | give | praise.

mf 9 Awake up my glory ✶ awáke | lute and | harp : I mysélf | will a- | -wake right | early.

10 I will give thanks unto thee, O Lórd a- | -mong the | people : and I will síng unto | thee a- | -mong the | nations.

11 For the greatness of thy mercy, réacheth | unto · the | heavens : ánd thy | truth | unto · the | clouds.

12 Set up thyself, O Gód a- | -bove the | heavens : and thy glóry a- | -bove | all the | earth.

EASTER DAY. MORNING (continued).

P. HUMPHREYS.

PSALM CXI.—*Confitebor tibi.*

mf I WILL give thanks unto the Lórd with my | whole | heart : secretly among the fáithful, and | in the | congre- | -ga- tion.

2 The wórks of the | Lord are | great : sought out of all thém | that have | pleasure · there- | -in.

3 His work is worthy to be práised, and | had in | honour : and his ríghteous- | ness en- | -dúreth · for | ever.

4 The merciful and gracious Lord hath so dóne his | marvellous | works : that they óught to be | had | in re- | membrance.

5 He hath given méat unto | them that | fear him : he shall éver be | mind- ful | of his | covenant.

6 He hath shewed his people the pówer | of his | works : that he may gíve them the | heritage | of the | heathen.

7 The works of his hands are vérity | and | judgement : áll | his com- | -mand- ments · are | true.

8 They stand fást for | ever · and | ever : ánd are | done in | truth and | equity.

9 He sent redémption | unto · his | people : he hath commanded his covenant for ever * hóly and | reverend | is his | Name.

10 The fear of the Lórd is the be- | ginning · of | wisdom : a good under- standing have all they that do thereafter * the práise of | it en- | dureth · for | ever.

EASTER DAY. EVENING.

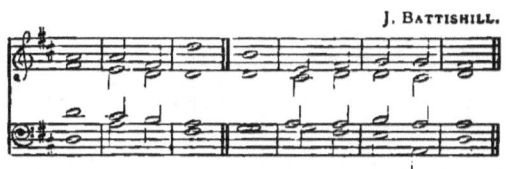

J. BATTISHILL.

PSALM CXIII.—*Laudate, pueri.*

F. f PRÁISE the | Lord ye | servants : O práise the | Name | of the | Lord.

F. 2 Blessed be the Náme | of the | Lord : from this time | forth for | ever- | more.

3 The Lórd's | Name is | praised : from the rising up of the sun, unto the góing | down | of the | same.

4 The Lord is high a- | -bove all | heathen : ánd his | glory · a- | -bove the | heavens.

5 Who is like unto the Lord our God * that háth his | dwelling · so | high : **and** yet humbleth himself to behold the thíngs that | are in | heaven and | earth ?

6 He taketh up the símple | out · of the | dust : and lífteth the | poor | out · of the | mire ;

7 That he may sét him | with the | princes : even wíth the | princes | of his | people.

8 He maketh the barren wóman to | keep | house : and to bé a | **joyful** | mother · of | children.

EASTER DAY. EVENING (*continued*).

Tonus Peregrinus.

PSALM CXIV.—*In exitu Israel.*

F.mf WHEN Is\|ra el came \| out of \| Egypt : and the house of Jacob fróm a- \| -mong the \| strange \| people,

F. 2 Júdah \| was his \| sanctuary : ánd \| Israel \| his do- \| -minion.

3 The séa saw \| that, and \| fled : Jór- \| dan was \| driven \| back.

4 The móuntains \| skipped · like \| rams : and the líttle \| hills like \| young \|\| sheep.

5 What aileth thee, O thou séa \| that

thou \| fleddest : and thou Jórdan \| that \| thou wast \| driven \| back ?

6 Ye mountains, that ye \| skipped like \| rams : and ye little \| hills like \| young \| sheep ?

7 Tremble thou earth, at the pré- sence \| of the \| Lord : at the présence \| of the \| God of \| Jacob ;

8 Who turned the hard róck into a \| standing \| water : and the flint-stone \| into · a \| springing \| well.

Verses 1 to 14. R. GOODSON.   *Verse 15 to end.* Dr. T. A. WALMISLEY.

PSALM CXVIII.—*Confitemini Domino.*

f O GIVE thanks unto the Lórd, for \|\| he is \| gracious : becáuse his \| mercy · en- \| -dureth · for \| ever.

2 Let Israel now confess that \| he is \| gracious : and thát his \| mercy · en- \| dureth · for \| ever.

3 Let the house of Aáron \| now con- fess : thát his \| mercy · en- \| -dureth · for \| ever.

4 Yea, let them now that féar the \| Lord con- \| -fess : thát his \| mercy · en- \| dureth · for \| ever.

mf 5 I called upón the \| Lord in \| trouble : and the Lórd \| heard \| me at \| large.

6 The Lórd is \| on my \| side : I will not féar what \| man · doeth \| unto \| me.

7 The Lord taketh my párt with \|\| them that \| help me : therefore shall I sée my de- \| -sire up- \| -on mine \| enemies.

8 It is better to trúst \| in the \| Lord : than to pút any \| confi- \| -dence in \| man.

9 It is better to trúst \| in the \| Lord : than to pút any \| confi- \| -dence in \| princes.

10 All nations compassed me \| round a- \| -bout : but in the Náme of the \| Lord will \| I de- \| -stroy them.

11 They kept me in on every side * they kept me in, I sáy, on \| every \| side : but in the Náme of the \| Lord will \| I de- stroy them.

12 They came about me like bees * and are extinct even as the fíre a- \| -mong the \| thorns : for in the Náme of the \| Lord I \| will de- \| -stroy them.

13 Thou hast thrust sore at mé, that \| I might \| fall : bút the \| Lord \| was my \| help.

14 The Lord is my stréngth \| and my \| song : and ís be- \| -come \| my sal- \| vation.

15 The voice of joy and health is in the dwéllings \| of the \| righteous : the right hand of the Lórd bringeth \| mighty \| things to \| pass.

16 The right hand of the Lórd \| hath · the pre- \| -eminence : the right hand of the Lórd bringeth \| mighty \| things to \| pass.

17 I shall not \| die but \| live : and declare the \| works \| of the \| Lord.

18 The Lord hath chástened and cor- \| rected \| me : but he hath not gíven me \| over \| unto \| death.

19 Open me the \| gates of \| righteous- ness : that I may go into them * ánd give \| thanks \| unto · the \| Lord.

20 This is the gáte \| of the \| Lord : the ríghteous shall \| enter \| into \| it.

21 I will thánk thee for \| thou hast \| heard me : and árt be- \| -come \| my sal- \| vation.

22 The same stóne which the | you good luck ☀ ye that áre of the |
builders · re- | -fused : is becóme the | house | of the | Lord.
head-stone | in the | corner.

23 This is the | Lord's | doing : ánd it
is | márvellous | in our | eyes.

24 This is the dáy which the | Lord
hath | made : we will rejóice | and be |
glad in | it.

25 Hélp me | now O | Lord : O Lórd |
send us | now pros- | -perity.

26 Blessed be he that cometh in the
Náme | of the | Lord : we have wished

27 God is the Lórd who hath | shewed·
us | light : bind the sacrifice with cords ☀
yea, even únto the | horns | of the |
altar.

28 Thou art my Gód, and | I will |
thank thee : thóu art my | God, and | I
will | praise thee.

29 O give thanks unto the Lórd. for |
he is | gracious : ánd his | mercy · en- |
dureth · for | ever.

ASCENSION DAY. MORNING.

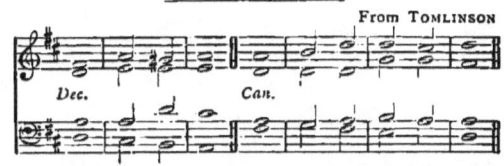

From TOMLINSON

PSALM VIII.—*Domine, Dominus noster.*

f O LORD our Governour ☀ how excellent is thy Náme in|all the|world : thou that bast sét thy | glory · a-|-bove the | heavens.

2 Out of the mouth of very babes and sucklings hast thou ordained strength ☀ becáuse | of thine | enemies : that thou mightest stíll the | enemy | and · the a- | -venger.

3 For I will consider thy heavens ☀ even the wórks | of thy | fingers : the moon and the stárs | which thou | bast or- | -dained.

4 What is man, that thóu art | mindful · of | him : and the són of man | that thou | visitest | him?

5 Thou madest him lówer | than the |
angels : to crówn | him with | glory · and |
worship.

6 Thou makest him to have dominion
of the wórks | of thy | hands : and thou
hast put all things ín sub- | -jection |
under · his | feet ;

7 A'll | sheep and | oxen : yéa and
the | beasts | of the | field ;

8 The fowls of the air, and the físhes |
of the | sea : and whatsoever walketh
through the | paths | of the | seas.

9 O' | Lord our | Governour : how
excellent ís thy | Name in | all the |
world !

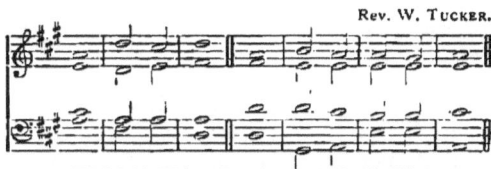

Rev. W. TUCKER.

PSALM XV.—*Domine, quis habitabit?*

mf LORD, who shall dwéll in thy |
taber- | nacle : or who shall rést up- | -on
thy | holy | hill?

2 Even he that léadeth an | uncorrupt | life : and doeth the thing which is
right ☀ and spéaketh the | truth | from his |
heart.

3 He that hath used no deceit in his
tongue ☀ nor done évil | to his | neighbour : ánd | hath not | slandered · his |
neighbour.

4 He that setteth not by himself ☀
but is lówly in his | own | eyes : and maketh múch of | them that | fear the | Lord.

5 He that sweareth unto his neighbour ☀ and dísap- | -pointeth · him | not :
though it | were · to his | own | hindrance.

6 He that hath not given his móney
up- | -on | usury : nor táken re- | -ward
a- | -gainst the | innocent.

7 Whóso | doeth · these | things :
shall | nev- | -er | fall.

ASCENSION DAY. MORNING (*continued*).

Dr. R. Woodward.

PSALM XXI.—*Domine, in virtute tua.*

mf THE King shall rejóice in thy | strength O | Lord : exceeding glád shall he | be of | thy sal- | -vation.

2 Thou hast given him his | heart's de- | -sire : and hast not denied him the re- | -quest | of his | lips.

3 For thou shalt prevent him wíth the | blessings · of | goodness : and shalt set a crówn of pure | gold up-|-on his | head.

4 He asked life of thee ✶ and thou gávest him a | long | life : éven for | ever | and | ever.

5 His honour is gréat in | thy sal- | -vation : glory and great wórship | shalt thou | lay up- | -on him.

6 For thou shalt give him éver- | -lasting · fe- | -licity : and make him glád with the | joy | of thy | countenance.

7 And why ✶ because the King putteth his trúst | in the | Lord : and in the mercy of the Most Híghest | he shall | not mis- | carry.

8 All thine énemies shall | feel thy | hand : thy right hánd shall | find out | them that | hate thee.

9 Thou shalt make them like a fiery oven in tíme | of thy | wrath : the Lord shall destroy them in his displeasure ✶ ánd the | fire | shall con- | -sume them.

10 Their fruit shalt thou róot | out · of the | earth : and their séed from a- | -mong the | children · of | men.

11 For they inténded | mischief · a- | -gainst thee : and imagined such a device as they áre not | able | to per- | form.

12 Therefore shalt thou pút | them to | flight : and the strings of thy bow shalt thou make réady a- | -gainst the | face of | them.

2nd part 13 Be thou exalted, Lórd in thine | own | strength : só will we | sing and | praise thy | power.

ASCENSION DAY. EVENING.

J. Barnby.

PSALM XXIV.—*Domini est terra.*

F. ƒ THE earth is the Lord's ✶ and áll that | therein | is : the compass of the wórld, and | they that | dwell there- | -in.

F. 2 For he hath fóunded it up-|-on the | seas : and prepáred | it up-|-on the | floods.

3 Who shall ascend into the híll | of the | Lord : or who shall rise úp | in his | holy | place ?

4 Even he that hath clean hánds and a | pure | heart : and that hath not lift up his mind unto vanity ✶ nor swórn | to de- | -ceive his | neighbour.

5 He shall receive the bléssing | from the | Lord : and righteousness fróm the | God of | his sal- | -vation.

6 This is the generátion of | them that | seek him : even of thém that | seek thy | face O | Jacob.

7 Lift up your heads O ye gates ✶ and be ye lift up ye éver- | -lasting | doors : and the Kíng of | glory | shall come | in.

8 Whó is the | King of | glory : it is the Lord strong and mighty ✶ éven the | Lord | mighty · in | battle.

9 Lift up your heads O ye gates ✶ and be ye lift up ye éver- | -lasting | doors : and the Kíng of | glory | shall come | in.

10 Whó is the | King of | glory : even the Lord of hósts | he · is the | King of | glory.

ASCENSION DAY. EVENING (*continued*).

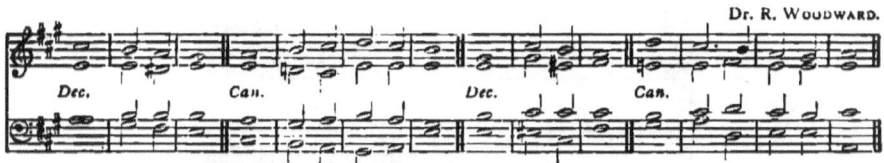

Dr. R. Woodward.

PSALM XLVII.—*Omnes gentes, plaudite.*

F. f O CLAP your hands togéther | all ye | people : O sing unto Gód | with the. | voice of | melody.

F. 2 For the Lord is hígh and | to be | feared : he is the great Kíng up- | -on | all the | earth.

3 He shall subdue the péople | under | us : ánd the | nations | under · our | feet.

4 He shall choose óut an | heritage | for us : even the wórship of | Jacob | whom he | loved.

5 God is gone úp with a | merry | noise : and the Lórd with the | sound | of the | trump.

6 O sing praises, sing práises | unto · our | God : O sing práises sing | praises | unto · our | King.

7 For God is the Kíng of | all the | earth : síng ye | praises · with | under- | standing.

8 God réigneth | over · the | heathen : God sítteth up- | -on his | holy | seat.

2nd part. 9 The princes of the people ✶ are joined unto the péople of the | God of | Abraham : for God which is very high exalted ✶ doth defend the éarth as it | were | with a | shield.

W. Russell.

PSALM CVIII.—*Paratum cor meum.*

mf O GOD my heart is réady, my | heart is | ready : I will sing and give praise with the bést | member | that I | have.

2 Awáke, thou | lute and | harp : I mysélf | will a- | -wake right | early.

3 I will give thanks unto thee O Lórd, a- | -mong the | people : I will sing práises unto | thee a- | -mong the | nations.

4 For thy mercy is gréater | than the | heavens : and thy trúth | reacheth | unto · the | clouds.

5 Set up thyself O Gód, a- | -bove the | heavens : and thy glóry a- | -bove | all the | earth.

6 That thy belóved may | be de- | livered : let thy right hand sáve | them, and | hear thou | me.

7 God hath spóken | in his | holiness : I will rejoice therefore and divide Sichem ✶ and méte | out the | valley · of | Succoth.

8 Gilead is míne, and Ma- | -nasses · is | mine : Ephraim also ís the | strength | of my | head.

2nd part. 9 Judah is my law-giver, ✶ Móab | is my | wash-pot : over Edom will I cast out my shoe ✶ upón Phi- | -listia | will I | triumph.

10 Who will lead me ínto the | strong | city : and whó will | bring me | into | Edom ?

11 Hast not thou forsáken | us O | God : and wilt not thou, O Gód, go | forth | with our | hosts ?

12 O hélp us a- | -gainst the | enemy : for váin | is the | help of | man.

13 Through Gód we shall | do great | acts : and it is hé that shall | tread | down our | enemies.

WHITSUNDAY. MORNING.

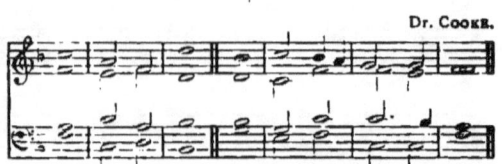
Dr. COOKE.

PSALM XLVIII.—*Magnus Dominus.*

f GREAT is the Lord, and highly | to be | praised : in the city of our God ✱ éven up- | -on his | holy | hill.

2 The hill of Sion is a fair place ✱ and the jóy of the | whole | earth : upon the north-side lieth the city of the great King ✱ God is well known in her pálaces | as a | sure | refuge.

3 For lo, the kíngs | of the | earth : are gáthered and | gone | by to- | -gether.

4 They márvelled to | see such | things : they were astónished and | sudden- - -ly | cast | down.

5 Fear came thére upon | them and | sorrow : as upón a | woman | in her | travail.

6 Thou shalt break the shíps | of the | sea : through | — the | east- | -wind.

7 Like as we have heard ✱ so have we seen in the city of the Lord of hosts ✱ in the cíty | of our | God : Gód up- | -holdeth ⋅ the | same for | ever.

8 We wait for thy lóving- | -kindness ⋅ O | God : ín the | midst of | thy | temple.

9 O God according to thy Name ✱ so is thy praise únto the | world's | end : thy right | hand is | full of | righteousness.

10 Let the mount Sion rejoice ✱ and the daúghter of | Judah ⋅ be | glad : bé- | -cause of | thy | judgements.

11 Walk about Sion, and gó | round a- | bout her : ánd | tell the | towers there- | -of.

12 Mark well her bulwarks, sét | up her | houses : that ye may téll | them that | come | after.

13 For this God is our Gód for | ever ⋅ and | ever : he shall bé our | guide | unto | death

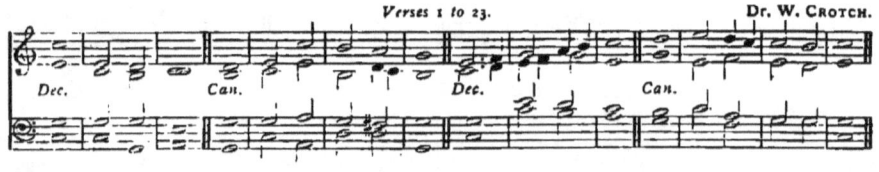
Verses 1 to 23. Dr. W. CROTCH.

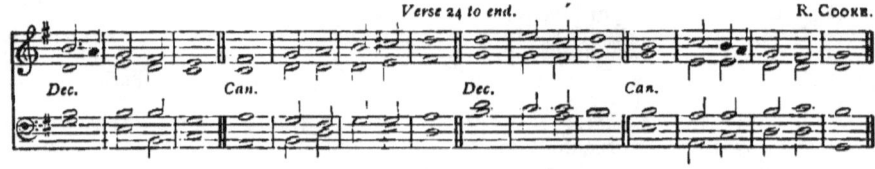
Verse 24 to end. R. COOKE.

PSALM LXVIII.—*Exurgat Deus.*

f LET God arise, and let his éne- | mies be | scattered : let them álso that | hate him | flee be- | -fore him.

2 Like as the smoke vanisheth, ✱ so shalt thou drive | them a- | -way : and like as wax melteth at the fire ✱ so let the ungodly pérish | at the | presence ⋅ of | God.

3 But let the righteous be glád and re- | -joice be ⋅ fore | God : lét them | also ⋅ be | merry ⋅ and | joyful.

4 O sing unto God, and sing práises | | unto ⋅ his | Name : magnify him that ridetb upon the heavens as it were upon an horse ✱ praise him in his Name JA'H | and re- | -joice be- | -fore him.

5 He is a Father of the fatherless ✱ and defendeth the cáuse | of the | widows : even Gód in his | holy | habit- | -ation.

6 He is the God that maketh men to be of one mind in an house ✱ and bringeth the prisoners | out of ⋅ cap- | -tivity : but letteth the runagátes con- | -tinue | in | scarceness.

WHITSUNDAY. MORNING (*continued*). 157

7 O God, when thou wentest fórth be- | -fore the | people : whén thou | wentest | through the | wilderness,

8 The earth shook, and the heavens dropped át the | presence · of | God : even as Sinai also was moved at the presence of Gód, who | is the | God of | Israel.

9 Thou, O God, sentest a gracious ráin upon | thine in- | -heritance : and refréshedst | it when | it was | weary.

10 Thy congregátion shall | dwell there- | -in : for thou, O God, hast of thy góodness pre- | -pared | for the | poor.

11 The Lórd | gave the | word : gréat was the | company | of the | preachers.

12 Kings with their armies did flee and | were dis- | -comfited : and théy of the | household · di- | -vided · the | spoil.

13 Though ye have lain among the pots ✶ yet shall ye be as the wíngs | of a | dove : that is covered with silver wíngs | and her | feathers · like | gold.

14 When the Almighty scattered kíngs | for their | sake : thén were they as | white as | snow in | Salmon.

15 As the hill of Basan, só is | God's | hill : even an hígh hill | as the | hill of | Basan.

16 Why hop ye so ye high hills ✶ this is God's hill, in the which it pléaseth | him to | dwell : yea the Lórd will a- | -bide in | it for | ever.

17 The chariots of God are twenty thousand ✶ éven | thousands · of | angels : and the Lord is among them ✶ as ín the | holy | place of | Sinai.

18 Thou art gone up on high ✶ thou hast led captivity captive, and recéived | gifts for | men : yea, even for thine enemies ✶ that the Lórd | God might | dwell a- | -mong them.

19 Praised bé the | Lord | daily : even the God who helpeth us, and póureth his | bene- | -fits up- | -on us.

20 He is our God ✶ even the Gód of | whom | cometh · sal- | -vation : God is the Lórd by | whom · we es- | -cape | death.

21 God shall wound the héad | of his | enemies : and the hairy scalp of such a one as góeth on | still | in his | wickedness.

22 The Lord hath said ✶ I will bring my people agáin as I | did from | Basan : mine own will | bring again ✶ as I did sometime fróm the | deep | of the | sea.

2nd part 23 That thy foot may be dipped in the blóod | of thine | enemies : and that the tongue of thy dógs may be | red | through the | same.

24 It is well seen O Gód | how thou | goest : how thou, my God and Kíng | goest | in the | sanctuary.

25 The singers go before ✶ the mínstrels | follow | after : in the midst are the dámsels | playing | with the | timbrels.

26 Give thanks O Israel, unto God the Lórd in the | congre- | -gations : fróm the | ground | of the | heart.

27 There is little Benjamin their ruler ✶ and the prínces of | Judah · their | counsel : the princes of Zabúlon | and the | princes · of | Nepthali.

28 Thy God hath sént forth | strength for | thee : stablish the thing, O Gód that | thou hast | wrought in | us,

29 For thy temple's sáke | at Je- | rusalem : so shall kíngs bring | presents | unto | thee.

30 When the company of the spearmen, and multitude of the mighty ✶ are scattered abroad among the beasts of the people ✶ so that they húmbly bring | pieces · of | silver : and when he hath scattered the péople | that de- | -light in | war ;

31 Then shall the princes cóme | out of | Egypt : the Morians' land shall soon stretch óut her | hands | unto | God.

ff 32 Sing unto God, O ye kíngdoms | of the | earth : O" sing | praises | unto · the | Lord ;

33 Who sitteth in the heavens over áll | from · the be- | -ginning : lo, he doth send out his voice ✶ yéa and | that a | mighty | voice.

34 Ascribe ye the power to Gód | over | Israel : his wórship and | strength is | in the | clouds.

35 O God, wonderful art thóu in thy | holy | places : even the God of Israel ✶ he will give strength and power unto his péople, | blessed | be | God.

WHITSUNDAY. EVENING.

PSALM CIV.—*Benedic, anima mea.*

F. ⨏ PRAISE the Lórd | O my | soul : O Lord my God, thou art become exceed-ing glorious ✱ thou art clóthed with | majes- | -ty and | honour.

F. 2 Thou deckest thyself with light as it wére | with a | garment : and spreadest óut the | heavens | like a | curtain.

3 Who layeth the beams of his chám-bers | in the | waters : and maketh the clouds his chariot ✱ and walketh upón the | wings | of the | wind.

4 He máketh his | angels | spirits : and his minis- | -ters a | flaming | fire.

5 He laid the foundátions | of the | earth : that it néver should | move at | any | time.

6 Thou coveredst it with the deep, like as | with a | garment : the wáters | stand | in the | hills.

7 At thý re- | -buke they | flee : at the vóice of thy | thunder · they | are a- | -fraid.

8 They go up as high as the hills ✱ and dówn to the | valleys · be- | -neath : even unto the pláce which | thou · hast ap- | -pointed | for them.

9 Thou hast set them their bóunds which they | shall not | pass : neither túrn a- | -gain to | cover · the | earth.

10 He sendeth the springs | into · the | rivers : which | run a- | -mong the | hills.

11 All beasts of the field | drink there- | -of : and the wild | asses | quench their | thirst.

12 Beside them shall the fowls of the áir have their | habit- | -ation : ánd | sing a- | -mong the | branches.

13 He watereth the hílls | from a- | bove : the earth is filled with the | fruit | of thy | works.

14 He bringeth forth gráss | for the | cattle : and green hérb | for the | service · of | men;

15 That he may bring food out of the earth ✱ and wine that maketh glád the | heart of | man : and oil to make him a cheerful countenance ✱ and bréad to | strengthen | man's | heart.

16 The trees of the Lord álso are full of | sap : even the cedars of Liban-us which | he hath | planted;

17 Wherein the birds | make their | nests : and the fir-trees áre a | dwelling | for the | stork.

18 The high hills are a refúge for the | wild | goats : and so are the stóny | rocks | for the | conies.

19 He appointed the móon for | cer-tain | seasons : and the sún | knoweth · his | going | down.

20 Thou makest darkness ✱ thát it | may be | night : wherein all the béasts | of the | forest · do | move.

21 The lions róaring | after · their | prey : do | seek their | meat from | God.

WHITSUNDAY. EVENING (continued). 159

22 The sun ariseth * and they get them a- | -way to- | -gether : and lay them | down | in their | dens.

23 Man goeth forth to his work, and | to his | labour : un- | -til the | even- | -ing.

ff 24 O Lord, how manifold | are thy | works : in wisdom hast thou made them all * the earth is | full | of thy | riches.

25 So is the great and | wide sea | also : wherein are things creeping innumerable * both | small and | great | beasts.

f 26 There go the ships * and there is | that Le- | -viathan : whom thou hast made to | take his | pastime · there- | -in.

27 These wait | all up- · -on | thee : that thou mayest give them | meat in | due | season.

28 When thou givest it them they | gather | it : and when thou openest thy hand | they are | filled · with | good.

mp 29 When thou hidest thy face | they are | troubled : when thou takest away their breath they die * and are turned a- | -gain | to their | dust.

mf 30 When thou lettest thy breath go forth they | shall be | made : and thou shalt renew the | face | of the | earth.

f 31 The glorious Majesty of the Lord shall en- | -dure for | ever : the Lord shall re- | -joice | in his | works.

32 The earth shall tremble at the | look of | him : if he do but touch the | hills | they shall | smoke.

33 I will sing unto the Lord as | long as · I | live : I will praise my God | while I | have my | being.

34 And so shall my | words | please him : my joy shall | be | in the | Lord.

35 As for sinners, they shall be consumed out of the earth * and the ungodly shall | come · to an | end : praise thou the Lord, O my soul, | praise | —the | Lord.

R. COOKE.

PSALM CXLV.—*Exaltabo te, Deus.*

mf I WILL magnify thee O | God my | King : and I will praise thy | Name for | ever · and | ever.

2 Every day will I give thanks | unto | thee : and praise thy | Name for | ever · and | ever.

3 Great is the Lord, and marvellous * worthy | to be | praised : there is no | end | of his | greatness.

4 One generation shall praise thy works | unto · an- | -other : and de- | clare | thy | power.

5 As for me, I will be talking | of thy | worship : thy glory, thy | praise and | wondrous | works ;

6 So that men shall speak of the might of thy | marvellous | acts : and I will also | tell | of thy | greatness.

7 The memorial of thine abundant kindness | shall be | shewed : and men shall | sing | of thy | righteousness.

8 The Lord is | gracious · and | merciful : long-suffering, | and of | great | goodness.

9 The Lord is loving unto | every | man : and his mercy is | over | all his | works.

10 All thy works praise | thee O | Lord : and thy saints give | thanks | unto | thee.

11 They shew the glory | of thy | kingdom : and | talk | of thy | power ;

12 That thy power, thy glory, and mightiness | of thy | kingdom : might be | known | unto | men.

13 Thy kingdom is an ever- | -lasting | kingdom : and thy dominion en- | -dureth · through- | -out all | ages.

14 The Lord upholdeth all | such as | fall : and lifteth up all | those | that are | down.

15 The eyes of all wait upon | thee O | Lord : and thou givest them their | meat in | due | season.

16 Thou openest | thine | hand : and fillest | all things | living · with | plenteousness.

17 The Lord is righteous in | all his | ways : and | holy · in | all his | works.

18 The Lord is nigh unto all them that | call up- | -on him : yea, all such as | call up- | -on him | faithfully.

19 He will fulfil the desire of | them that | fear him : he also will hear their | cry | and will | help them.

20 The Lord preserveth all | them that | love him : but scattereth a- | -broad | all · the un- | -godly.

2nd part 21 My mouth shall speak the praise | of the | Lord : and let all flesh give thanks unto his holy | Name for | ever · **and** | ever.

TRINITY SUNDAY. MORNING.

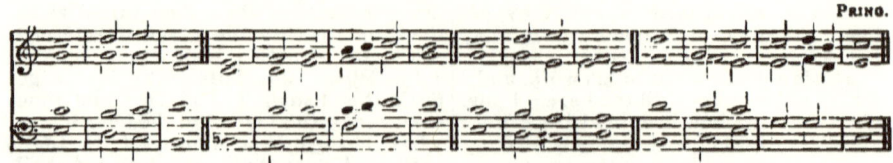

PSALM XXIX.—*Afferte Domino.*

BRING unto the Lord, O ye mighty ✴ bring young ráms | unto · the | Lord : ascribe unto the Lórd | worship | and | strength.

2 Give the Lord the honour dúe | unto · his | Name : wórship the | Lord with | holy | worship.

3 It is the Lórd that com· | -mandeth · the | waters : it is the glórious | God that | maketh · the | thunder.

4 It is the Lord that ruleth the sea ✴ the voice of the Lord is mighty in | oper· | -ation : the voice of the Lórd | is a | glorious | voice.

5 The voice of the Lórd | breaketh · the | cedar-trees : yéa, the Lord | breaketh · the | cedars · of | Libanus.

6 He maketh them also to skíp | like a | calf : Libanus also and Sírion, | like a | young | unicorn.

7 The voice of the Lord divideth the flames of fire ✴ the voice of the Lórd | shaketh . the | wilderness : yea, the Lord sháketh the | wilder- | -ness of | Cades.

8 The voice of the Lord maketh the hinds to bring forth young ✴ and discóvereth the | thick | bushes : in his temple doth évery man | speak | of his | honour.

9 The Lord sítteth a- | -bove the | water-flood : and the Lórd re- | -maineth · a | King for | ever.

10 The Lord shall give strength | unto · his | people : the Lord shall give his | people · the | blessing · of | peace.

W. LEE.

PSALM XXXIII.—*Exultate, justi.*

mf REJOICE in the Lórd | O ye | righteous : for it becometh wéll the | just | to be | thankful.

2 Práise the | Lord with | harp : sing praises unto him with the lute ✴ and instru- | -ment of | ten | strings.

3 Sing unto the Lórd a | new | song : sing praises lustily unto hím | with a | good | courage.

4 For the wórd of the | Lord is | true : ánd | all his | works are | faithful.

5 He loveth ríghteous- | -ness and | judgement : the earth is fúll of the | goodness | of the | Lord.

6 By the word of the Lórd were the | heavens | made : and all the hosts of them bý the | breath | of his | mouth.

7 He gathereth the waters of the sea together ✴ as it wére up- | -on an | heap : and layeth úp the | deep as | in a | treasure-house.

8 Let all the éarth | fear the | Lord : stand in awe of him ✴ all yé that | dwell | in the | world.

9 For he spáke, and | it was | done : he commánded, | and it | stood | fast.

10 The Lord bringeth the cóunsel of the | heathen · to | nought : and maketh the devices of the people to be of none effect ✴ and cásteth | out the | counsels · of | princes.

11 The counsel of the Lórd shall en- | dure for | ever : and the thoughts of his heart from géner- | -ation · to | gener- | ation.

12 Blessed are the people, whose Gód is the | Lord Je- | -hóvah : and blessed are the folk that he hath chosen to hím to | be | his in- | -heritance.

13 The Lord looked down from heaven ✴ and behéld all the | children · of | men : from the habitation of his dwelling ✴ he considereth all thém that | dwell | on the | earth.

14 He fashioneth áll the | hearts of | them : and únder- | -standeth | all their | works.

15 There is no king that can be saved

TRINITY SUNDAY. MORNING (continued).

by the múltitude | of an | host : neither is any mighty mán de- | -livered · by | much | strength.

16 A horse is counted but a váin thing to | save a | man : neither shall he delíver ány man | by his | great | strength.

17 Behold the eye of the Lord is upón | them that | fear him : and upou them that pút their | trust | in his | mercy.

18 To delíver their | soul from | death :

and to féed them | in the | time of | dearth.

19 Our soul hath patiently tárried | for the | Lord : for hé is our | help | and our | shield.

20 For our héart shall re- | -joice in | him : because we have hóped | in his | holy | Name.

21 Let thy merciful kindness O Lórd | be up- | -on us : like as wé do | put our | trust in | thee.

TRINITY SUNDAY. EVENING.

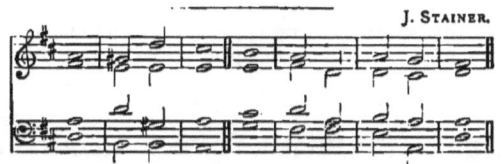

J. STAINER.

PSALM XCIII.—*Dominus regnavit.*

F. f THE Lord is King * and hath put on glóri- | -ous ap- | -parel : the Lord hath put on his appárel and | girded · him- | -self with | strength.

F. 2 He hath máde the round | world so | sure : thát it | cannot | be | moved.

3 Ever since the world began hath thy séat | been pre- | -pared : thóu | art from | ever- | -lasting.

4 The floods are risen O Lord * the flóods have lift | up their | voice : the | floods lift | up their | waves.

5 The waves of the sea are mighty and | rage | horribly : but yet the Lórd who | dwelleth · on | high is | mightier.

6 Thy testimonies O Lórd are | very | sure : hóliness be- | -cometh · thine | house for | ever.

J. TURLE.

PSALM XCVII.—*Dominus regnavit.*

f THE Lord is King * the éarth may be | glad there- | -of : yea, the multitude of the ísles | may be | glad there- | -of.

2 Clouds and dárkness are | round a- | -bout him : righteousness and judgement are the hábit- | -ation | of his | seat.

3 There shall gó a | fire be- | -fore him : and burn úp his | ene · mies on | every | side.

4 His lightnings gave shíne | unto · the | world : the éarth | saw it · and | was a- | -fraid.

5 The hills melted like wax * at the présence | of the | Lord : at the presence of the Lórd | of the | whole | earth.

6 The héavens have de- | -clared · his | righteousness : and áll the | people · have | seen his | glory.

7 Confounded be all they that wor-

ship carved images * and that delíght in : vain | gods : wórship | him | all ye | gods.

8 Sion héard of it | and re- | -joiced : and the daughters of Judah were glad * becáuse of thy | judgements | O | Lord.

9 For thou Lord, art higher than áll that are | in the | earth : thou art exálted | far a- | -bove all | gods.

10 O ye that love the Lord * see that ye hate the thíng | which is | evil : the Lord preserveth the souls of his saints * he shall deliver them fróm the | hand of | the un- | -godly.

11 There is sprung up a lfght | for the | righteous : and joyful gládness for | such as | are true- | -hearted.

12 Rejóice in the | Lord ye | righteous : and give thanks * fór a re- | -membrance | of his | holiness.

TRINITY SUNDAY. EVENING (continued).

P. HUMPHREYS.

PSALM CL.—*Laudate Dominum.*

f O PRAISE Gód | in his | holiness : praise him in the | firmament | of his | power.

2 Práise him in his | noble | acts : praise him according | to his | excellent | greatness.

3 Praise him in the sóund | of the | trumpet : práise him up- | -on the | lute and | harp.

4 Práise him in the | cymbals and | dances : práise him up- | -on the | strings and | pipe.

5 Praise him upon the wéll- | -tuned | cymbals : práise him up- | -on the | loud | cymbals.

F. 6 Let évery thing | that hath | breath : praise | — — | — the | Lord.

THE TRANSFIGURATION. MORNING.

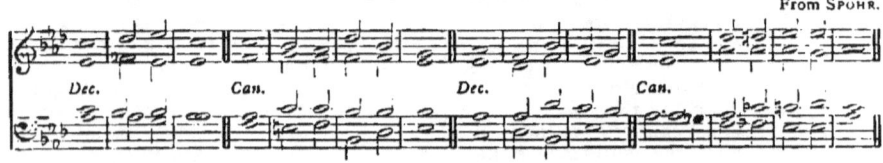
From SPOHR.

PSALM XXVII.—*Dominus illuminatio.*

F. mf THE Lord is my light and my salvation ∗ whóm then | shall I | fear : the Lord is the strength of my life ∗ of whóm then | shall I | be a- | -fraid ?

F. 2 When the wicked ∗ even mine enemies and my foes ∗ came upon me to éat | up my | flesh : théy | stumbled | and | fell.

3 Though an host of men were laid against me ∗ yet shall not my héart | be a- | -fraid : and though there rose up war against me ∗ yét will I | put my | trust in | him.

4 One thing have I desired of the Lórd which I | will re- | -quire : even that I may dwell in the house of the Lord all the days of my life ∗ to behold the fair beauty of the Lórd | and to | visit · his | temple.

5 For in the time of trouble, he shall hide me in his | taber- | -nacle : yea in the secret place of his dwelling shall he hide me ∗ and set me úp up- | -on a | rock of | stone.

6 And now shall he lift | up mine | head : abóve mine | enemies | round a- | bout me.

7 Therefore will I offer in his dwelling, an oblátion with | great | gladness : I will sing and speak | praises | unto · the | Lord.

mp 8 Hearken unto my voice, O Lord ∗ when I crý | unto | thee : have mércy up- | -on me | and I | hear me.

9 My heart hath talked of thee ∗ Séek | ye my | face : Thý | face Lord | will I | seek.

10 O hide not thóu thy | face | from me : nor cast thy sérvant a- | -way | in dis- | -pleasure.

11 Thóu hast | been my | succour : leave me not, neither forsáke me, O | God of | my sal- | -vation.

12 When my fáther and my | mother · for- | -sake me : the Lórd | taketh | me | up.

13 Téach me thy | way O | Lord : and lead me in the right wáy be- | -cause of | mine | enemies.

14 Deliver me not over into the will | of mine | adversaries : for there are false witnesses risen up against me, ánd | such as | speak | wrong.

15 I should útterly | have | fainted : but that I believe verily to see the goodness of the Lórd in the | land | of the | living.

16 O tárry thou the | Lord's | leisure : be strong, and he shall comfort thine heart ∗ and pút thou thy | trust | in the | Lord.

THE TRANSFIGURATION. MORNING (*continued*).

From BEETHOVEN.

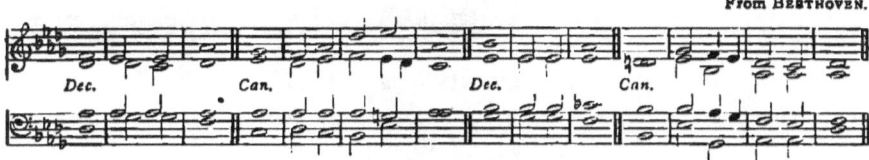

PSALM LXI.—*Exaudi, Deus.*

mf HEAR my | crying • O | God : gíve | ear | unto • my | prayer.

2 From the ends of the éarth will I | call up • on | thee : whĕn my | heart | is in | heaviness.

3 O set me up upon the rŏck that is | higher • than | I : for thou hast been my hope * and a strong tówer for | me a- | gainst the | enemy.

4 I will dwell in thy táber- | -nacle • for | ever : and my trust shall be únder the | covering | of thy | wings.

5 For thou, O Lord, hast héard | my de- | -sires : and hast given an heritage únto | those that | fear thy | Name.

6 Thou shalt grant the Kíng a | long | life : that his years may endúre throughout | all | gener- | -ations.

7 He shall dwĕll before | God for | ever : O prepare thy loving mercy and fáithfulness | that they | may pre- | -serve him.

8 So will I alway sing práise | unto • thy | Name : that I˘ may | daily per- | form my | vows.

E. J. HOPKINS.

PSALM XCIII.—*Dominus regnavit.*

F. f THE Lord is King * and hath put on glóri- | -ous ap- | -parel : the Lord hath put on his appárel and | girded • him- | -self with | strength.

F. 2 He hath máde the round | world so | sure : thát it | cannot | be | moved.

3 Ever since the world began hath thy séat | been pre- | -pared : thŏu | art from | ever- | -lasting.

4 The floods are risen O Lord * the flóods have lift | up their | voice : thĕ | floods lift | up their | waves.

5 The waves of the sea are míghty and | rage | horribly : but yet the Lŏrd who | dwelleth • on | high is | mightier.

6 Thy testimonies, O Lŏrd, are | very | sure : hŏliness be- | -cometh • thine | house for | ever.

Sir George Elvey.

PSALM LXXXIV.—*Quam dilecta!*

mf O HOW ámiable | are thy | dwellings : | thóu | Lord | of | hosts !

2 My soul hath a desire and longing ✱ to enter into the cóurts | of the | Lórd : my heart and my flesh rejóice | in the | living | God.

3 Yea, the sparrow hath found her an house ✱ and the swallow a nest, where shé may | lay her | young : even thy altars, O Lord of hósts, my | King | and my | God.

4 Blessed are they that dwéll | in thy | house : théy will be | alway | praising | thee.

5 Blessed is the man whose stréngth | is in | thee : ín whose | heart | are thy | ways.

6 Who going through the vale of misery úse it | for a | well : ánd the | pools are | filled ⋅ with | water.

2nd part 7 They will gó from | strength to | strength : and unto the God of gods appeareth évery | one of | them in | Sion.

8 O Lord God of hósts | hear my | prayer : héarken | O | God of | Jacob.

9 Behold, O Gód | our de- | -fender : and look upón the | face of | thine A- | nointed.

10 For one dáy | in thy | courts : ís | better | than a | thousand.

11 I had rather be a door-keeper in the hóuse | of my | God : than to dwéll in the | tents | of un- | -godliness.

12 For the Lord God is a líght | and de- | -fence : the Lord will give grace and worship ✱ and no good thing shall he withhold from thém that | live a | godly life.

13 O Lórd | God of | hosts : blessed is the mán that | putteth ⋅ his | trust in | thee.

A. R. Reinagle.

PSALM XCIX.—*Dominus regnavit.*

f THE Lord is King ✱ be the people néver | so im- | -patient : he sitteth between the cherubims ✱ be the éarth | never | so un- | -quiet.

2 The Lórd is | great in | Sion : ánd | high a- | -bove all | people.

3 They shall give thánks | unto ⋅ thy | Name : which is gréat | wonder- | -ful and | holy.

4 The king's power loveth judgement ✱ thóu hast pre- | -pared | equity : thou hast executed júdgement and | righteous- | -ness in | Jacob.

5 O mágnify the | Lord our | God : and fall down before his fóotstool, | for | he is | holy.

6 Moses and Aaron among his priests ✱ and Samuel among such as cáll up- | -on his | Name : these called upón the | Lord | and he | heard them.

7 He spake unto them óut of the | cloudy | pillar : for they kept his testimonies ✱ ánd the | law | that he | gave them.

8 Thou héardest them O | Lord our | God : thou forgavest them O God ✱ and púnish- | -edst their | own in- | ventions.

9 O magnify the Lord our God ✱ and worship him upón his | holy | hill : fór the | Lord our | God is | holy.

THE TRANSFIGURATION. EVENING (continued).

Sir JOHN GOSS.

PSALM CXXXIII.—*Ecce, quam bonum!*

mf BEHOLD, how good and joyful a | thing it | is : bréthren. to | dwell to- | gether · in | unity !

2 It is like the precious ointment upon the head ✶ that ran down | unto · the | beard : even unto Aaron's beard ✶ | and went dówn to the | skirts | of his | clothing.

3 Líke as the | dew of | Hermon : which fell up- | -on the | hill of | Sion.

4 For there the Lórd | promised · his | blessing : ánd | life for | ever- | -more.

ST. MICHAEL AND ALL ANGELS. MORNING.

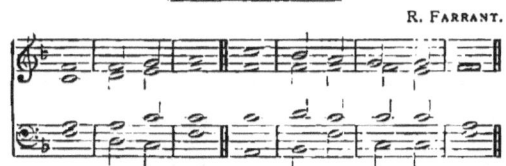

R. FARRANT.

PSALM XCI.—*Qui habitat.*

mf WHOSO dwelleth under the defénce of the | most | High : shall abíde under the | shadow · of | the Al- | -mighty.

2 I will say unto the Lord ✶ Thou art my hópe | and my | stronghold : my Gód, in | him | will I | trust.

3 For he shall deliver thee from the snáre | of the | hunter : ánd | from the | noisome | pestilence.

4 He shall defend thee under his wings ✶ and thou shalt be sáfe | under · his | feathers : his faithfulness and trúth shall | be thy | shield and | buckler.

5 Thou shalt not be afráid for any | terror · by | night : nór for the | arrow · that | flieth · by | day ;

6 For the péstilence that | walketh · in | darkness : nor for the síckness that de- | -stroyeth | in the | noonday.

7 A thousand shall fall beside thee ✶ and ten thóusand at | thy right | hand : but it shall | not come | nigh | thee.

8 Yea, with thine éyes shalt | thou be- | -hold : and sée the re- | -ward of | the un- | -godly.

9 For thou, Lórd | art my | hope : thou hast set thine hóuse of de- | -fence | very | high.

10 There shall no evil háppen | unto | thee : neither shall ány | plague come | nigh thy | dwelling.

11 For he shall give his angels chárge | over | thee : to kéep | thee in | all thy | ways.

12 They shall béar thee | in their | hands : that thou húrt not thy | foot a- | gainst a | stone.

13 Thou shalt go upón the | lion and | adder : the young lion and the dragon shált thou | tread | under · thy | feet.

14 Because he hath set his love upon me ✶ therefore will I' de- | -liver | him : I will set him up ✶ becáuse | he hath | known my | Name.

15 He shall call upon mé, and | I will | hear him : yea, I am with him in trouble ✶ I will delíver him and | bring | him to ! honour.

16 With long lífe will I | satisfy | him : ánd | shew him | my sal- | -vation.

166 ST. MICHAEL AND ALL ANGELS. MORNING (*continued*).

J. S. Smith.

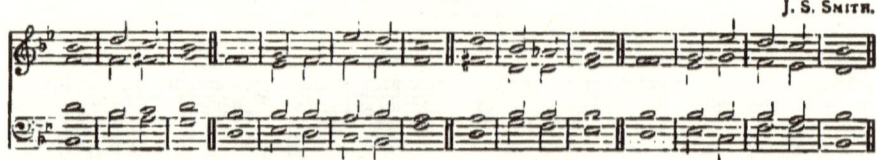

PSALM CIII.—*Benedic, anima mea.*

f PRAISE the Lórd | O my | soul : | and all that is withín me | praise his | holy | Name.

2 Praise the Lórd | O my | soul : ánd for- | -get not | all his | benefits ;

3 Who forgíveth | all thy | sin : and héaleth | all | thine in- | -firmities ;

4 Who saveth thy lífe | from de- | struction : and crowneth thée with | mercy • and | loving- | -kindness ;

5 Who satisfieth thy móuth with | good | things : making thee yóung and | lusty | as an | eagle.

6 The Lord executeth ríghteous- | ness and | judgement : for all thém that | are op- | -pressed • with | wrong.

7 He shewed his wáys | unto | Moses : his wórks | unto • the | children of | Israel.

8 The Lord is fúll of com- | -passion • and | mercy : long-súffering, | and of | great | goodness.

9 He will not | alway • be | chiding : neither kéepeth | he his | anger • for | ever.

10 He hath not déalt with us | after • our | sins : nor rewárded us ac- | -cording | to our | wickednesses.

11 For look how high the heaven is in compárison | of the | earth : so great is his mercy álso | toward | them that | fear him.

12 Look how wide also the éast is | from the | west : so fár hath he | set our | sins | from us.

13 Yea, like as a fáther pítieth his | own | children : even so is the Lord mér- ciful | unto | them that | fear him.

14 For he knoweth wheréof | we are | made : he remémbereth | that we | are but | dust.

mp 15 The days of mán are | but as | grass : for he flourisheth ás a | flower | of the | field.

16 For as soon as the wind goeth óver it | it is | gone : and the place theréof shall | know it | no | more.

mf 17 But the merciful goodness of the Lord ✱ endureth for ever and éver upon | them that | fear him : and his ríghteousness up- | -on | children's | children ;

18 Even upon súch as | keep his | covenant : and thínk upon | his com- | mandments • to | do them.

f 19 The Lord hath prepáred his | seat in | heaven : and his kíngdom | ruleth | over | all.

20 O praise the Lord, ye angels of his ✱ yé that ex- | -cel in | strength : ye that fulfil his commandment ✱ and hearken únto the | voice | of his | word.

21 O praise the Lórd, all | ye his | hosts : ye sérvants of | his that | do his | pleasure.

22 O speak good of the Lord, all ye works of his ✱ in all pláces of | his do- | minion : práise thou the | Lord | O my | soul.

ST. MICHAEL AND ALL ANGELS. EVENING.

Dr. Dupuis.

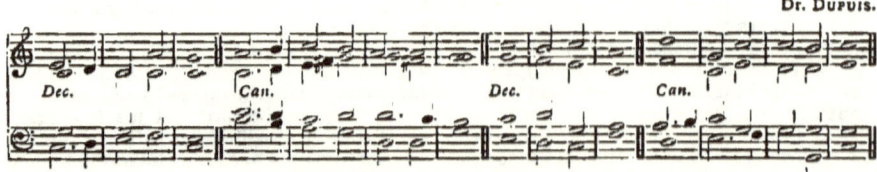

PSALM XXXIV.—*Benedicam Domino.*

mf I WILL alway give thánks | unto • the | Lord : his práise shall | ever • be | in my | mouth.

2 My soul shall make her bóast | in the | Lord ; the humble shall héar there- | -of | and be | glad.

3 O práise the | Lord with | me : and let us mágni- | -fy his | Name to- | -gether.

4 I sought the Lórd| and he|heard me: yea, he delivered me | out of | all my | fear.

5 They had an eye unto hím | and

ST. MICHAEL AND ALL ANGELS. EVENING (continued). 167

were | lightened : ánd their | faces · were | not a- | -shamed.

6 Lo the poor crieth, and the Lórd | heareth | him : yea, and sáveth him | out of | all his | troubles.

7 The angel of the Lord tarrieth róund about | them that | fear him : ánd | — de- | -livereth | them.

8 O taste and see how grácious the | Lord | is : blessed ís the | man that | trusteth · in | him.

9 O fear the Lord, yé that | are his | saints : for théy that |fear him| lack |nothing.

10 The lions do láck and | suffer | hunger : but they who seek the Lord, shall want no mánner of | thing | that is | good.

11 Come, ye children, and héarken | unto | me : I will téach you the | fear | of the | Lord.

12 What man is hé that | lusteth · to | live : ánd would | fain | see good | days ?

13 Kéep thy | tongue from | evil : and | thy lips | that they | speak no | guile.

14 Eschew évil and | do | good : séek | peace | and en- | -sue it.

15 The eyes of the Lórd are | over · the | righteous : and his éars are | open | unto · their | prayers.

16 The countenance of the Lord is against thém that | do | evil : to root out the remémbrance | of them | from the | earth.

17 The righteous cry, and the Lórd | heareth | them : and delívereth them | out of | all their | troubles.

18 The Lord is nigh unto them that áre of a | contrite | heart : and will sáve such as | be · of an | humble | spirit.

19 Great are the tróubles | of the | righteous : but the Lórd de- | -livereth · him | out of | all.

20 He kéepeth | all his | bones : só that not | one of | them is | broken.

21 But misfortune shall sláy | the un- | godly : and they that háte the | righteous | shall be | desolate.

22 The Lord delivereth the sóuls | of his | servants : and all they that put their trúst in | him shall | not be | destitute.

E. J. HOPKINS.

PSALM CXLVIII.—Laudate Dominum.

ƒ O PRÁISE the | Lord of | heaven : práise | — him | in the | height.

2 Praise him, áll ye | angels · of | his : práise | — him | all his | host.

3 Práise him, | sun and | moon : práise him, | all ye | stars and | light.

4 Práise him, | all ye | heavens : and | ye wáters that | are a- | -bove the | heavens.

5 Let them praise the Náme | of the | Lord : for he sp ake the word, and they were made ✱ he commánded, | and they | were cre- | -ated.

6 He hath made them fást for | ever | and | ever : he hath given them a láw | which shall | not be | broken.

7 Praise the Lórd up- | -on | earth : yé | dragons · and | all | deeps ;

8 Fire and háil | snow and | vapours : wínd and | storm ful- | -filling · his | word ;

9 Móuntains and | all | hills : frúitful trees and | all | cedars ;

10 Béasts and | all | cattle : wórms | — and | feathered | fowls ;

11 Kings of the éarth and | all | people : princes and áll | judges | of the | world ;

12 Young men and maidens, old men and children ✱ praise the Náme | of the | Lord : for his Name only is excellent ✱ and his práise a- | -bove | heaven and | earth.

2nd part. 13 He shall exalt the horn of his people ✱ áll his | saints shall | praise him : even the children of Israel ✱ éven the | people · that | serveth | him.

ALL SAINTS' DAY. MORNING.

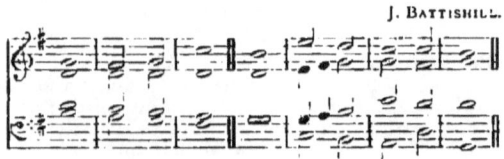

J. BATTISHILL.

PSALM I.—*Beatus vir, qui non abiit.*

mf BLESSED is the man that hath not walked in the counsel of the ungodly ∗ nor stood in the | way of | sinners : and hath not sât in the | seat | of the | scornful.

2 But his delight is in the láw | of the | Lord : and in his law will he exercîse him- | -self | day and | night.

3 And he shall be like a tree planted by the | water | side : that will bring fôrth his | fruit in | due | season.

4 His léaf also | shall not | wither : and look, whatsoéver he | doeth | it shall | prosper.

5 As for the ungodly, it is nót | so with | them : but they are like the chaff ∗ which the wind scattereth awáy from the | face | of the | earth.

6 Therefore the ungodly shall not be able to stánd | in the | judgement : neither the sinners in the côngre- | -gation | of the | righteous.

7 But the Lord knoweth the wáy | of the | righteous : and the wáy of the un- | godly | shall | perish.

Dr. E. G. MONK.

[music]

PSALM XV.—*Domine, quis habitabit?*

mf LORD, who shall dwéll in thy | taber- | -nacle : or who shall rést up- | -on thy | holy | hill?

2 Even he that léadeth an | uncorrupt | life : and doeth the thing which is right ∗ and spéaketh the | truth | from his | heart.

3 He that hath used no deceit in his tongue ∗ nor done évil | to his | neighbour : ánd | hath not | slandered · his | neighbour.

4 He that setteth not by himself ∗ but is lówly in his | own | eyes : and maketh múch of | them that | fear the | Lord.

5 He that sweareth unto his neighbour ∗ and dísap- | -pointeth · him | not : though it | were · to his | own | hindrance.

6 He that hath not given his móney up- | -on | usury : nor táken re- | -ward a- | -gainst the | innocent.

7 Whóso | doeth · these | things : shall | nev- | -er | fall.

J. COWARD.

PSALM CXLVI.—*Lauda, anima mea.*

mf PRAISE the Lord, O my soul ∗ while I líve will I | praise the | Lord : yea, as long as I have any being ∗ I will síng | praises | unto · my | God.

2 O put not your trust in princes ∗ nor in ány | child of | man : fôr there is | no | help in | them.

3 For when the breath of man goeth forth ∗ he shall túrn again | to his | earth : and thén | all his | thoughts | perish.

4 Blessed is he that hath the God of Jácob | for his | help : and whose hópe is | in the | Lord his | God;

5 Who made heaven and earth ∗ the sea, and áll that | therein | is : whô keepeth · his | promise · for | ever;

ALL SAINTS' DAY. MORNING (continued).

6 Who helpeth them to ríght that | suffer|wrong: whó | feed- | -eth the | hungry.

7 The Lórd looseth mén | out of | prison : the Lórd giveth | sight | to the | blind.

8 The Lord helpeth thém | that are | fallen : the Lórd | careth | for the | righteous.

9 The Lord careth for the strangers ✷ he defendeth the fáther- | -less and | widow : as for the way of the ungódly, he | turneth · it | upside | down.

10 The Lord thy God ◠ Sion, shall be Kíng for | ever- | -more : ánd throughout | all | gener- | -ations.

ALL SAINTS' DAY. EVENING.

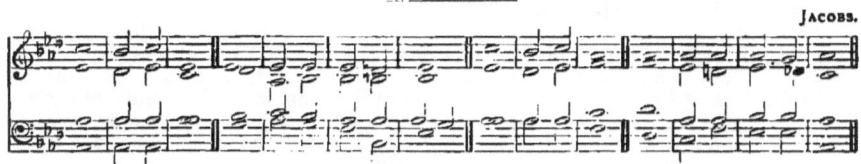

JACOBS.

PSALM CXII.—*Beatus vir.*

mf BLESSED is the mán that | feareth . the | Lord : he hath gréat de- | -light in | his com- | -mándments.

2 His seed shall be míghty up- | -on | earth : the generátion of the | fáithful | shall be | blessed.

3 Riches and plenteousness shall bé | in his | house : and his ríghteous- | -ness en- | -dureth · for | ever.

4 Unto the godly there ariseth up líght | in the | darkness : hé is | merciful | loving · and | righteous.

5 A good man is mérci- | -ful and | lendeth : and will gúide his | words | with dis- | -cretion.

6 For hé shall | never · be | moved :

and the righteous shall be hád in | ever- | lasting · re- | -membrance.

7 He will not be afráid of any | evil | tidings : for his heart standeth fást, and be- | -lieveth | in the | Lord.

8 His heart is stáblished, and | will not | shrink : until he sée his de- | -sire up- | -on his | enemies.

9 He hath dispersed abroad ✷ and gíven | to the | poor : and his righteousness remaineth for ever ✷ his hórn shall | be ex- | -alted · with | honour.

10 The ungodly shall sée it, and | it shall | grieve him : he shall gnash with his teeth, and consume away ✷ the desíre of the un- | -godly | shall | perish.

Dr. G. C. MARTIN.

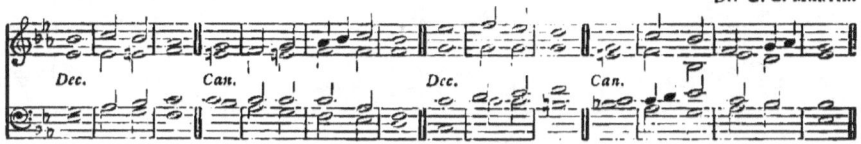

PSALM CXXI.—*Levavi oculos.*

mf I WILL lift up · mine éyes | unto · the | hills : fróm | whence | cometh · my | help.

2 My help cometh éven | from the | Lord : whó hath | made | heaven and | earth.

3 He will not suffer thy fóot | to be | moved : and hé that | keepeth · thee | will not | sleep.

4 Behold, hé that | keepeth | Israel : shall | neither | slumber · nor | sleep.

5 The Lord himsélf | is thy | keeper : the Lord is thy defénce up- | -on thy | right | hand ;

6 So that the sun shall not búrn thee by | day : neither the | moon | by | night.

7 The Lord shall presérve thee from | all | evil : yea, it is even hé | that shall | keep thy | soul.

8 The Lord shall preserve thy going out ✷ and thy | coming | in : from this time | forth for | ever- | -more.

ALL SAINTS' DAY. EVENING (continued).

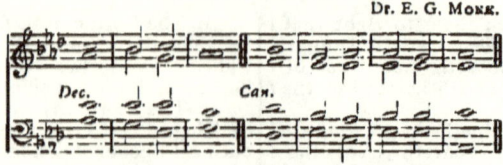
Dr. E. G. Monk.

PSALM CXLIX.—*Cantate Domino.*

f O SING unto the Lórd a | new | song : let the cóngre- | -gation · of ‖ saints | praise him.

2 Let Israel rejóice in | him that | made him : and let the children of Síon be | joyful ‖ in their | King.

3 Let them praise his Náme | in the | dance : let them sing praises únto | him with | tabret · and | harp.

4 For the Lord hath pleasure | in his | people : ánd | helpeth · the | meek- | hearted.

5 Let the sáints be | joyful · with | glory : lét them re- | -joice ‖ in their | beds.

6 Let the praises of Gód be | in their | mouth : and a twó-edged | sword | in their | hands ;

7 To be avénged | of the | heathen : ánd | to re- | -buke the | people ;

8 To bínd their | kings in | chains : ánd their | nobles · with | links of | iron.

9 That they may be avenged of thém | as it · is | written : Súch | honour · have | all his | saints.

BURIAL OF THE DEAD.

I. Rev. F. A. J. Hervey.

Alternative Chants.

II. Rev. W. Felton.   III. T. Purcell.

From PSALMS XXXIX and XC.

p LORD, let me know mine end * and the númber | of my | days : that I may be certified how | long I ‖ have to | live.

2 Behold, thou hast made my days as it wére a | span | long : and mine age is even as nothing in respect of thee * and verily, every man living is | alto- | -gether | vanity.

3 For man walketh in a vain shadow * and disquíeteth him- | -self in | vain : he heapeth up riches, and cánnot tell | who shall | gather | them.

4 And now, Lórd what | is my | hope : trúly my | hope is | even · in | thee.

5 Deliver me from áll | mine of- | fences ; and make me nót a re- | -buke | unto · the | foolish.

6 When thou with rebukes dost chasten man for sin * thou makest his beauty to consume away * like as it were a móth | fretting · a | garment : évery man | therefore | is but | vanity.

7 Hear my prayer O Lord * and with thine éars con- | -sider · my | calling : hold not thy | peace ‖ at my | tears.

8 For I * am a | stranger · with | thee : and a sójourner, as | all my | fathers | were.

BURIAL OF THE DEAD (continued).

2nd part 9 O spare me a little * that I' may re- | -cover · my | strength : before I go hence, and | be no | more | seen. Ps. xxxix. 5-9, 12-15.

p 10 Lord thou hast | been our | refuge : from óne gener- | -ation | to an- | -other.

11 Before the mountains were brought forth * or ever the éarth and the | world were | made : thou art God from ever- lásting and | world with- | -out | end.

12 Thou turnest mán | to de- | -struc- tion : again thou sayest, Cóme a- | -gain ye | children · of | men.

13 For a thousand years in thý sight | are but · as | yesterday : seeing that is pást as a | watch | in the | night.

14 As soon as thou scatterest them * they are éven | as a | sleep : and fáde away | suddenly | like the | grass.

15 In the morning it is gréen and | groweth | up : but in the evening it is cut dówn | dried | up and | withered.

16 For we consume awáy in | thy dis- | pleasure : and are afráid at thy | wrath- ful | indig- | -nation.

17 Thou hast sét our mis- | -deeds be- | fore thee : and our secret síns in the | light | of thy | countenance.

18 For when thou art angry, áll our | days are | gone : we bring our years to an end * as it wére a | tale | that is | told.

19 The days of our age are threescore years and ten * and though men be so strong that they cóme to | fourscore | years : yet is their strength then but labour and sorrow * so soon pásseth it a- | -way and | we are | gone.

2nd part 20 So téach us to | number · our | days : that we may applý our | hearts | unto | wisdom. Ps. xc. 1-10, 12.

F. f Glory be to the Fáther, | and · to the | Son : ánd | to the | Holy | Ghost ;

F. As it was in the beginning * is nów, and | ever | shall be : wórld without | end. | A· | -men.

CHURCHING OF WOMEN.

Dr. Camidge.

From PSALM CXVI.—*Dilexi, quoniam.*

mf I' AM | well | pleased : that the Lord hath héard the | voice of | my | prayer ;

2 That he hath inclined his éar | unto | me : therefore will I call upon hím as | long | as I | live.

3 I found trouble and heaviness * and I called upon the Náme | of the | Lord : O Lord, I beséech | thee de- | -liver my | soul.

4 Gracious ís the | Lord and | right- eous : yéa, our | God is | merci- | -ful.

5 What reward shall I gíve | unto · the | Lord : for all the benefits that hé hath | done | unto | me ?

6 I will receive the cúp | of sal- | vation : and cáll upon the | Name | of the | Lord.

2nd part 7 I will pay my vows unto the Lord * in the síght of | all his | people : in the courts of the Lord's house * even in the midst of thee O Jerúsalem | Praise | — the | Lord.

F. f Glory be to the Fáther, | and · to the | Son : ánd | to the | Holy | Ghost ;

F. As it was in the beginning * is nów, and | ever | shall be : wórld without | end. | A· | -men.

THANKSGIVING DAY.

¶ *Instead of* O come, let us sing, &c., *the following shall be said or sung.*

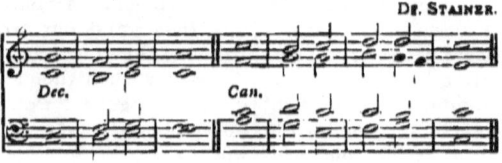

PSALM CXLVII. 1-3, 8, 9, 12-14.

F. f PRAISE ye the Lord * for it is good to sing práises | unto · our | God : fór it is | pleasant · and | praise is | comely.

F. 2 The Lord doth búild | up Je- | rusalem : he gathereth togéther the | out- | -casts of | Israel.

3 He healeth thóse that are | broken · in | heart : ánd | bindeth | up their | wounds.

4 He covereth the heaven with clouds * and prepareth ráin | for the | earth : he maketh the gráss to | grow up- | on the | mountains.

5 He gíveth to the | beast his | food : ánd to the | young | ravens · which | cry.

6 Praise the Lórd | O Je- | -rusalem, práise thy | God | O | Sion.

7 For he hath strengthened the bárs | of thy | gates : hé hath | blessed · thy | children · with- | -in thee.

8 He maketh péace | in thy | borders : and filleth thee wíth the | finest | of the | wheat.

F. f Glory be to the Father, | and · to the | Son : ánd | to the | Holy | Ghost ;

F. As it was in the beginning * is nów, and | ever | shall be : world without | end. | A- | -men.

CONSECRATION OF CHURCHES.

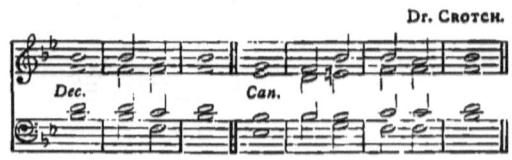

PSALM XXIV.—*Domini est terra.*

f THE earth is the Lord's * and áll that | therein | is : the compass of the wórld, and | they that | dwell there- | -in.

2 For he hath fóunded it up- | -on the | seas : and prepáred | it up- | -on the | floods.

3 Who shall ascend into the híll | of the | Lord : or who shall rise úp | in his | holy | place ?

4 Even he that hath clean hánds and a | pure | heart : and that hath not lift up his mind unto vanity * nor swórn | to de- | -ceive his | neighbour.

5 He shall receive the bléssing | from the | Lord : and righteousness fróm the | God of | his sal- | -vation.

6 This is the generátion of | them that | seek him : even of thém that | seek thy | face O | Jacob.

7 Lift up your heads O ye gates * and be ye lift up ye éver- | -lasting | doors : and the Kíng of | glory | shall come | in.

8 Whó is the | King of | glory : it is the Lord strong and mighty * éven the | Lord | mighty · in | battle.

9 Lift up your heads O ye gates * and be ye lift up ye éver- | -lasting | doors : and the Kíng of | glory | shall come | in.

10 Whó is the | King of | glory : even the Lord of hósts | he · is the | King of | glory.

CONSECRATION OF CHURCHES (continued).

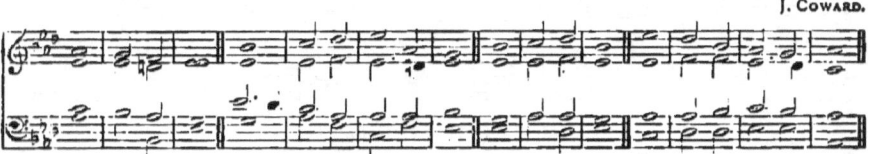

J. COWARD.

PSALM LXXXIV.—*Quam dilecta!*

F. mf O HOW ámiable | are thy | dwellings : thôu | Lord | of | hosts |

F. 2 My soul hath a desire and longing ✻ to enter into the côurts | of the | Lord : my heart and my flesh rejoíce | in the | living | God.

3 Yea, the sparrow hath found her an house ✻ and the swallow a nest, where shê may | lay her | young : even thy altars, O Lord of hôsts, my | King | and my | God.

4 Blessed are they that dwéll | in thy | house : théy will be | alway | praising | thee.

5 Blessed is the man whose stréngth | is in | thee : in whose | heart | are thy | ways.

6 Who going through the vale of misery úse it | for a | well : ánd the | pools are | filled · with | water.

2nd part 7 They will gó from | strength to | |

strength : and unto the God of gods appeareth évery | one of | them in | Sion.

8 O Lord God of hôsts | hear my | prayer : héarken | O | God of | Jacob.

9 Behold, O Gód | our de- | -fender : and look upón the | face of | thine A- | -nointed.

10 For one dáy | in thy | courts : ís | better | than a | thousand.

11 I had rather be a door-keeper in the hoúse | of my | God : than to dwéll in the | tents | of un- | -godliness.

12 For the Lord God is a líght | and de- | -fence : the Lord will give grace and worship ✻ and no good thing shall he withhold from thém that | live a | godly | life.

13 O Lórd | God of | hosts : blessed is the mán that | putteth · his | trust in | thee.

A. R. REINAGLE.

PSALM CXXII.—*Lætatus sum.*

mf I WAS glad when they sáid | unto | me : We will gó into the | house | of the | Lord.

2 Our feet shall stánd | in thy | gates : O˘ | — Je- | -rusa- | -lem.

3 Jerusalem is búilt | as a | city : that ís at | unity | in it- | -self.

4 For thither the tribes go up ✻ even the tríbes | of the | Lord : to testify unto Israel ✻ to give thánks unto the | Name | of the | Lord.

5 For thére is the | seat of | judgement : even the séat | of the | house of | David.

6 O pray for the péace | of Je- | rusalem : théy shall | prosper · that | love | thee.

7 Péace be with- | -in thy | walls : and plénteous- | -ness with- | -in thy | palaces.

8 For my bréthren and com- | panions' | sakes : I˘ | will | wish | thee pros- | -perity.

9 Yea, because of the hoúse of the | Lord our | God : I˘ will | seek to | do thee | good.

CONSECRATION OF CHURCHES (*continued*).

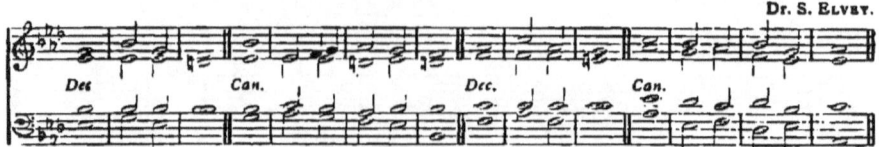

Dr. S. Elvey.

PSALM CXXXII.—*Memento, Domine.*

mf LORD, re- | -member | David : ånd | all | his | trouble ;

2 How he swâre | unto · the | Lord : and vowed a vow únto the Al- | -mighty | God of | Jacob ;

3 I will not come within the táber- nacle | of mine | house : nôr | climb up | into · my | bed ;

4 I will not suffer mine eyes to sléep, nor mine | eye-lids · to | slumber : neither the temples of my héad to | take | any | rest ;

5 Until I find out a place for the témple | of the | Lord : an habitation fôr the | mighty | God of | Jacob.

6 Lo, we héard of the | same at | Ephrata : ånd | found it | in the | wood.

7 We will gó into his | taber- | -nacle : and fall lów on our | knees be- | -fore his | footstool.

8 Arise, O Lórd | into · thy | resting- place : thôu and the | ark | of thy | strength.

9 Let thy priests be | clothed · with | righteousness : and lét thy | saints | sing with | joyfulness.

10 For thy sérvant | David's | sake : turn not awáy the | presence · of | thine A- | -nointed.

11 The Lord hath made a faithful óath | unto | David : ånd he | shall not | shrink | from it.

12 Of the frúit | of thy | body : shåll I | set up- | -on thy | seat.

13 If thy children will keep my cove- nant ✱ and my téstimonies that | I | shall | learn them : their children also shall sit upón thy | seat for | ever- | -more.

14 For the Lord hath chosen Sion to be an habitation | for him- | -self : hê hath | longed | for | her.

15 This shall bé my | rest for | ever : here will I dwell ✱ fôr I | have · a de- light there- | -in.

16 I will bléss her | victuals · with | increase : and will sátis- | -fy her | poor with | bread.

17 I will déck her | priests with | health : and her sáints | shall re- | -joice, and | sing.

18 There shall I make the hórn of | David · to | flourish : I have ordáined a | lantern · for | mine A- | -nointed.

2nd part. 19 As for his enemies ✱ I shall clóthe | them with | shame : but upon himsélf | shall his | crown | flourish.

INSTITUTION OF MINISTERS.

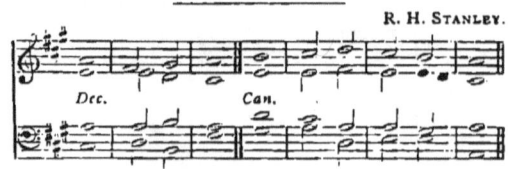

R. H. Stanley.

PSALM CXXII.—*Lætatus sum.*

mf I WAS glad when they sâid | unto | me : We will gó into the | house of the | Lord.

2 Our feet shall stånd | in thy | gates : O' | — Je- | -rusa- | -lem.

3 Jerusalem is búilt | as a | city : that is at | unity | in it- | -self ;

4 For thither the tribes go up ✱ even the tribes | of the | Lord : to testify unto Israel ✱ to give thånks unto the | Name | of the | Lord.

5 For thére is the | seat of | judge- ment : even the séat | of the | house of | David.

6 O pray for the péace | of Je- | rusalem : théy shall | prosper · that | love | thee.

7 Péace be with- | -in thy | walls : and plénteous- | -ness with- | -in thy | palaces.

8 For my bréthren and com- | panions' | sakes : I" will | wish | thee pros- | -perity.

9 Yea, because of the hóuse of the | Lord our | God : I" will | seek to | do thee | good.

INSTITUTION OF MINISTERS (*continued*).

D_r S. Elvey.

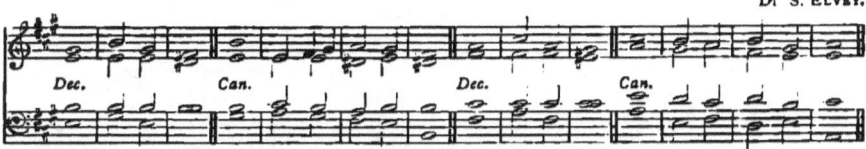

PSALM CXXXII.—*Memento, Domine.*

mf LORD, re- | -member | David : ánd | all | his | trouble;

2 How he swáre | unto · the | Lord : and vowed a vow únto the Al- | -mighty | God of | Jacob;

3 I will not come within the táber- nacle | of mine | house : nór | climb up | into · my | bed ;

4 I will not suffer mine eyes to sléep, nor mine | eye-lids · to | slumber : neither the temples of my héad to | take | any | rest ;

5 Until I find out a place for the témple | of the | Lord : an habitation fór the | mighty | God of | Jacob.   ·

6 Lo, we héard of the | same at | Ephrata : ánd | found it | in the | wood.

7 We will gó into his | taber- | -nacle : and fall lów on our | knees be- | -fore his | footstool.

8 Arise, O Lórd | into · thy | resting- place : thóu and the | ark | of thy | strength.

9 Let thy príests be | clothed · with | righteousness : and lét thy | saints | sing with | joyfulness.

10 For thy sérvant | David's | sake : turn not awáy the | presence · of | thine A- | -nointed.

11 The Lord hath made a faithful óath | unto | David : ánd he | shall not | shrink | from it.

12 Of the frúit | of thy | body : sháll I | set up- | -on thy | seat.

13 If thy children will keep my cove- nant * and my téstimonies that | I shall ! learn them : their children also shall sit upón thy | seat for | ever- | -more.

14 For the Lord hath chosen Sion to be an habitátion | for him- | -self : hé hath | longed | for | her.

15 This shall bé my | rest for | ever : here will I dwell * fór I | have · a de- | light there-.| -in.

16 I will bléss her | victuals · with | increase : and will sátis- | -fy her | poor with | bread.

17 I will déck her | priests with | health : and her sáints | shall re- | -joice and | sing.

18 There shall I make the hórn of | David · to | flourish : I have ordáined a | lantern · for | mine A- | -nointed.

19 As for his enemies * I shall clóthe | them with | shame : but upon himsélf | shall his | crown | flourish.

John Foster.

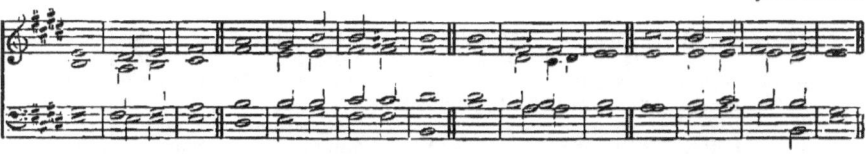

PSALM CXXXIII.—*Ecce, quam bonum!*

mf BEHOLD, how good and jóyful a | | thing it | is : bréthren, to | dwell to- | gether · in | unity !

2 It is like the precious ointment upon the head * that ran dówn | unto · 'he | beard : even unto Aaron's beard *

and went dówn to the | skirts | of his | clothing.

3 Like as the | dew of | Hermon : which féll up- | -on the | hill of | Sion.

4 For there the Lórd | promised · his | blessing: ánd | life for | ever- | -more.

INSTITUTION OF MINISTERS (continued).

(Special Psalm after Institution.)

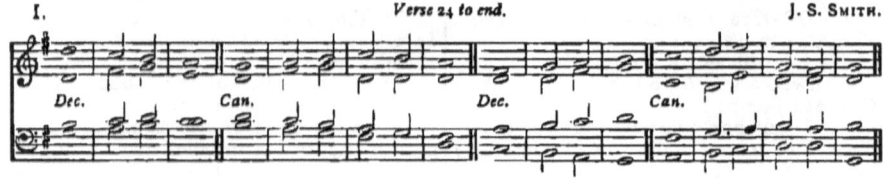

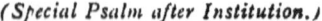

Alternative Chants.

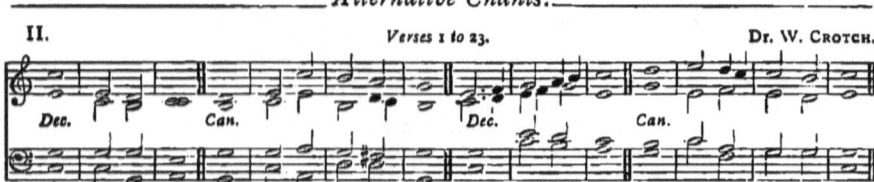

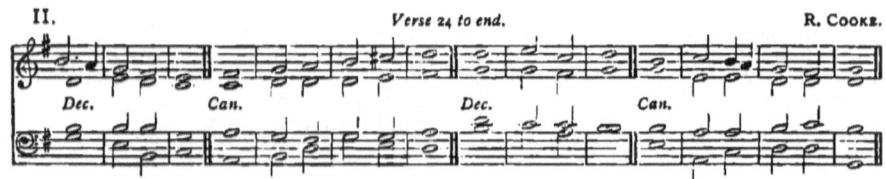

PSALM LXVIII.—*Exurgat Deus.*

ƒ LET God arise, and let his éne- | mies be | scattered : let them álso that | hate him | flee be- | -fore him.

2 Like as the smoke vanisheth, ✱ so shalt thou drǐve | them a- | -way : and like as wax melteth at the fire ✱ so let the ungodly pérish | at the | presence · of | God.

3 But let the righteous be glád and re- | -joice be · fore | God : lět them | also · be | merry · and | joyful.

4 O sing unto God, and sing práises | unto · his | Name : magnify him that rideth upon the heavens as it were upon an horse ✱ praise him in his Name JAʼH | and re- | -joice be- | -fore him.

5 He is a Father of the fatherless ✱ and defendeth the cáuse | of the | widows : even Gód in his | holy | habit- | ation.

6 He is the God that maketh men to be of one mind in an house ✱ and bringeth the prísoners | out of . cap- | -tivity : but letteth the runagátes con- | -tinue | in | scarceness.

7 O God, when thou wentest fórth be- | -fore the | people : whěn thou | wentest | through the | wilderness,

8 The earth shook, and the heavens dropped át the | presence · of | God : even as Sinai also was moved at the presence of Gód, who | is the | God of | Israel.

9 Thou, O God, sentest a gracious ráin upon | thine in- | -heritance : and re-fréshedst | it when | it was | weary.

10 Thy congregátion shall | dwell there- | -in : for thou, O God, hast of thy góodness pre- | -pared | for the | poor.

11 The Lórd | gave the | word : gréat was the | company | of the | preachers.

12 Kings with their armies did flée and | were dis- | -comfited : and théy of the | household · di- | -vided . the | spoil.

13 Though ye have lain among the pots ✶ yet shall ye be as the wíngs | of a | dove : that is covered with silver wíngs | and her | feathers . like | gold.

14 When the Almighty scattered kíngs| for their | sake : thén were they as | white as | snow in | Salmon.

15 As the hill of Basan, só is | God's | hill : even an hígh hill | as the | hill of | Basan.

16 Why hop ye so ye high hills ✶ this is God's hill, in the which it pléaseth | him to | dwell : yea, the Lórd will a- | -bide in | it for | ever.

17 The chariots of God are twenty thousand ✶ éven | thousands · of | angels : and the Lord is among them ✶ as ín the | holy | place of | Sinai.

18 Thou art gone up on high ✶ thou hast led captivity captive, and recéived | gifts for | men : yea, even for thine enemies ✶ that the Lórd | God might | dwell a- | -mong them.

19 Praised bé the | Lord | daily : even the God who helpeth us, and póureth his | bene- | -fits up- | -on us.

20 He is our God ✶ even the Gód of whom | cometh · sal- | vation : God is the Lórd by | whom · we es- | -cape | death.

21 God shall wound the héad | of his | enemies : and the hairy scalp of such a one as góeth on | still | in his | wickedness.

22 The Lord hath said ✶ I will bring my people agáin as I | did from | Basan : mine own will I bring again ✶ as I did sometime fróm the | deep | of the | sea.

2nd part 23 That thy foot may be dipped in the blóod | of thine | enemies : and that the tongue of thy dógs may be | red | through the | same.

24 It is well seen, O Gód, | how thou | goest : how thou, my God and Kíng, | goest | in the | sanctuary.

25 The singers go before ✶ the mínstrels | follow | after : in the midst are the dámsels | playing | with the | timbrels.

26 Give thanks O Israel, unto God the Lórd in the | congre- | -gations : fróm the | ground | of the | heart.

27 There is little Benjamin their ruler ✶ and the princes of | Judah · their | counsel : the princes of Zabúlon | and the | princes · of | Nephthali.

28 Thy God hath sént forth | strength for | thee : stablish the thing, O Gód that | thou hast | wrought in | us,

29 For thy temple's sáke | at Je- | rusalem : so shall kings bring | presents | unto | thee.

30 When the company of the spearmen, and multitude of the mighty ✶ are scattered abroad among the beasts of the people ✶ so that they húmbly bring | pieces · of | silver : and when he hath scattered the péople ! that de- | -light in | war ;

31 Then shall the princes cóme | out of | Egypt : the Morians' land shall soon stretch óut her | hands | unto | God.

ff 32 Sing unto God, O ye kíngdoms | of the | earth : O' sing | praises | unto · the | Lord ;

33 Who sitteth in the heavens over áll | from · the be- | -ginning : lo, he doth send out his voice ✶ yéa and | that a | mighty | voice.

34 Ascribe ye the power to Gód | over | Israel : his wórship and | strength is | in the | clouds.

35 O God, wonderful art thóu in thy | holy | places : even the God of Israel ✶ he will give strength and power unto his péople, | blessed | be | God.

fF.Glory be to the Fáther | and · to the | Son : ánd | to the | Holy | Ghost ;

F.As it was in the beginning ✶ is nów, and | ever | shall be : wórld without | end. | A | -men.

INSTITUTION OF MINISTERS (*continued*).

Or this Psalm.

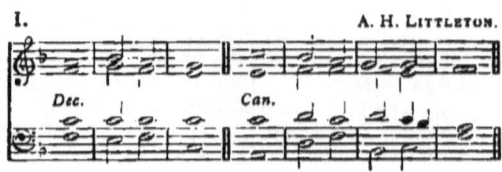

Alternative Chant.

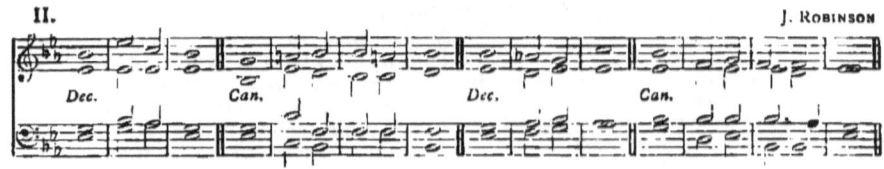

PSALM XXVI.—*Judica me, Domine.*

mp BE thou my Judge O Lord * for I′ have | walked | innocently : my trust hath been also in the Lórd | therefore | shall I · not | fall.

2 Exámine me O | Lord and | prove me : try óut my | reins | and my | heart.

3 For thy loving-kindness is éver be- | -fore mine | eyes : and I′ will | walk | in thy | truth.

4 I have not dwélt with | vain | persons : neither will I have féllowship | with | the de- | -ceitful.

5 I have hated the congregátion | of the | wicked : and wíll not | sit a- | -mong · the un- | -godly.

6 I will wash my hands in ínnocency | O | Lord : and só will I | go | to thine | altar ;

7 That I may shew the vóice of | thanks- | -giving : and téll of | all thy | wondrous | works.

8 Lord, I have loved the habitátion | of thy | house : and the pláce | where thine | honour | dwelleth.

9 O shut not up my sóul | with the | sinners : nor my lífe | with the | blood- | thirsty ;

10 I′n whose | hands is | wickedness : and their ríght | hand is | full of | gifts.

11 But as for me * I′ will | walk | in nocently : O deliver me, ánd be | merciful | unto | me.

12 My fóot | standeth | right : I will praise the Lórd | in the | congre- i -gations.

F. f Glory be to the Fáther, | and · to the | Son : ánd | to the | Holy | Ghost ;

F. As it was in the beginning * is nów, and | ever | shall be : wórld without | end. | A- | -men.

SELECTIONS OF PSALMS.

SELECTION FIRST.

S. WESLEY.

PSALM I.—*Beatus vir, qui non abiit.*

mf BLESSED is the man that hath not walked in the counsel of the ungodly ∗ nor stóod in the | way of | sinners : and hath not sât in the | seat | of the | scornful.

2 But his delight is in the lâw | of the | Lord : and in his law will he exercíse him- | -self | day and | night.

3 And he shall be like a tree planted bý the | water | side: that will bring fórth his | fruit in | due | season.

4 His léaf also | shall not | wither : and look, whatsoéver he | doeth | it shall | prosper. |

5 As for the ungodly, it is nôt | so with | them : but they are like the chaff ∗ which the wind scattereth away from the | face | of the | earth.

6 Therefore the ungodly shall not be able to stánd | in the | judgement : neither the sinners in the cóngre- | -gation | of the | righteous.

2nd part 7 But the Lord knoweth the wáy | of the | righteous : and the **way of the un-** | godly | shall | perish.

Dr. STAINER.

PSALM XV.—*Domine, quis habitabit?*

mf LORD, who shall dwéll in thy | taber- | -nacle : or who shall rést up- | -on thy | holy | hill ?

2 Even he that léadeth an | uncorrupt | life : and doeth the thing which is right ∗ and spéaketh the | truth | from his | heart.

3 He that hath used no deceit in his tongue ∗ nor done évil | to his | neighbour : ánd | hath not | slandered · his | neighbour.

4 He that setteth not by himself ∗ but is lówly in his | own | eyes : and maketh múch of | them that | fear the | Lord.

5 He that sweareth unto his neighbour ∗ and dísap- | -pointeth · him | not : though it | were · to his | own | hindrance.

6 He that hath not given his móney up- | -on | usury : nor táken re- | -ward a- | -gainst the | innocent.

7 Whóso | doeth · these | things : shâll | nev- | -er | fall.

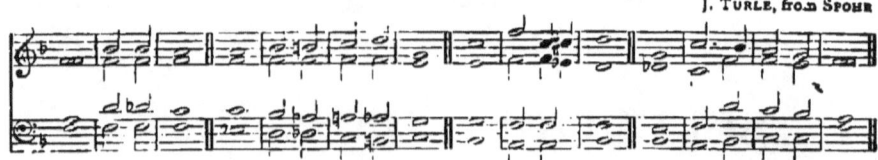

J. TURLE, from SPOHR

PSALM XCI.—*Qui habitat.*

mf WHOSO dwelleth under the defénce of the | most | High : shall abíde under the | shadow · of | the Al- | -mighty.

2 I will say unto the Lord ✱ Thou art my hópe | and my | stronghold : my Gód, in | him | will I | trust.

3 For he shall deliver thee from the snáre | of the | hunter : ánd | from the | noisome | pestilence.

4 He shall defend thee under his wings ✱ and thou shalt be sáfe | under · his | feathers : his faithfulness and trúth shall | be thy | shield and | buckler.

5 Thou shalt not be afráid for any | terror · by | night : nôr for the | arrow · that | flieth · by | day ;

6 For the pêstilence that | walketh · in | darkness : nor for the síckness that de- | -stroyeth | in the | noonday.

7 A thousand shall fall besíde thee ✱ and ten thoúsand at | thy right | hand : bût it shall | not come | nigh | thee.

8 Yea, with thine éyes shalt | thou be- | -hold : and sée the re- | -ward of | the un- | -godly.

9 For thou, Lórd | art my | hope : thou hast set thine hóuse of de- | -fence | very | high.

10 There shall no evil háppen | unto | thee : neither shall ány | plague come | nigh thy | dwelling.

11 For he shall give his angels chárge | over | thee : to kéep | thee in | all thy | ways.

12 They shall béar thee | in their | hands : that thou húrt not thy | foot a- | -gainst a | stone.

13 Thou shalt go upón the | lion and adder : the young lion and the dragon snált thou | tread | under · thy | feet.

14 Because he hath set his love upón me ✱ therefore will I' de- | -liver | him : I will set him up ✱ becáuse | he hath | known my | Name.

15 He shall call upon mé, and | I will | hear him : yea, I am with him in trouble ✱ I will delíver him and | bring | him to | honour.

16 With long lífe will I | satisfy | him : ánd | shew him | my sal- | -vation.

SELECTION SECOND.

J. TURLE.

PSALM IV.—*Cum invocarem.*

mf HEAR me when I call, O Gód | of my | righteousness : thou hast set me at liberty when I was in trouble ✱ have mercy upon mé, and | hearken | unto · my | prayer.

2 O ye sons of men ✱ how lóng will ye blas- | -pheme mine | honour ; and have such pleasure in vánity and | seek | after | falsehood ?

3 Know this also ✱ that the Lord hath chosen to himself the mán | that is | godly : when I cáll upon the | Lord | he will | hear me.

4 Stánd in | awe and | sin not : com- mune with your own heart ✱ and in your | chamber | and be | still.

5 Offer the sácri- | -fice of | righteous- ness : and pút your | trust | in the | Lord.

6 Thére be | many · that | say : Whó will | shew us | any | good ?

7 Lórd | lift thou | up : the líght of thy | counte- | -nance up- | -on us.

8 Thou hast put gládness | in my | heart : since the time that their córn and | wine and | oil in- | -creased.

2nd part 9 I will lay me down in péace, and | take my | rest : for it is thou, Lord, ónly that | makest · me | dwell in | safety.

SELECTION SECOND (*continued*).

J. TURLE

PSALM XXXI.—*In te, Domine, speravi.*

mf IN thee, O Lórd, have I | put my | trust : let me never be put to con-fúsion, de- | -liver . me | in thy | righteousness.

2 Bow dówn thine | ear to | me : make háste | to de- |-liver | me.

3 And be thou my strong rock, and hóuse | of de- | -fence : thát | thou . mayest | save | me.

4 For thou art my strong róck | and my | castle : be thou also my guide ✱ and léad me | for thy | Name's | sake.

5 Draw me out of the net that they have láid | privily | for me : fór | thou | art my | strength.

6 Into thy hánds I com- | -mend my | spirit : for thou hast redeemed me ✱ O'| Lord thou | God of | truth.

J. TURLE, from SPOHR.

PSALM XCI.—*Qui habitat.*

mf WHOSO dwelleth under the defénce of the | most | High : shall abíde under the | shadow · of | the Al- | -mighty.

2 I will say unto the Lord ✱ Thou art my hópe | and my | stronghold : my Gód, in | him | will I | trust.

3 For he shall deliver thee from the snáre | of the | hunter : ánd | from the | noisome | pestilence.

4 He shall defend thee under his wings ✱ and thou shalt be sáfe | under · his | feathers : his faithfulness and trúth shall | be thy | shield and | buckler.

5 Thou shalt not be afráid for any | terror · by | night : nór for the | arrow . that | flieth · by | day;

6 For the péstilence that | walketh · in | darkness : nor for the síckness that de- | -stroyeth | in the | noonday.

7 A thousand shall fall beside thee ✱ and ten thoúsand at | thy right | hand : bút it shall | not come | nigh | thee.

8 Yea, with thine éyes shalt | thou be- |-hold : and sée the re- | -wárd of | the un- | -godly.

9 For thou, Lórd | art my | hope : thou hast set thine hóuse of de- | -fence | very | high.

10 There shall no evil háppen | unto | thee : neither shall ány | plague come | nigh thy | dwelling.

11 For he shall give his angels chárge | over | thee : to kéep | thee in | all thy | ways.

12 They shall béar thee | in their | hands : that thou húrt not thy | foot a- | gainst a | stone.

13 Thou shalt go upón the | lion and | adder : the young lion and the dragon shált thou | tread | under · thy | feet.

14 Because he hath set his love upon' me ✱ therefore will I'. de- | -liver | him : I will set him up ✱ becáuse | he hath | known my | Name.

15 He shall call upon mé, and | I will | hear him : yea, I am with him in trouble ✱ I will delíver him | and | bring | him to | honour.

16 With long lífe will I | satisfy | him : ánd | shew him | my sal- | -vation.

SELECTION SECOND (continued).

J. BARNBY.

PSALM CXXXIV.—*Ecce nunc.*

mf BEHÓLD, now | praise the | Lord :|
áll ye | servants | of the | Lord ;
  2 Ye that by night stand in the hóuse | of the | Lord ; even in the cóurts of the | house of | our | God.

  3 Lift up your hánds | in the | sanc- tuary : ánd | praise | — the | Lord.
  4 The Lórd that made | heaven . and | earth : gíve thee | blessing | out of | Sion.

SELECTION THIRD.

Dr. BOYCE.

PSALM XIX.—*Cæli enarrant.*

THE heavens declàre the | glory · of | God : and the fírmament | sheweth · his | handy- | -work.
  2 One dáy | telleth · an- | -other : and one níght | certi- | -fíeth · an- | -other.
  3 There is neíther | speech nor | language : bút their | voices · are | heard a- | -mong them.
  4 Their sound is gone óut into | all | lands : and their wórds into the | ends | of the | world.
  5 In them hath he set a tábernacle | for the | sun : which cometh forth as a bridegroom out of his chamber * and re- jóiceth as a | giant · to | run his | course.
  6 It goeth forth from the uttermost part of the heaven * and runneth about unto the énd of | it a- | -gain : and there is nothing híd | from the | heat there- | -of.
  7 The law of the Lord is an undefiled láw con- | -verting · the | soul : the testi- mony of the Lord is sure * and gíveth | wisdom | unto · the | simple.
  8 The statutes of the Lord are rìght and re- | -joice the | heart : the command- ment of the Lord is pure * and gíveth | light | unto · the | eyes.
  9 The fear of the Lord is cléan and en- | -dureth · for | ever : the judgements of the Lord are trúe, and | righteous | alto- | -gether.
  10 More to be desired are they than gold * yéa than | much fíne | gold : sweeter álso than | honey | and the | honey- comb.
  2nd part. 11 Moreover, by thém is thy | servant | taught : and in keepiug of them | there is | great re- | -ward.
  mp 12 Who can téll how | oft · he of- | fendeth : O cleanse thou mé | from my | secret | faults.
  13 Keep thy servant also from pre- sumptuous sins * lest they get the do- mínion | over | me : so shall I be unde- filed, and ínnocent | from the | great of- | fence.
  14 Let the words of my mouth * and the meditátion | of my | heart : be álway ac- | -ceptable | in thy | sight,
  15 O | — | Lord : mý | strength and | my re- | -deemer.

Dr. CROTCH.

PSALM XXIV.—*Domini est terra.*

f THE earth is the Lord's * and áll that | therein | is : the compass of the wórld, and | they that | dwell there- | -in.
  2 For he hath fóunded it up-|-on the | seas : and prepáred | it up-|-on the | floods
  3 Who shall ascend into the híll | of

the | Lord : or who shall rise up | in his | holy | place ?

4 Even he that hath clean hánds and a | pure | heart : and that hath not lift up his mind unto vanity * nor sworn | to de- | -ceive his | neighbour.

5 He shall receive the blessing | from the | Lord : and righteousness from the | God of | his sal- | -vation.

6 This is the generation of | them that | seek him : even of them that | seek thy | face O | Jacob.

7 Lift up your heads O ye gates * and be ye lift up ye ever- | -lasting | doors : and the King of | glory | shall come | in.

8 Who is the | King of | glory : it is the Lord strong and mighty * even the | Lord | mighty · in | battle.

9 Lift up your heads O ye gates * and be ye lift up ye ever- | -lasting | doors : and the King of | glory | shall come | in.

10 Who is the | King of | glory : even the Lord of hosts | he · is the | King of | glory.

J. BATTISHILL.

PSALM CIII.—*Benedic, anima mea.*

f PRAISE the Lórd | O my | soul : and all that is within me | praise his | holy | Name.

2 Praise the Lórd | O my | soul : ánd for- | -get not | all his | benefits ;

3 Who forgíveth | all thy | sin : and héaleth | all | thine in- | -firmities ;

4 Who saveth thy lífe | from de- | struction : and crowneth thée with | mercy · and | loving- | -kindness ;

5 Who satisfieth thy móuth with | good | things : making thee yóung and | lusty | as an | eagle.

6 The Lord execúteth ríghteous- | ness and | judgement : for all thém that | are op- | -pressed · with | wrong.

7 He shewed his wáys | unto | Moses : his wórks | unto · the | children of | Israel.

8 The Lord is fúll of com- | -passion · and | mercy : long-súffering, | and of | great | goodness.

9 He will not | alway · be | chiding : neither kéepeth | he his | anger · for | ever.

10 He hath not déalt with us | after · our | sins : nor rewárded us ac- | -cording | to our | wickednesses.

11 For look how high the heaven is in compárison | of the | earth : so great is his mercy álso|toward|them that |fear him.

12 Look how wide also the éast is | from the | west : so fár hath he | set our | sins | from us.

13 Yea, like as a father pítieth | his | own | children : even so :s the Lord mérciful | unto | them that | fear him.

14 For he knoweth wheréof | we are | made : he rememberèd | that we | are but | dust.

mp 15 The days of mán are | but as | grass : for he flourisheth ás a | flower | of the | field.

16 For as soon as the wind goeth óver it | it is | gone : and the place theréof shall | know it | no | more.

mf 17 But the merciful goodness of the Lord * endureth for ever and éver upon | them that | fear him : and his righteousness up- | -on | children's | children ;

18 Even upon súch as | keep his | covenant : and think upon | his com- | -mandments · to | do them.

f 19 The Lord hath prepared his | seat in | heaven : and his kíngdom | ruleth | over | all.

20 O praise the Lord, ye angels of his * yé that ex- | -cel in | strength : ye that fulfil his commandment * and hearken únto the | voice | of his | word.

21 O praise the Lórd, all | ye his | hosts : ye sérvants of | his that | do his | pleasure.

22 O speak good of the Lord, all ye works of his * in all pláces of | his do- | minion : práise thou the | Lord | O my | soul.

SELECTION FOURTH.

Dr CROTCH.

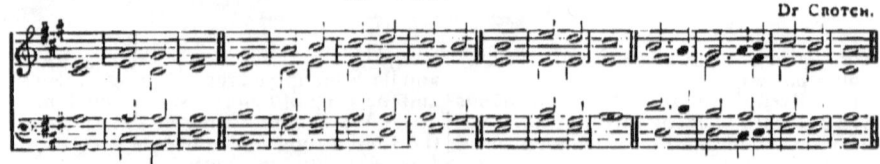

PSALM XXIII.—*Dominus regit me.*

mp THE Lórd | is my | shepherd : thére- | fore | can I | lack | nothing.

2 He shall féed me in a | green | pasture : and lead me fórth be- | -side the | waters · of | comfort.

3 Hé shall con- | -vert my | soul : and bring me forth in the paths of right- eousness | for his | Name's | sake.

4 Yea, though I walk through the valley of the shadow of death * I' will |

tear no | evil : for thou art with me * thy ród and thy | staff | comfort | me.

5 Thou shalt prepare a table before me * against thém that | trouble | me : thou hast anointed my head with óil, and my | cup | shall be | full.

6 But thy loving-kindness and mercy * shall follow me all the dáys | of my | life : and I will dwell in the hóuse | of the | Lord for | ever.

J. BATTISHILL.

PSALM XXXIV.—*Benedicam Domino.*

mf I WILL alway give thánks | unto · the | Lord : his práise shall | ever · be | in my | mouth.

2 My soul shall make her bóast | in the | Lord : the humble shall héar there- | of | and be | glad.

3 O práise the | Lord with | me : and let us mágni- | -fy his | Name to- | -gether.

4 I sought the Lórd | and he | heard me : yea, he delivered me | out of | all my | fear.

5 They had an eye unto hím | and were | lightened : ánd their | faces · were | not a- | -shamed.

6 Lo the poor crieth, and the Lórd | heareth | him : yea, and sáveth him | out of | all his | troubles.

7 The angel of the Lord tarrieth róund about | them that | fear him : ánd | — de- | -livereth | them.

8 O taste and see how grácious the | Lord | is : blessed ís the | man that | trusteth · in | him.

9 O fear the Lord, yé that | are his | saints : for théy that | fear him | lack | nothing.

10 The lions do láck and | suffer | hunger : but they who seek the Lord, shall want no mánner of | thing | that is | good.

11 Come, ye children, and héarken | unto | me : I will téach you the | fear | of the | Lord.

12 What man is hé that | lusteth · to | live : ánd would | fain | see good | days?

13 Kéep thy | tongue from | evil : and thy lips | that they | speak no | guile.

14 Eschew évil and | do | good : séek | peace | and en- | -sue it.

15 The eyes of the Lórd are | over · the | righteous : and his éars are | open | unto · their | prayers.

16 The countenance of the Lord is against thém that | do | evil : to root out the remémbrance | of them | from the | earth.

17 The righteous cry, and the Lórd | heareth | them : and delívereth them | out of | all their | troubles.

18 The Lord is nigh unto them that áre of a | contrite | heart : and will sáve such as | be · of an | humble | spirit.

19 Great are the tróubles | of the | righteous : but the Lórd de- | -livereth · him | out of | all.

20 He kéepeth | all his | bones : só that not | one of | them is | broken.

21 But misfortune shall sláy | the un- | godly : and they that háte the | righteous | shall be | desolate.

22 The Lord delivereth the sóuls | of his | servants : and all they that put their trúst in | him shall | not be | de- stitute.

SELECTION FOURTH (continued).

Dr. Garrett.

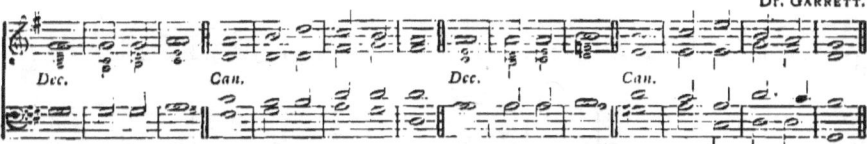

PSALM LXV.—*Te decet hymnus.*

F. mf THOU, O God art | praised · in | Sion : and unto thee shall the vow be per- | -formed | in Je- | -rusalem.

F. 2 Thou that | hearest · the | prayer : unto | thee shall | all flesh | come.

3 My misdeeds pre- | -vail a- | -gainst me : O" be thou | merciful | unto · our | sins.

4 Blessed is the man, whom thou choosest, and receivest | unto | thee : he shall dwell in thy court ✱ and shall be satisfied with the pleasures of thy house ✱ even | of thy | holy | temple.

5 Thou shalt shew us wonderful things in thy righteousness ✱ O God of | our sal- | -vation : thou that art the hope of all the ends of the earth ✱ and of them that remain | in the | broad | sea.

6 Who in his strength setteth | fast the | mountains : and is | girded · a- | bout with | power.

7 Who stilleth the raging | of the | sea : and the noise of his waves and the | madness | of the | people.

8 They also that dwell in the uttermost parts of the earth ✱ shall be afraid | at thy | tokens : thou that makest the outgoings of the morning and | evening · to | praise | thee.

9 Thou visitest the earth and | blessest | it : thou | makest · it | very | plenteous.

10 The river of God is | full of | water : thou preparest their corn ✱ for so thou pro- | -videst | for the | earth.

11 Thou waterest her furrows ✱ thou sendest rain into the little | valleys · there- | -of : thou makest it soft with the drops of rain and | blessest · the | increase | of it.

12 Thou crownest the year | with thy | goodness : and thy | clouds | drop | fatness.

13 They shall drop upon the dwellings | of the | wilderness : and the little hills shall re- | -joice on | every | side.

14 The folds shall be | full of | sheep : the valleys also shall stand so thick with corn that | they shall | laugh and | sing.

SELECTION FIFTH.

John Foster.

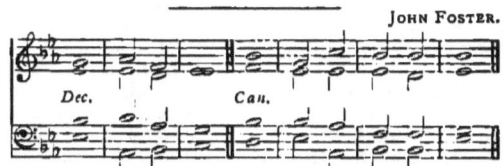

PSALM XXVI.—*Judica me, Domine.*

mp BE thou my Judge O Lord ✱ for I" have | walked | innocently : my trust hath been also in the Lord | therefore | shall I · not | fall.

2 Examine me O | Lord and | prove me : try out my | reins | and my | heart.

3 For thy loving-kindness is ever be- | -fore mine | eyes : and I" will | walk | in thy | truth.

4 I have not dwelt with | vain | persons : neither will I have fellowship | with | the de- | -ceitful.

5 I have hated the congregation | of the | wicked : and will not | sit a- | -mong · the un- | -godly.

6 I will wash my hands in innocency | O | Lord : and so will I | go | to thine | altar ;

7 That I may shew the voice of | thanks- | -giving : and tell of | all thy | wondrous | works.

8 Lord, I have loved the habitation | of thy | house : and the place | where thine | honour | dwelleth.

9 O shut not up my soul | with the | sinners : nor my life | with the | blood- | thirsty ;

10 I"n whose | hands is | wickedness : and their right | hand is | full of | gifts.

11 But as for me ✱ I" will | walk | innocently : O deliver me, and be | merciful | unto | me.

12 My foot | standeth | right : I will praise the Lord | in the | congre- | -gations.

SELECTION FIFTH (continued).

JACKSON.

PSALM XLIII.—*Judica me, Deus.*

mf GIVE sentence with me O God * and defend my cause against the un- | -godly | people : O deliver me from the de- | -ceitful · and | wicked | man.

2 For thou art the God of my strength * why hast thou | put me | from thee : and why go I so heavily * while the | ene · my op- | -presseth | me ?

3 O send out thy light and thy truth, that | they may | lead me : and bring me unto thy holy | hill and ! to thy | dwelling.

4 And that I may go unto the altar of God * even unto the God of my | joy and | gladness : and upon the harp will I give thanks unto thee O | God | my | God.

5 Why art thou so heavy | O my | soul : and why art thou so dis- | -quiet- | -ed with- | -in me ?

6 O put thy | trust in | God : for I will yet give him thanks * which is the help of my | countenance | and my | God.

J. L. BROWNSMITH.

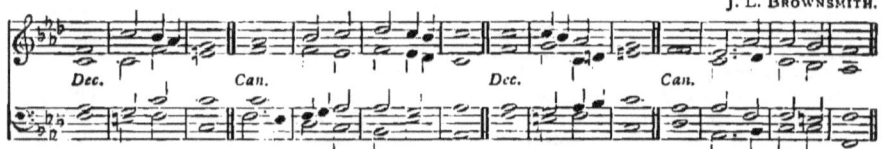

PSALM CXLI.—*Domine, clamavi.*

mp LORD, I call upon thee * haste thee | unto | me : and consider my voice when I | cry | unto | thee.

2 Let my prayer be set forth in thy sight | as the | incense : and let the lifting up of my hands | be an | evening | sacrifice.

3 Set a watch, O Lord, be- | -fore my | mouth : and keep the | door | of my | lips.

4 O let not mine heart be inclined to any | evil | thing : let me not be occupied in ungodly works with the men that work wickedness * lest I eat of such | things as | please | them.

5 Let the righteous rather | smite me | friendly : and | — re- | -prove | me.

6 But let not their precious balms | break my | head : yea, I will pray | yet a- | -gainst their | wickedness.

7 Let their judges be overthrown in | stony | places : that they may hear my | words for | they are | sweet.

8 Our bones lie scattered be- | -fore the | pit : like as when one breaketh and heweth | wood up- | -on the | earth.

9 But mine eyes look unto thee, O | Lord | God : in thee is my trust, O | cast not | out my | soul.

10 Keep me from the snare that they have | laid for | me : and from the traps | of the | wicked | doers.

2nd part 11 Let the ungodly fall into their own | nets to- | -gether : and let | me | ever · es- | -cape | them.

SELECTION SIXTH.

R. FARRANT.

PSALM XXXII.—*Beati, quorum.*

F. mp BLESSED is he whose unrighteousness | is for- | -given : and whose | sin | is | covered.

F. 2 Blessed is the man unto whom the Lord im- | -puteth · no | sin : and in whose | spirit · there | is no | guile.

SELECTION SIXTH (continued).

3 For whilst I | held my | tongue : my bones consumed awáy | through my | daily · com- | -plaining.

4 For thy hand is heavy upon me | day and | night : and my móisture is | like the | drought in | summer.

5 I will acknowledge my sín | unto | thee : and mine unrighteousness | have I | not | hid.

6 I said, I will confess my síns | unto · the | Lord : and so thou forgávest the | wickedness | of my | sin.

7 For this shall every one that is godly make his prayer unto thee ✻ in a time when thou | mayest · be | found : but in the great wáter-floods | they shall | not come | nigh him.

8 Thou art a place to hide me in ✻ | thou shalt presérve | me from | trouble : thou shalt compass me abóut with | songs | of de- | -liverance.

9 I will inform thee, and teach thee in the wáy wherein | thou shalt | go : and I' will | guide thee | with mine | eye.

10 Be ye not like to horse and mule ✻ which háve no | under- | -standing : whose mouths must be held with bit and brídle | lest they | fall up- | -on thee.

11 Great plagues remáin | for · the un- | -godly : but whoso putteth his trust in the Lord ✻ mercy embráceth | him on | every | side.

12 Be glad O ye righteous ✻ and rejóice | in the | Lord : and be joyful all yĕ | that are | true of | heart.

J. TURLE, from H. PURCELL.

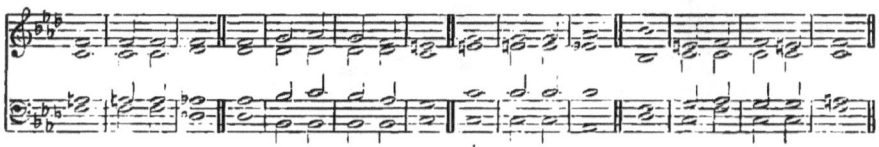

PSALM CXXX.—*De profundis.*

p OUT of the deep have I called únto | thee O | Lord : Lórd | hear | my | voice.

2 O let thine éars con- | -sider | well : thĕ | voice of | my com- | -plaint.

3 If thou, Lord, wilt be extreme to márk what is | done a- | -miss : O Lórd | who | may a- | -bide it ?

4 Fór there is | mercy · with | thee : thérefore | shalt | thou be | feared.

5 I look for the Lord ; my sóul doth | wait for | him : ín his | word | is my | trust.

6 My soul fléeth | unto · the | Lord : before the morning watch, I sáy, be- | -fore the | morning | watch.

7 O Israel, trust in the Lord ✻ for with the Lórd | there is | mercy : ánd with | him is | plenteous · re- | -demption.

8 And hĕ shall re- | -deem | Israel : fróm | all | his | sins.

J. TURLE.

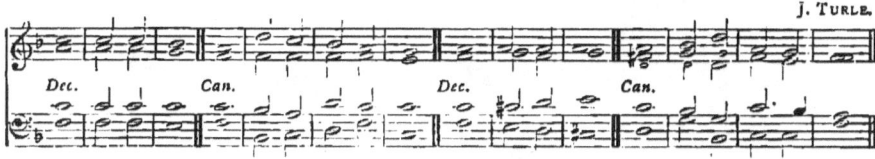

Dec.   Can.   Dec.   Can.

PSALM CXXI.—*Levavi oculos.*

mf I WILL lift up mine éyes | unto · the | hills : fróm | whence | cometh · my | help.

2 My help cometh éven | from the | Lord : whó hath | made | heaven and | earth.

3 He will not suffer thy fóot | to be | moved : and hé that | keepeth · thee | will not | sleep.

4 Behold, hé that | keepeth | Israel : sháll | neither | slumber · nor | sleep.

5 The Lord himsélf | is thy | keeper : the Lord is thy defénce up- | -on thy | right | hand ;

6 So that the sun shall not búrn | thee by | day : néither the | moon | by | night.

7 The Lord shall presérve thee from | all | evil : yea, it is even hé | that shall | keep thy | soul.

8 The Lord shall preserve thy going out ✻ ánd thy | coming | in : from thís time | forth for | ever- | -more.

SELECTION SEVENTH.

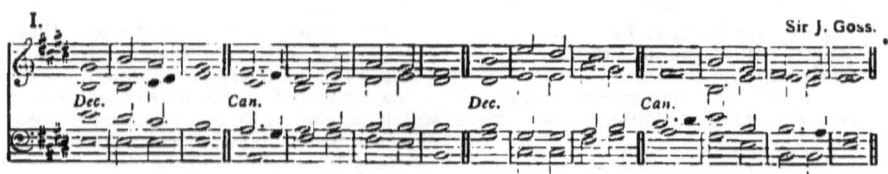

Alternative Chants.

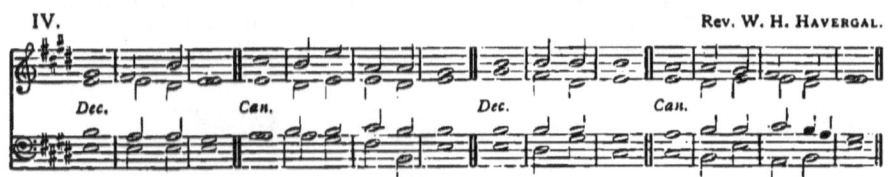

PSALM XXXVII.—*Noli æmulari.*

F. mf FRET not thyself becáuse of | the un- | -godly : neither be thou énvious a- | gainst the | evil- | -doers.

F. 2 For they shall soon be cut dówn | like the | grass : and be wíthered | even . as the | green | herb.

3 Put thou thy trust in the Lórd and be | doing | good : dwell in the lánd, and | verily . thou | shalt be | fed.

4 Delíght thou | in the | Lord : and he shall give | thee thy | heart's de- | -sire.

5 Commit thy way unto the Lord ✷ and pút thy | trust in | him : ánd | he shall | bring it . to | pass.

6 He shall make thy righteousness as cléar | as the | light : and thy júst | deal- ing | as the | noonday.

7 Hold thee still in the Lord ✷ and abide pátient- | -ly up- | -on him : but grieve not thyself at him whose way doth prosper ✷ against the man that dóeth | after | evil | counsels.

SELECTION SEVENTH (continued).

8 Leave off from wráth and let | go dis- | -pleasure : fret not thyself ✱ élse shalt thou be | moved · to | do | evil.

9 Wicked doers sháll be | rooted | out : and they that patiently abide the Lórd | those · shall in- | -herit · the | land.

10 Yet a little while ✱ and the ungódly shall be | clean | gone : thou shalt look after his pláce, and | he shall | be a- | way.

11 But the meek-spirited sháll pos- | sess the | earth : and shall be refréshed in the | multi- | -tude of | peace. .

12 The ungodly seeketh cóunsel a- | gainst the | just : and gnásheth up- | -on him | with his | teeth.

13 The Lord shall láugh | him to | scorn : for he hath séen | that his | day is | coming.

14 The ungodly have drawn out the swórd and have | bent their | bow : to cast down the poor and needy ✱ and to slay such as áre of a | right | conver-|-sation.

15 Their sword shall go thróugh their | own | heart : ánd their | bow | shall be | broken.

16 A small thing thát the | righteous | hath : is better than gréat | riches · of | the un- | -godly.

17 For the arms of the ungódly | shall be | broken : ánd the | Lord up- | -hold- eth · the | righteous.

18 The Lord knoweth the dáys | of the | godly : and their inhéritance | shall en- | -dure for | ever.

19 They shall not be confóunded in the | perilous | time : and in the days of déarth | they shall | have e- | -nough.

20 As for the ungodly they shall perish ✱ and the enemies of the Lord shall consúme as the | fat of | lambs : yea, even as the smóke shall | they con- | -sume a- | -way.

21 The ungodly borroweth, and páy- eth | not a- | -gain : but the ríghteous is | merci- | -ful and | liberal.

22 Such as are blessed of Gód shall pos- | -sess the | land : and they that are | cúrsed of him | shall be | rooted | out.

23 The Lord órdereth a | good man's | going : and maketh his wáy ac- | -ceptable | to him- | -self.

24 Though he fall ✱ he shall nót be | cast a- | -way : for the Lórd up- | -holdeth him | with his | hand.

25 I have been yóung, and | now am | old : and yet saw I never the righteous forsaken ✱ nór his | seed | begging · their | bread.

26 The righteous is ever mérci- | -ful and | lendeth : ánd his | seed | is | blessed.

27 Flee from evil ✱ and do the thíng | that is | good : ánd | dwell for | ever-|-more.

28 For the Lord loveth the thíng | that is | right : he forsaketh not his that be gódly but | they are · pre- | served · for | ever.

29 The unrighteous | shall be | pun- ished : as for the seed of the ungódly, | it · shall be | rooted | out.

30 The righteous shall in- | -herit · the | land : ánd | dwell there- | -in for | ever.

31 The mouth of the righteous is éxer- | -cised · in | wisdom : and his tóngue | will be | talking of | judgement.

32 The law of his Gód is | in his | heart : ánd his | goings | shall not | slide.

33 The ungódly | seeth · the | righteous : ánd | seeketh · oc- | -casion · to | slay him.

34 The Lord will not léave him | in his | hand : nór con- | -demn him | when · he is | judged.

35 Hope thou in the Lord, and keep his way ✱ and he shall promote thee that thóu shalt pos- | -sess the | land : when the ungódly shall | perish | thou shalt | see it.

36 I myself have seen the ungódly in | great | power : and flóurishing | like a | green | bay-tree.

37 I went by, and lo | he was | gone : I sought him, but his pláce could | no- | where be | found.

38 Keep innocency ✱ and take heed unto the thíng | that is | right : for that shall bríng a man | peace | at the | last.

39 As for the transgressors, théy shall | perish · to- | -gether : and the end of the ungodly is ✱ they shall be róoted | out | at the | last.

40 But the salvation of the righteous cómeth | of the | Lord : who is also their stréngth | in the | time of | trouble.

_{2nd}
part. 41 And the Lord shall stánd by | them and | save them : he shall deliver them from the ungodly ✱ and shall save them, becáuse they | put their | trust in | him.

SELECTION EIGHTH.

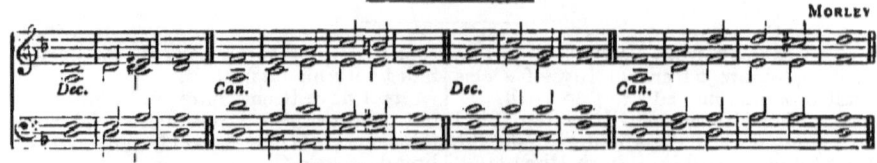

MORLEY

PSALM LI.—*Miserere mei, Deus.*

p HAVE mercy upon me O God * áfter thy | great | goodness : according to the multitude of thy mercies, dó a- | -way | mine of- | -fences.

2 Wash me thróughly | from my | wickedness : ánd | cleanse me | from my | sin.

3 For I*ac- | -knowledge · my | faults : ánd my | sin is | ever · be- | -fore me.

4 Against thee only have I sinned * and done this évil | in thy | sight : that thou mightest be justified in thy sáying and | clear when | thou art | judged.

5 Behóld I was | shapen · in | wickedness : and in sín hath my | mother · con- | ceived | me.

6 But lo, thou requirest trúth in the | inward | parts : and shalt make me to únder- | -stand | wisdom | secretly.

7 Thou shalt purge me with hyssop * ánd I | shall be | clean : thou shalt wash me * ánd I | shall be | whiter · than | snow.

8 Thou shalt make me héar of | joy and | gladness : that the bones which thóu hast | broken | may re- | -joice.

9 Turn thy fáce | from my | sins : and pút out | all | my mis- | -deeds.

10 Make me a cléan | heart O | God : ánd re- | -new a · right | spirit · with- | -in me.

11 Cast me not awáy | from thy | presence : and táke not thy | holy | Spirit | from me.

12 O give me the cómfort of thy | help a- | -gain : and stáblish me | with thy | free | Spirit.

2nd part 13 Then shall I teach thy wáys | unto · the | wicked : and sinners shall bé con- | verted | unto | thee.

14 Deliver me from blood-guiltiness, O God * thou that art the Gód | of my | health : and my tóngue shall | sing | of thy | righteousness.

15 Thou shalt ópen my | lips O | Lord : ánd my | mouth shall | shew thy | praise.

16 For thou desirest no sacrifice * élse would I | give it | thee : but thou delíghtest | not in | burnt- | -offerings.

17 The sacrifice of Gód is a | troubled | spirit : a broken and contrite heart, O Gód, | shalt thou | not de- | -spise.

18 O be favourable and grácious | unto | Sion : búild thou the | walls | of Je- | -rusalem.

19 Then shalt thou be pleased with the sacrifice of righteousness * with the burnt-ófferings | and ob- | -lations : then shall they óffer young | bullocks · up- | -on thine | altar.

J. TURLE.

PSALM XLII.—*Quemadmodum.*

mf LIKE as the hárt de- | -sireth · the | water-brooks : so longeth my sóul | after | thee O | God.

2 My soul is athirst for God * yea, éven for the | living | God : when shall I come to appear be- | -fore the | presence · of | God ?

3 My tears have been my méat | day and | night : while they daily sáy unto me | Where is | now thy | God ?

4 Now when I think thereupon * I pour out my héart | by my- | -self : for I went with the multitude * and brought them fórth | into · the | house of | God ;

2nd part 5 In the voice of práise and | thanks- | giving : amóng | such as | keep | holyday.

6 Why art thou so full of héaviness | O my | soul : and why art thou só dis- | quiet- | -ed with- | -in me ?

7 Pút thy | trust in | God : for I will yet give him thanks for the | help | of his | countenance.

8 My God, my sóul is | vexed · with- | in me : therefore will I remember thee concerning the land of Jordan * ánd the | little | hill of | Hermon.

SELECTION EIGHTH (continued).

9 One deep calleth another * because of the nóise | of the | water-pipes : all thy waves and stórms are | gone | over | me.

10 The Lord hath granted his loving-kíndness | in the | day-time : and in the night-season did I sing of him * and made my prayer únto the | God | of my | life.

11 I will say unto the God of my strength * Why̆ hast thou for- | -gotten | me : why go I thus heavily * whíle the | ene · my op- | -presseth | me ?

12 My bones are smitten asúnder | as · with a | sword : while mine enemies that tróuble me | cast me | in the | teeth ;

13 Namely, while they say dáily | unto | me : Whére | — is | now thy | God ?

14 Why art thou so véxed | O my | soul : and why art thou só dis- | -quiet- | -ed with- | -in me ?

15 O pút thy | trust in | God : for I will yet thank him * which is the hélp of my | countenance | and my | God.

SELECTION NINTH.

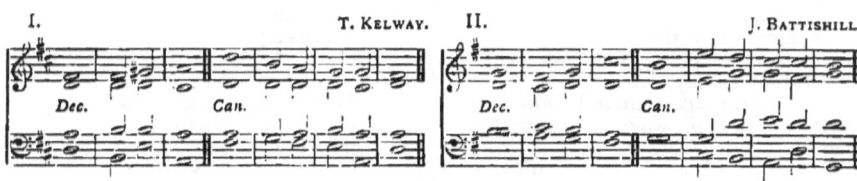

I. T. Kelway.   II. J. Battishill.

PSALM LXXII.—Deus, judicium.

f GIVE the Kíng thy | judgements · O | God : and thy ríghteousness | unto · the | King's | son.

2 Then shall he judge thy people accórding | unto | right: ánd de-|-fend | the | poor.

3 The mountains álso shall | bring | peace : and the little hills | righteousness | unto · the | people.

4 He shall keep the símple folk | by their | right : defend the children of the póor, and | punish · the | wrong- | -doer.

5 They shall fear thee, as long as the sún and | moon en- | -dureth : from óne gener- | -ation | to an- | -other.

6 He shall come down like the ráin into a | fleece of | wool : éven as the | drops that | water · the | earth.

7 In his tíme shall the | righteous | flourish : yea, and abundance of péace, so | long · as the | moon en- | -dureth.

8 His dominion shall be also from the óne sea | to the | other: and from the flóod | unto · the | world's | end.

9 They that dwell in the wílderness shall | kneel be- | -fore him : his éne- | -mies shall | lick the | dust.

10 The kings of Tharsis and of the ísles shall | give | presents: the kings of Arábia and | Saba | shall bring | gifts.

11 All kings shall fáll | down be- | -fore him : áll | nations · shall | do him | service.

12 For he shall deliver the póor | when he | crieth : the needy álso and | him that | hath no | helper.

13 He shall be favourable tó the | simple · and | needy : and shall presérve the | souls | of the | poor.

14 He shall deliver their sóuls from | falsehood · and | wrong : and déar shall their | blood be | in his | sight.

15 He shall live * and unto him shall be given of the góld | of A- | -rabia : prayer shall be made ever unto hím, and | daily · shall | he be | praised.

16 There shall be an heap of corn in the earth * hígh up- | -on the | hills: his fruit shall shake like Libanus * and shall be green in the cíty like | grass up- | -on the | earth.

17 His Name shall endure for ever * his Name shall remain under the sún a- | mongst the · pos- | -terities : which shall be blessed through hím, and | all the | heathen · shall | praise him.

18 Blessed be the Lord God * éven the | God of | Israel : which ónly | doeth | wondrous | things;

2nd part. 19 And blessed be the Name of his Májes- | -ty for | ever : and all the earth shall be filled with his Májesty. | Amen. | A-|-men.

SELECTION NINTH (continued).

I. W. RUSSELL

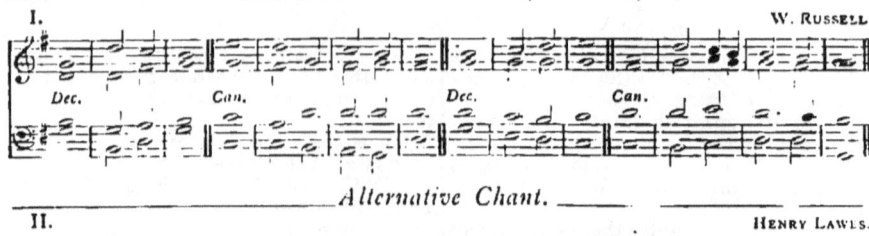

Alternative Chant.

II. HENRY LAWES.

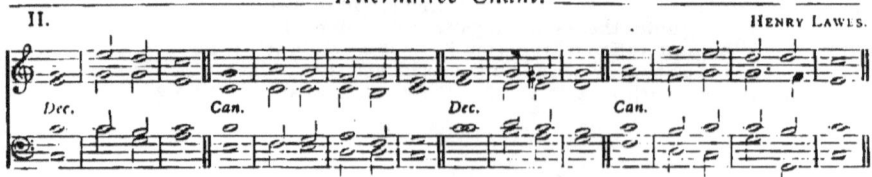

PSALM XCVI.—*Cantate Domino.*

f O SING unto the Lórd a | new | song : sing unto the Lórd | all the | whole | earth.

2 Sing unto the Lórd and | praise his | Name : be telling of hís sal- | -vation · from | day to | day.

3 Declare his hónour | unto · the | heathen : and his wónders | unto | all | people.

4 For the Lord is great ✶ and cannot wórthi- | -ly be | praised : he is móre to be | feared · than | all | gods.

5 As for all the gods of the héathen, | they are · but | idols : but it ís the | Lord that | made the | heavens.

6 Glory and wórship | are be- | -fore him : power and | honour · are | in his | sanctuary.

7 Ascribe unto the Lord ✶ O ye kíndreds | of the | people : ascribe unto the Lórd | worship | and | power.

8 Ascribe unto the Lord the honour dúe | unto · his | Name : bring présents and | come | into · his | courts.

9 O worship the Lórd in the | beauty · of | holiness : let the whole éarth | stand in | awe of | him.

10 Tell it out among the héathen that the | Lord is | King : and that it is he who hath made the round world so fast ✶ that it cannot be moved ✶ and how that hé shall | judge the | people | righteously.

11 Let the heavens rejóice and let the | earth be | glad : let the sea make a nóise, and | all that | therein | is.

12 Let the field be jóyful and | all that · is | in it : then shall all the trees of the wóod re- | -joice be- | -fore the | Lord.

2nd part. 13 For he cometh, for he cómeth to | judge the | earth : and with righteousness to judge the wórld and the | people | with his | truth.

SELECTION TENTH.

I. Dr. T. S. DUPUIS. II. J. FOSTER.

PSALM LXXVII.—*Voce mea ad Dominum.*

mp I WILL cry unto Gód | with my | voice : even unto God will I cry with my voice ✶ and hé shall | hearken | unto | me.

2 In the time of my tróuble I | sought the | Lord : my sore ran, and ceased not in the nightseason ✶ mý | soul re- | -fused | comfort.

3 When I am in heaviness ✶ I' will | think up · on | God : when my héart is | vexed · I | will com- | -plain.

4 Thou hóldest mine | eyes | waking: I am so féeble | that I | cannot | speak.

5 I have considered the | days of | old : ánd the | years | that are | past.

6 I cáll to re- | -membrance · my | song : and in the night I commune with mine own héart, and | search | out my | spirits.

7 Will the Lord absént him-|-self for | ever : and will he|be no|more in-|-treated ?

SELECTION TENTH (continued).

8 Is his mercy cléan | gone for | ever : and is his promise come utterly tó an | end for | ever- | -more ?

9 Hath God forgótten | to be | gracious : and will he shut up his lóving-|-kindness | in dis- | -pleasure ?

10 And I said, It ís mine | own in- | firmity : but I will remember the years of the right hánd | of the | most | Highest.

f 11 I will remember the wórks | of the | Lord : and call to mínd thy | wonders · of | old | time.

12 I will think álso of | all thy | works : and my tálking shall | be of | thy | doings.

13 Thy wáy O | God is | holy : who is so gréat a | God as | our | God ?

14 Thou art the Gód that | doeth | wonders : and hast decláred thy | power a- | -mong the | people.

15 Thou hast míghtily de- | -livered . thy | people : éven the | sons of | Jacob and | Joseph.

16 The waters saw thee O God * the waters sáw thee and | were a- | -fraid : the dépths | also | were | troubled.

17 The clouds poured out wáter the | air | thundered : and thine | arrows | went a- | -broad.

18 The voice of thy thunder was héard | round a- | -bout : the lightnings shone upon the ground * the éarth was | moved . and | shook with- | -al.

19 Thy way is in the sea * and thy páths in the | great | waters : ánd thy | footsteps | are not | known.

20 Thou léddest thy | people · like | sheep :·bý the | hand of | Moses and | Aaron.

SELECTION ELEVENTH.

Dr. Dupuis.

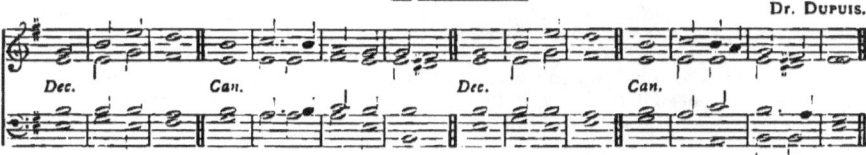

PSALM LXXX.—*Qui regis Israel.*

mf HEAR, O thou Shepherd of Israel * thou that leadest Jóseph | like a | sheep · shew thyself also * thóu that | sittest · up- | -on the | cherubims.

2 Before Ephraim, Bénjamin | and Ma- | -nasses : stir úp thy | strength and | come and | help us.

3 Túrn us a- | -gain O | God : shew the light of thy cóuntenance | and we | shall be | whole.

4 O Lórd | God of | hosts : how long wilt thou be ángry | with thy | people · that | prayeth ?

5 Thou feedest them wíth the | bread of | tears : and givest them plénteous- | -ness of | tears to | drink.

6 Thou hast made us a very strífe | unto · our | neighbours : and our énemies | laugh | us to | scorn.

7 Turn us agáin thou | God of | hosts : shew the light of thy cóuntenance | and we | shall be | whole.

8 Thou hast brought a víne | out of | Egypt : thou hast cast óut the | heathen · and | planted | it.

9 That mádest | room for | it : and when it had tákenlroot itlfilled . the | land.

10 The hills were covered wíth the | shadow | of it : and the boughs theréof were | like the | goodly | cedar-trees.

11 She stretched out her bránches | unto · the | sea : ánd her | boughs | unto the | river.

p 12 Why hast thou then bróken | down her | hedge : that all théy that go | by pluck | off her | grapes ?

13 The wild boar out of the wóod doth | root it | up : and the wild béasts of the | field de- | -vour it.

14 Turn thee again, thou God of hósts look | down from | heaven : behóld and | visit | this | vine ;

15 And the place of the vineyard that thy ríght | hand hath | planted : and the branch that thou mádest so | strong | for thy- | -self.

16 It is burnt with fíre and | cut | down : and they shall perish át the re- | buke | of thy | countenance.

17 Let thy hand be upon the mán of thy | right | hand : and upon the son of man * whom thou madest so stróng | for thine | own | self.

18 And so will not wé go | back from | thee : O let us live * and wé shall | call up- | -on thy | Name.

mf 19 Turn us again, O Lórd | God of | hosts : shew the light of thy cóuntenance | and we | shall be | whole.

SELECTION ELEVENTH (*continued*).

Dr. CROTCH

PSALM LXXXI.—*Exultate Deo.*

f SING we merrily únto | God our | | strength : make a cheerful nóise | unto , the | God of | Jacob.

2 Take the psálm, bring | hither · the|tabret : the mérry|harp|with the | lute.

3 Blow up the trúmpet in the | new | moon : even in the time appointed * ánd up- | -on our | solemn | feast-day.

4 For this was made a | statute · for | Israel : and a law | of the | God of | Jacob.

2nd part 5 This he ordained in Jóseph | for a | testimony : when he came out of the land of Egypt * ánd had | heard a | strange | language.

6 I eased his shóulder | from the | burden : and his hands were de- | -livered · from | making · the | pots.

7 Thou calledst upon me in troubles * and I' de- | -livered | thee : and heard thee what tíme as the | storm | fell up- | on thee.

8 I' | proved · thee | also : át the | waters | of | strife.

9 Hear, O my people * and I will assúre | thee O | Israel : íf thou wilt | hearken | unto | me.

10 There shall no strange gód | be in | thee : neither shalt thou wórship | any | other | god.

11 I am the Lord thy God * who brought thee óut of the | land of | Egypt : open thy mouth | wide and | I shall | fill it.

mf 12 But my people wóuld not | hear my | voice : and I'srael | would | not o- | -bey me.

13 So I gave them up unto their ówn hearts' | lusts : and let them fóllow their | own im- | -agin- | -ations.

mf 14 O that my people would have héarkened | unto | me : for if I'srael had | walked | in my | ways,

15 I should sóon have put | down their | enemies : and túrned my | hand a- | -gainst their | adversaries.

16 The haters of the Lord shóuld have been | found | liars : but théir time | should have · en- | -dured · for | ever.

17 He should have fed them álso with the | finest | wheat-flour : and with honey out of the stony róck should | I have | satisfied | thee.

SELECTION TWELFTH.

J. S. SMITH.

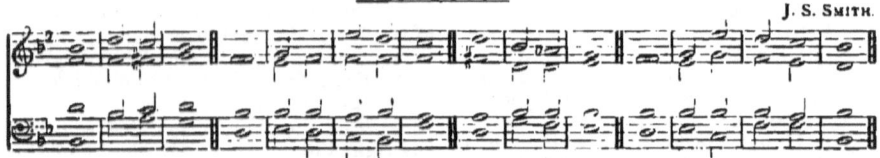

PSALM LXXXIV.—*Quam dilecta!*

mf O HOW ámiable | are thy | dwellings : thóu | Lord | of | hosts !

2 My soul hath a desire and longing * to enter into the cóurts | of the | Lord : my heart and my flesh rejóice | in the | living | God.

3 Yea, the sparrow hath found her an house * and the swallow a nest, where she may | lay her | young : even thy altars, O Lord of hósts, my | King | and my | God.

4 Blessed are they that dwéll | in thy | house : théy will be | alway | praising | thee.

5 Blessed is the man whose stréngth | is in|thee : ín whose|heart|are thy | ways.

6 Who going through the vale of misery úse it | for a | well : ánd the | pools are | filled · with | water.

2nd part 7 They will gó from | strength to | strength : and unto the God of gods appeareth évery | one of | them in | Sion.

8 O Lord God of hósts | hear my | prayer : héarken | O | God of | Jacob.

9 Behold, O Gód | our de- | -fender : and look upón the|face of|thine A-|-nointed.

10 For one dáy | in thy | courts : ís better | than a | thousan

SELECTION TWELFTH (*continued*).

11 I had rather be a door-keeper in | worship * and no good thing shall he
the hóuse | of my | God : than to dwéll in | withhold from thém that | live a | godly |
the | tents | of un- | -godliness. | life.
12 For the Lord God is a líght | and | 13 O Lórd | God of | hosts : blessed
de- | -fénce : the Lord will give grace and | is the mán that | putteth · his | trust in | thee.

Dr. G. C. MARTIN.

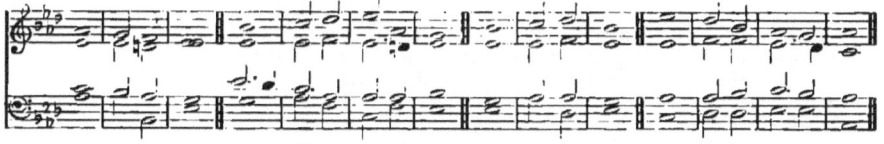

PSALM CXXII.—*Lætatus sum*.

mf I WAS glad when they sáid | unto | 6 O pray for the péace | of Je- |
me : We will gó into the | house of the | Lord. rusalem : théy shall | prosper · that |
2 Our feet shall stánd | in thy | gates : love | thee.
O' | — Je- | -rúsa- | -lem. 7 Péace be with- | -in thy | walls :
3 Jerusalem is búilt | as a | city : that and plénteous- | -ness with- | -in thy |
is at | unity | in it- | -self. palaces.
4 For thither the tribes go up * even 8 For my bréthren and com- |
the tríbes | of the | Lord : to testify unto panions' | sakes : I* will | wish | thee
Israel * to give thánks unto the | Name | pros- | -perity.
of the | Lord. ²ⁿᵈ 9 Yea, because of the hóuse of the |
5 For thére is the | seat of | judge- Lord our | God : I* will | seek to | do
ment : even the séat | of the | house of | David. | thee | good.

J. COWARD.

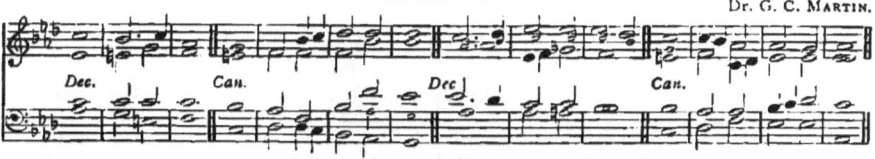

PSALM CXXXIV.—*Ecce nunc*.

mf BEHÓLD, now | praise the | Lord : | 3 Lift up your hánds | in the | sanc-
áll ye | servants | of the | Lord ; tuary : ánd | praise | — the | Lord.
2 Ye that by night stand in the 4 The Lórd that made | heaven ·
hóuse | of the | Lord : even in the cóurts and | earth : give thee | blessing | out of |
of the | house of | our | God. Sion.

SELECTION THIRTEENTH.

Dr. G. C. MARTIN.

PSALM LXXXV.—*Benedixisti Domine*.

mp LORD, thou art become grácious | 4 Turn us thén O | God our |
unto · thy | land : thou hast turned awáy Saviour : and lét thine | anger | cease |
the cap- | -tivi- | -ty of | Jacob. from us.
2 Thou hást forgiven the offénce | of 5 Wilt thou be displéased at | us for |
thy | people : ánd | covered | all their | ever : and wilt thou stretch out thy wrath
sins. from óne gener- | -ation | to an- | -other ?
3 Thou hast taken awáy all | thy 6 Wilt thou not turn agáin, and |
dis- | -pleasure : and turned thysélf from quicken | us : that thy péople I may re-
thy | wrathful | indig- | -nation. joice in | thee ?

SELECTION THIRTEENTH (*continued*).

Dr. G. C. MARTIN

7 Shéw us thy | mercy ⋅ O | Lord : and | grant us | thy sal- | -vation.

8 I will hearken what the Lord God will sáy con- | -cerning | me : for he shall speak peace unto his people and to his saints ✶ that they | turn | not a- | gain.

9 For his salvation is nígh | them that | fear him : that glóry may | dwell | in our | land.

10 Mercy and trúth are | met to- | gether : rīghteousness and | peace have | kissed ⋅ each | other.

11 Truth shall flóurish | out ⋅ of the earth : and rīghteousness hath | looked | down from | heaven.

12 Yea, the Lord shall shéw | lovingkindness : ánd our | land shall | give her increase.

13 Rīghteousness shall | go be- | -fore him : and he shall diréct his | going | in the | way.

Sir GEORGE ELVEY.

PSALM XCIII.—*Dominus regnavit.*

F. f THE Lord is King ✶ and hath put on glóri- | -ous ap- | -parel : the Lord hath put on his appárel and | girded ⋅ him- | self with | strength.

F. 2 He hath máde the round | world so | sure : that it | cannot | be | moved.

3 Ever since the world began hath thy séat | been pre- | -pared : thóu | art from | ever- | -lasting.

4 The floods are risen, O Lord ✶ the flóods have lift | up their | voice : thé | floods lift | up their | waves.

5 The waves of the sea are mīghty and | rage | horribly : but yet the Lórd who | dwelleth ⋅ on | high is | mightier.

6 Thy testimonies, O Lórd are | very | sure : hóliness be- | -cometh ⋅ thine | house for | ever.

Sir G. A. MACFARREN.

PSALM XCVII.—*Dominus regnavit.*

f THE Lord is King ✶ the éarth may be | glad there- | -of : yea, the multitude of the ísles | may be | glad there- | -of.

2 Clouds and dárkness are | round a- | -bout him : righteousness and judgement are the hábit- | -ation | of his | seat.

3 There shall gó a | fire be- | -fore him : and burn úp his | ene ⋅ mies on | every | side.

4 His lightnings gave shíne | unto ⋅ the | world : the éarth | saw it ⋅ and | was a- | -fraid.

5 The hills melted like wax ✶ at the présence | of the | Lord : at the presence of the Lórd | of the | whole | earth.

6 The héavens have de- | -clared ⋅ his | rīghteousness : and áll the | people ⋅ have | seen his | glory.

7 Confounded be all they that worship carved images ✶ and that delīght in | vain | gods : wórship | him | all ye | gods.

8 Sion héard of it | and re- | -joiced : and the daughters of Judah were glad ✶ becáuse of thy | judgements | O | Lord.

9 For thou Lord, art higher than áll that are | in the | earth : thou art exálted | far a- | -bove all | gods.

10 O ye that love the Lord ✶ see that

SELECTION THIRTEENTH (continued).

ye hate the thing I which is I evil : the
Lord preserveth the souls of his saints ✱
he shall deliver them from the I hand of I
the un- I -godly.

11 There is sprung up a light I for the I righteous : and joyful gladness for I such as I are true- I -hearted.

12 Rejoice in the I Lord ye I righteous:
and give thanks ✱ for a re- I -membrance I
of his I holiness.

SELECTION FOURTEENTH.

I.   Dr. S. S. Wesley.   II.   Dr. W. Hayes.

PSALM CII.—*Domine, exaudi.*

F. mp HEAR my I prayer O I Lord : and let my crying I come I unto I thee.

F. 2 Hide not thy face from me in the time I of my I trouble : incline thine ear unto me when I call ✱ O hear I me and I that right I soon.

3 For my days are consumed a- I -way like I smoke : and my bones are burnt up I as it I were a I firebrand.

4 My heart is smitten down and I withered · like I grass : so that I' for- I -get to I eat my I bread.

5 For the voice I of my I groaning : my bones will scarce I cleave I to my I flesh.

6 I am become like a pelican I in the I wilderness : and like an owl I that is I in the I desert.

7 I have watched ✱ and am even as it I were a I sparrow : that sitteth a- I -lone up- I -on the I house-top.

8 Mine enemies revile me I all the · day I long : and they that are mad upon me are I sworn to- I -gether · a- I -gainst me.

9 For I have eaten ashes I as it · were I bread : and I mingled · my I drink with I weeping ;

10 And that because of thine indig- I -nation and I wrath : for thou hast taken me I up and I cast me I down.

11 My days are gone I like a I shadow : and I' am I withered I like I grass.

12 But thou, O Lord, shalt en- I -dure for I ever : and thy remembrance through- out I all I gener- I -ations.

13 Thou shalt arise, and have mercy up- I -on I Sion : for it is time that thou have mercy upon her, I yea the I time is I come.

14 And why ✱ thy servants think up- I -on her I stones : and it pitieth them to I see her I in the I dust.

15 The heathen shall fear thy I Name O I Lord : and all the kings I of the I earth thy I Majesty ;

16 When the Lord shall I build up I Sion : and when his I glory I shall ap- I -pear ;

17 When he turneth him unto the prayer of the I poor I destitute : and de- I -spiseth · not I their de- I -sire.

18 This shall be written for those that I come I after : and the people which shall be I born shall I praise the I Lord.

19 For he hath looked down I from his I sanctuary : out of the heaven did the I Lord be- I -hold the I earth ;

20 That he might hear the mourning of such as are I in cap- I -tivity : and de- liver the children ap- I -pointed I unto I death ;

21 That they may declare the Name of the I Lord in I Sion : and his I worship I at Je- I -rusalem ;

22 When the people are I gathered · to- I -gether : and the kingdoms I also · to I serve the I Lord.

23 He brought down my strength I in my I journey : and I shortened I my I days.

24 But I said ✱ O my God, take me not away in the midst I of mine I age : as for thy years, they endure throughout I all I gener- I -ations.

mf 25 Thou, Lord, in the beginning ✱ hast laid the foundation I of the I earth : and the heavens are the I work of I thy I hands.

26 They shall perish, but thou I shalt en- I -dure : they all shall wax I old as I doth a I garment ;

27 And as a vesture shalt thou change them ✱ and they I shall be I changed : but thou art the same, and thy I years I shall not I fail.

28 The children of thy servants I shall con- I -tinue : and their seed shall stand I fast I in thy I sight.

SELECTION FIFTEENTH.

Alternative Chants.

PSALM CVII.—*Confitemini Domino.*

mf O GIVE thanks unto the Lórd, for | he is | gracious : ánd his | mercy · en- | dureth · for | ever.

2 Let them give thanks whom the Lórd | hath re- | -deemed : and delivered fróm the | hand | of the | enemy ;

3 And gathered them out of the lands * from the éast and | from the | west : fróm the | north and | from the | south.

4 They went astray in the wílderness | out · of the | way : ánd | found no | city . to | dwell in ;

5 Húngry | and | thirsty : théir | soul fainted | in them.

6 So they cried unto the Lórd | in their | trouble : and he delívered them from | their dis- | -tress.

7 He led them fórth by the | right

SELECTION FIFTEENTH (continued).

way : that they might gó to the ! city ǀ where they ǀ dwelt.
 F. 8 O that men would therefore praise the Lórd ǀ for his ǀ goodness : and declare the wonders that he dóeth ǀ for the ǀ children · of ǀ men !
 9 For he satisfíeth the ǀ empty ǀ soul : and fílleth the ǀ hungry ǀ soul with ǀ goodness.
 10 Such as sit in darkness ✴ and ín the ǀ shadow · of ǀ death : being fast bóund in ǀ mise- ǀ -ry and ǀ iron ;
 11 Because they rebelled against the wórds ǀ of the ǀ Lord : and lightly regarded the cóunsel ǀ of the ǀ most ǀ Highest ;
 12 He also brought dówn their ǀ heart through ǀ heaviness : they fell dówn, and ǀ there was ǀ none to ǀ help them.
 13 So when they cried unto the Lórd ǀ in their ǀ trouble : he delívered them ǀ out of ǀ their dis- ǀ -tress.
 _{2nd part} 14 For he brought them out of darkness ✴ and óut of the ǀ shadow · of ǀ death : ánd ǀ brake their ǀ bonds in ǀ sunder.
 F. 15 O that men would therefore praise the Lórd ǀ for his ǀ goodness : and declare the wonders that he dóeth ǀ for the ǀ children . of ǀ men !
 16 For he hath bróken the ǀ gates of ǀ brass : and smítten the ǀ bars of ǀ iron . in ǀ sunder.
 17 Foolish men are plágued for ǀ their of- ǀ -fence : ánd be- ǀ -cause of ǀ their ǀ wickedness.
 18 Their soul abhórred all ǀ manner · of ǀ meat : and they were éven ǀ hard at ǀ death's ǀ door.
 19 So when they cried unto the Lórd ǀ in their ǀ trouble : he delívered them ǀ out of ǀ their dis- ǀ -tress.
 20 He sent his wórd, and ǀ healed ǀ them : and théy were ǀ saved · from ǀ their de- ǀ -struction.
 F. 21 O that men would therefore praise the Lórd ǀ for his ǀ goodness : and declare the wonders that he dóeth ǀ for the ǀ children · of ǀ men !
 22 That they would offer unto him the sácrifice of ǀ thanks- ǀ -giving : and téll ǀ out his ǀ works with ǀ gladness !
 23 They that go dówn to the ǀ sea in ǀ ships : and óccupy their ǀ business · in ǀ great ǀ waters ;
 24 These men see the wórks ǀ of the ǀ Lord : ánd his ǀ wonders ǀ in the ǀ deep.
 25 For at his word the stórmy ǀ wind a- ǀ -riseth : which lífteth ǀ up the ǀ waves there- ǀ -of.
 26 They are carried up to the heaven ✴ and dówn again ǀ to the ǀ deep : their soul melteth awáy be- ǀ -cause ǀ of the ǀ trouble.
 27 They reel to and fro ✴ and stagger like a ǀ drunken ǀ man : ánd are ǀ at their ǀ wits' ǀ end.
 28 So when they cry unto the Lórd ǀ in their ǀ trouble : he delívereth them ǀ out of ǀ their dis- ǀ -tress.
 29 For he máketh the ǀ storm to ǀ cease : só that the ǀ waves there- ǀ -of are ǀ still.
 30 Then are they glad, becáuse they ǀ are at ǀ rest : and so he bringeth them unto the háven ǀ where they ǀ would ǀ be.
 F. 31 O that men would therefore praise the Lórd ǀ for his ǀ goodness : and declare the wonders that he dóeth ǀ for the ǀ children · of ǀ men !
 32 That they would exalt him also in the congregátion ǀ of the ǀ people : and práise him in the ǀ seat ǀ of the ǀ elders !
 33 Who turneth the flóods ǀ into · a ǀ wilderness : ánd ǀ drieth ǀ up the ǀ water springs.
 34 A fruitful lánd ǀ maketh · he ǀ barren : for the wickedness of ǀ them that ǀ dwell there- ǀ -in.
 35 Again, he maketh the wilderness a ǀ standing ǀ water : and wáter-springs ǀ of a ǀ dry ǀ ground.
 36 And thére he ǀ setteth · the ǀ hungry : that théy may ǀ build · them a ǀ city · to ǀ dwell in ;
 37 That they may sow their lánd, and ǀ plant ǀ vineyards : tó ǀ yield them ǀ fruits of ǀ increase.
 38 He blesseth them ✴ so that they múlti- ǀ -ply ex- ǀ -ceedingly : and suffereth nót their ǀ cattle ǀ to de- ǀ -crease.
 39 And again ✴ when they are minished and ǀ brought ǀ low : through oppréssion, through ǀ any ǀ plague or ǀ trouble ;
 40 Though he suffer them to be évil in- ǀ treated · through ǀ tyrants : and let them wander óut of the ǀ way ǀ in the ǀ wilderness ;
 41 Yet helpeth he the póor ǀ out of ǀ misery : and maketh him hóuseholds ǀ like a ǀ flock of ǀ sheep.
 42 The righteous will consider thís ǀ and re- ǀ -joice : and the móuth of all ǀ wickedness ǀ shall be ǀ stopped.
 _{2nd part} 43 Whoso is wíse will ǀ ponder · these ǀ things : and they shall understánd the loving- ǀ -kindness ǀ of the ǀ Lord.

SELECTION SIXTEENTH.

Verses 1 to 14. F. KINKEE.
Verse 15 to end. TRAVERS.

PSALM CXVIII.—*Confitemini Domino.*

f O GIVE thanks unto the Lórd, for | he is | grácious : becáuse his | mercy · en- | -dureth · for | ever.

2 Let Israel now conféss that | he is | gracious : and thát his | mercy · en- | dureth · for | ever.

3 Let the house of Aáron | now con- | fess : thát his | mercy · en- | -dureth · for | ever.

4 Yéa, let them now that féar the | Lord con- | -fess : thát his | mercy · en- | dureth · for | ever.

mf 5 I called upón the | Lord in | trouble : and the Lórd | heard | me at | large.

6 The Lórd is | on my | side : I will not féar what | man · doeth | unto | me.

7 The Lord taketh my párt with | them that | help me : therefore shall I sée my de- | -sire up- | -on mine | enemies.

8 It is better to trúst | in the | Lord : than to pút any | confi- | -dence in | man.

9 It is better to trúst | in the | Lord : than to pút any | confi- | -dence in | princes.

10 All nations cómpassed me | round a- | -bout : but in the Náme of the | Lord will | I de- | -stroy them.

11 They kept me in on every side * they kept me in | say on | every | side : but in the Náme of the | Lord will | I de- | -stroy them.

12 They came about me like bees * and are extinct even as the fire a- | -mong the | thorns : for in the Náme of the | Lord I | will de- | -stroy them.

13 Thou hast thrust sore at mé, that | I might | fall : but the | Lord | was my | help.

14 The Lord is my stréngth | and my | song : and is be- | -come | my sal- | -vation.

15 The voice of joy and health is in the dwéllings | of the | righteous : the right hand of the Lórd bringeth | mighty | things to | pass.

16 The right hand of the Lórd | hath · the pre- | -eminence : the right hand of the Lórd bringeth | mighty | things to | pass.

17 I shall not | die but | live : and declare the | works | of the | Lord.

18 The Lord hath chástened and cor- | rected | me : but he hath not gíven me | over | unto | death.

19 O'pen me the | gates of | righteous- ness : that I may go into them * and give | thanks | unto · the | Lord.

20 This is the gáte | of the | Lord : the ríghteous shall | enter | into | it.

21 I will thánk thee, for | thou hast | heard me : and árt be- | -come | my sal- | vation.

22 The same stóne which the | builders · re- | -fused : is become the | head-stone | in the | corner.

23 This is the | Lord's | doing : and it is | marvellous | in our | eyes.

24 This is the day which the | Lord hath | made : we will rejóice | and be | glad in | it.

25 Help me | now O | Lord : O Lórd send us | now pros- | -perity.

26 Blessed be he that cometh in the Náme | of the | Lord : we have wished you good luck * ye that áre of the | house | of the | Lord.

27 God is the Lórd who hath | shewed · us | light : bind the sacrifice with cords * yea, even únto the | horns | of the | altar.

28 Thou art my Gód, and | I will | thank thee : thóu art my | God, and | I will | praise thee.

29 O give thanks unto the Lórd, for | he is | gracious : ánd his | mercy · en- | dureth · for | ever.

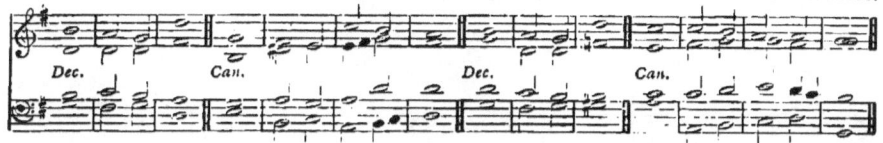

Dr. GARRETT.

PSALM CXXIII.—*Ad te levavi oculos meos.*

mp UNTO thée lift I | up mine | eyes : O | thóu that | dwellest | in the | heavens.

2 Behold, even as the eyes of servants look unto the hand of their masters ✶ and as the eyes of a maiden unto the hánd | of her | mistress : even so our eyes wait upon the Lord our God ✶ until | he have | mercy · up- | -on us.

3 Have mercy upon us, O Lórd, have | mercy · up- | -on us : for wé are | utter- | -ly de- | -spised.

4 Our soul is filled with the scornful reproof | of the | wealthy : and with the de- | -spiteful · ness | of the | proud.

PSALM CXXIV.—*Nisi quia Dominus.*

mp IF the Lord himself had not been on our side ✶ nów may | Israel | say : If the Lord himself had not been on our síde, when | men rose | up a- | gainst us ;

2 They had swállowed | us up | quick : when they were so wráthful- | -ly dis- | -pleased | at us.

3 Yea, the wáters had | drowned | us : and the stréam had | gone | over · our | soul.

4 The déep waters | of the | proud : had góne | even | over · our | soul.

mf 5 But práised | be the | Lord : who hath not given us over fór a | prey | unto · their | teeth.

6 Our soul is escaped ✶ even as a bird out of the snáre | of the | fowler : the snare is bróken, | and we | are de- | -livered.

2nd part 7 Our help standeth in the Náme | of the | Lord : whó hath | made | heaven and | earth.

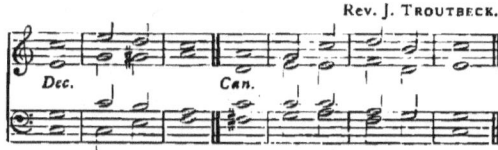

Rev. J. TROUTBECK.

CXXV.—*Qui confidunt.*

mf THEY that put their trust in the Lord shall be éven as the | mount | Sion : which may not be remóved, but | standeth | fast for | ever.

2 The hills stánd a- | -bout Je- | rusalem : even so standeth the Lord round about his people ✶ from thís time | forth for | ever- | -more.

3 For the rod of the ungodly cometh not into the lót | of the | righteous : lest the righteous pút their | hand | unto | wickedness.

4 Dó ! well O | Lord : unto thóse that are | good and | true of | heart.

5 As for such as turn báck unto their | own | wickedness : the Lord shall lead them forth with the evil-doers ✶ but péace shall | be up- | -on | Israel.

SELECTION EIGHTEENTH.

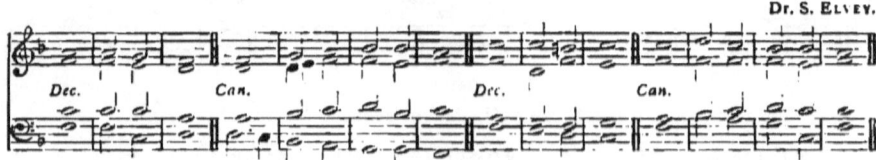

Dr. S. ELVEY.

PSALM CXXXIX.—*Domine, probasti.*

mf O LORD, thou hast séarched me | out and | known me : thou knowest my down-sitting and mine uprising * thou understándest my|thoughts|long be-|-fore.

2 Thou art about my páth, and a-| bout my | bed : ánd | spiest · out | all my | ways.

3 For lo, there is not a wórd | in my | tongue : but thou, O Lórd | knowest it | alto- | -gether.

4 Thou hast fashioned me behínd | and be- | -fore : ánd | laid thine | hand up- | -on me.

5 Such knowledge is too wónderful | and | excellent | for me : I cánnot at- | tain | unto | it.

6 Whither shall I gó then | from thy | Spirit : or whíther shall I | go then | from thy | presence ?

7 If I climb up into héaven | thou art | there : if I go down to héll | thou art | there | also.

8 If I take the wíngs | of the | morning : and remain in the úttermost | parts | of the | sea ;

9 Even there álso shall | thy hand | lead me : ánd | thy right | hand shall hold me.

10 If I say, Peradventure the dárk- ness shall | cover | me : thén shall my | night be | turned · to | day.

11 Yea, the darkness is no darkness with thee * but the night is as cléar | as the | day : the darkness and líght to | thee are | both a- | -like.

12 Fór my | reins are | thine : thou hast cóvered me | in my | mother's | womb.

13 I will give thanks unto thee * for I am fearfully and wónder- | -fully | made : marvellous are thy works * and thát my | soul | knoweth · right | well.

14 My bónes are not | hid from | thee : though I be made secretly * and fáshioned be- | -neath | in the | earth.

15 Thine eyes did see my sùbstance, yet | being · im- | -perfect : and in thy book were | all my | members | written ;

16 Which dáy by | day were | fash- ioned : when as yét | there was | none of | them.

17 How dear are thy counsels únto | me O ! God : O how gréat | is the | sum of | them !

18 If I tell them * they are more in number | than the | sand : when I wake úp | I am | present · with | thee.

19 Wilt thou not sláy the | wicked · O | God : depart from mé, ye | blood- | thirsty | men.

20 For they speak unrìghteous- | -ly a- | -gainst thee : and thine énemies | take thy | Name in | vain.

21 Do not I hate them, O Lórd, that | hate | thee : and am not I grieved with thóse that | rise | up a- | -gainst thee ?

22 Yea, I háte | them right | sore : éven as | though they | were mine | enemies.

23 Try me O God, and seek the gróund | of my | heart : próve me, | and ex- | -amine · my | thoughts.

24 Look well if there be any wáy of | wickedness | in me : and léad me in the | way | ever- | -lasting.

SELECTION EIGHTEENTH (*continued*).

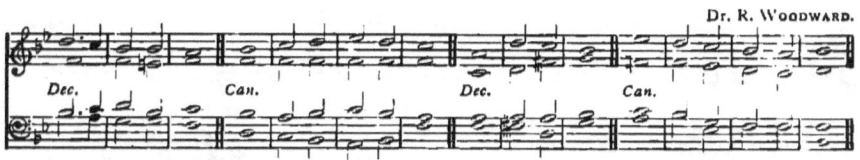

Dr. R. Woodward.

PSALM CXLV.—*Exaltabo te. Deus.*

mf I WILL magnify thée O | God my | | King : and I will práise thy | Name for | ever · and | ever.

2 Every day will I give thánks | unto | thee : and práise thy | Name for | ever · and | ever.

3 Great is the Lord, and marvellous ✱ wórthy | to be | praised : there ís no | end | of his | greatness.

4 One generation shall praise thy wórks | unto · an- | -other : ánd de- | clare | thy | power.

5 As for me, I will be tálking | of thy | worship : thy glóry, thy | praise and | wondrous | works ;

6 So that men shall speak of the might of thy | marvellous | acts : and I will álso | tell | of thy | greatness.

7 The memorial of thine abundant kíndness | shall be | shewed : and mén shall | sing | of thy | righteousness.

8 The Lórd is | gracious · and | merciful : long-súffering, | and of | great | goodness.

9 The Lord is loving únto | every | man : and his mércy is | over | all his | works.

10 All thy works práise | thee O | Lord : and thy sáints give | thanks | unto | thee.

11 They shew the glóry | of thy | kingdom : ánd | talk | of thy | power ;

12 That thy power, thy glory, and míghtiness | of thy | kingdom : might be | known | unto | men.

13 Thy kingdom is an éver- | -lasting | kingdom : and thy domínion en- | -dureth · through- | -out all | ages.

14 The Lord uphóldeth all | such as | fall : and lifteth úp all | those | that are | down.

15 The eyes of all wáit upon | thee O | Lord : and thou gívest them their | meat in | due | season.·

16 Thou ópenest | thine | hand : and fíllest | all things | living · with | plenteousness.

17 The Lord is ríghteous in | all his | ways : ánd | holy · in | all his | works.

18 The Lord is nigh unto all thém that | call up-| -on him : yea,·áll such as | call up- | -on him | faithfully.

19 He will fulfil the desíre of | them that | fear him : he also will héar their | cry | and will | help them.

20. The Lord presérveth all | them that | love him : but scáttereth a- | -broad | all · the un- | -godly.

2nd part 21 My mouth shall speak the práise | of the | Lord : and let all flesh give thanks unto his hóly | Name for | ever · and | ever.

SELECTION NINETEENTH.

I. Right Rev. Bishop Turton. II. E. J. Hopkins.

PSALM CXLVII.—*Laudate Dominum.*

F. 1 O PRAISE the Lord ✶ for it is a good thing to sing práises | unto · our | God : yea, a joyful and pleasant thing it | is to | be | thankful.

F. 2 The Lord doth búild | up Je- | rusalem : and gather togéther the | out- | casts of | Israel.

3 He healeth thóse that are | broken · in | heart : and gíveth | medicine · to | heal their | sickness.

4 He telleth the númber | of the | stars : and cálleth them | all | by their | names.

5 Great is our Lord ✶ and gréat | is his power : yéa, and his | wisdom | is | infinite.

6 The Lórd setteth | up the | meek : and bringeth the ungódly | down | to the | ground.

7 O sing unto the Lórd with | thanks- | giving : sing praises upón the | harp | unto · our | God.

8 Who covereth the heaven with clouds ✶ and prepareth ráin | for the | earth : and maketh the grass to grow upon the mountains ✶ and hérb | for the | use of | men.

9 Who giveth fódder | unto · the | cattle : and feedeth the yóung | ravens · that | call up- | -on him.

10 He hath no pleasure in the stréngth | of an | horse : neither delígheth | he in | any · man's | legs.

11 But the Lord's delight is in | them that | fear him : and pût their | trust | in his | mercy.

12 Praise the Lórd | O Je- | -rusalem : práise thy | God , O | Sion.

13 For he hath made fast the bárs | of thy | gates : and hath | blessed · thy | children · with- | -in thee.

14 He maketh péace | in thy | borders : and filleth thee | with the | flour of | wheat.

15 He sendeth forth his commánd- ment up- | -on | earth : and his wórd | runneth | very | swiftly.

16 He gíveth | snow like | wool : and scáttereth the | hoar- | -frost like | ashes.

17 He casteth fórth his | ice like | morsels : who is áble | to a- | -bíde his | frost ?

18 He sendeth out his wórd, and | melteth | them : he bloweth with his wind | and the | waters | flow.

19 He sheweth his wórd | unto | Jacob : his statutes and órdinances | unto | Isra- | -el.

20 He hath not dealt só with | any | nation : neither have the héathen | know- ledge | of his | laws.

I. J. BATTISHILL.   II. R. GOODSON.

PSALM CXLVIII.—*Laudate Dominum.*

O PRÁISE the | Lord of | heaven : práise | — him | in the | height.

2 Praise him, áll ye | angels · of | his : práise | — him | all his | host.

3 Práise him, | sun and | moon : práise him, | all ye | stars and | light.

4 Práise him, | all ye | heavens : and ye wáters that | are a- | -bove the | heavens.

5 Let them praise the Náme | of the | Lord : for he spake the word, and they were made ✶ he commánded, | and they | were cre- | -ated.

6 He hath made them fást for | ever · and | ever : he hath given them a láw | which shall | not be | broken.

7 Praise the Lórd up- | -on | earth : yè | dragons · and | all | deeps ;

8 Fire and háil | snow and | vapours : wínd and | storm ful- | -filling · his | word ;

9 Móuntains and | all | hills : frúitful | trees and | all | cedars ;

10 Béasts and | all | cattle : wórms | — and | feathered | fowls ;

11 Kings of the éarth and | all | people : princes and áll | judges | of the | world ;

12 Young men and maidens, old men and children ✶ praise the Náme | of the | Lord : for his Name only is excellent ✶ and his práise a- | -bove | heaven and | earth.

13 He shall exalt the horn of his people ✶ áll his | saints shall | praise him : even the children of Israel ✶ éven the | people · that | serveth | him.

I. J. TURLE.   II. A. R. REINAGLE.

PSALM CXLIX.—*Cantate Domino.*

ƒ O SING unto the Lórd a | new | song : let the cóngre- | -gation · of | saints | praise him.

2 Let Israel rejóice in ' him that made him : and let the children of Sion be | joyful | in their | King.

3 Let them praise his Náme | in the | dance : let them sing praises únto | him with | tabret · and | harp.

4 For the Lord hath pléasure | in his | people : ánd | helpeth · the | meek- | hearted

5 Let the sáints be | joyful · with | glory : lét them re- | -joice | in their | beds.

6 Let the praises of Gód be | in their | mouth : and a twó-edged | sword | in their | hands ;

7 To be avénged | of the | heathen : ánd | to re- | -buke the | people ;

8 To bínd their | kings in | chains : ánd their | nobles · with | links of | iron.

9 That they may be avenged of thém | as it · is | written : Súch | honour · have | all his | saints.

PSALM CL.—*Laudate Dominum.*

ff O PRAISE Gód | in his | holiness : praise him in the | firmament | of his | power.

2 Práise him in his | noble | acts : praise him according | to his | excellent | greatness.

3 Praise him in the sóund | of the | trumpet: praise him up- | -on the | lute and | harp.

4 Práise him in the | cymbals · and | dances : praise him up- | -on the | strings and | pipe.

5 Praise him upon the wéll- | -tuned | cymbals : praise him up- | -on the | loud | cymbals.

F. 6 Let évery thing | that hath | breath praise | — — | — the | Lord

www.ingramcontent.com/pod-product-compliance
Lightning Source LLC
Chambersburg PA
CBHW021813230426
43669CB00008B/744